YORKSHIRE ODDITIES

YORKSHIRE ODDITIES
INCIDENTS
AND
STRANGE EVENTS

BY
S. BARING-GOULD

Illustrated by
RON TINER

SMITH SETTLE
1987

First published in 1874
This edition published from the Fifth edition
of 1900 in 1987 by
SMITH SETTLE
Ilkley Road, Otley
West Yorkshire LS21 3JP

Reprinted 1987, 1988, 1989

Text and Illustrations ©Smith Settle 1987

ISBN Paperback 1 870071 13 1

Designed, printed and bound by
SMITH SETTLE
Ilkley Road, Otley
West Yorkshire LS21 3JP

"There be such a company of wilful gentlemen within Yorkshire as there be not in all England besides" — *Abbot of York to Cromwell, 1556, Rolls House MS.*

PREFACE

A RESIDENCE of many years in Yorkshire, and an inveterate habit of collecting all kinds of odd and out-of-the-way information concerning men and matters, furnished me, when I left Yorkshire in 1872, with a large amount of material, collected in that county, relating to its eccentric children.

A friend, when he heard that I was collecting such material, exclaimed, "What are you about? Every other Yorkshireman is a character!" Such is the case. No other county produces so much originality — and that originality, when carried to excess, is eccentricity.

I look back with the greatest pleasure to the kindness and hospitality I met with in Yorkshire, where I spent some of the happiest years of my life. I venture to offer this collection of memoirs of odd people, and narrative of strange events, as a humble contribution to the annals of the greatest, not perhaps only in extent, of our English counties, and a slight return for the pleasant welcome it afforded a migratory penman from the South.

S. Baring-Gould.

CONTENTS

YORKSHIRE
ODDITIES AND INCIDENTS.

THE GHOST OF TRINITY CHURCH, YORK.

SOME years ago I heard mention made of an apparition said to have been seen in Trinity Church, Micklegate, York, which at the moment excited my curiosity. But as I heard no more about it, it passed out of my mind.

In 1869 I was invited to deliver a lecture at Middlesborough, when I met a clergyman who introduced himself to me as an old acquaintance. We had not met for some years, and then he had been a boy at school. About a week after I left Middlesborough I received from him the following letter:—

I.

"Easter Sunday Evening, 1869.

"DEAR MR. BARING-GOULD.

"I venture, from the slight acquaintance I am happy to have with you personally, and the deeper one I have with your tastes from external sources, to enclose for your perusal a narrative of a perfectly true event, drawn up by myself some few years ago, at the request of some friends who doubted the truth of the circumstances therein related. If you have ever heard anything of it, and can help me in explaining it, I shall be grateful, as it perplexes me, as one always is teased when something which one cannot account for has been brought to one's notice.

'Mr. S—— is going in a few Sundays to preach at the very church in York where this took place, and this bringing again before my mind the spectacle I then saw, caused me to apply to my friends for the account I gave them, and I now send it to you. I could, if you are interested, supply some minor details, but better by word of mouth, if ever we meet again. The only correction I should make is this: You will find that I relate a sequence of events, and I am not quite satisfied in my own mind that I have given the order of the incidents exactly as they occurred, and it is possible that I may have inverted them. At the time I was so startled that I was more intent on observing the figures than noting what was the succession in the scenes, if I may use the expression. Indeed, each reappearance was a surprise; and when I tried to recall each incident in the order in which it occurred, I found that though I could recall the appearance distinctly before my mind's eye, yet I could not swear to which scene preceded the other.

"This was the only occasion of my visiting the church. I confess the impression left on my nerves was not pleasant, and I do not think I should like to risk the effect of a repetition of it. Apologising for thus troubling you with my experiences,

"I remain, yours very truly,

"A.B.

"P.S. – The Incumbent, Mr. W——, has left, and another, Mr. M——, has now the living of Holy Trinity, Micklegate."

The following account, dated 1866, was enclosed in the letter:—

"While staying in York at this time last year (1865), or perhaps a little earlier, I first heard of the apparitions or ghosts supposed to be seen in Trinity Church, Micklegate. I felt curious to see a ghost, I confess, if such a thing is to be seen without the usual concomitants of a dark night and a lone house. Accordingly I went to the church for morning service on a blazing hot Sunday morning in August last, with a girl about thirteen years old and her little brother.

"The east window of the church, I must explain, is of stained glass, rather tawdry, and of no particular design, except that the colouring is much richer in the centre than at the sides, and that at the extreme edge there is one pane of unstained glass which runs all round the window.

"The peculiarity of the apparition is, that it is seen on the window itself, rather less than half-way from the bottom (as I saw it from the gallery), and has much the same effect as that of a slide drawn through a magic lantern when seen on the exhibiting sheet. The form seen – I am told invariably – is that of a figure dressed in white walking across the window, and gives the idea of some one passing in the churchyard in a surplice. I say a figure, for the number is generally limited to one, and I was told that only on Trinity Sunday did more than one appear, and that then there were three.

"But I can vouch for the larger number appearing on other occasions, as on the day I was there, which was one of the Sundays after Trinity, there were rarely fewer than three visible.

"The figures began to move across the window long before the commencement of the service, when in fact there was no one present but ourselves. They did so again before the service began, as well as during the 'Venite,' and subsequently as many as twenty or thirty times, I should suppose, till the conclusion of the sermon.

"Of the three figures two were evidently those of women, and the third was a little child. The two women were very distinct in appearance. One was tall and very graceful, and the other middle-sized; we called the second one the nursemaid, from her evident care of the child during the absence of the mother, which relationship we attributed to the tall one, from the passionate affection she exibited towards the child, her caressing it, and the wringing of her hands over it.

"I may add that each figure is perfectly distinct from the others, and after they had been seen once or twice are at once recognisable.

"The order of their proceedings, with slight variation, was this: The mother came alone from the north side of the window, and having gone about half-way across, stopped, turned round, and waved her arm towards the quarter whence she had come. This signal was answered by the entry of the nurse with the child. Both figures then bent over the child, and seemed to bemoan its fate; but the taller one was always the most endearing in her gestures. The mother then moved towards the other side of the window taking the child with her, leaving the nurse in the centre of the window, from which she gradually retired towards the north corner, whence she had come, waving her hand, as though making signs of farewell, as she retreated.

"After some little time she again appeared, bending forward, and evidently anticipating the return of the other two, who never failed to reappear from the south side of the window where they had disappeared.

"The same gestures of despair and distress were repeated, and then all three retired together to the north side of the window.

"Usually they appeared during the musical portions of the service, and especially during one long eight-line hymn, when – for the only occasion without the child – the two women rushed on (in stage phrase), and remained during the whole hymn, making the most frantic gestures of despair. Indeed, the louder the music in that hymn, the more carried away with their grief did they seem to be.

"Nothing could be more emphatic than the individuality of the several figures; the manner of each had its own peculiarity. I do not doubt that if the stained glass were removed, a much plainer view would be obtained. I think so, because the nearer the centre of the window, where the stained glass was thickest, there the less distinct were the forms. It was like catching glimpses of them through leaves. But nearer the edge of the window, where the colours were less bright, they were *perfectly* distinct; and still more so on the pane of unstained glass at the edge. There they seemed most clear, and gave one the impression of being real persons, not shadows.

"Indeed, by far the most remarkable and perplexing incident in the whole spectacle was this, that on one occasion, when the mother and child had taken their departure, the medium figure – the nurse – waved her hands, and after walking slowly to the *very edge* of the window, turned round *whilst on the pane of unstained glass,* and waved her arm towards the other two with what one would call a stage gesture, and then I most distinctly saw, and I emphatically declare I did see the arm bare nearly to the shoulder, with beautiful folds of white drapery hanging from it like a picture on a Greek vase. Nothing could be plainer than the drag of the robes on the ground after the figures as they retired at the edge of the window where the clear glass was, previous to going out. The impression produced was that one saw real persons in the churchyard; for though the figures were seen on the window, yet they gave one the impression of walking past the window outide, and not moving upon the glass.

"No one in the church seemed to be in the smallest degree attracted or discomposed by all this, or, indeed, to observe it.

"I talked a great deal on the subject with Miss C——, daughter of the late Dr. C——, of York, and she told me that Mr. W——, the Incumbent of Trinity Church, would give anything to get rid of it, or discover the imposture, if imposture there be. She told me that he and his family had watched day and night without being able to find any clue to the mystery. Their house is in the churchyard and opposite the east window, and therefore very favourably placed for such an investigation. I am not inclined to think that the trees outside the church at the east end can originate the appearance by any optical illusions produced by waving branches. I could see their leaves rustling in the air, and their movement was evidently unconnected with the appearance and movement of the figures.

"A.B."

This curious communication led to my making inquiries, and I speedily heard of several persons who had seen the "ghosts" at a later date. Friends to whom I applied have sent me the following letters, written independently of one another. They naturally shrink from having their names published, but I can testify to these accounts being perfectly *bona fide:*—

II.

South Parade, York,
March 22nd, 1871.

"Dear Mr. Baring-Gould,

"I promised to send you an account of the ghost at Holy Trinity, Micklegate, and I now forward you the enclosed, written by a friend on whose word you may perfectly rely.

"I heard another account a few days ago from a lady who saw it on Sunday, the 19th February last. She described the figure – for she saw only one – as being dressed in a shining white garment, and says that it crossed the east window twice, with a slightly 'skipping' step. It appeared to be outside the church, as she saw it distinctly through the stained glass.

"I have never seen it myself, though I have been several times to the church.

"There are four lights in the east window, and the glass of the two central lights is of a darker tint than that in the side ones. There are, however, narrow panes of transparent glass in each of the lights, so that a person passing across the window outside could be distinctly seen by anyone sitting in the west gallery.

"The sill of the east window is about five feet from the ground outside, and about seven feet from the pavement inside; about ten yards from the east wall separating the churchyard from a private garden.

"Yours very truly,

"R.T."

This is the enclosure alluded to by my friend "R.T.":—

III.

"Having heard from several people of the ghost at the Church of the Holy Trinity, Micklegate, York, on Sunday, at the end of September, 1869, a friend and myself made up our minds to go and see if we also could be favoured with a sight of this wonderful apparition.

"Well, we went up into the gallery, the only place whence they say it is to be seen. You may, perhaps, already know that the gallery faces the east window, which is filled with modern stained glass.

"I am afraid that our attention rambled somewhat from the service, for we were looking out for the ghostly visitant. However, we watched and watched, as we began to think, in vain, until at the very end of the second lesson, when, just before the beginning of the 'Jubilate Deo,' I saw a figure, I should say of a shortish woman, with something white folded over her, covering even her head and face, but still I could see what it was. The figure appeared to walk very fast across the two middle lights of the east window, from right to left (i.e., from south to north), and seemed to be at some distance from the window.

"The strange thing is, that I saw it clearly through the thick painted glass.

"The whole thing happened so suddenly, and really surprised me so much, that for some time I could hardly get up from the seat or find my place at the beginning of the chant. Just as it disappeared my friend said, 'Did you see that?' To which, of course, I answered, 'Yes; did you?' that was all we saw; and a lady who was there at the same time, whom we knew, saw it also, exactly as we did, only apparently not with the same distinctness.

"Many persons have seen a great deal more. I believe that the figure is generally seen to walk across the window in the reverse way to that which my friend and I saw, and returns with a child, some say with two.

"We examined outside the window. It is a good deal above the ground, about five feet, I should think, and at the side of it is a very old gravestone, with no inscription on the headstone as far as I could make out. I believe it is currently reported that the apparition issues from that grave.

"Some people thought that it might be a shadow caused in some peculiar manner by the trees that grew outside; but it was not, for the trees were cut down about three years ago, and the apparition is still seen, as it has been, I have been told, for a century.

"I have nothing to add, except that this is a true and unexaggerated account of what I saw."

IV

YORK, *March 28th*, 1874.

"SIR,

"Owing to severe illness in my family, I was not able to reply to your note earlier. I will now try and tell you what I have seen and been told on the subject of the ghosts at Holy Trinity, Micklegate.

"A York lady, now dead, told me she remembered seeing it when a child, and that she once read an account of it in an old History of York: she thought the book must have been published in the seventeenth century.

"We now live in the parish of Holy Trinity, and attend the church regularly. A part of my family sit in the gallery, therefore I will tell you, in as matter-of-fact a manner as possible, what I myself have seen, and leave one of my daughters, if she likes, to give you her experiences.

"I must state also that the ghost is seen more or less distinctly as you happen to be seated in the centre or side of the gallery; as a rule, the former is the best place.

"As I have no faith in ghosts, I have been most wishful to have the matter cleared up. At present I cannot account for the appearance in any way.

"I went many times to the gallery in hopes of seeing the phenomenon, but was repeatedly disappointed. At last, one dull day, hopeless for the purpose as I thought – rain was falling at the time – I was startled by seeing something.

"There are two east windows – one on the right, filled with common green glass, the organ in front of it. From the outside of this window I saw something move, and immediately a graceful figure of a girl of eighteen or twenty years crossed the outside of the stained east window with a light, free step. She was entirely covered with a fine lace veil which, as she walked and met the air, showed the outline of the head and figure; the features I could not distinguish, but could see a shade through the veil where they naturally would be.

"The veil was of a pure white, flowing back as a train as she walked. In two or three minutes the figure returned, the robe flowing back in the same way, and disappeared behind the organ window.

"The figure appeared to me to be decidedly outside the window, and at a greater distance than was possible for any one to be; in the first place, because the east window is high up, and therefore anyone walking past it, to be seen at all, must be at some little distance from it; and, secondly, because there is a dead wall within a few yards of the window.

"The pure white of the robe quite obliterated the colours in the window, but the lead work was distinct enough, and the figure appeared behind it. The distinct outline of the figure is most striking.

"The apparition always returns to the organ window. I have seen this several times since the first. Owing to the dull day and the darkness of the windows, the appearance on the first occasion was the more remarkable. Two or three other figures also appear, but I never thought them as distinct as the first, and I thought the second and third might be reflections of the first. The two or three often move quickly back and forwards with a dancing movement somewhat like the reflection of the sun on a wall, but taking the form of human figures. However, it was dull and raining when first I saw the apparition, so that on that occasion there could have been no reflection of sunlight.

"These appearances are sometimes not seen for weeks and months; then they appear once or twice on succeeding days or Sundays. No one can be sure of seeing them if they go to the church for that purpose. I do not believe the apparition takes place at one more favoured time than another, though some people like to think so. The present rector wished to abolish the 'ghosts,' and was advised to cut down one or two trees. This was done; all thought that the ghosts were banished. Ten months after there was a gay wedding; my daughters went into the gallery to witness the ceremony, and lo! the 'ghost or ghosts' were there also. They had not been seen for nine or ten months. That was the first occasion since the cutting down of the trees on which they reappeared.

"The Sunday-school children who sit in the gallery see the form so often as to be quite familiar with the sight, and call them 'the mother, nurse, and child.'

"The legend I have heard told of it is that a family, consisting of a father, mother, and only child, lived here once upon a time. The father died, and was buried at the east end of the church, under or near the organ window. After a while the plague broke out in York and carried off the child, and it was buried outside the city, as those who died of plague were not allowed to be laid in the churchyards for fear of communicating the infection.

"The mother died afterwards, and was laid in her husband's grave, and now, as in her lifetime, continues to visit the grave of her child and bemoan the separation. The child is brought from its grave in the plague-pit by the mother and nurse, and brought to the grave of its father, and then it is taken back to where it lies outside the walls."

"L.S."

V.

The following appeared in the "Newcastle Daily Chronicle" a couple of years after the publication of my book, in 1874:—

"SIR, – On Good Friday last I went to Holy Trinity Church, York, for morning service at 11 o'clock, and repaired with a friend to the gallery, being anxious to see a certain apparition which is said to haunt the place.

"The gallery is situated at the extreme west end of the building, and faces the east window, from which it is distant some 50 feet or so. It is said that in the aisle and body of the church nothing is ever seen. The gallery was full, but no one seemed to have come there especially for the ghost, and though many of them afterwards said they saw it, they were not in the least affected by the apparition, treating it as a matter of course, to which they were well accustomed.

"I kept my eyes fixed upon the east window for nearly the whole of the hour and a half during which the service lasted, but was not favoured with a sight of the phenomenon; although others saw it cross the window and return, and my friend who knows it well, called my attention to the fact, at the moment, yet I could not perceive nothing. I therefore left the place as unbelieving as ever, and supposed that either I was the victim of a hoax, or that it required a great stretch of imagination to fancy that a passing shadow was the desired object. However, not liking to discredit the statements of many friends who were used to seeing it almost every Sunday, I consented on Easter Day to go to the same place and pew. The seat I occupied was not an advantageous one, a large brass chandelier being between me and the lower panes of the window. In the middle of the service my eyes, which had hardly once moved from the left or north side of the window, were attracted by a bright light formed like a female robed and hooded passing from north to south with a rapid gliding motion outside the church apparently at some distance. The window is Gothic, and I fancy, from 20 to 25 feet high, by 12 to 15 feet wide at the base. The panes through which the ghost shines are about 5 feet high and about half-way between the top and bottom. There are four divisions in the window, all of stained glass, of no particular pattern, the outer on right and left being of lighter colour than the two centre panes, and at the edge of each runs a rim of plain transparent white glass, about two inches wide, and adjoining the stone work. Through this rim, especially, could be seen what looked like a form transparent, but yet thick, (if such a term can be used) with light. It did not resemble linen, for instance, but was far brighter, and would, no doubt, have been dazzling to a near observer. The robe was long, and trailed. The figure was of course not visible when it had crossed the window and passed behind the wall. My friend whispered to me that it would return, must return, and at the end of five minutes or so, the same figure glided back from right to left, having turned round while out of sight. About half an hour later it again passed across from north to south, and having remained about ten seconds only, returned with what I believe to have been the figure of a young child, and stopped at the last pane but one, where both vanished. I did not see the child again, but a few seconds afterwards the women reappeared, and completed the passage, behind the last pane, very rapidly. Nothing more was seen during the service, and no other opportunity presented itself to me for making observations. During each time, the chandelier prevented me from obtaining a complete view but there could be no doubt as to the shape, a certain amount of indistinctness, however, being caused by the stained glass. On the reappearance for the last time, I saw the head, which was, I believe, that of the child, move up and down distinctly, as if nodding. The figure shone with dazzling brightness, and appeared to be at a considerable distance, say thirty yards or so, though at the same time as distinct as possible, considering the obstruction of coloured glass. Each time the level upon which it glided was precisely the same, and afterwards, on carrying a straight line from the spot in the gallery where I sat, through the part of the glass where the feet of the figure shone, and continuing that line (in my mind's eye, with all the objects before me, except the ghost, whose position I had taken good notice of), I found that it would traverse a thick holly tree eight or nine feet high at about four feet from the ground, and at two or three feet from the ground a low wall about four feet high, and would reach the ground itself in the middle of a gravel yard belonging to the back premises of the house, called the vicarage, at a distance of twelve or fifteen yards from the window. Any person walking between the window and the holly tree would barely be seen at all, much less be seen in the place which the apparition occupies; and any one on the further side of the tree would be almost if not quite invisible on account of the holly and other bushes and the dead wall. Any one about there at all can easily be seen from the many houses on all sides.

"If it were a shadow thrown upon the glass of the window it would, of course, be seen by those who sit in the body of the church as well as those in the gallery.

"It cannot be a reflection on the principle of Pepper's Ghost, which is produced by the figure actually being in a very strong light and appearing reflected on glass in a darkish spot. The lights both inside and outside of the church at York which might be thought to produce the ghost, are precisely the reverse, and any figure required to be reproduced by reflection on the east window would have to be standing or walking in the centre of the aisle.

"For the above facts I can vouch, and I have no reason to believe that the following are either incorrect or exaggerated.

"It is said to appear very frequently on Trinity Sunday, and to bring two other figures on to the scene, another female, called the nurse, and the child. It is often seen as distinctly on a dark, rainy, or snowy day, as when the sun is shining. When I saw it the sun was not bright.

"The motion is even, not at all jerky. Sometimes it glides swiftly; at other times slowly. It cannot be a mere accidental reflection, from a door or window, for instance, for the figure faces different ways, according to the direction in which it is going; and it is not always alone, nor do the figures always act in concert.

"One of my friends, with a companion, has watched outside on the wall, where he had a full view of the whole place around, during morning service. The ghost has been seen from the inside while outside nothing was visible.

"It is said to have haunted the church for 150, 200, and some authorities say 300 years, and there are many pretty legends connected with it.

"One of the many traditions says that 300 years ago, during religious disturbances, a party of soldiers came to sack the convent attached to this church; that the abbess, a women of great virtue and courage, stopped them, as they were entering, declaring that they should enter over her dead body only, and that, should they succeed in their sacrilegious purpose, as they afterwards did, her spirit would haunt the place until the true Church were re-established, and a convent built on the same spot. Another story relates that during the plague, some two hundred years ago, a nurse and child died of the pestilence, and were necessarily buried outside the city walls, while the unfortunate mother of the child, at her death, was interred in Holy Trinity Churchyard. Here the mother waits and receives the nurse and child, weeping and wringing her hands before parting with them. The same scene is often enacted several times during the same say, and even during the same service.

"Whatever may have been the circumstances under which the ghost (if it is one, which it is hard to believe in these matter-of-fact days) commenced its peculiar promenade, I would recommend those who have the chance to go to Holy Trinity Church, York, and see for themselves, though an audience of the apparition cannot always be assured. A ghost in broad daylight does no harm, frightens no one, and ought to interest everybody. – I am, &c.,   H.G.F.T."

Finally the Rector of Holy Trinity, York, intervened; he wrote to the "York Herald":—

"I think the time has come when it is perhaps necessary for me to give a word of explanation in regard to this imaginary apparition. The fact is simply this: Any one seated in the gallery of the church which is at the west end, can see through the east window any person, or persons, walking in the vicarage garden. The wall at the east end of the church, below the east window, is too high to allow anyone in the body of the church to see either the garden or anyone in it. This fact explains at once the reason, how it is absolutely necessary for anyone to be in the gallery in order to see the 'ghost.' This is the real truth of the matter. What is seen is not a 'ghost;' it is not a 'reflection,' but is a living being, or beings, walking in a garden. Of course the east window being of stained glass and of a rather peculiar pattern, a distinct form is not always visible. And I may say that this simple explanation has been attested and verified over and over again both by myself and others. One argument of proof is all, I think, that I need give. The Vicarage House was at one time empty for about 12 months, during which time the 'ghost' was neither seen nor heard of, and then it was let to a person with a large family; and on the very first Sunday after the family took possession of the premises, I was told by a simple-minded youth that the ghost had returned, and five or six young ghosts with it. After what I have here stated, I need hardly say that all the sensational matter in regard to vivid lights, mother, nurse, and child, extraordinary displays on Trinity Sunday, &c., &c., is as pure an invention as ever was fabricated by a morbid imagination. And I will add that I sincerely hope that the people of York will not take the advice of one of your voluminous correspondents, and will not go to the church for the mere purpose of seeing this purely imaginative ghost. I trust that all who go will remember it is God's house, intended to be a house of prayer, and not a place for gratifying an idle curiosity."

This letter called forth a sharp animadversion from another correspondent who signed himself "Novocastrensis," to which H.G.F.T. replied: – "I have read Mr. Gould's accounts since I saw the 'ghost,' and find that though they differ considerably in the details from my description, in the essential points they agree with and corroborate it. I should like to state here distinctly that the story was not adapted for my 'own' or any other's 'purpose' from 'Yorkshire Oddities,' but is an unprejudiced, and to the best of my belief, an unexaggerated and true account and description of what I myself saw. It is not my desire to raise a discussion, but the injustice implied in the letter is the excuse I urge for thus trespassing upon your space. – I am, &c.

"H.G.F. T

"Newcastle-upon-Tyne, 6th May, 1876."

This provoked another letter from a fresh correspondent: – "SIR, – I was in York when the letters appeared in the *Chronicle* and the *Journal* about the ghost in Holy Trinity Church. A lady, a member of the congregation, who has frequently seen the ghost, gave me the following simple explanation. Opposite the window there is a cottage, in one of the windows of which there is a swing pane of glass. The tenant of the cottage can cause the ghost to appear and disappear at pleasure by simply opening and shutting it, thus causing reflected sunlight to fall on the church window: – I am, &c,,   J.L.

"May 9th, 1876."

Another correspondent rushed into print: – "SIR, – though I am not one of those who can boast of having seen the York ghost, yet even to me the explanation published in today's *Journal*, in a letter signed 'J.L.' seems utterly inadequate to explain the matter. The fact of a swing window opening and shutting might throw sunlight upon the church window, but it is perfectly clear that in such a case the reflection would not be confined perpetually to the same identical part of the window, the angles caused by the sun and the swing window being of course varied, according to the time of day. It strikes me that by those means the figures could not be reversed on their return as is always the case, according to the story. Again, the apparition is often seen in dull weather, when no sunbeam could be reflected. If the light were actually turned on to the stained glass, the congregation seated in the body of the church would be able to see it as well as those in the gallery, but they do not. I should like to see the matter explained. Yet a reason such as 'J.L.' gives for it is altogether unsatisfactory, and may be taken for what it is worth, which is not much, considering the evidence against him, and the fact that his information is only second-hand – I am, &c.,   R.H.H.

"Newcastle-on-Tyne."

VI

"M—— Rectory, York,

"Aug. 11th, 1875.

"DEAR SIR, – Having had the pleasure of reading your interesting book 'Yorkshire Oddities,' I recognised an old acquaintance in the 'Trinity Ghost.' Happening to have found out an apparent explanation of the ghost, I thought you would be interested in hearing what I know about it.

"In 1869 I went to school at Mr. Metcalfe's, the present incumbent of the church. For my first year I saw and heard nothing about the ghost. We used to sit in two pews in the body of the church under the gallery. In 1870 we changed to a pew in the front of the gallery and the one behind it. Soon after we changed our seats, some of us saw the ghost, and the next Sunday we looked for it, and most of us saw it. The attempt was made known to find out what the ghost was. In 1871 my curiosity being rather excited by the frequent appearances of the ghost, I and a boy of the name of Yewdall determined to find out what it was. The appearance of the ghost was, as one of your informants describes it, that of a figure in a surplice, and it always went across the window from left to right, and returned from right to left. The east window is a pattern window of a good deal of red and blue glass, and beyond the window there is a small strip of churchyard and then a wall. Beyond the wall is the yard of the old parsonage house. On the left hand side of this yard is the parsonage which is rented to a few poor families who used to take in lodgers. On the other side are the offices.

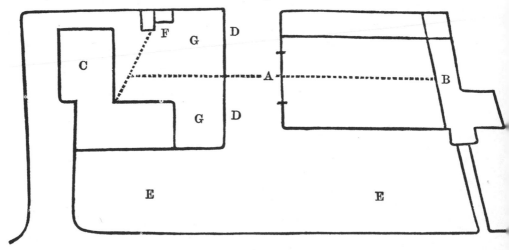

A East window
B Gallery
C Parsonage
D Wall
E Churchyard
F Ashpit, &c.
G yard formerly garden

"As we used to teach at the Sunday School which was held in a large room jutting out from the parsonage towards the church, we often noticed the women and children of the house going across the yard to the ashpits; and it struck us that this might be the ghost. So we went into the church directly the doors were opened and went up into the gallery while another of us walked across the churchyard in front of the east window. Curiously enough, at the same time we saw him going across the window near the bottom, the ghost went across higher up. This goes a good way to proving my supposition, as is drawn in the following diagram.

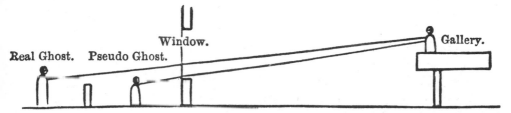

"I have forgotten to state that the ghost was always seen best in sunny weather, but it is also to be seen in cloudy weather as well as bright sunshine. Usually one ghost appeared, but I have often seen two, and a few times as many as eight children with the two big ones. This was, I suppose, the husband and wife of one of the families surrounded by the children. In 1862 (I believe the date is correct) Mr. Saul was the Incumbent, but upon his death, on vacation of the living, the parsonage house was uninhabited. During this time I have been told that the church was delivered from the ghost, but the very first Sunday the new rector came the ghosts reappeared as before. – I remain, yours truly, ——."

The name I have not given, though the letter was signed.

PETER PRIESTLY,

THE WAKEFIELD PARISH CLERK.

IN the middle of the last century there lived in Wakefield a certain Peter Priestly, who for many years was sexton of the parish church of All Saints. The then vicar was Michael Bacon, D.D., a tall, portly man, a commanding presence, who wore a large bushy wig, as was the wont of many old divines of that date. He was a man of rather a warm temperament, and was apt at times, when matters did not flow quite according to his will, to grow a little irritable, and whilst in that condition his habit was frequently to thrust his right hand in a testy, impetuous way under his wig. This habit destroyed the symmetry of that capital ornament, and made it protrude considerably on the right side; and this protrusion grew greater the longer the wig was worn.

The vicar's wigs were inherited and worn by the sexton, whose venerable and awe-inspiring appearance was much enhanced thereby. Mrs. Priestly in vain endeavoured to reduced the protuberance of hair on the right side, so as not to betray the origin of the wig. The horse-hair resumed its elasticity in spite of her efforts, and the congregation in the parish church were amused to see the stately Doctor in his reading-desk with a deformed wig, and below him the scarcely less stately clerk in a wig the counterpart of that of the Doctor. But what amused the wags not a little was to observe the fact that when the Doctor's wig was perfectly symmetrical, instantly the sexton's assumed the most exaggerated inequality in the sides. The secret, of course, was that the Doctor had donned a new wig, and had given his old one to the clerk. But after a while the irascible vicar had succeeded in brushing out the tufts of his false head of hair on the right, and simultaneously the continued efforts of Mrs. Priestly had reduced the right-hand protuberance in the wig of her husband. Consequently, as one bush grew, the other shrank into itself. But there were points – like the equinoxes – when both wigs were alike.

Now it fell out that Doctor Bacon had determined to present himself with a new wig one Easter, and he had accordingly given Peter Priestly his old wig, which had arrived at its maximum of extension on the right-hand side.

Peter had heard it said that on S. Mark's Eve the spirits of all those who are to die during the year may be seen in the church. Half believing this popular superstition and half in doubt about the truth of it, and thinking, moreover, that if it might be so, he should like to know whether trade would be brisk for him during the rest of the year, he decided that anyhow he would go to the church and see what would happen; and not wishing to spend his time idly, he determined to occupy himself with lettering some grave-stones which he had not completed. The place in which he carried on this work was the base of the church tower, which was shut off from the nave by a large boarded partition, against which stood the west gallery of the church. The opening from the tower into the nave consisted of large folding-doors.

Now, according to the story, on S. Mark's Eve a train of all those who are to die before the ensuing S. Mark's Eve come into the church through one of the doors in their winding-sheets, each carrying a corpse-candle. A ghostly priest precedes the weird procession, and dolefully intones the burial service.

When Peter had finished his supper on that eventful evening, he said to his wife: "I think, lass, I'll go and do a bit o' my lettering; so gi'e me my lantern wi' a can'le in it. I happen shan't be so varry long; but I think I'll just go for a bit. Howsomever, if I should stop a middling while, ye needn't be flayed (frightened), for I want to finish them two stoanes."

It was not without some trepidation that Peter took up his place in the tower, and left the folding-doors ajar that he might look into the nave and see the awful train sweep in.

Peter was not a nervous man, or at least he did not think himself so, and he began his work, whistling a psalm tune. He was engaged on a large grave-stone on which he had already completed about half the inscription. It was standing raised upon tressels to the required height; and at this he worked diligently for a long while, with his face towards the east and the folding-doors, and every now and then he stole to the doors and peeped through into the nave. All was perfectly dark and silent. He returned to his work with lighter heart after each glance into the great dark church. He had taken the candle out of his lantern, and had put it into an old rusty candlestick, which he kept there for the purpose in order that he might have a better light.

The church clock, with many premonitory groanings, had struck the hours of ten and eleven, and Peter still pursued his work. The eventful ghostly hour was approaching when the graves reveal their secrets. As this hour drew nigh Peter's courage began to fail. It flashed across his mind that perhaps the spectral procession would enter the church, not through the south porch, as he had at first conjectured, but through the western tower-door; in which case it would be upon him, envelop him, before he knew where he was.

This caused great agitation in Peter's breast, and made him turn his head every now and then to see if anything were stirring. But all remained still; the only sound that broke the silence was the pulse of time, the old clock throbbing above in the tower, and that sound seemed to grow more monotonous and weary.

Twelve o'clock drew near, and Peter's heart began to beat quicker. "I arn't flayed," he said to himself, "but I'm varry hot; t' work ha' made me so, I reckon. There's nowt to be flayed at, for there's nowt to be seen. I'll just wait while it strikes twelve, and then I'll go home."

So on he worked, but his hand was not as steady as usual, and he made a blunder in the letter he was cutting; and this annoyed him.

"I doan't know how it is," he said; "I think I mun be getting ow'd, for my hand rather shakes, and I can't see as weel as I used." He wiped his spectacles and snuffed the candle which stood at his right hand, and drew it closer to him. At that moment the striking apparatus of the clock groaned and prepared for twelve. Peter looked round over his shoulder. The quarter began to strike, and then with a great whirr the first stroke of the ominous hour sounded – the second – the third. How slow they did strike – surely slower than usual. At each stroke he turned his head and glanced behind him. Twice he started. Surely there was a little sharp sound for a moment, like an unearthly hiss. He raised himself and looked about him. There was nothing.

He bent himself again over his work, and the clock had reached the eleventh stroke. The twelfth followed. He turned sharply round, and on the instant such a rush sounded close to his right ear – such a strange, super-natural light glared suddenly through the tower – such a breath of hot air fanned his cheek – that he thought surely the ghostly train was passing. Over went the candle, and was extinguished. Down fell mallet and chisel. The old man stumbled out of the tower, rushed through the church-yard, and ran home, never looking behind him till he reached his door.

His house stood at the north-east corner of the church-yard. Opening his door, he ran through the room, and, pale and breathless, sank into his old arm-chair by the side of the fire. For a moment or two his mouth opened and gasped inarticulate words. Then, extending his trembling hand, he said to his alarmed wife, "Gi'e me my pipe, lass – gi'e me my pipe."

"Why, Peter," said his loving spouse, "whativer is t'matter wi' thee? Thou looks right flayed."

"Gi'e me my pipe, lass – gi'e me my pipe," he gasped again.

She went to the clock-case and took the pipe down from a ledge at the side of it, where it always rested when not in use, and reached down the tobacco-box from the delf-case against the wall; and bringing them to the old man, said, as she gained a closer view of him, "Why, Peter, whativer hast thou been doing? Thou'st burn't ommost half t' hair off t' right side o' thy wig!"

"What?" said Peter, with a sudden feeling of relief from his fright.

"Why, tak'thy wig off, and thou'll soon see," said the wife.

Doing as he was bid, he sat studying the precious wig. The great bunch of hair ruffled out by the vicar's hand was consumed to the roots.

Peter burst out laughing; the mystery was solved. But he made no more visits to the church at midnight on S. Mark's Eve.

Peter was remarkable for many witty sayings, but most of these have been forgotten.

He was lettering a grave-stone in the churchyard one day, when a physician came by, who, looking at the inscription, which was partly cut, said, "Why Peter, you've spelt it wrong."

"Have I, Doctor?" said he, sharply. "Then how should it be?"

When he was told how to correct his blunder, he looked slyly into the physician's face and said, "Well, well, pass it over, Doctor – pass it over. I've covered up monny a blot o' yours."

He one day stood listening to a Methodist local preacher in the market-place. The preacher was attempting an oratorical effect, and exclaimed, "My brethren, if every field in the world was thrown into one field, what a great field that would be! "Ah!" said Peter, loud enough to be heard, "if every jackass i' t' world was one jackass, what a big jackass that 'ud be!"

PROPHET WROE.

JOHN WROE was born at Bowling, in the parish of Bradford, Yorkshire, on September 19th, 1782, and was baptised in the old parish church of Bradford. He was put to school, but from want of capacity or of application he made such poor progress that when he left it he read very imperfectly, and he never acquired a facility of reading.

He was brought up to follow his father's employment, which was that of worsted manufacturer, combined with farming and the proprietorship of a coal-pit. In course of time his father gave him a share in his business, and articles of partnership were drawn up, but were never signed. John's natural incapacity for application to business probably obliged his father to place his brother Joseph in his room as partner, and John afterwards often complained of being hardly treated by his father and brothers. It is evident, however, that this treatment he brought on himself, and that his father acted with judgment in not entrusting the conduct of business into his hands.

His grandfather is said to have declared that "the Lord would raise up a minister from among his offspring." To fulfil this prophecy Wroe placed his youngest son Thomas in a school to be educated for the ministry in the Church, but was prevented from applying to the Archbishop of York for ordination for him, as the Vicar of Bradford and a friend dissuaded him from doing so, on account of Thomas labouring from an impediment in his speech.

John's irritation against his brother Joseph brought him to the verge of committing a dreadful crime. He procured a pistol and lay in wait for his brother, intending to shoot him, but his conscience reproached him, and he did not put his murderous purpose into execution.[1]

John and his father in course of time came to an open rupture about some wool that had been bought by the latter, and John determined to set up for himself. He applied for a farm in Tory Street, and the landlord would have accepted him, but his father intercepted the letter, and took the farm himself for three years. John, highly incensed, moved into the farm-house, and maintained his position there during all that time. His father wished to dispossess him, but not liking to summons his own son, he thought it better to suffer him to remain there.

On his way one night to Adwalton he was attacked by two men, who robbed

[1] This he mentions in his tract, "A Vision of an Angel," Bradford, Inkersley, 1820.

19

him of eighteen pounds. The men were apprehended but not convicted, and John never recovered the money.

He took up wool-combing as a business, and engaged apprentices. One of his apprentices, Benjamin Lockwood, involved him in losses, according to his own account, and this led him to bankruptcy.

I give the next passage from his memoirs as it stands. It is vaguely worded, and I do not profess to understand it. "He was about five years an housekeeper previous to his marriage with the daughter of Benjamin Appleby, of Fasseley Mills, near Leeds."

In 1819 John Wroe was attacked by fever, and was pronounced in danger. Dr. Field, who attended him, advised Mrs. Wroe to prevail on him to settle his affairs. The thought of death so moved and alarmed Wroe that he entreated that some Methodist preacher might be brought to visit and pray with him; but they refused, although his wife sent to four of them. She then asked him if she had better not send for his parish priest, or some of the clergymen of the Church; but he declined, saying it was too late, and he begged her to read to him some chapters from the Bible; "and," said he, "I will see what I can do for myself."

He gradually recovered his bodily health, but not his ease of mind, and for some months he continued wandering about the fields with his Bible in his hand, sitting down under the hedges, and spelling out easy passages for himself; but still found no comfort.

Soon after this he fell into epileptic fits, and saw visions. In these trances he became completely rigid, his eyes remained closed – the eyelids as fast together as if they had grown to one another, and his tongue stiff in his mouth. In this condition he remained sometimes seven, twelve, twenty-four, or even thirty-six hours. After one of his fits, his eyes remained closed for six days, but he recovered the use of his tongue. The first of his trances came on in the morning of November 12th, 1819, at two o'clock, before dawn, as he was rambling in the fields. He says: "A woman came to me, and tossed me up and down in the field. I endeavoured to lay hold of her, but could not; I therefore knew it was a spirit." Could this not have been his wife, impatient at him leaving his bed and rambling about so early?

After this he was taken and put to bed. Whom by? Was it by this woman who tossed him about? In bed he remained twelve hours.

On the 19th November, six days after his shaking, he had a fit, and lost his sight and power of speech. On his returning to consciousness, he wrote on a black board, in rude letters and abject spelling, the revelations he had been allowed to behold. It consisted of oxen running down a lane, tossing their horns, which frightened him to tears. "I thought that I walked about a mile among these beasts, until I returned to my former place, and there an angel met me, and he took me to a large place, where I saw a great number of books, placed on their edges, having gilt letters. There also appeared large altars, full of letters, but I could not read them. I begged that I might be enabled to read and understand what I had seen; and there appeared another, the letters of which were black print or old English, with the word Jeremiah on the top of it, and the letter L. I wrote on the wall with my fingers at the time, as I lay in bed; the people who were present observing me, concluded that I wished to write (I was dumb, for my tongue was fastened in my mouth as before); they gave me a piece of board and chalk, and I wrote Jeremiah, 50th chapter. I had never read this chapter, or heard it read, or seen it before, to my recollection; but when I came to myself, I could, without looking at it, repeat nearly every word in it."

On the 29th of November following he had another epileptic fit accompanied with visions; and on the 14th of December "I was again struck blind at about ten o'clock in the forenoon, and remained more like a corpse than a living man for twenty-four hours, when I came to myself by degrees, but continued blind for five days. After many things, the angel said to me, 'Thou shalt be blind for six days, and on the seventh day thy father shall come to thee, and many people with him; he shall lay his right thumb on thy right eye, and his fourth finger on thy left, as a token that he remembers his former sins and wickedness; and if not, it will be a witness against him at the Day of Judgment, and thou shalt receive thy sight.' During the six days that I was blind my wife at one time was reading a hymn for me; when she had read it I desired her to read it again; but before she had done so I fainted, and saw the elements separated, and there appeared before me a large open square; I saw our Saviour nailed on the cross and the tears trickling down his face, and at that time I thought he was weeping for the wicked people upon the earth. An Angel then appeared holding a man by a single hair of his head, who had a very large sword in his hand, which he waved backward and forward. I then saw a pair of large scales let down to the earth, and a great bundle, which was placed in one side of it, which I thought was the sins of the people, and then saw a great number of weights placed in the other; but the bundle was so much heavier that the weights bounced out, and the scales were drawn up into heaven. Then the man that was held by the hair of his head by the angel brandished his sword six or seven times, as formerly, and disappeared. I afterwards saw Moses and Aaron, accompanied by a great number of people, attended by angels, and I heard such delightful music as it would be impossible to describe. There was darkness over the place soon after, and I lost sight of all in a moment."

He continued with his eyes shut for exactly six days, and on the seventh his father came and placed his thumb on his right eye, and his fourth finger on his left, whereupon John Wroe opened his eyes and then fainted away. As soon as he received his sight the people surrounding him asked if he really saw clearly. He found that with one eye he saw as distinctly as before, but with the other only imperfectly, and this he attributed to some one having three days before endeavoured to force the eyelids open.

Wroe tells us in his Autobiography that his father, placing his thumb and finger on his eyes in the manner indicated beforehand by the angel, filled every one with astonishment; but from Joseph Wroe, his cousin, we learn that the father did this according to the express orders of John.

Samuel Muff, a spectator, says: "During the twenty-four hours that John Wroe was in his trance reports of the circumstance frequently reached my house, adding that he was likely to die. I accordingly went to see him, and he came to himself when I was in the house, but was entirely blind. On hearing my voice, he communicated many things to me which I cannot at present recollect; but I remember his having said that he was blind, but that he would yet see. He wrote me a few lines in the course of his six days' blindness, desiring that I would come and see him at the time his eyes were opened, and which he asserted would be at the end of the six days; the letter was sent to me by one of my neighbours, who declared he saw him write it; and stone blind as he then was, it is the best piece of his writing I ever saw. I complied with his desire, and actually saw his eyes open in the manner already related. After his father had placed his thumb and finger on his eyes, he appeared to me for some time as if he were dead. He afterwards came to himself, sat up in the chair, and his eyes instantly opened. He and I were brought up within a quarter of a mile of each other, and were schoolfellows, but the master who instructed us never could teach him to spell or read, nor even to speak plainly."

Joseph Wroe, John's cousin, says: "The first time I met with John Wroe after the commencement of his visions, which was in the street in Bradford, I said, 'I have been informed that thou has begun to preach.' He replied, 'Well, I do not know much about preaching, but I have begun talking, and people may call it what they please.' I said, in a contemptuous manner, 'I have also been informed that thou has been visited with visions or trances; what hast thou seen?' He replied, 'I have seen a great deal too much to relate here.' He appeared reserved, and would say no more. Some time after this a person came to my house, and inquired of me whether I had seen my cousin John, adding, 'People say he is blind, and has been so for three or four days.' I went to see him on the following Sunday, with many others. At his desire I led him to the door, and accompanied him to the house of a neighbour, named Abraham Holmes: it was this man who wrote his visions, and part of which was done on that occasion. We delayed there until it was dark, and I led him back to his house. When I was about to return home he laid hold of my hand, and would not suffer me to proceed until I had promised him to return next day, as he asserted that he would then receive his sight. I accordingly attended the same day; several persons did the same, and one of them said to John, 'Art thou not afraid that thou wilt never see any more?' He replied, 'No, I have not a doubt about it. I am as firm as a rock in the belief that my sight will be restored at the appointed time.' A few minutes before the time he requested that some person would lead him to a private place, where he might have an opportunity for prayer. I accordingly led him into the parlour, and withdrew; he soon after returned, and ordered a chair to be placed in the middle of the room, so that every person present might observe what was to be done. He then called his father, directing him to lay his thumb and finger on his eyes, and he did so. John said, 'You have done enough; take away your hand.' He then stretched out his legs and feet, his head and arms fell back, and he fainted, and his countenance appeared like that of a person who was dead. He remained so for about a minute, when his eyelids began to move, and suddenly opened: he came to himself and said, 'I can see.' I inquired of him, 'How wast thou before thy sight was restored?' He replied, 'I got a glance of that glorious place, and at that instant my sight returned.' "

The following night he prayed that he might be guided in the choice of a sect to which to belong. At about two in the morning he woke, and saw on the tester of his bedstead a black board, on which appeared in gilt letters, "A.A. Rabbi, Rabbi, Rabbi." He awoke his wife, and told her what he had seen. He thought at first that Rabbi was the name of a town, and that he was perhaps to go to that place and declare there what he had seen; but afterwards concluded it was a sign that he was to go and testify to the Jews. Afterwards he conceived himself to be commanded to testify in England for three years, "with his hat on his head," and at the expiration of that time to join the Jews.

Accordingly, in the same year, 1820, Wroe went to Liverpool by Huddersfield, to visit the Jews there. At Huddersfield he was well received by three Methodist preachers, who helped him on his way with money. On reaching Manchester he lodged in a house, and was asked by the person who let him his lodging whether he knew John Wroe, as he understood that he came from Bradford. Wroe having answered in the affirmative, the man continued – "What sort of a fellow is he?" John replied, "Some give him a very indifferent character; but time proves all things." He was then asked if he were John Wroe, and when he said he was, he was told that he should be heartily welcome to his lodging and victuals gratuitously as long as he stayed there.

The accomplishment of some predicitions made by Wroe tended greatly to increase his fame and impress the ignorant and superstitious with belief in his supernatural mission. But it is as easy to account for the accomplishment of these prophecies as it is to vindicate the natural origin of his fits and visions. He predicted the speedy death of his wife's brother, and he sent his wife to her brother, Joseph Appleby, to inform him that before long he would be dead. Appleby was at the time ill in bed: there is little doubt that the fright caused by receiving this message killed him.

In the spring of 1821 the cousin of John Wroe, who employed him as a wool-comber, refused to engage him or have any more of his badly-executed work, telling him he was more fit to be a preacher than a wool-comber. Thereupon John fell back in a fit against a bale of wool, and when he recovered called all to witness what he said – "Take notice of that young man," said he, pointing to the son of his employer, who had been foremost in his complaints and abuse; "he will never do any work; he will never again pay any man wages." The young man was immediately taken ill and died. In this case the lad was no doubt killed by fright.

On the 14th of August, 1822, came the final summons to Wroe to go to the Jews. As he was sitting in conversation with some dupes or believers he asserted that he heard thrice a voice which cried, "Go to my people Israel, and speak the words that I command thee." It continued speaking for about a quarter of an hour, and was succeeded by beautiful music. "He inquired of the aforenamed persons," we are told in his Autobiography, "whether they heard anything? and when they answered in the affirmative, and appeared alarmed, one of them said, 'The voice came from beneath the second bar of the fire-grate.' Wroe said, 'This voice is not come for my sake, but for yours.'" One regrets to hear this, for hitherto Wroe seems to have been acting in sincere good faith, believing in his visions; but on this occasion there is apparent deception. His neglect had lost him his livelihood, and he was obliged to prey on those deluded people who regarded him as a prophet, and to keep up the delusion had recourse to artifice.

He was now convinced of the truth of the great revelation of Joanna Southcott. Already, in August, 1820, he had had an interview with George Turner, the prophet of that sect, on his visiting Bradford, on which Wroe had informed Turner that he (Wroe) was sent exclusively to the public, and that Turner was sent exclusively to the elect of the Society; and on this understanding Turner had consented to shake hands with him.

But in 1822 the Society of Joanna Southcott was in a state of expectancy, awaiting the advent of the promised Shiloh on the 14th October in that year, and it seems to have entered into Wroe's head to take advantage of this, and announce himself to the Society as a prophet in place of Turner, who, he had the shrewdness to see, would be discredited by the failure of the appearance of the Shiloh. He was accordingly visited with trances, in which he saw Joanna "transfigured before him in the open firmament, in the day-time, with the Child in her left arm."

Accordingly, Wroe attended a meeting of the Society at Bradford on August 25th, 1822, and he announced: "You are expecting Shiloh to appear and be amongst you on a certain day; but I tell you He will not; and many of the believers will fall off, not merely one or two in a society, but whole societies will fall away. Yet I do not doubt that the visitation to George Turner is of God; and as a testimony of which, I will give in my name among you."

On the following Sunday evening he had one of his epileptic fits in the meeting, and lay as if dead. On recovering he announced that he had seen an angel, who had commissioned him to act as prophet. But only two persons at the meeting believed in him, and the whole of the Society at Bradford never thoroughly accepted him. He then went to Almondbury, where was a meeting of the Southcottites, where also he met with indifferent success.

On Sunday evening he reappeared in Bradford, and adopted the following extraordinary expedient to impress the congregation: – Unknown to the members, he caused to men to stand, and on each side of the archway leading into the second room of the meeting-house – the house being divided into three parallel apartments, which opened into each other by an archway in each partition, thus forming a sort of narthex, nave, and chancel. Each man held a sword, and the swords were united at the points, so that the Friends, to enter, had to pass under the swords. Wroe entered last of all. Then the men pointed their swords at his breast saying, "The sword of the Lord is against thee." Wroe instantly fell on his knees, and prayed aloud that if his mission were not Divine, the swords might fall and smite him asunder.

Wroe then stood up and walked to the second archway, the men with the swords stepping backwards before him, still with their swords at his breast. Thus he stood and preached on his mission to the congregation, who were amazingly impressed at this solemn farce. When all was over, he bade those of the Bradford Society who believed in him to pass under the swords; and the great majority of the congregation did so. This naturally created a schism in the body.

Letters were written by the Committee of the Society at Bradford, by Wroe's direction, to the Societies at Ashton-under-Line, Stockport, Sheffield, and Colne, to inform them of what had taken place, and requesting them to delegate to men from each congregation to come to Bradford and examine the truth concerning the mission of Wroe. The Societies at Stockport and Sheffield declined the invitation, but in the following year nearly the whole of the body at Sheffield accepted the prophetic mission of Wroe, and some at Stockport believed.

It was time now for Wroe to begin his mission to the Jews. He had a large following, and was provided liberally with money by his dupes, which he was not, however, suffered to touch himself.

After having visited Jews at Liverpool and London without success, on April 27th he embarked in the brig *Doris* at Liverpool for Gibraltar, in the company of Robert Harling, of Thornhill, and reached there on the 20th May. But there Harling's heart failed, whether at the sight of the "abominable idolatries" of the people, or because his faith was shaken in Wroe, does not transpire. On the day following their landing Harling returned to England in a vessel that was ready to sail; but John, having visited and converted the local Methodist preacher, remained with him two months. This preacher, Cooke, was greatly exercised in spirit on the arrival of the Prophet; but having prayed earnestly to the Lord, as he tells us, "The Lord opened my eyes to see," and he became an enthusiastic believer.

On Saturday, the 31st, Wroe appeared in the synagogue of the Jews and delivered his testimony. The Governor of Gibraltar declined to permit him to preach in public; consequently Wroe departed, having been offered a free passage to England. Before he did so he had been turned out of the synagogue, and had invaded the Roman Catholic Churches, where he deposited his prophecies on the altar in Spanish. This is one of them: –

" I, Jesus from heaven, command thee, John Wroe, to warn the kingdom of Spain that if they return not from their wicked ways of worshipping images made with men's hands, and bowing before them, I will draw my two-edged sword against them, and it shall turn every way till I have destroyed them. But who is this that has caused them to err? They have hearkened unto their priests instead of hearkening unto me. Now, I will tell you what I will do unto your priests: I will chase them as hounds chase a fox, until I utterly destroy them, and the remnant that is left shall slay your king, and they shall know that I have sent this unto them by my servant.''

He began to address the Irish Roman Catholic soldiers on the Rock, but the adjutant turned him out. In the two months he was at Gibraltar he had succeeded in making many enemies. A women threw a pitcher out of a window at his head, but fortunately missed him, and he was several times threatened with a pistol. One day that he was creating disorder in the cathedral the priests took him by the shoulders, thrust him out, and locked the doors behind him.

Wroe reached Liverpool on August 23rd, and then visited Ashton and Birmingham. On October 12th he again sailed for the Continent, and reaching Paris on the 16th, he began to preach his mission to the Jews in the Palais Royal.

From Paris he and his companion, William Lees, went to Strasburg, where they ''attended the meeting of the Jews in their synagogue. These Jews, not understanding English, conducted them to the house of the Rabbi, who was not at home. His daughter could speak some English, but not sufficient to admit of her understanding the whole of what John and William wished to communicate. The Jews therefore requested to have the purport of the message given to them in writing, which was accordingly done. They behaved very well. On the following day, Sunday, John was so ill that he was confined to the house, and sent William to the Hebrews to receive their answer to his letter. William found a man who could speak English. He said 'he had read the letter to the Rabbi, who was very angry, and said he had power to imprison them for two years, but had pity on them, thinking they were deranged.' ''

After visiting Vienna, they proceeded to Trieste. One would like to know what they thought of that glorious road over the Sommering Pass, and down the valleys of the Murz and the Save, by Laibach and the weird ashey-grey dolomite peaks of the Terglou and Dobartz; but no allusion to the scenery escapes these dull travellers, except that they ''durst not proceed by night, through the apprehension of robbers, the road being over the mountains.''

At Trieste they visited the Jews and a Roman Catholic priest, who treated them with good-natured contempt; and they went on to Venice, where they again testified to the Jews. At Verona they left a letter addressed to the Roman Catholic priests, on the altars. At Vicenza their letter to the priests was returned to them unanswered. At *table d'hôte* at the inn, where about forty gentlemen of different nations were present, ''the spirit of the Lord rested on John, and he stood up and addressed them, and gave them two letters. *They appeared much astonished.*''

From Milan they made their way to Paris, distributing tracts and prophecies among the Jews and Catholics, and strewing them on the altars of the churches. Having deposited one of these prophecies, not couched in the most sanguine and complimentary terms, addressed to the French priest, upon the high altar at Amiens, they nearly got into trouble. They were arrested at Calais, and their baggage overhauled by the police, who had received orders from the Minister of the Interior to search them for papers against the Government. But the police-officer, having looked through their budget of tracts, observed, contemptuously, that "they were all on religious subjects," and let them depart.

John then took all that remained of his tracts and denunciations of woe against the idolators, in Italian and French, and tore them into small pieces, which he scattered about the streets of Calais, saying "he was commanded to do so as a testimony against them." On the 17th December they embarked on the French mail, a sailing packet, and had a very rough passage. It blew so hard that they could not reach Dover, but stood off Deal beach, and a boat conveyed the mail and the passengers ashore. They had to pay fifteen shillings each to the watermen, exclusive of their fare in the packet. They were well drenched with salt water, but John cheered on William by assuring him that before they reached home he would see the young woman who was to become his wife.

On reaching London, Wroe visited some of the Believers, and prepared the way for a future visit, when he would meet George Turner face to face. He assembled the Friends at Gravesend and Chatham, and prophesied before them, and William Lees at the former place saw the enchanting Cordelia Chenne, whom he afterwards married, thus fulfilling the prediciton of Wroe in the billy-boat. The following year was an eventful one.

In January he received a communication "from the Spirit" that he was to spend forty days in a dark hole, and eat nothing but butter and honey, and drink milk. On the 29th he was publicly baptised in the river Aire, above Apperley Bridge, by John Brunton, of Bradford, in the presence of some thirty thousand spectators.

"Both sides of the river were lined with persons of various ages and denominations. The Spirit had given John a sign – that on his entering the water the sun should shine; for during the two preceding days the weather was extremely cold, with severe frost accompanied with snow. The Sunday forenoon on which the ceremony was to take place continued very wet till noon, and when Wroe arrived at the brink of the river, the sun was still veiled. He walked down the river, intending to delay till the clouds broke; but the people, thinking that he was afraid of the cold water, roared at him, 'he dussn't go in! He's runnin' away!' They were all disposed to view the fun, and they endeavoured to stop Wroe's further progress. Some friends followed him, urging him not to disappoint the crowd, and he found that he had better put a bold face on it, and go in. The sun just then shone forth with a degree of warmth most unusual at that season of the year. The musicians and singers began to play and sing, and he descended into the water. But when preparing to do so, a cry was raised by the multitude, 'Drown him!' The same words were uttered by some young men who had placed themselves on the branches of a tree adjacent to the river. John commanded them, in the name of the Lord, to come down. One of them, named Hudson, who was formerly John's apprentice, cursed him. Immediately that part of the bank on which the tree grew gave way, and all were precipitated into the river. None of them were drowned, but some had five or six miles to travel home in their wet clothes; and Hudson, who had cursed John, died within a few days after. When John came out of the water the musicians and singers again performed."

The mob then set on Wroe with sticks, pelted him with mud, and he and his band of Believers were obliged to beat a precipitate retreat.

On April 17th, in the same year, he was *publicly circumcised.* This function was introduced and announced by the band of singers of Ashton-under-Line marching in procession through the village, playing and singing the whole way. In the evening the highly unedifying performance was performed in the meeting-house of the Friends, "in the presence of the congregation."

On August 30th he was again baptised in the river Medlock, near Park Bridge, and on coming out of the river he stood with one foot in the water, the other on the land, raised his hands to heaven, and swore that there should be no more time – in imitation of the angel described in Revelation (x., 5, 6).

He seems now to have enjoyed circumcision on all male adherents, and reports circulated that several children had died in consequence. "But," says the Autobiography, "these reports, with one exception, were entirely false." The child who died was the son of Robert Grimshaw, of Hurst Brook, near Ashton. The poor child died six days after the operation. An inquest was held by the coroner, and a verdict of manslaughter was returned against Henry Lees, the operator. He was, however, acquitted at the Assizes, as the medical evidence was not conclusive that the wound occasioned by circumcision had caused the child's death.

On the 11th September Wroe received a call to wander in the fields for fourteen days, and live on nuts, wheat, blackberries, hips, herbs, and water. But these, as may well be believed, did not satisfy his hunger. At the end of this time, which he spent in wandering to Huddersfield and Oakenshaw, he told his wife "he had a command from God that she should destroy all pictures, portraits, or likenesses of anything he had created or caused to grow, whether of iron, stone, wood, cloth, or paper, and everything of a black colour that could be found within the house." Which command she, like a dutiful but foolish wife, obeyed.

He then proceeded to Bradford, and on Sunday the 26th addressed a large congregation which crowded into the chapel to hear him. It ended in a riot. "John left the room, accompanied by Elizabeth Elsworth and Mary Brear, with whom he walked about two hundred yards, when one of the females received a blow and was pushed aside. John was also forced along for some distance. However, they reached the New Inn, where there were two horses in readiness for John and his friend. Many of the people were about to enter, but were prevented by the landlord. Some persons already in the house said the two females were 'John's women,' and that he was picking poor people's pockets. The horses being got ready, the people in the house rushed out, crying to their persecuting companions, 'Now, lads, he's going!' on which they closed the yard gate. John, however, escaped by another passage. Having succeeded in getting on the road leading to Great Horton, a cry was raised, 'Kill him! kill him!' He was then pursued by the mob, amounting to thousands, some crying out, 'That's the devil who says he's been living on hips and haws, wheat and nuts, for fourteen days!' He was surrounded, and prevented from proceeding. By being preceded by Joseph Brear, he soon after succeeded in clearing his way, and proceeding a little further. But he was stopped, the mob pulling his horse and tearing his clothes. Joseph again succeeded in clearing the way a little, but was presently knocked off his horse by a stone; when remounted, they proceeded a short distance. John then turned and said something to the people. John and his horse were then pulled down and struck; the bridle and girth were broken in pieces. He at length succeeded in getting on the causeway, and resumed his journey on foot; stones and other missiles were showered against him in all directions. Some of his companions entertained fears that he never would reach Horton with his life.

The bursting of a storm of rain fortunately dispersed the mob, and the Prophet escaped. "On arriving at Moses Elsworth's nearly his whole body was black; he had also one of his eyes much discoloured, and received a cut on his face from a stone." On the following day he obtained warrants against nineteen of the mob, who appeared before the magistrate, were bound over to keep the peace for twelve months, and had to pay all expenses.

Prophet Wroe now deemed it expedient to visit London. Accordingly he had a revelation in August, 1825: "Go thou to Tozer, and stand before him, and prophesy, with thy rod in thy hand, and say, 'Thus saith the Lord, the Lord thy God has showed thee many things; and for this end wast thou born. The seal thou hast received thou shalt be able to retain; but thy body shall go to the dust, and thou shalt put on incorruption at the first resurrection. . . . Thou shalt be a witness for Joanna, and thou shalt come with her, and at that day thou shalt be great unto the ends of the earth."

On the 28th August, John Wroe, with his faithful ally, William Lees, visited the chapel of Mr. Lindsay, a prophet of the congregation of Joanne Southcott in London. Lindsay received them cordially, and announced to his congregation that "Brother Wroe" was to have full liberty to use the chapel morning and afternoon.

Now Tozer was the right-hand man of Lindsay – his faithful witness, who wrote down the oracles that dropped from his lips. He was, in fact, to Lindsay what William Lees was to John Wroe. It was to this Tozer that Wroe bore the message given above, which was a speech wrapped up in the most flattering and complimentary language, but a snub for all that. Mr. Tozer was wont to designate himself, "The man clothed in linen, with the writer's inkhorn," and believed himself, or endeavoured to induce others to believe, that he was the person spoken of by the Prophet Ezekiel (ix., 2); and when Mr. Lees appeared on the scene with a white surplice on and an ink-bottle at his left side it was a distinct throwing down of the gauntlet, and was likely to lead to unpleasant results. Foreseeing which, Wroe wrestled in prayer before the congregation that "Satan might be rebuked within *them* walls that day." Then Wroe stood up and said with a loud voice, "Thus saith the Lord, There are in this place those whose places shall be taken by others who have mocked and despised them. None shall enter but such as are circumcised or married." Lindsay turned red, trembled, and knocked over his inkstand. Tozer got up and said, "Friends, what must be my feelings at this time? This day of the month, this day of the week, eleven years ago, I addressed 1500 people in this city, and since that time the visitation has been trodden under foot. Eleven days were spoken of by the Woman – take them to mean years – (see the book, and find it). God grant that this may be the beginning of the Gathering." The people answered "Amen." It is evident he was overawed by Wroe and Lee in his white surplice and ink-pot.

In the afternoon Wroe was again at the chapel, and again hinted that there was now a new outpouring upon himself, and that the old prophets were to yield to him. "Thus saith the Lord, Many in this place that are first shall be last." Tozer and Lindsay looked uneasy. "If you will sign for Satan's destruction, let a man be deputed to Ashton on the 17th of next month. Many dreams have been interpreted there; let the same be sent to those who profess to be visited, and see who will get an answer in truth."

Lindsay walked backward and forward, in and out of the room, whilst John Wroe spoke, but said nothing. At the conclusion of Wroe's speech, Lindsay, who was greatly agitated, said, "I have received an order from above to go and see the Living Skeleton now exhibiting in Pall Mall, at three o'clock to-morrow, and John, with others, must go with me. And let so-and-so take his clarionette and play a tune before the skeleton, but for what purpose I know not."

John Wroe answered – "If the Lord hath commanded me to go, I will go; if not, I cannot go."

This Living Skeleton was Claude Ambroise Seurat, born in 1797, who was exhibited in London in 1825. His flesh had wasted completely away, and when he had attained his full height he presented the extraordinary spectacle of a skeleton covered with skin, alive and able to move and converse. A portion of Mr. Hones' description of him must be quoted here: – "He seemed another 'Lazarus come forth,' without his grave-clothes, and for a moment I was too consternated to observe more than his general appearance. My eye then first caught the arm as the most remarkable limb; from the shoulder to the elbow it is like an ivory German flute, somewhat deepened in colour by age; it is not larger, and the skin is of that hue, and not having a trace of muscle, it is as perfect a cylinder as a writing-rule. Amazed by the wasted limbs, I was still more amazed by the extraordinary depression of the chest. Its indentation is similar to that which an over-careful mother makes in the pillowed surface of an infant's bed for its repose. Nature has here inverted her own order, and turned the convex inwards, while nobler organs, obedient to her will, maintain life by the gentle exercise of their wonted functions in a lower region. If the integument of the bowels can be called flesh, it is the only flesh on the body; for it seems to have wholly shrunk from the limbs, and where the muscles that have not wholly disappeared remain, they are also shrunk.''

That this emaciated object, whose appearance in London created a sensation, should have been supposed by superstitious people, eagerly looking out for portents and realisations of wild prophecies, to be sent into the world with some peculiar significance, is not to be wondered at.

Lindsay seems to have resolved to put Wroe's apostleship to the proof by a visit to the extraordinary phenomenon, then exhibiting in the Chinese Pavilion, in Pall Mall. The Living Skeleton was to have decided between them, and confounded him who was the false prophet and imposter.

But Wroe would not go through this ordeal: he slunk away, conscious, perhaps, that he was an imposter, and with superstitious fear of the Walking Skeleton. He escaped to Greenwich, where he pretended to be ill.

Lindsay, finding Wroe was not at the exhibition, pursued him to Greenwich, and an angry meeting ensued.

Next Sunday, Wroe again invaded the chapel of Lindsay, who began to prophesy against him, saying, ''I say, in the name of the Lord, you shall shave!'' Then John Wroe took the prophetic rod, and thrusting it towards Lindsay, thundered forth, ''Dost thou come to defy Israel? The Lord rebuke thee, Satan!''

Lindsay was silent, but presently tried to create a diversion by setting Wroe and his follower Lees at variance, for he pointed to the latter and said, ''Thus saith the Lord, This man shall shave, and shall prophesy against his master.'' ''When will he shave off his beard?'' asked Wroe indignantly. ''When thine is plucked up by the roots,'' answered Lindsay. The scene was becoming undignified. The prophets seemed to be aware of it, and that it was necessary to patch the matter up; so Lindsay said, ''You see the spirits seem to differ a little; it is we who do not understand how they work and move.''

By degrees Wroe succeeded in obtaining recognition as the Prophet from the majority of Joanne Southcott's congregations. The faithful men wore long beards, ''the city mark,'' as it was called, and white linen vestments at the religious meetings in their tabernacles.

George Turner had succeeded Joanne Southcott; he was succeeded by William Shaw, and then Wroe received general acknowledgement. He announced that his mission would last forty years, and that at the expiration of this perod Shiloh would come.

As soon as he was acknowledged as Prophet, he had a power in his hands which he did not fail to exercise. In 1830 he announced that he had received orders from heaven that seven virgins should be delivered to him to comfort and cherish him, and three of his believers at once gave up to him their daughters. With these poor girls and some married women Wroe wandered from place to place. They were with him in Kent, in Devonshire, in Lancashire, and Yorkshire – wherever Wroe pretended that he was called. The matter became scandalous, and the confidence of several of the members of the community was shaken. The girls were questioned, and made shocking disclosures. Two of the Society, named Masterman and Walker, rose in the congregation at Ashton, on February 27th, 1831, and charged him with profligacy. Wroe could not stand against the storm; he escaped through a trap-door in the orchestra, amidst cat-calls, jeers, and howls. He remained secreted in Ashton a few days, and then left the place for ever.

The confidence of his faithful disciple Lees was somewhat dashed shortly before this by an exposure of the Prophet at Manchester. Lees had a friend at Manchester with whom he did business. Wroe used to spend much of his time in Lees' house. The Prophet announced to Lees that he was called by the Spirit on a mission, but that he had no money. Lees called a covenant meeting, and the sum of eighty pounds was raised, and placed at the disposal of the Prophet, who departed with it. Now it happened that Lees' friend did business at a certain public-house in Manchester, and having noticed Wroe there, and being shortly after at Ashton, he asked Lees where the Prophet was. Lees told him that had gone on a mission. His friend laughed, and said, "Come with me and you shall see him."

With difficulty he persuaded Lees to get into a cab with him and drive to Manchester to the public-house. The two men went in, opened the door into a back parlour, and found the Prophet sitting by the fire, in his low-crowned brown hat and long coat, between two low women, drinking hot whiskey and water with them. The landlord informed them that Wroe had been there several days. Lees went home, burned his white robe, destroyed all his books and tracts belonging to the Society, shaved off his beard, and next Sunday was in the parish church, which he had been in the habit of attending before he fell under the influence of Wroe.

But his humiliation did not end here. His daughter gave promise of becoming a mother by Wroe. In vain did the Prophet assure him that the child that would be born was the promised Shiloh. It turned out to be a girl. Lees put Wroe out of his doors.

It was soon after this that the Prophet was met by Masterman and Walker, and the scandal of the virgins was exposed.

Lees, hearing that Wroe was coming to Ashton, exasperated at the dishonour of his daughter and the dupe that had been made of himself, stationed himself behind a chimney and fired a gun at Wroe. The ball whizzed past his hat, and fortunately did him no injury. But the rumour of these scandals and the death of a child named Wood whom he had circumcised, caused a riot at Bradford when he visited it shortly after. The mob broke into the tabernacle, tore up the benches, smashed the windows, and would have maltreated Wroe if they could have caught him; but the wary Prophet made his escape in time.

One day in July he had a vocation to go on a mission. He was then living at Pudsey. His followers raised a handsome sum to defray his expenses, and he departed. After he had gone, it was observed that his wife passed a certain public-house in the neighbourhood every day. This was unusual, and it was agreed to watch her. After John Wroe had been gone fourteen days, she was followed at a distance. She went down a lane to a corn-field and made a signal, whereupon Wroe was observed to creep out of the standing corn. His wife opened her basket and produced a dish of new potatoes and a mutton-chop, and a four-ounce bottle of wine. The Prophet drew a horse-rug from out of the corn, and prepared to seat himself on it and enjoy his dinner, when the spies rushed upon him, carried him in triumph into Pudsey, set him on a donkey, rode him through the town, then tied a rope round his body, threw him into a horse-pond, pulled him out, and threw him in again and again; till the women, seeing him nearly exhausted, interfered and begged that he might be spared.

When he was living at Bowling he had a trance which lasted ten or twelve days. He lay apparently insensible on a stump bedstead, and people came from far and wide to see him. At the foot of the bed was a basket in which the visitors deposited silver and copper; and all who came were expected to give a trifle. There was a fixed hour at which the cottage door was opened and closed, and when it was closed the key was turned in the lock, and no one was admitted on any excuse.

It unfortunately happened that one night Mrs. Wroe went out for some purpose or other, and left the door unfastened behind her, intending to return in a minute. A man named Holt and his son lived close by. As they saw Mrs. Wroe go out, they and a neighbour who was with them thought the opportunity was not to be neglected, and opened the door of Wroe's house and peeped cautiously in. To their surprise John was sitting very comfortably in the ingle-nook, eating beef-steak, pickled cabbage, and oat-cake.[1] Next day he was laid on his bed as usual in a trance, and so he continued for three or more days. One of the visitors wished to thrust a needle under Wroe's nail, to prove if he were perfectly sensible, but his wife would not permit it.

Another of his devices for raising money was not more honest. He announced that the Lord had declared to him that every member of the Society of the house of Israel was to wear a gold ring of the value of £1 3s. 6d., which was to be procured from the Prophet, and it was to be a sign and a seal to them that they were the elect. This was in 1856, and all the members were supplied with gold rings by 1857. At this time the number of the members was thought to be about 6000, of whom 700 were in Ireland.

Unfortunately for the credit of the Prophet, towards the end of 1856 one of the members, who had not wholly lost his common-sense, thought it advisable

[1] My informant, who knew Wroe well, says: "J. Holt, the young man who saw this, told it me. He is now living at Bradford."

to have his gold ring tested with nitric acid, and the startling discovery was made that the rings were not of gold at all, not worth a florin each. Wroe threw the blame on the goldsmith who had provided him with them, and ordered that no more should be issued.

About 1854 John Wroe said he had a command from the Lord to build a mansion. The treasury of the "House of Israel" was empty; so the pillars of the Church met, and on consultation agreed to let Wroe have the Flying Roll money. This was a fund to which, after the death of Joanna Southcott, all sealed members paid according to their income or ability. It was a sacred fund retained by the Society for the purpose of publishing the Eternal Gospel and sending it to all parts of the world, proclaiming the millenium, the outpouring of the Spirit, and the Great Desolation. This eternal Gospel was to be published forty years after the Death of Joanna.[1] The sum amounted to a large amount – over two thousand pounds.

Wroe bought a piece of land on a height near Wakefield, and on this began to build. The house, said Wroe, was to be dedicated to the Lord, and was to belong to the members of the "House of Israel" gathered out of all nations. No architect was to be employed. It was to be built as the Spirit directed.

Subscription-books were issued to all the sanctuaries. Every member's contribution was to be entered separately, and no man was to know what his neighbour gave. The poorest workman was to contribute not less than 10 per cent. of his earnings.[2] All extra gifts were to be sent to John Wroe at Wrenthorpe, near Wakefield, and those who did not wish to pay to the local treasurers might send their subscriptions direct to the Prophet.

During 1855 and 1856 post-office orders poured in from all parts, and it was said in Wakefield at the time that Wroe had more orders cashed than all the tradesmen of the town put together.

The female members of the Society were to furnish the mansion. They were not to tell their husbands how much they gave; and many put down their names for sums which they really could not pay, and had to sell goods and borrow cash to keep up their payments to the end of 1856.[3]

The land was bought of Mr. William Ramsden, farmer, of Wrenthorpe, and was conveyed by Mr. Haigh, solicitor, of Horbury, to John Wroe, and not to the

---

[1] Is it more than a coincidence that the Southcottites should reproduce the forms and terminology of a heresy of the fourteenth century? The Abbot Joachim was the prophet then, and his "Eternal Gospel" proclaimed precisely the same doctrines as the "Eternal Gospel" of Joanna. This heresy invaded the ranks of the Franciscans, and produced a tremendous schism, which ended in the prescription of the Fraticelli. For an account of the Abbot Joachim and the Eternal Gospel see Hahn, "Ketzer Geschichte," ii. and iii.; and Dean Milman's "Latin Christianity."

[2] The members were obliged to keep books of their earnings, and exhibit them, to prove that they paid 10 per cent. to Wroe.

[3] This information comes from some of those who were thus victimised. Some members turned total abstainers, others vegetarians, to economise money in order to pay their subscriptions.

Society. A farm of upwards of a hundred acres was bought in addition, and was conveyed to himself.

The rumour of this produced some uneasiness among the members, and twenty of them waited on the Prophet to question him about the conveyance. He spoke them fair, assured them that the mansion and land would go to the Society, and in their presence drew up a will wherein he devised the whole estate to the Society. Messrs. Snell, Currey, Gill, and Farren, leading members and pillars of the Church, witnessed it, and departed in satisfaction to their homes. A fortnight after, Wroe sent for a solicitor of Wakefield, and privately drew up a new will, cancelling the old one, and in this latter will he devised the mansion and ninety-eight acres of land to his grandson, James Wroe; and to his daughters, Susanna and Sarah, property producing about £50 per annum to each; and to his only son Joseph property of the value of £60 per annum.

The mansion was designed somewhat in the style of Melbourne Town Hall. It cost upwards of £2000, but need not have cost half as much. When Wroe saw how the money poured in, he had the north east wing taken completely down, and enlarged the building. Much of the work was done two or three times over. The glazier (Mr. Slater) had a contract to do all the glazing, and as soon as his contract was finished, Wroe contracted with Mr. Slater to take every square of glass out again, and put good plate-glass into the windows instead.

Wroe found he could not get on without an architect, and therefore employed Mr. Thorpe, of Wakefield, and worried him out of all endurance. Wroe visited Australia in 1850, 1854, 1859, and 1862. He was in America in 1840, 1848, 1853, and 1859. His wife died May 16th, 1853, aged seventy-four years, a fortnight after he left for America. He is said to have treated her badly. On his travels he assumed different names; sometimes he called himself Johanan Asrael, sometimes Yokkow or Yockaman.

He obtained the name of "Pudding Wroe" among the urchins of Wakefield and Bradford; and the origin of this was as follows: – After one of his long trances, he began to walk about, and was asked by acquaintances concerning his health and appetite, and "What could he eat or fancy?" His invariable answer was, "Nowt but pudding."

The boys used to shout after him – "Pudding Wroe," or "Nowt but pudding," and this highly incensed the Prophet. One day, after he had had this cry ringing in his ears, he came home, and, standing in the door, saw the table laid for dinner, and his wife and children ready in their places. "What is for dinner to-day?" asked Wroe.

"Nowt but pudding!" shouted the incautious children. Wroe flew into a passion, and said to his wife, "I'll tell thee what, lass, I wi'nt have yon stuff called pudding ony more."

"Why, lad!" said Mrs. Wroe, "what are t' bairns to call it, then?"

"They mun call it *soft meat*," answered John.

Wroe purchased a handsome mule with a long flowing tail, and a basket carriage. The harness was of the best kind, with silver buckles, &c. One day when Wroe drove to Sandal, and left his mule and carriage outside the house where he had business, some evil-disposed persons shaved the mule's tail. Wroe raved and threatened, but could not find the guilty parties. He never went near Sandal afterwards.

The following is Wroe's receipt for curing a cold: – Put two gallons of boiling water in a large bottle, and place a funnel on the neck; put your face in the mouth of the funnel, and throw a blanket over your head; thus you inhale the steam, and are thrown into a perspiration.

Wroe would put a pillow in the oven, lay his head on it, and let the oven be heated as hot as he could bear it, to drive away a head cold.

In his last voyage to Australia, in 1862, he fell upon the deck of the ship when it was rolling, and dislocated his shoulder. The doctor set it, but it soon fell out of place again, and never was right after.

On the day of his death, which occurred at Fitzroy, in Australia, he had been out walking as usual, and seemed in his wonted health. On his return from a walk he seated himself in his chair, and suddenly fell forward on the floor, and was taken up a corpse. He had been collecting money in Australia; and directly it was rumoured that Wroe was dead, all the members in Melbourne demanded back their money, and threatened to roughly handle Benjamin Eddow, Wroe's companion and secretary, unless he restored the subscriptions. He was obliged to surrender some of the cash, and to conceal himself. He got away the following day, and remained hidden in a blacksmith's shop till he could find a ship on which to get back to England. He brought with him between six and seven hundred pounds. The Melbourne Society complained that Wroe had not kept faith with them, for he had promised them he would never die!

BISHOP-DYKE POND[1]

On the Monday following Palm Sunday, being the 14th of April, 1690, William Barwick, a man living in Cawood, a village a few miles south of York, on the Ouse, below its junction with the Wharfe, took his wife a stroll along a pleasant lane leading to Bishop Wood, then an extensive tract of forest trees, and even now one of the wildest and most picturesque spots in the neighbourhood of Selby.

Mary Barwick was expecting her confinement at no great distance of time. William made her walk before him; they crossed the little bridge over Bishop's Dyke, and entered a close or field where was a pond. It was surrounded by thick rushes, and the willows were covered with their silken tufts, unrifled by the children for "palms" on the preceding day.

William Barwick looked round. No one was in sight. He seized his wife, threw her into the pond, and did not let go his hold till she was drowned. When he was quite satisfied that life was extinct, he drew the body out of the water, and concealed it among the rushes which lay between the water and the quickwood hedge. He then returned home.

At dusk he revisited the spot, and taking a hay-spade from a rick that stood in the field, he made a hole by the side of the pond, and there buried the poor woman in her clothes. What was the motive which actuated William Barwick does not transpire.

Next day Barwick visited his brother-in-law at Rufforth, three miles east from York, a man named Thomas Lofthouse, who had married the sister of poor Mary Barwick, and told him that his wife Mary had gone to his uncle, Richard Harrison, in Selby, where she was likely to remain for some time.

Lofthouse gave no thought to this announcement. Whether he supposed that Barwick was in difficulties, and it was likely to prove advantageous to his wife that she sould be confined in Selby instead of at home, where she could have more comforts; or whether he thought there had been a quarrel, and the announcement of Barwick intimated a separation, I do not know. At all events, the statement of Barwick caused no surprise to his brother-in-law, nor did it arouse any suspicion of foul play in his mind.

Exactly a week after that visit, on Tuesday in Easter week, about half-past

---

[1] J. Aubery, in his "Miscellanies upon Various Subjects," 1696, gives the particulars of this curious story.

twelve o'clock in the afternoon, Thomas Lofthouse, having occasion to water a quickset hedge not far from his house, brought water for the purpose in a pail. As he was going for the second pailful, he suddenly observed a woman, in shape like his sister-in-law, going before him towards the pond. He was startled, but hardly thought at the moment that he saw a ghost. The figure glided before him, and seated itself on a rising green bank right over against the pond; he walked before her as he went to the pond, and as he returned with the pail full of water he looked sideways to see if the figure were still there. He saw the face – it was that of Mary Barwick, but deadly pale; the lips bloodless, the teeth showing, and the eyes fixed on something white, which he thought was a bag at the time, but afterwards supposed to be a baby, which she seemed to be dandling. As soon as he had emptied the pail, he went into his yard, and stood still to see if the figure were still in the same spot; but by this time it had vanished.

Lofthouse said nothing about what he had seen till evening. He was saying family prayers that night before retiring to rest, when, in praying for their friends and relations, he came to the name of his sister-in-law. He faltered, trembled, his voice broke down, and he could scarcely conclude his devotions.

When he went to bed he told his wife everything, and the poor woman was dreadfully alarmed. She implored her husband next day to go to Selby and see Richard Harrison, at whose house Barwick had said his wife was staying. He promised to do so, and on the morning early saddled his horse and rode to Selby. His nearest road was by York, Cawood, and Wiston; but he had no mind to meet William Barwick, and he therefore took the high road from York by Escrick, Riccal, and Barlby.

On reaching Selby he soon ascertained that poor Mary Barwick had never been there. On his return he went to the Lord Mayor of York; and having obtained a warrant, got Barwick apprehended and bought before the Mayor. The wretched man then acknowledged what he had done, and his confession was written down and signed in the presence of the Lord Mayor. To this were annexed the depositions of Lofthouse, and Barwick was consigned to York Castle.

These depositions are of sufficient interest to be here given verbatim:—

"The information of Thomas Lofthouse, of Rufforth, taken upon oath, the twenty-fourth day of April, 1690; who sayeth and deposeth,——

"That one William Barwick, who lately married this informant's wife's sister, came to this informant's house about the 14th instant, and told this informant he had carried his wife to one Richard Harrison's house in Selby, who was uncle to him, and would take care of her; and this informant, hearing nothing of the said Barwick's wife, his said sister-in-law, imagined he had done her some mischief, did yesterday go to the said Harrison's house in Selby, where he said he had carried her to; and the said Harrison told this informant he knew nothing of the said Barwick or his wife; and this informant doth verily believe the said Barwick to have murdered her.

"THOMAS LOFTHOUSE.

"Jurat die et anno super dicto coram me.

"S. DAWSON, Mayor."

"The examination of the said William Barwick, taken the day and year abovesaid, who sayeth and confesseth,—

"That he, this examinant, on Monday was seventh night, about two o'clock in the afternoon, this examinant was walking in a close betwixt Cawood and Wiston; and he farther sayeth that he threw his said wife into the pond, where she was drowned; and the day following, towards evening, got a hay-spade at a hay-stake in the said close, and made a grave beside the said pond, and buried her.

"WILLIAM BARWICK.

"Exam. capt., die et anno super dict. coram me.

"S. DAWSON, MAYOR."

"The examination of William Barwick, taken the twenty-fifth day of April, 1690, who sayeth and confesseth,—

"That he carried his wife over a certain wain-bridge, called Bishop-Dyke Bridge, betwixt Cawood and Sherborne, and within a lane about one hundred yards from the said bridge, and on the left hand of the said bridge, he and his wife went over a stile, on the left-hand side of a certain gate entering into a certain close, on the left hand of the said lane; and in a pond in the said close, adjoining to a quickwood hedge, did drown his wife, and upon the bank of the said pond did bury her; and further, that he was within sight of Cawood Castle, on the left hand; and that there was but one hedge betwixt the said close where he drowned his wife and the Bishop-slates belonging to the said castle.

"WILLIAM BARWICK.

"Exam. capt. die et anno super dict. coram me.

"S. DAWSON, Mayor."

William Barwick was tried and convicted before Sir John Powell, Knight, at the Summer Assizes held in York on the 18th of September, 1690.

"On Tuesday, September the seventeenth, 1690, at York Assizes, Thomas Lofthouse, of Rufforth, within three miles of York city, sayeth,—

"That on Easter Tuesday last, about half an hour after twelve o'clock in the daytime, he was watering quickwood, and as he was going for the second pail there appeared, walking before him, an apparition in the shape of a woman. Soon after, she sat down over against the pond, on a green hill; he walked by her as he went to the pond, and as he came with the pail of water from the pond, looking sideways to see if she sat in the same place, which he saw she did; and had on her lap something like a white bag, a-dandling of it (as he thought), which he did not observe before. After he had emptied his pail of water, he stood in his yard to see if he could see her again, but could not. He says her apparel was brown cloathes, waistcoat and petticoat, a white hood, such as his wife's sister usually wore, and her face looked extreme pale, her teeth in sight, no gums appearing, her visage being like his wife's sister, and wife to William Barwick.

(Signed)   "THOMAS LOFTHOUSE."

When Barwick ascended the gallows to be hung, he told the hangman that he hoped the rope was strong enough, as if it should break with his weight he would fall to the ground and become a cripple for life. His apprehensions, however, were soon quieted, for the hangman assured him he might venture upon it with perfect confidence.

After he was dead the body was hung in chains by the pond where the murder had been committed.

SNOWDEN DUNHILL,

THE CONVICT.

THE following life of a thief and housebreaker, written by himself, is curious and sad.[1] The talent it exhibits, and the real feeling which peeps out here and there, show that the man, had he been better brought up, and subjected in early youth to religious influences, might have become something very superior to the ordinary agricultural labourer. The man cannot have been difficient in his secular education. His style is singularly good for one in his class, but of moral education he had none. The only religion he knew of was that of his wife, Sally Dunhill, a fanatic, who combined hysterical piety with gross dishonesty:—

"I was born at a small village on the Wolds in the East Riding of Yorkshire. The earliest circumstance of which I have any remembrance is that of following bare-headed and on foot, a waggon containing furniture belonging to a farmer who was removing to the village of Spaldington, near Howden. Of my parents I have but an indistinct remembrance, for I never returned to them, but continued to reside in the village of my adoption, and principally in the house of the family I had accompanied.

"Spaldington is a secluded and purely agricultural village. My earliest recollections are connected with the old hall at that place, a fine building, erected in the time of Queen Elizabeth. This house, with its peaked roof ornamented with large round stones, its moats, its rookery, and the reputation of being haunted by a fairy, is yet strongly impressed upon my memory. But the old seat of the De la Hayes, the Vescis, and the Vavasours totters to its fall.

"I well remember the tradition which prevailed in the village, that one of the De Vescis was a competitor for the crown of Scotland, he having married a daughter of the King of that country. The burthen of an old song, which is supposed to relate to some eventful battle in which De Vesci bore a conspicuous part, still clings to my memory, and now, with a world between me and the spot, I often catch myself humming the chorus—

[1] "The Life of Snowden Dunhill, written by Himself." Howden, 1833

"'And the drums they did beat, and the trumpets did sound,
  And the cannons did roar fit to tear up the ground;
  For its oh! brave, gallant, and brave,
  For the honour of England's crown.'

Snowden Dunhill's youth was spent much as that of other rural bumpkins; he wrestled, played football, and was passionately fond of cock-fighting.

One day, when only six years old, he saved the life of a little companion with whom he was playing by the side of the moat round the Old Hall at Spaldington. The child fell into the water, sank, and rose for the last time, when little Snowden, with great pluck, jumped in after his playmate, and caught him by the dress. The two children struggled in the water, and the drowning boy nearly dragged little Snowden under. But Snowden maintained his hold, and succeeded in dragging his comrade to the bank.

At fourteen or fifteen Snowden Dunhill, being a strong lad, was taken into a small farmhouse to work for his food and clothes.

His master died shortly after, but his widow carried on the farm. She was very poor, the farm was small, and the widow took her meals with the farm servants in the kitchen.

Dunhill was given no pocket-money, and, as he kept fighting-cocks and liked occasionally to go to the public-house to have a game of balls, he was driven to obtain money by theft.

"During this time I practised a variety of petty thefts without being suspected. I took apples, eggs, or anything I could lay my hands on, and the corn which ought to have been given to the horses found its way to my game cocks, of which I had several. These acts, which are generally practised by farmers' servants, were confirmed into a habit before I had begun to think them wrong. The education of this class is so utterly neglected, and their morals so little attended to, that I have long been satisfied that the honesty of the rural districts is very much inferior to that of the towns.

"My next step in life – the most important one to all – was marriage, and mine assuredly deepened the darkest shades of my character. It was not a conection of the heart, but one almost of fear, for the woman to whom I paid my addresses was the being who ruled me from the first moment of our acquaintance. Had it been my fortune to have met with an honest and industrious woman, my destiny might have been different. But if, as the proverb says, 'Marriages are made in heaven,' it does not become me to complain.

"We lived a short time in the village of Spaldington, but one farmer missed his corn, the wife of another her poultry, a third her apples, and a fourth her bees; when the bees were missed I fancy they thought nothing could escape us. They were easily moved and carried into our cottage, but the buzzing, the stinging, and the bother of the business, determined me never again to attempt a similar undertaking. The proverb of running your head into a swarm of bees has ever since appeared to me the most forcible in the English language.

"We were then put into a house in the lanes of Spaldington, in the road between Howden and Market-Weighton, apart from any other residence, and in the very best situation that could have been chosen if the farmers had wished us to continue our system of plunder. I had never been accustomed to work, and I had now very little wish to learn. The new connexions which I speedily formed put me in the way of obtaining a better though more precarious subsistence.

"I continued to live in the cottage above alluded to, and my family increasing rapidly, rendered it necessary to extend my operations. The farmers in the neighbourhood were at first the greatest sufferers, and there was scarcely a barn or granary within several miles which I had not the means of entering when I chose. Either from discarded servants, or from labourers who were daily about the farm houses, I got all the information I wanted.

"At this time I was master of two good horses, and I had a numerous connexion among servants and labourers. But what I found most useful was a secret understanding with two or three millers, by whose means I got rid of all the corn which I stole. Millers are generally reputed to be great rogues, but in their dealings with me I found them quite the contrary. The most dishonest persons with whom I had dealings were the attorneys, and they stripped me of the fruits of my toil with most surprising expedition and facility. This, however, will be seen in the sequel.

"About this time I was concerned in a robbery at Bubwith, by which I obtained a considerable sum of money. After our arrangements were made, a comrade entered the house through a back window, by taking an iron bar out of the frame, the wood being quite rotten from age and damp. In scrambling in he kicked from the shelf a large earthenware vessel, and immediately after he himself tumbled head foremost into the pantry, a depth of six or seven feet. The uproar occasioned by his fall caused us to take to our heels and make to our horses, which were at no great distance, in a large field behind the house. We laid down and listened for a considerable time, and hearing nothing, we approached the house again by degrees, and eventually got up to the very window. A low whistle from me was instantly answered, which at once told us all went well. We found the back door open for us, and our comrade, no way alarmed, busy rummaging some drawers, and putting into a sack everything he took a fancy to.

"As I had formerly lived in the service of a near relation of the old lady to whom the house belonged (I had forgotten to say it was a widow lady's house we took the liberty with), I found no difficulty in laying my hands upon the tinder-box, candles, and everything else. It was an exceedingly stormy night, or I think we must have been heard, for we carried a chest of drawers out of the house and actually beat them to pieces, not being able to open them. I knew that she had a considerable sum of money, and I hoped we had found it, but it turned out to be a box of farthings; and I was afterwards exceedingly provoked on learning that we had missed three hundred guineas in gold which the old lady had in her lodging room. I also learned that she had a presentiment that she would be robbed, and made an observation to that effect the day before – one of those curious anticipating feelings which I know not how to account, but which have in several instances happened to myself when coming events, as it were, cast their shadows before.

"But to return to our adventure. After helping ourselves to such things as we thought of most value, and such as could be most easily conveyed away on our horses, and drinking the good old lady's health in some excellent home-made wine, we mounted our horses, with four sacks filled with many things of value. We took a route so as to avoid the toll-bars and public roads, and reached my house just as the sun was beginning to chase away the darkness which had proved so propitious to us. Having instantly buried all the things, my companions departed, and all was soon ready for the reception of any of those enemies of my profession, the constables, should they pay us a visit. However, none came, and though I was generally supposed to be the person who did the deed, no steps were taken to make it out against me. This is one of the very few exploits of the kind I was ever engaged in, and as to highway robberies, I never dreamed of committing one.

"I had now accumulated a considerable sum of money, which I lent out on note to several farmers in the neighbourhood, most of whom, from fear or other considerations, were glad to be on good terms with me. Such occurences as the following frequently happened: – 'Well, Snowden, how do you do?' would farmer —— say, meeting me in the street towards dusk on a market-day. 'Are you going home to-night?' 'Aye, my lad,' was my general reply. 'I wanted to see you', retorted the farmer; 'I have just received fifty pounds for some oats; I wish you would take care of it for me, and I will ask you for it again some day when I meet you' I took charge of the money, and was ever most punctual in returning it. I could not help laughing, however, at the odd mixture of feelings that must have dictated such a choice of banker. I dare say some of these very farmers have since met with bankers not quite so punctual in their payments as I was in mine.

"I was once busily employed in coursing a hare when I was pounced upon by a Mr. ——. He came suddenly upon me, with so many violent denunciations that I was for a time really in a fright. However, I eventually recovered my recollection, and had the good sense to leave him without giving way to any abusive language in reply. I secretly, however, resolved to have my revenge, and that in a way at once in accordance with my profession and my own interest. I ordered two or three of the persons I could place the most reliance in to be ready to accompany me with their horses to Foggathorpe, the village in which I think the gentleman resided. I had long had a key of his granary, in which I knew he had recently stored a quantity of wheat of the finest quality, and for which the soil of that village is much famed.

"We had already been up to the granary once with our horses, having taken them loaded away, and secreted several sacks of wheat in a wood a little from the turnpike road, and about three miles from the house. We had filled our sacks a second time, and got them upon the horses, having previously placed everything in the granary as we found it, or as nearly so as we could. I had just thrown my legs over my horse, then standing near the steps of the granary, I being the last of the party, when I heard the gentleman's voice, which I at once knew, for neither his early habit of rising nor the tone of his voice were unknown to me. It was quite dark, and I proceeded with great care on the way towards the high road till I reached a gate about seventy or eighty yards from his house. By some mismanagement on my part, I had no sooner passed through the gate than it fell back into its place with considerable noise. I again heard his voice, but I made the best of my way with my load, and I felt no little relief when I found myself in the Market-Weighton turnpike road. Though I had no very great opinion of the gentleman's courage, I felt quite sure he would have used every endeavour to make out the charge against me had his suspicions of what had taken place been once roused. As to his following me alone at that moment I had not the most distant fear, for I knew well the care he always took of himself. However, the whole affair passed over. I never heard that he missed what we took away, and the reason probably was, that he at that very time had a large stock of wheat on hand for the purpose of speculation, as I afterwards learned. I remember this wheat was of such singularly good quality that I sold it for the great sum of one guinea and ninepence the bushel, a price I scarcely ever remember to have equalled.

"The next thing that occurs to me worthy of remark, and which I had good cause to remember, nearly terminated fatally for myself. I expected a good booty from the information I had previously received. This was an attack upon the property of two bachelors who resided in the same house, in a village about a mile and a half from Howden. The House was very near to the river Ouse, and we had prepared a boat to carry the gains of the night down the river as far as Swinefleet, this being considered, for many reasons, the readiest mode of moving it from the premises, and I had some friends in that place in whom I placed the greatest confidence. Between one and two o'clock we arrived at the house, and were preparing all things in readiness for the business in hand. I was crossing from the bank of the river over a garden, and so on to the back of the premises. In my way I came to a piece of dead fence, over which I was passing, and which gave a crackling sound under my tread. At that moment I heard a dog bark, and instantly after a shot was fired from the upper part of the eastern end of the house. I had my face at the time rather turned away from the place whence the shot proceeded, and I received the whole of the contents in my back and shoulders. I instantly fell; and I well remember that I thought all was over with me, as I lay for some time with my head in the ditch and my feet upon the dead thorns over which I had just passed, and to which I attributed my mishap; for the night was so dark I could not be seen, and the shot must have been directed by the noise I made in getting over the fence. As I lay there I could distinctly hear a whispering from a small door in the end of the house, and I greatly feared lest the inmates should sally forth and take me in my defenceless state. With my head laid upon the ground, the sensation produced upon me by the striking of two o'clock by the church of Howden, I well remember. All was now calm, quiet, and dark; and I actually felt the earth vibrate under my ear as the hollow bell threw over the land its sullen sound. I have understood, since I came here, that savages in America always resort to this mode of listening for the approach of a friend or an enemy. But to return to myself again.

"I at length contrived with great difficulty to get upon my feet; and, with still greater exertion and much loss of blood, I reached the boat, where I found my men in great consternation and alarm. One of them pushed the boat adrift, and the tide soon carried it away with the waters. They then supported me at a slow pace to Howden, where I arrived almost in a state of insensibility, from the combined effects of pain and loss of blood. By my desire they took me to the house of a medical man of my acquaintance, and knocked at his door. He soon came down, and without asking a single question, stripped me; and during the night he extracted no fewer than thirty-eight large shot corns from my back and shoulders.

"I cannot even now recall the agony I suffered without a shudder; and my general health and strength never recovered from the shock I received. I remained secluded for a considerable time, but thanks to the attentive care of my wife, and my own sober habits, for I never was an habitual drunkard, I speedily was able to get out again. In all my night excursions after this adventure I employed the greatest circumspection.

"My inward disposition was accurately betokened by my countenance and outward appearance. I was tall and large-limbed, but neither clumsy nor powerfully made. I speak now of forty years of age; for sufferings, mental and bodily, have entirely changed my face and figure. My hair was light, my eyes a bluish grey, my countenance round and somewhat florid. In my looks I always fancied that I resembled two men of no little celebrity – I mean Sir Walter Scott and William Cobbett, who certainly bear a considerable resemblance to each other. But this may be my vanity, for the best of us are not free from it.

"In my manners I was boisterous, and in tone familiar with all, and overbearing with most. However, my general appearance promised anything but cruelty and dishonesty; and, thank God, no one can charge me with the former, whatever may be said of the latter.

"I must, however, plead guilty to one or two acts of apparent cruelty towards my horses, but which rather rose from necessity of self-preservation than from any other cause. It has often happened to me, for the purpose of reaching a given place by a certain hour of the night, to be compelled to strain my horse to the full extent of his speed. I knew so well the general opinion entertained towards me, that I felt I must find the greatest difficulty in clearing myself from anything like a reasonable suspicion of crime.

"I distinctly remember once having upon me a considerable sum of money, and I was riding at full speed upon a narrow strip of green sward by the road side, which was nearly covered by the extended branches of the trees. The moon was shining beautifully through them, and in contemplating her I felt a soothing calmness spread over my soul, which I cannot account for or explain the cause of. My musings were suddenly cut short by a deep-drawn sigh from my horse, then a slight shudder, and the next moment he was dead under me. I cried like a child. I raised his head, but all in vain, no trace of life remained.

"By the moon's rays, which at that instant shot through an opening in a dark Scots fir immediately over his head, I saw the film of death rapidly spread over his eyes, and felt his limbs stiffen under my grasp. I had to travel several miles on foot, pretty well loaded, and through a very lonely and suspicious-looking part of the country. However, I reached the house of one of my friends towards morning, to his no small astonishment, he thinking me fifty miles distant in a different direction.

"My horse was soon recognised; and had a robbery been perpetrated within a reasonable distance of the place where he fell, of course it must have been done by me. The common question of the whole neighbourhood was, 'What had I been doing?' However, this never transpired. I ever afterwards tied a piece of raw beef round the bit of my bridle when about to make hard use of my horse, and I always thought that it afforded him considerable help. I need not observe that this was done in imitation of poor Dick Turpin, whose history is infinitely better known than mine can ever pretend to be.

"On the night of the 25th of October, 1812, I felt a presentiment that something sinister was about to happen to me. Few men have passed through life, particularly those of an excitable temperament, who have not felt some boding of this kind. I was seated in my chair by the fire, taking my accustomed pipe – an indulgence I never omitted the last thing at night – when this sudden impression came over me. My wife observed that something was the matter, and questioned me on the subject. However, as I knew she would only laugh at me, I did not tell her the cause.

"In the middle of the forenoon, whilst I was listening to my daughter Rose, who was my favourite, she suddenly looked up and said, in a hurried tone, 'Father, there are several men coming to the house.' It instantly occurred to me that something had happened during the past night, and that my forebodings would not prove vain. However, as my whole family knew that I had not stirred out during the night, I had little fear; and this circumstance even led me to suppose that it might be some mistake.

"By this time the party had arrived at the door of the cottage, and one of them gave me to understand that he had a justice's search-warrant, and that I was their prisoner. I submitted at once to be taken into custody, and I was immediately secured. Some of the party then began to rummage every drawer and corner of the house, amidst the very voluble abuse of my wife. They, however, found nothing they came to search for, which, as I sooned learned, was some wheat stolen during the last night from a neighbouring farmer.

"On this information I felt considerable relief, conscious of my innocence; but my wife became perfectly outrageous when the constable refused to take her word that I had never stirred over my threshold since six o'clock of the preceding evening. She, poor woman, swore she would take the law of them threatened writs, indictments, justices, and I know not what; and I verily believed she would have inflicted summary vengeance on the head of the constable with the poker, so furious had she become, from a consciousness that the accusation was without foundation.

"However, in spite of all her threats and rage, I was speedily conveyed before the justice who granted the warrant, and on the oath of a person, who swore that he was going along a road near my house and towards the farm-house in question, about two o'clock in the morning, that he saw a horse and two men returning from it, and that he was quite sure I was one of them, my commitment was made out for the House of Correction at Beverley.

"All this took so short a time that I scarcely attempted to defend myself; and indeed I scarcely even know now how I could effectually have done so. For I could only bring the members of my own family to prove that I had not been out of my cottage, and of course they would not have been believed against the positive evidence of the witness who swore to my person, though he was, according to his own statement, fifty yards distant from me – in addition to this, at two o'clock in the morning."

The prosecutor of Snowden Dunhill was Mr. Barnard Clarkson, of Holme, at that time a partner in the Howden Bank.

The consciousness that her husband was ignorant of the robbery imputed to him caused Sally Dunhill to regard him as a martyr. Her Ranting enthusiasm was excited, and she wrote a long letter to the prosecutor, denouncing him, in Biblical terms, as one who "compassed about" the righteous man "with words of hatred, and fought against him without a cause"; and announced to him that she had given herself up to prayer against him (Clarkson), and invoked the malediction of heaven upon his head – "Let his posterity be cut off; and in the generations following let their name be blotted out." And she concluded this strange epistle with the words of the Palmist: "Let them curse, but bless thou: when they arise, let them be ashamed; but let thy servant rejoice. Let mine enemies be clothed with shame, and let them cover themselves with their own confusion as with a mantle. I will greatly praise the Lord with my mouth; yea I will praise him among the multitude, for he shall stand at the right hand of the poor, to save him from those that condemn his soul."

Snowden Dunhill continues in his Autobiography:—

"I now, for the first time, become an inmate of a prison, an event I had always held in the greatest horror. As it was well known that I had plenty of money, I had very soon the proffered and apparently disinterested assistance of an attorney. My situation was maturely considered, and it was soon determined that a writ of habeas corpus should be put in, for the purpose of taking my trial at the approaching Assizes at York, in preference to Beverley.

"I was in consequence taken up to London in custody, after the writ was obtained, and my trial was appointed to take place at York, principally on this ground, as urged by counsel, that my character was so notorious in the East Riding of Yorkshire that no unprejudiced jury could there be impannelled. The reader may be sure that all this was done at no slight expense; but perhaps he will not believe me when I assure him that by the time my counsel had received his fee for the approaching defence I had scarcely a shilling left in the world.

"The March Assizes of 1813 at length arrived, when I gave myself up to the gaoler of the Castle, and I was soon placed in the dock. My eyes were cast on the ground, and I for a time felt stupefied. However, I at last raised them to the objects before me, and the first that caught them was the judge himself, then the counsel, and then the immense crowd of spectators who had assembled to hear my trial. I soon was calm enough to discover in the gallery the faces of many persons I knew, and I endeavoured to put on a forced courage by nodding familiarly at them, and by appearing to be utterly careless of what was going forward.

"The indictment was read over to me, and I was called upon to hold up my hand and plead guilty or not guilty; though I uttered the latter with a loud voice, it was with a full conviction that my doom was sealed. I felt – and I suppose all persons similarly circumstanced feel the same – that not only the assembled people, but that the whole world has combined to destroy me.

"The facts above narrated were stated shortly to the jury. The witness swore to my person, and accounted for his being there at that hour, naturally enough, by stating that he had been to visit his sweetheart. The farmer swore to having missed the corn on the night in question. Though my counsel tried to confound the first witness by fierce looks and bullying questions, and by dwelling upon the impossibility of his being able to swear to a person at the distance of fifty yards and at two in the morning, yet he stuck to his oath immovably. I was asked what I wished to say, and all that I could state was that I was innocent; that I was in bed at the time, and that all the family knew this to be the fact. My wife was anxious to speak for me, but my counsel insisted upon her holding her tongue, which she at last consented to do on his assuring her that she would do my case more harm than good. The jury without the slightest hesitation found me guilty, and the judge at once sentenced me to seven years' transportation.

"I was immediately conveyed back to my cell, and a few days afterwards I was forwarded to the hulks. In this miserable banishment I passed six years, embittered by the most dreadful account of my family, every member of it, even in the roughest degree, having transgressed the laws of his country, and was then undergoing for his offences the punishment awarded to him. Could hope under any form have presented herself to me, I felt that I might yet be a reclaimed man, but I could not catch the most distant glimpse of her. My years passed on in the midst of misery the most distressing, till they at last came to an end. I obtained my discharge or pardon a short time before the expiration of my full term, for I had been guilty of no violence, or insolence, or excess, since my arrival.

"I left this abode of vice and misery without a friend on the face of the earth, and unconscious where to find even a momentary place of refuge. There are many unfortunate individuals who, had they a house or employment to fly to after having undergone their periods of punishment, would be glad to betake themselves to habits of honesty and industry. But, unluckily for them, they are turned out without a refuge to resort to, and necessity, and not inclination, drives them to the commission of fresh crimes.

"As to myself, I returned to Spaldington, but the change which my worldly prospects and circumstances had undergone was in the extreme overwhelming. Some of these misfortunes I well knew, but to others I was an entire stranger, and I cannot at this day lay blame to anyone but myself for them. My evil example pointed out the way of lawless depredation to my children, in characters so legible that they could not fail to read and study them.

"The farmers of the village had thought it right to clear my cottage of every one connected with me in name, relationship, or blood.

"I felt at a great loss where to fix, or to what object to turn myself for a livelihood and bare subsistence. As to my children and connections, they were scattered in every direction, and for the most part undergoing the punishment due to their crimes.

"My daughter, my favourite daughter, Rose, had been committed, and sentenced to confinement in York Castle. During her imprisonment she was delivered of a bastard-child; what its fate may be, heaven alone can tell! She was visited in the Castle by a gentleman from Howden, for the purpose of proffering her some assistance in her necessitous situation. This I have understood she indignantly refused. Holding up her new-born babe to his gaze, she said, 'See! he has hands to help himself, and if ever there was a true-born rogue, here he is!'' Thus, like Hannibal towards Rome, was this poor child devoted from its earliest infancy to war against all the settled institutions of society.

"After her release from York the reader will readily imagine from this anecdote of her, that she would speedily fall into another scrape. This soon happened. She was committed to Wakefield House of Correction, again tried and found guilty, and I have never since heard of her. She had cohabited with two different men, both of whom passed as her husband. Their names were M'Dowel and Connor, and they both have been transported.

"My daughter, Sarah Dunhill, after having been confined in York Castle, was tried at the East Riding Sessions at Beverley, and imprisoned one year. She was subsequently tried at the Borough Sessions at Beverley for picking the pocket of a gentleman named Scholfield, and stealing from him a considerable sum of money.

"During her trial she made a moving appeal to the barristers present, stating that she had always found them her best friends; that their ingenuity had often assisted her in the hour of need, and she yet reposed faith in their kindness, and proudly left her honesty and honour in their keeping. The Recorder, startled into momentary confusion at the nature of this appeal, speedily recovered his dignity, and inflicted on her the doom of the law. She was at this time residing at Hull, and had come over to Beverley fair that morning for the purpose of depredation. For this offence she was transported for seven years. She had three husbands, named James Stanhope, William Rhodes, and James Crossland, all of whom were severally transported, one after the other.

"My son, William Dunhill, was transported at the York Assizes for the term of fourteen years. He, poor fellow, died immediately on his arrival in New South Wales. He was the most promising of my family, and with different examples before him, and good advice, would probably have proved an ornament to society.

"Robert Taylor, son of my wife by a former husband, and who lived under the same roof with us for several years, was also transported.

"I think I omitted to state that my wife at the time I married her was a widow, and her name was Taylor. Her husband was shot in attempting to commit a robbery shortly before I married her, a circumstance which was not known to me, and which she never mentioned.

"As to my wife, she was also transported, after having contrived innumerable depredations, and been the cause of those fatal events which befell herself, myself, and the rest of the family.

"A robbery committed at Howden was readily traced home to the inmates of our house; suspicion fell at once upon them, and the furniture, watches, coins, and many other stolen articles were found on my premises. But as this and many other things happened during my absence, and as I never again saw several members of my family, I am the less particular in narrating them, from my great anxiety that nothing should appear in this history of myself for which I cannot vouch the truth."

Snowden returned to Spaldington, found his family dispersed, his cottage occupied by other tenants, and no one in the village disposed to receive him with open arms. The farmers naturally viewed his return with alarm, and he found none in the neighbourhood disposed to give him work, had he cared to take it. But steady work was distasteful to him. Had he sought it in other parts of Yorkshire he might readily have found it. Instead of this he loafed about, sulky and angry with society. By degrees he formed new connections, in Hull and Lincolnshire, and resumed his former dishonest practices in concert with them.

"I had heard much of the easy lives led by the convicts in New South Wales; and, moreover, some members of my family were already there, and I felt impelled to make an endeavour to join them.

"I had not long to wait for the gratification of this wish, for I was soon traced to the commission of a paltry crime. I was apprehended, tried, and convicted;

my character did the rest, and readily procured for me that banishment from England on which I had set my heart. My trial took place at a district Quarter sessions in the north of Lincolnshire, in the goal of which I was only detained a few days when, with several others, I was transmitted, pinioned and loaded with irons, to London, there to await a ship to convey me to Botany Bay.

"It was a cold, bleak morning when I was put upon the coach in the court-yard of the prison, before daylight, with the rain and sleet falling in abundance. The coach remained half-an-hour or more in the yard of the prison till all was in readiness, when the gates were thrown open and we commenced our inauspicious journey. I cannot at all describe the feelings of loneliness and of heartrending distress which came over me at this moment, in which I felt that I was rushing from certain misery to something that might be even still worse, and yet in my despair I felt a clinging to existence. I have never met with – nay, I have never heard of – a bad man who could look death unflinchingly in the face. On ascending the first rise of the ground in our journey towards London a breeze from the north suddenly sprung up, which scattered to the loaded clouds, and the sun burst forth in all its glory. There appeared before me, as if a veil had been taken off the earth by magic power, a wide-spread picture. The Humber, glorying in its Scythian name, rolling to the ocean its mass of waters; and in the distance the winding Trent and Ouse, stealing onward like two wily serpents; and I could just discover the broad expanse where they became united.

"The beautiful Lincolnshire hills on my left, and the still more beautiful hills, dales, and woods of my own native Yorkshire to the north, lent their charms to form a landscape I never saw equalled, and in casting my last lingering gaze upon it I felt that the inanimate beauties of creation must now to me ever be a blank. I strained my eyes to catch as much of it as I could, feeling the prospect, as it were, a part of myself, and necessary to my very existence, for there it had commenced, and little at one time did I think at how great a distance I was doomed to end it.

"Arrived at Botany Bay, I was soon disposed of, and commenced in good earnest the life of a slave. Hard-worked, half-starved, ill-fed, and worse clothed, such is the fate of the hapless convict."

Whilst in confinement, Snowden Dunhill wrote his Autobiography, and much wished to send it to his native village that it might be printed there for circulation. But it was some time before an opportunity presented itself.

One October day, 1830, as he was wheeling earth and stones near the pier of Sydney, in the harbour of Port Jackson, he rested for a moment to look at the beautiful bay before him, and compare it with one of the lake-like reaches of the Humber, when he was roused from his musings by a tap on the shoulder, and the salutation of "Well, Snowden, how are you?"

He touched his cap, and looked up. Before him stood a sailor, who grasped his hand and shook it warmly. The sailor was the little boy whose life he had saved in the moat of Spaldington Old Hall so many years before.

The sailor gave him some money, and told him he was about to return to Hull. Dunhill at once produced his little Autobiography, and entreated him to take it back to Yorkshire, and get it printed there. The sailor readily promised to do this, and to his fulfilment of the promise we owe the existence of the curious little memoir presented to the reader.

In August, 1833, Snowden Dunhill was seen by another Howden man, who was at Hobart Town, Van Dieman's Land. His account of Dunhill is that he was "a tall, stout man, bent and stooping with suffering and privation more than from natural infirmity, but with the step and assurance of his old self."

The Howden man would not have known Dunhill had not the convict heard his name mentioned, and introduced himself to him: "Ye're one of ——'s sons i' Howden?" in the broadest East Riding Yorkshire. Then, when the stranger answered that he was, Dunhill's eyes filled with tears, and had begun to sob.

"In external appearance he was not very much altered. The boisterous and overbearing manners of former years yet remained, unsoftened and unrepressed by the sufferings he had undergone. An habitual stoop had bent down his person, and somewhat taken away from the portly and blustering gait of early life. The small, grey, quick, and piercing eye still retained its cunning and prying character. His dress was much the same as he wore in England."

Dunhill had received his ticket of freedom at Sydney two or three years before this, and had then removed to Van Dieman's Land, where his wife and daughter were settled.

There is a strange irony in facts. Sally Dunhill, who had been unable to rear one of her own children in morality and honesty, so impressed on the people of Hobart Town that she was a saintly woman by her vociferous prayers and familiarity with Holy Scripture, that she was employed in teaching at a day-school and was entrusted with the education of children in those paths she had never trodden herself. The residue of her time was spent in making penny pies, which Snowden hawked about the town.

Snowden Dunhill gradually sank into habitual drunkenness, and was suspected of reverting to his old tricks of petty larceny. When he died is not known.

JAMES NAYLOR,

THE QUAKER.[1]

JAMES NAYLOR was born at East Ardsley, near Wakefield, in 1616. He was the son of a small farmer, whose house was near the old church. He received a passable education in reading, writing, and arithmetic. In 1628, when he was aged twenty-two, he married, and settled in Wakefield parish. He was a diligent reader of the Scriptures, and zealous as an Independent. He spent about three years at Wakefield, and then joined the Parliamentary army as a private in 1641. He rose to become quartermaster of his regiment under Major-General Lambert, but in 1649, on account of ill health, he was obliged to leave the army and return to Wakefield. The pulpits of the Established Church were now in the hands of Independent ministers, and that of Horbury, near Wakefield, was occupied by the "godly and painful Master Marshall," under whom James Naylor sat and groaned with unction.

But Naylor relaxed his religious exercises on visits to a Mrs. Roper at Horbury, a lady whose husband had been for some time absent. When this lady became a mother by James Naylor, the Rev. Mr. Marshall thought it necessary to expose him, and Naylor, indignant with his Independent minister, joined the sect of the Quakers, then founded by George Fox. In 1652 he went on a religious visitation to the West, and in 1655 he visited London, in which city a meeting of Quakers had been established by the ministry of Edward Burrough and Francis Howgill, two men of Westmoreland.

Naylor prophesised in the meeting with so great applause that several women began to exalt him above Burrough and Howgill, and disturbed the latter when they attempted to speak. The two ministers reproved the women, and they in dudgeon complained to Naylor, and he encouraged them in their opposition to Burrough and Howgill. Two of these women, Martha Symonds

---

[1] Authorities: — "The Grand Imposter Examined; or, the Life, Trial, and Examination of James Naylor, London, 1656," reprinted in the Harleian Misc., vi., 424. Johannis Lussenii "Hist. u. Schrifftmässige Erörterung der vor wenigh Zeit in Engelland entstandenen secte der Quäcker," in "Quäcker Grueuel," published by authority of the magistrates of Hamburg, 1702. "The Recantation of James Naylor," in Somers' Tracts," vi., 22 pub. 1659. "Naylor's Writings Collected," 8vo, 1716. Sewell's "Hist. of the Quakers," 1714. Sewell was personally accquainted with Hannah Stranger, one of Naylor's followers. "The Journals of the House of Commons," vi., p. 448 – 59. Blome's "Fanatick History." J. Whiting's "Account."

and Hannah Stranger, became his most devoted adherents, and followed him in all his wanderings.

In 1656 he revisited the West, prophesised in Cornwall, and on passing through Exeter was arrested under the sweeping charge of vagrancy, and committed to gaol. There he was visited by many devout females, amongst others by one Dorcas Erbury, who fell into a swoon, and was revived by Naylor, who cried over her, "Tabitha, I say unto thee, arise!" She awoke, and the faithful believed that Naylor had restored her from death to life.

He was released at length by order of Council and then travelled to Bristol at the head of six believers. On reaching Bedminster, a village a mile from Old Bristol, though now a suburb of the town, Naylor and his party formed in procession, intending to produce a scene in the streets of Bristol.

One of his disciples, a young man with bare head, led the horse by the bridle upon which Naylor was mounted; two men followed in single file on horseback, each with his wife on a pillion behind him; and one woman walked on the causeway. As they went forward the six shouted, "Holy, holy, holy, Lord God of Sabaoth!" till they came to the almshouse in the suburbs of Bristol, "when one of the women alighted, and she, with the other of her own sex, lovingly marched on each side of Naylor's horse." The road was deep in mud and rain was falling, but neither mud nor rain damped the ardour of the enthusiasts. On reaching Redcliffe Gate, Timothy Wedlock, a Devonshire man of the company, bareheaded, and Martha Symonds holding the bridle on one side and Hannah Stranger holding it on the other, advanced, chanting their hymn of praise.

Naylor wore a broad-brimmed hat and a long sad-coloured mantle. He was of a moderate height, ruddy complexion, had a slightly arched nose, large brown eyes, was a remarkably handsome man, and was thought by many to resemble the traditional type of face attributed to our Lord. Martha Symonds was the wife of Thomas Symonds, book-binder of London; and Hannah Stranger was the wife of John Stranger, combmaker in London. The two other women accompanying Naylor were Dorcas Erbury, whom he had raised from the dead, and her mother.

In this way the solemn procession advanced to the High Cross at Bristol, and after that to the White Hart, Broad Street, where lodged two Quakers, Dennis Hollister and Henry Row.

The magistrates at once apprehended the party, and committed them to prison.

The following is the examination of the prisoners, somewhat condensed:—

EXAMINATION OF JAMES NAYLOR.

Being asked his name, he replied, "The men of this world call me James Naylor."

Q. "Art not thou the man that rid on horseback into Bristol, a woman leading thy horse, and others saying before thee, 'Holy, holy, holy, Hosannah to the Son of David'?''

A. ''I did ride into a town, but what its name was I know not; and by the Spirit a woman was commanded to hold my horse's bridle, and some there were that cast down clothes and sang praises to the Lord, such songs as the Lord put into their hearts; and it is like it might be the song, 'Holy, holy, holy,' &c.''

Q. ''Whether or not didst thou reprove these women?''

A. ''Nay; but I bade them take heed that they say nothing but what they were moved to by the Lord.''

Q. ''Dost thou own this letter which Hannah Stranger sent unto thee?''

A. ''Yes, I do own that letter.''

Q. ''Art thou (according to that letter) the fairest of ten thousand?''

A. ''As to the visible, I deny any such attribute to be due unto me; but if as to that which the Father hath begotten in me, I shall own it.''

Two letters were then produced and read; we need only give one:—

''JAMES NAYLOR,

''Oh! thou fairest of ten thousand, thou only begotten Son of God, how my heart panteth after thee! O stay me with flaggons and comfort me with wine. My beloved, thou are like a roe or young hart upon the mountains of spices, where thy beloved spouse hath long been calling thee to come away, but hath been but lately heard of thee. Now it lies something upon me that thou mindest to see her, for the spirit and power of God is with her, and there is given to her much of excellent and innocent wisdom arisen and arising in her, which will make all the honest-hearted to praise the Lord alone, and no more set up self. And therefore let not my lord and master have any jealousy against her, for she is highly beloved of the Lord, and that shall all see who comes to know the Lord. And now He doth bless them that bless His, and curse them that curse His; for this hath the Lord showed me, that her portion is exceedingly large in the Lord, and as her sorrow hath been much, so shall her joy be much more; which rejoiceth my heart to see her walk so valiantly and so faithfully in the work of the Lord, in this time of so great trials as hath been upon her especially.

''And I am,

''HANNAH STRANGER.

''*The Postscript.*

''Remember my dear love to thy master. The name is no more James, but Jesus.

JOHN STRANGER.''

''Remember my love to these friends with thee. The 17th day of 8th month, superscribed to the hands of James Naylor.''

Q. "Art thou the only Son of God?"

A. "I am the son of God; but I have many brethren."

Q. "Have any called thee by the name of Jesus?"

A. "Not as unto the visible, but as Jesus, the Christ that is in me."

Q. "Dost thou own the name of the King of Israel?"

A. "Not as a creature; but if they gave it to Christ within, I own it, and have a kingdom, but not of this world; my kingdom is of another world, of which thou wotest not."

Q. "Whether or no art thou the prophet of the Most High?"

A. "Thou hast said I am a prophet."

Q. "By whom were you sent?"

A. "By Him who hath sent the Spirit of His Son in me to try, not as to carnal matters, but belonging to the kingdom of God, by the indwelling of the Father and the Son, to judge all spirits, to be guided by none."

Q. "Is not the written Word of God the guide?"

A. "The written Word declares of it, and what is not according to that is not true."

Q. "Who is thy mother? or whether or no is she a virgin?"

A. "Nay, according to the natural birth."

Q. "Who is thy mother acording to thy spiritual birth?"

A. "No carnal creature."

Q. "Who then?"

He returned no answer.

Q. "Art thou the everlasting Son of God?"

A. "When God is manifest in the flesh there is the everlasting Son; and I do witness God in the flesh. I am the Son of God, and the Son of God is but one."

Q. "Art thou the everlasting Son of God, the King of Righteousness?"

A. "I am; and the everlasting righteousness is wrought in me; if ye were acquainted with the Father ye would also be acquainted with me."

Q. "Do any kiss thy feet?"

A. "It might be they did, but I minded them not."

Q. "How dost thou provide for a livelihood?"

A. "As do the lilies, with care, being maintained of my Father."

Q. "What business hast thou at Bristol, or that way?"

A. "I was guided and directed by my Father."

Q. "Where were you born?"

A. "At Arderslow, in Yorkshire."

Q. "Where lives thy wife?"

A. "She whom thou callest my wife lives in Wakefield."

Q. "Why dost thou not live with her?"

A. "I did till I was called to the army."

Q. "Under whose command didst thou serve in the army?"

A. "First under him they call Lord Fairfax."

Q. "Who then?"

A. "Afterwards with the man called Colonel Lambert. And then I went into Scotland, where I was quartermaster, and returned sick to my earthly habitation."

Q. "What wentest thou for to Exeter?"

A. "I went to Launceston to see the Brethren."

Q. "What estate hast thou?"

A. "Take no care for that."

Q. "Wherefore camest thou in such an unusual posture as two women leading thy horse; others saying, 'Holy, holy, holy!' &c., with another before thee bareheaded, knee-deep in the highway mud, when thou mightest have gone on the causey; and at such a time that, it raining, thy companions received the rain at their necks, and vented it at their hose and breeches?"

A. "It tended to my Father's praise and glory; and I ought not to slight anything which the Spirit of the Lord moves."

Q. "Wherefore didst thou call Marthy Symonds 'Mother,' as George Fox affirms?"

A. "George Fox is a liar and a firebrand of hell; for neither I, nor any with me, called her so."

Q. "Thou hast a wife this time?"

A. "A woman I have, who by the world is called my wife, and some children I have, which according to the flesh are mine."

MARTHA SYMONDS' EXAMINATION.

"She contendeth she knew James Naylor formerly, for he is now no more James Naylor, but refined to a more excellent substance; and so she saith she came with him from Eccles to Bristol."

Q. "What made thee lead his horse into Bristol, and cry, 'Holy, holy, holy!' and to spread thy garment before him?"

A. "I was forced thereto by the power of the Lord."

Q. "Whether didst thou kneel before him?"

A. "I was forced thereto by the power of love."

Q. "Dost thou own him to be the Prince of Peace?"

A. "He is a perfect man; and he that is a perfect man is the Prince of Peace."

Q. "Hast thou a husband?"

A. "I have a man which thou callest my husband."

Q. "What made thee leave him, and to follow James Naylor?"

A. "It is our life to praise the Lord, and the Lord my strength is manifest in James Naylor."

Q. "Oughtest thou to worship James Naylor upon thy knees?"

A. "Yea, I ought so to do."

Hannah Stranger, Thomas Stranger, and Timothy Wedlock were next examined. It is not necessary to reproduce their interrogations; they much resemble what has been given above.

Dorcas Erbury was next called. She was widow of William Erbury, once a minister.

Q. "Where dost thou live?"

A. "With Margaret Thomas."

Q. "Wherefore dost thou sing, 'Holy, holy, holy'?"

A. "I did not at that time; but those that sang did it discharging of their duty."

Q. "Dost thou own him to be the Holy One of Israel?"

A. "I do, and with my blood will seal it."

Q. "And dost thou own him for the Son of God?"

A. "He is the only begotten son of God."

Q. "Wherfore didst thou pull off his stockings, and lay thy clothes beneath his feet?"

A. "He is worthy of it, for he is the Holy One of Israel."

Q. "Christ raised those that had been dead; so did not he?"

A. "He raised me."

Q. "In what manner?"

A. "He laid his hand on my head after I had been dead two days, and said, 'Dorcas, arise!' and I arose, and live, as thou seest."

Q. "Where did he this?"

A. "At the gaol in Exeter."

Q. "What witness hast thou for this?"

A. "My mother, who was present."

Q. "His power being so much, wherefore opened he not the prison doors and escaped?"

A. "The doors shall open when the Lord's wish is done."

The Bristol magistrates sent Naylor and his deluded followers to London, to be examined before Parliament.

On the 31st October it was ordered that a Committee should be appointed to consider the information given touching "the misdemeanour and blasphemies of James Naylor and others at Bristol and elsewhere, and to report thereon."

The Committee met next day, and on December 2nd it was resolved that the report of the Committee should be brought in and read on the following Friday, December 5th. On that day it was read by the reporter, – it consisted of thirteen sheets of paper – and the debate on the report began on the 6th, when James Naylor was called to the bar of the House. He came with his hat on, but it was removed by the Sarjeant. The report was read to him, and he was demanded whether each particular was true, and he acknowledged that it was so.

The debate was adjourned to Monday, the 8th, and it occupied Parliament till the 20th December. The House resolved "that James Naylor was guilty of horrid blasphemy, and that he was a grand imposter and seducer of the people," and his sentence was, "that he should be set on the pillory, with his head in the pillory, in the Palace Yard, Westminster, during the space of two hours, on Thursday next, and be whipped by the hangman through the streets from Westminster to the Old Exchange, London; and there, likewise, he should be set on the pillory, with his head in the pillory, for the space of two hours, between the hours of eleven and one, on Saturday next, in each place wearing a paper containing an inscription of his crimes; and that at the Old Exchange his tongue should be bored through with a hot iron, and that he should be there also stigmatised in the forehead with the letter B; and that he should afterwards be sent to Bristol, to be conveyed into and through the city on horseback, with his face backwards, and there also should be whipped the next market-day after he came thither; and that thence he should be committed to prison in Bridewell, London, and there be restrained from the society of all people, and there to labour hard till he should be released by Parliament; and during that time he should be debarred the use of pen, ink, and paper, and should have no relief but what he earned by his daily labour."

The women were ordered to be kept in confinement. The severity of this atrocious sentence deserves notice. The Independents, who had suffered under Laud and the Star Chamber, now that they were in the power, had no idea of tolerating the Quakers, who read their Bibles differently from themselves. Cromwell was especially prejudiced against them, and it is probable that the Protector had something to do with the severity of the sentence on Naylor.

One Robert Rich, a merchant of London, wrote to the Parliament, on December 15, a petition in favour of Naylor: "If I may have liberty of those that sit in Parliament, I do here attend at this door, and am now ready out of the Scriptures of truth to show that not anything that James Naylor hath said or done is blasphemy, &c."

Sentence was pronounced by the Speaker, Sir Thomas Widdrington. Naylor on hearing it said, "I pray God He may not lay it to your charge." On December 20th, 1656, Naylor suffered a part of his sentence, standing two hours in the pillory, and receiving at the cart's tail three hundred and ten stripes. "The executioner gave him three hundred and ten stripes," says Sewell. "and would have given him one more, as he confessed to the Sherrif, but his foot slipping, the stroke fell upon his own hand, which hurt him much. Naylor was hurt with the horses treading on his feet, whereon the prints of the nails were seen. His wounds were washed by R. Travers, who certified, 'there was not the space of a man's nail free from stripes and blood, from his shoulders near to his waist; his right arm sorely striped; his hands much hurt by the cords that they bled and were swelled: the blood and wounds of his back did very little appear at first sight, by reason of abundance of dirt that covered them, till it was washed off.'"

Another petition in his favour was presented, signed by about a hundred persons, to Parliament, requesting the remission of the rest of his sentence, and as this was refused, appeal was made to Cromwell the Protector, with like want of success.

Five Independent ministers visited Naylor in prison, and vainly urged him to recant.

Rich besieged the doors of Parliament on December 27th, from eight o'clock till eleven, imploring a respite, but all in vain. Naylor was then brought out to undergo the rest of his sentence; he was again pilloried, his tongue bored through, and his forehead branded. Rich held the hand of the unhappy man whilst his tongue was pierced, and the red-hot iron applied to his brow, and he licked the wounds to allay the pain. Thousands who witnessed the execution of the sentence exhibited their respect by removing their caps. There was no reviling, and nothing thrown at Naylor, but all stood silent and sympathetic.

James Naylor was then sent to Bristol, and whipped from the middle of St. Thomas' Street to the middle of Broad Street, and taken back to his prison in Bridewell. There he wrote his recantation, in epistles addressed to the Quakers. In one of these he says: "Dear brethren, my heart is broken this day for the offence which I have occasioned to God's truth and people, and especially to you, who in dear love followed me, seeking me in faithfulness to God, which I rejected, being bound wherein I could not come forth, till God's hand brought me, to whose love I now confess. And I beseech you forgive wherein I evil requited your love in that day. God knows my sorrow for it, since I see it, that ever should offend that of God in any, or reject his counsel; and I greatly fear further to offend or do amiss, whereby the innocent truth of people of God should suffer, or that I should disobey therein."

He was confined about two years, and was then set at liberty. He thereupon went to Bristol, where in a public meeting he made confession of his offence and fall so movingly as to draw tears from most of those present; and he was then restored to the community of the Quakers, from which he had been excluded by George Fox at Exeter for his presumption and pride.

Charges of the most gross immorality have been brought against James Naylor, whether truly or falsely who can now decide? It is possible that the language of the women who followed him, in speaking of him, their letters to him, one of which has been quoted, may have given rise to these reports. Naylor, however, never would admit that there had been anything unseemly in his behaviour towards the women who followed him from London into Cornwall, and from Cornwall to Bristol; and Sewell, who knew Hannah Stranger, repudiates the charge as utterly false. But it is curious to notice how that religious fantacism and sensuality so frequently run together. It was so in that outburst of mysticism in the Middle Ages – the heresy of the Fraticelli; it was so with at least one branch of the Hussites in Bohemia; and in the sixteenth and seventeenth centuries, when the great convulsion of the Reformation had set minds naturally predisposed to religious excitement in a ferment, this was most conspicuous, as in the ferocious licentiousness of John Bockelson, the Anabaptist King of Sion, or the more cautious profligacy, under a cloak of religion, of Ludwig Hetzer and David Joris.

James Naylor quitted London finally in 1660, intending to return to

Wakefield; but was found by a countryman one evening in a field near Holm and King's Rippon, in Huntingdonshire, having been robbed and left bound. He was taken to Holm, and his clothes were changed. To those who kindly cared for him he said, "You have refreshed my body; the Lord refresh your souls."

He shortly after died there of the rough handling he had received from the highwaymen who had plundered him, and was buried in a Quaker's cemetery belonging to Thomas Parnel, a physician.

Two hours before he died he uttered the touching and eloquent speech: – "There is a spirit which I feel that delights to endure all things, in hope to enjoy its own in the end. Its hope is to outlive all wrath and contention, and to weary out all exultation and cruelty, or whatever is of a nature contrary to itself. It sees to the end of all temptations. As it bears no evil in itself, so it conceives none in thoughts to any other. If it be betrayed, it bears it; for its ground and spring are the mercies and forgiveness of God. Its crown is meekness; its life is everlasting love, unfeigned, and takes its kingdom with entreaty and not with contention, and keeps it by lowliness of mind. In God alone it can rejoice, though none else regard it or can own its life. It is conceived in sorrow, and brought forth without any to pity it; nor doth it murmur at grief and oppression. It never rejoiceth but through sufferings; for with the world's joy it is murdered. I found it alone, being forsaken; I have fellowship therein with them who lived in dens and desolate places in the earth; who through death obtained their resurrection, and eternal, holy life."

A more beautiful and true description of the Christian spirit was never uttered. It is a passage meriting a place beside the famous definition of charity by St. Paul. The man who used such words was no hypocrite when he used them. If he had erred greatly, he had also repented; if he had fallen, he had risen after his fall. One is glad to turn away the eye from the blemishes of the unfortunate Quaker's career to the spot of pure light that rests on his death-bed.

His writings were collected and published in an octavo volume in 1716. They are very unequal. Some passages of great beauty, almost comparable to that given above, may be found, but there is also much that is as involved in style and confused in thought as the specimen quoted earlier from his recantation.

"OLD THREE LAPS."

AT Laycock, two miles west of Keighley, at a farm called "The Worlds," lived a close-fisted yeoman named Sharp, at the end of last century and the beginning of this. He carried on a small weaving business in addition to his farm, and amassed a considerable sum of money. The story goes that on one occasion old Sharp brought a piece of cloth to the Keighley tailor and told him to make a coat for him out of it. The tailor on measuring the farmer pronounced the cloth to be insufficient to allow of tails to the coat, and asked what he was to do under the circumstances. "Tho' mun make it three laps," – *i.e., any way*. The expression stuck to him, and till the day of his death the name of "Three Laps" adhered to him, when it passed to his still more eccentric son.

This son, William Sharp, for a while followed the trade of a weaver, but was more inclined to range the moors with his gun than stick to his loom; and the evenings generally found him in the bar of the "Devonshire Inn" at Keighley, the landlord of which was a Mr. Morgan. Young Three Laps was found of chaffing his boon companions. On one occasion he encountered a commercial traveller in the timber trade, and began his banter by asking him the price of a pair of mahogany "laithe" (barn) doors. The traveller, prompted by Mr. Morgan, drew him out, and booked his order.

After some weeks the invoice of mahogany barn-doors, price upwards of £30, was forwarded to William Sharp. Young Three Laps was beside his wits with dismay, and had recourse to Mr. Morgan, and through his intervention the imaginary mahogany barn-doors were not sent.

The barmaid of the "Devonshire" was a comely, respectable young woman, the daughter of a neighbouring farmer named Smith. William Sharp fell desperately in love with the girl, proposed, and was accepted. The day for the wedding was fixed, and the young man went to Keighley Church at the appointed hour to be married. But the bride was not there. At the last moment a difficulty had arisen about the settlements. Mr. Smith could not induce Old Three Laps to bestow on his son sufficient money to support him in a married condition, and the two old men had quarrelled and torn up the settlements.

The blow was more than the mind of William Sharp could bear. He returned to "The Worlds" sulky, went to bed, and never rose from it again. For forty-nine years he kept to his bed, and refused to speak to anyone. He was just thrity years old when he thus isolated himself from society and active life, and he died in his bed at the age of seventy-nine, on March 3rd, 1856.

The room he occupied measured nine feet long and was about the same breadth. The floor was covered with stone flags, and was generally damp. In one corner was a fire-place which could be used only when the wind blew from one or two points of the compass; the window was permanently fastened, and where some of the squares had been broken, was carefully patched with wood. At the time of his death, this window had not been opened for thirty-eight years. The sole furniture comprised an antique clock, minus weight and pendulum, the hands and face covered with a network of cobwebs; a small round table of dark oak, and a plain unvarnished four-post bedstead, entirely without hangings. In this dreary cell, whose only inlet for fresh air during thirty-eight years was the door occasionally left open, did this strange being immure himself. He obstinately refused to speak to anyone, and if spoken to even by his attendants would not answer. All trace of intelligence gradually faded away; the only faculties which remained in active exercise were those he shared with the beasts.

His father by his will made provision for the temporal wants of his eccentric son, and so secured him a constant attendant. He ate his meals regularly when brought to him, and latterly in a very singular manner, for in process of time his legs became contracted and drawn towards his body, and when about to eat his food he used to roll himself over and take his meals in a kneeling posture. He was generally cleanly in his habits. During the whole period of his self-imposed confinement he never had any serious illness, the only case of indisposition those connected with him could remember being a slight loss of appetite, caused apparently by indigestion, for two or three days – and this, notwithstanding that he ate on an average as much as any farm labourer. He certainly, physically speaking, did credit to his food, for though arrived at the age of seventy-nine years, his flesh was firm, fair and unwrinkled, save with fat, and he weighed about 240 lbs. He showed great repugnance to being seen, and whenever a stranger entered his den he immediately buried his head in the bed-clothes. About a week before his death his appetite began to fail; his limbs became partially benumbed, so that he could not roll himself over to take his food in his accustomed posture.

From this attack he seemed to rally, and no apprehensions were entertained that the attack would prove fatal, till the evening before his death.

However, during the night he rapidly became worse, and expired at four a.m. on Monday, March 3rd, 1856.

Shortly before he expired he was heard to exclaim – "Poor Bill! poor Bill! poor Bill Sharp!" – the most connected sentence he had been known to utter for forty nine years.

He was buried in Keighley Churchyard on the 7th of March, amidst crowds who had come from all parts of the neighbourhood to witness the scene. The coffin excited considerable attention from its extraordinary shape, as his body could not be straightened, the muscle of the knees and thighs being contracted.

It was an oak chest, two feet four inches in depth. The weight was so great that it required eight men with strong ropes to lower it into the grave. It was thought to weigh with its contents 480 lbs.

A gentleman who visited Old Three Laps before his death has given the following account of what he saw: –

"If you change to go a-skating 'to the Tarn,' and want a fine bracing walk, keep on the Sutton road about a mile, and you will come to an avenue of larch, not in a very thriving state, but sufficient to indicate that some one had an idea of the picturesque who planted the trees, although the house at the top of the avenue has not a very attractive appearance. You have now reached 'World's End,' and save here and there a solitary farm, with its cold stone buildings and treeless fields, there are few signs of life between you and the wide and boundless moors of Yorkshire and Lancashire. On the opposite hill, right up in the clouds, is 'Tewett Hall,' the residence of a Bradford Town Councillor. He alone, in this part, seems to follow Three Laps' ancestors' plan of planting, and in a few years we may expect to see a fine belt of timber on the verge of the horizon, a sight that will cheer the heart of some future Dr. Syntax when in search of the picturesque. At this place Three Laps 'took his bed,' and in a little parlour, with a northern light, the sill of which is level with the field, the floor cold and damp, and meanly furnished, it was my privilege to see Three Laps some twenty-five years ago. To gain admission we had some difficulty; but with the assistance of the farmer and a tin of tobacco to the nurse, who was an inveterate smoker, we were shown into his bedroom. As soon as he heard strangers, he pulled the bed-clothes over his head, which the nurse with considerable force removed, and uncovered his body, which was devoid of every vestige of body linen. A more startling and sickening sight I never saw. Nebuchadnezzar rushed into my mind. Three Laps covered his face with his hands, his fingers being like birds' claws, while, with his legs drawn under his body, he had the appearance of a huge beast. He had white hair, and a very handsome head, well set on a strong chest. His body and all about him was scrupulously clean, and his condition healthy, as his nurse proudly pointed out, digging her fist furiously into his ribs. He gave no signs of joy or pain, but lay like a mass of inanimate matter. It struck me at the time that his limbs were stiff; but a neighbour of his, who after his dinner stole a peep into his bedroom window, told me that he found him playing with his plate in the manner of a Chinese juggler, and with considerable ability. On my informant tapping the window, he vanished under the bed-clothes.

"Such was the life of the strange man who for love of a woman never left this obscure room for nearly half a century."

The case of Old Three Laps is not unique.

In the early part of this century there lived in the neighbourhood of Caen, in Normandy, a Juge de Paix, M. Halloin, a great lover of tranquility and ease; so much so, indeed, that, as bed is the article of furniture most adapted to repose, he rarely quitted it, but made his bed-chamber a hall of audience, in which he exercised his functions of magistrate, pronouncing sentence with his head resting on a pillow, and his body languidly extended on the softest of feather beds. However, his services were dispensed with, and he devoted the remaining six years of his life to still greater ease. Feeling his end approach, M. Halloin determined on remaining constant to his principle, and showing to the world to what an extent he carried his passion for bed. Consequently, his last will contained a clause expressing his desire to be buried at night, in his bed, comfortably tucked in, with pillows and coverlets, as he had died.

As no opposition was raised against the execution of this clause, a huge pit was sunk, and the defunct was lowered into his last resting-place without any alteration having been made in the position in which death had overtaken him. Boards were laid over the bed, that the falling earth might not disturb this imperturbable quietist.

CHRISTOPHER PIVETT.

CHRISTOPHER PIVETT died at York, in 1796, at the advanced age of ninety-three years. He was by trade a carver and gilder, but in early life had served in the army, and been present in several battles – Fontenoy, Dettingen, and the siege of Carlisle.

After he settled at York, his house was accidently burnt down; and he then formed the singular resolution never again to sleep in a bed, lest he should be burned to death whilst asleep, or not have sufficient time to remove his property, should an accident again occur. This resolution he strictly adhered to for the remaining forty years of his life.

His practice was to repose upon the floor, or on two chairs, or sitting in a chair, but always dressed.

During the whole period he dwelt alone he was his own cook, and seldom suffered anyone to enter the house. He would not tell anyone where he had been born or to whom he was related, and there can be little doubt that the name of Pivett was an assumed one. Among other singularities, he kept a human skull in his house, and strictly ordered that it should be buried with him.

DAVID TURTON,

DAVID TURTON was born in Horbury, near Wakefield, A.D. 1768, and died August 19th, 1846.

He was by trade a weaver of flannel, and his loom, which was in the upper room of the cottage in which he lived, might be heard by passers-by going diligently from early morn to dewy eve. In this way he supplied his few earthly wants, for he was a man of a very simple and unobtrusive character; and he did not change either his dress or his habits with the growing luxury of the times.

In matter of diet he was frugal, and he was always stuck to the old oat-cake and oatmeal porridge he had been accustomed to from childhood. "Avver bread and avver me-al porritch" was what he called them, for he spoke the broadest Yorkshire. Alas! the delightful oat-cake, thin, crisp, is now a thing of the past in Horbury. There was an old woman made it, the last of a glorious race of avver bre-ad makers in Horbury, some years ago. But she has gone the way of all flesh; and the base descendants of the oat-cake crunchers, the little men of to-day, sustain their miserable lives on bakers' wheat bread.

David did not, as is the custom with Northerners now, speak two languages – English and Yorkshire, according to the company in which they find themselves; but on all occasions, and for all purposes, he adhered to that peculiarly racy and piquant tongue, both in pronunciation and phraseology, which was so well known to those who dwelt in the West Riding of Yorkshire half a century ago, and which still more or less prevails in that locality. Half a century ago every village had its own peculiarity of intonation, its own specialities in words. A Horbury man could be distinguished from a man of Dewsbury, and a Thornhill man from one of Batley. The railways have blended, fused these peculiar dialects into one, and taken off the old peculiar edge of provincialism, so that now it is only to be found in its most pronounced and perfect development among the aged.

The figure of David Turton was spare, his legs long and lean as clothes-line props. He wore drab breeches and white stockings, a long waistcoat of rather coarse black cloth, with a long coat of the same material, much the pattern of that now affected by our bishops.

His features were small and sharp, his eye especially bright and full of life;

and having lost nearly all his teeth at a comparitively early age, his pointed chin and nose inclined much towards each other.

Music was his great delight, and in that he spent all his spare time and money. He was a good singer, and could handle the violoncello creditably. All Handel's ontarios, besides many other works of the classical composers, he knew off by heart, and he was for a long time the chief musical oracle in the neighbourhood in which he lived. He even aspired to be a composer, and published a volume of chants and psalm tunes. Some of the former, but few of the latter, have survived. His chants have found their way into various collections of Anglican chants along with those of Dr Turton, Bishop of Ely, also a musician and composer of chants. But they have ceased to sound in his own parish church, where they have been displaced by Gregorians. Not one of his hymn tunes has found its way into the most popular collection of the day – "Hyms Ancient and Modern" – which is the more to be regretted, as Turton's tunes were often original, which is much more than can be said for a good many of the new tunes inserted in that collection.

A considerable number of choristers in cathedral and parish church choirs owed all their musical skill to the careful training of old David Turton.

His efficiency in music, together with the simple goodness of his character, made him a favourite among musical people in all grades of society, and there was seldom a gathering in the neighbourhood where any good class of music was performed in which his well-known figure was not to be seen.

On one occasion he went to Hatfield Hall, then the residence of Francis Maude, Esq., who was a great lover of music, and a friend and patron of old David.

His own account of his *débût* on that occasion is sufficiently characteristic to be given:-

"I went t' other day," said he, "to a gre-at meusic do at ou'd Mr. Maude's at 'Atfield 'All. Nah! when I gat theare, a smart looking chap o' a waiter told me I was to goa into t' parlour; soa I follows efter him doun a long passage till we commed to a big oppen place like, and then he oppens a doo-ar, and says to me, 'Cum in!' soa I walks in, and theare I seed t' place were right full o' quality (gentlefolks), and Mr. Maude comes to me and says, 'Now, David, haw are ye?' 'Middlin',' says I, 'thenk ye!' Soa then there comes a smart chap wi' a tray full of cups o' tea, and he says to me, 'Will ye hev sum?' 'Thenk ye,' says I, 'I'm none particular.' 'Why, then, help yer sen,' says he. Soa I taks a cup i' my hand; and then says he, 'Weant ye hev sum sugar and cre-am?' 'Aye, for sure,' says I; soa I sugars and creams it, and then there comes another chap wi' a tray full of bre-ad and butter, and cakes like, and says he, 'Will he hev sum?' 'I don't mind if I do,' says I. 'Well, then,' says he, 'tak sum wi'thy fingers.' Soa I holds t' cup and t' sawcer i' one hand, and taks a piece of spice cake i' t'other. 'Now, then,' thinks I, 'how am I ever to sup my te-a? I can't team (pour) it out into t' sawcer, for boath my hands is fast.' But all at once I sees a plan o' doin' it. I thowt I could hold t' cake i' my mouth while I teamed (poured) t' te-a into t' sawcer, and then claps th' cup on a chair while I supped my tea. But, bless ye, t' cake war so varry short (crumbling) that it brake off i' my mouth, and tum'led onto t' floor, and I were in a bonny tak-ing. Howsomever, I clapt t' cup and t' sawcer onto t' chair, and kneeled me down on t' floor, and sammed (picked) it all up as weel as I could; and then I sups up my tea as sharp as I could, and gave t' cup and t' sawcer to t' chap who cumed round again wi' his tray. 'Will ye hev some more?' says he. 'Noa,' says I, 'noa more, thenk ye.' For I thowt to mysen I had made maugrums (antics) enough, and all t' quality 'at war theare mun ha' thowt me a hawkard owd chap. Weel! when tea were finish'd we gat to th' music, and then, I promise ye, I war all reet, an' a rare do we had on it.''

David was returning through a pasture one day in which was a furious bull, who seeing old David with his red bag, made at him. The musician did not fly; that would not compart with his dignity, and his bass viol that he carried in the bag might be injured by a precipitate retreat over the hedge. The bull bellowed, and came on with lowered horns.

"Steady!" soliloquised the musician; "I reckon that was double B nat'ral."
Again the bull bellowed.

"I am pretty sure it were B," said David again, "but I'll mak' sure;" and opening his bag, he extracted the bass viol, set it down, and drawing his bow across the vibrating string, produced a sound as full of volume and of the same pitch as the tone of the infuriated beast.

"I thowt I were reet," said David, with a grim smile.

At the sound of the bass viol the bull stood still, raised his head, and glowered at the extraordinary object before him. David, having his viol out, thought it a pity to bag it again without a tune, and began the violoncello part in one of Handel's choruses. It was too much for the bull; he was out-bellowed, and turned tail.

When David was getting a little advanced in years he was coming home on a dark night from a musical gathering, and tumbling over a large stone which happened to be lying on the road, he fell down with great force and dislocated his hip.

This was a sore trial to him in many ways. In the first place, it quite prevented his going on with his customary means of obtaining his living, and, besides that, it deprived him of the pleasure of going about his musical friends.

For a long, weary time he was quite confined to his bed, and time hung heavy on his hands, for he had no other resources except his loom and his music. His constant companion in bed with his violoncello, and as he could not for a long time sit up sufficiently to enable him to use the bow, he spent a great part of the day in playing over pizzicato the music which he loved so well.

After some time he got about a little on crutches, and ultimately was able to go by the help of a stick. His little savings had now dwindled away, and poverty began to look him in the face. But at this crisis his musical friends came forward, and gave with great success for his benefit the oratorio of the "Messiah" in the town of Wakefield, and by this means raised for him the liberal sum of £70, of which they begged his acceptance.

He was afraid to have so large a sum in his own charge, and he therefore requested that it might be placed in the hands of the Vicar of Horbury, so that he might draw from time to time just as much as he needed. This was accordingly done, and by his careful expenditure of it, it sufficed to make him quite comfortable during the rest of his life, and to erect the simple memorial-stone which now stands over his grave in Horbury churchyard.

He had a married sister living in London who had often invited him to pay her a visit, and when he had recovered from his accident sufficiently to go about pretty well by the aid of a stick, and having now plenty of time at his disposal, on account of his being lame and unable to work at his loom, he determined to embark on the railway to London.

His sister lived in Kensington, and his own account of his visit, and of what he saw in the great city, was highly amusing:—

"I went up," said he, "on a Setterday, and o' t' Sunday-morn, while we was getting our breakfast, th' sister's hus-hand says to me across t' table, 'I reckon ye'll goa wi' us to chapel this forenoin,' for ye see they was chapel-folks. 'We'll see,' says I, 'efter a bit.' But I knew varry weel mysen what I were boun' to do, though I didn't say so to them.

"Soa I just watches my opportunity, an' when they was all gone out of the room, I nips out, as sharp as a lark, and goas to t' end o' t' entry. For t' sister's house war not to t' street, but up a bit on a entry like; and away I goas till I sees a homnibus, and I calls out to t' fellow, 'I say, are ye for Sant Paul's?' 'Aye,' says he.

"Why, then,' says I, 'ye're t' chap for me!' Soa he oppens t' door, an' I jumps in.

"'How much is it?' says I. 'Nobbut sixpence,' says he. Soa I rode all t' way thro' (from) Kensington to Sant Paul's – and ye know it's rare way – all for sixpence.

"Eh! and bless ye! we just hed a sarvice! Think nobbut o' me goin to their ou'd chapel, wi' nowt but a bit on a poor snuffin' hymn or two, an' some squealin' bairns and women to sing 'em, and a ram'lin, rantin' sarmon iver so long, when I had t' opportunity o' going to Sant Paul's to hear thinks done as they sud be done. Nay, nay! – I warn't sich a fooil as that nauther. I watn't born i' Yorkshire to know no better nor that, I'll uphou'd ye.

"Howsomever, when I gat back hoame, they was into me weel for giving 'em t' slip, an' turnin' my back, as they said, on t' blessed Gospel invitin' of me. But I let 'em say what they'd a mind to. When a beer barrel begins to fiz out o' t' bung hoil, tha' mun let it fiz a bit, thof't mak a mucky slop, or it'll bust t' barrel. I said nowt; I just set and thowt o' what I'd heard, and I played it ower again on my in'ards.

"T' next day I thowt I sud like to goa and hear t' band of t' Orse Guards. Now t' sister 'usband had a nephy 'at was one on 'em; soa I went wi' him. And after they'd played iver so many things – eh! an' bless ye, they just did play 'em – he says to t' leader o' t' band – 'Yon ow'd chap' – meaning' me – 'knows a bit about meusic.' Soa t' fellow says to me, 'Is there owt partickler ye'd like?' 'Nay,' says I, owt 'at ye've got'll be reight for me.'

"'Nay,' says he, 'owt' at ye've a mind to ax for.' Soa I picks two or three things 'at just comes to my mind like. And, bless ye! they play 'em like owt at all, and then I menshuned another or two, an' they were never fast wi owt till it was time for 'em to lap up. Soa they says, 'we mun goa now, but ye mun come agean another day!' 'I sall,' says I, 'ye may depend.' And I went reg'lar every day as long as I war i' London; and rared pleased they war wi' me an' all, and so ye mind war I wi' them.

"That, and Sant Paul's, an' Westminster Habbey, war t' main o' what I seed and heeard all t' time I war i London."

JOHN BARTENDALE,

THE PIPER.

In the reign of King Charles I. a strolling musician, a poor piper, named John Bartendale, was brought, in 1634, before the Assizes, and was convicted of felony.

He received sentence, and on March 27th was hung on the gallows, outside Micklegate Bar, York. There were no houses there at that time – it was open country. After he had remained swinging for three-quarters of an hour, and was to all appearance dead, he was cut down, and buried near the place of execution. The officers of justice had accomplished their work carelessly in both particulars, as it afterwards transpired, for he had been neither properly hung nor properly buried.

Earth has a peculiarly invigorating and restorative effect, as has been recently discovered; and patients suffering from debility are by some medical men now-a-days placed in earth baths with the most salutary effects. In the case of gangrened wounds a little earth has been found efficacious in promoting healthy action of the skin. John Bartendale was now to experience the advantages of an earth-bath.

That same day, in the afternoon, a gentleman, one of the Vavasours of Hazlewood, was riding by, when he observed the earth moving in a certain place. He ordered his servant to alight; he himself descended from his horse; and together they threw off the mould, and discovered the unfortunate piper alive. He opened his eyes, sat up, and asked where he was, and how he came there. Mr. Vavasour and his servants helped him out of his grave, and seated him on the side. The man was sent for water and other restoratives, and before long the news had spread about down Micklegate that the poor piper was come to life again. A swarm of wondering and sympathising people poured out to congratulate John the Piper on his resurrection, and to offer their assistance. A conveyance was obtained, and as soon as Bartendale was in a sufficient condition to be moved, he was placed in it, covered with Mr. Vavasour's cloak, – for he had been stripped by the executioner before he was laid in the earth – and was removed again to York Castle.

It was rather hard that the poor fellow, after he had obtained his release, should have been returned to his prison; but there was no help for it. The resurrection of the piper was no secret; otherwise Mr. Vavasour would doubtless have removed him privately to a place of security till he was recovered, and then have sent him into another part of the country.

At the following Assizes, Bartendale was brought up again. It was a nice point at law whether the man could be sentenced to execution again after the Sheriff had signed his affidavit that the man had been hung till he was dead. Mr. Vavasour was naturally reluctant to supply the one link in the chain of evidence which established the identity of the prisoner with the piper who had been hung and buried for felony; he made earnest intercession that the poor fellow might be reprieved, popular sympathy was on his side, the judge was disposed to mercy, and Bartendale was accorded a full and free pardon, the judge remarking that the case was one in which the Almighty seemed to have interfered in mercy to frustrate the ends of human justice, and that therefore he was not disposed to reverse the decree of Providence according to the piper a prolongation of his days on earth.

Drunken Barnaby in his "Book of Travels" alludes to Barterndale, when he stops at York:

> "Here a piper apprehended,
>   Was found guilty and suspended;
>   Being led to t' fatal gallows,
>   Boys did cry, 'Where is thy bellows?
>   Ever must thou cease thy tuning,'
>   Answered he, 'For all your cunning,
>   You may fail in your prediction.'
>   Which did happen without fiction;
>   For cut down, and quick interred,
>   Earth rejected what was buried;
>   Half alive or dead he rises,
>   Got a pardon next Assizes,
>   And in York continued blowing –
>   Yet a sense of goodness showing."

After his wonderful deliverance the poor fellow turned hostler, and lived very honestly afterwards.

When asked to describe his sensations on being hung, he said that when he was turned off, flashes of fire seemed to dart before his eyes, and were succeeded by darkness and a state of insensibility.

BLIND JACK OF KNARESBOROUGH.[1]

BLIND JACK METCALF is certainly one of the most remarkable characters that Yorkshire has produced. Afflicted with loss of sight, the indomitable energy of his true north-country character enabled him to carry on a successful business where many a south countryman would have failed.

He was born at Knaresborough on the 15th August, 1717, and was the son of a labourer. At the age of six he was seized with small-pox, and on his recovery it was found that he had become totally blind. Children speedily accommodate themselves to circumstances. Jack in six months was able to find his way from his father's cottage along the street of Knaresborough and back home without a guide, and in the course of three years could go to any part of the little town alone, could find the shops, and execute errands for his father or mother. He began also to associate with other boys in bird-nesting expeditions, and would climb the trees and throw down the nests to his companions. By accompanying the boys in their rambles he learned his way about the neighbourhood, and was in a short time perfectly acquainted with all the lanes, woods, and fields within a radius of two or three miles. As his father kept horses, he learned to ride, and in time became an able horseman. He was taught the fiddle, as it was thought that the only means open to him for obtaining a subsistence was that of strolling musician. But Jack Metcalf had more natural taste for the cry of a hound or a harrier than for the squeak of his fiddle.

A gentleman at Knaresborough, of the name of Woodburn, was owner of a pack of hounds. This gentleman encouraged young Metcalf by taking him to hunt with him, and Blind Jack kept five hounds of his own. Mr. Woodburn's hounds being seldom kennelled, Metcalf used to take several of them out secretly along with his own at night when the hares were out feeding in the fields; but one of them having destroyed a couple of lambs, he got into trouble, and was obliged to discontinue his midnight excursions.

When about fourteen years old, his activity of limb led him to imagine that he could undertake anything without danger, and with certainty of success. The following adventure, however, somewhat modified his opinion: –

A large plum-tree in the neighbourhood of Knaresborough having attracted the attention of Metcalf's companions, they with one consent repaired to the

[1] Chiefly from a Chapbook Life, written apparently shortly after his death. Published by Johnson, of Leeds.

place on a Sunday morning. In these cases Metcalf was always appointed to ascend for the purpose of shaking the trees. Accordingly, he was sent to his post; but his comrades being suddenly alarmed by the appearance of the owner of the tree, ran away, leaving Blind Jack up the tree. He, taking the alarm, dropped, and fell headlong into a gravel-pit belonging to Sir Henry Slingsby, cut his face, and lay for some time stunned in the pit.

Shortly after this, he and some other boys, one night between eleven and twelve o' clock, assembled in the church porch at Knaresborough – that being the usual place of meeting. They determined to rob an orchard. Having accomplished this feat with success, they returned to the church-porch to divide their booty. Now it happened that the door of Knaresborough church was opened by means of a ring, which turned the latch. One of the party took hold of it, and by way of bravado gave a loud rap, calling out, "A tankard of ale here!" A voice from within answered aloud, "You are at the wrong house!" The boys were so scared that for a moment or two none spoke or moved. At length Metcalf said, "Did not you hear something speak in the church?" Upon this, without answering, they all ran until they got out of the churchyard. They then held a consultation, all equally wondering at the voice, and equally unable to account satisfactorily for it.

Like true Yorkshire boys, they were not, however, to be scared away without knowing what had frightened them; and they stealthily returned to the porch. But no sooner had they reached it, than the ring turned, and the door began to open. This was to much even for their nerves, and they fled in all directions like wind. Only on reaching the outside of the churchyard wall did they venture to breathe freely and look back, and then, lo! the whole of the interior of the church was alight –

> ". . . Glimmering thro' the groaning trees,
> Kirk Alloway seem'd in a bleeze."

Uninspired, like Tam o' Shanter, with draughts of John Barleycorn, they did not venture nearer, but dispersed to their homes. The cause of this panic was as follows: – The remains of an old lady in the neighbourhood had been kept from interment until the arrival of her relations, who lived at a great distance. Immediately on their arrival the sexton was called up to dig the grave in the church, and had lighted a great number of candles.

About the year 1731, when Metcalf was fourteen years old, he began to learn swimming in the river Nidd, and soon became so expert, that he surpassed all his companions. About this time two men were drowned in the eddies of the Nidd. Metcalf was sent to dive for the bodies, and after four attempts succeeded in bringing up one of the corpses. The other body could not be found.

There are frequent floods in the river Nidd, and in the deep places there are eddies, which draw to the bottom any substance, however light, that comes within their sphere of action. Large pieces of timber were often carried down by the floods; these on coming over the deep places spun round, and then sank. Upon these occasions Metcalf would dive for them, and with the greatest of ease fix ropes to the wood, which was then drawn up by persons stationed on the banks.

In the year 1732, one John Barker kept an inn at the west end of the High Bridge, Knaresborough. This man was a manufacturer of linen cloth, and used to bleach his own yarn. At one time, having brought two packs of yarn to the river to wash, a sudden flood, occasioned by a heavy rain in the neighbourhood, swept them away, and carried them through the arches of the bridge, which stands on a rock. A little below was a sheet of still water, supposed to be twenty-one feet in depth; as soon as the yarn got to this it sank, except a little which caught on the edge of the rock in going down. Metcalf being intimate with Barker, and calling at his house a few days after the accident, found him lamenting his loss. Metcalf told him that he hoped to recover the yarn, but Barker smiled at the supposed absurdity of the proposal; finding, however, that his friend was resolved on trial, he consented. Metcalf then ordered some long cart-ropes to be procured, and fixing a hook at one end, the other being held by some persons on the High Bridge, he descended, and hooking as much of the yarn as he could at one time, gave orders for drawing up. In this way the whole was recovered with little damage.

At Bilton, two miles from Knaresborough, was a rookery, where boys had made many attempts to take the young birds; but the owner wishing to preserve them, they were prevented. Metcalf determined to make a trial, sent one of his comrades in the day-time to reconnoitre the position of the nests, and having received his information, they set out in the dead of night and brought away seven dozen and a half, excepting the heads, which they left under the trees. The owner of the rooks finding the heads, offered a reward of two guineas for the discovery of the offenders; but the secret was kept until long afterwards.

A person at Knaresborough having occasion to go to Borough Bridge, which is about seven miles distant, and having left something behind, sent his son for it. Metcalf being about the same age as this boy, chose to accompany him. When they got to the place the boy missed the key, which he had lost from his pocket by the way, and being afraid to return, he consulted Metcalf how they should proceed. Metcalf was for entering the house at all events, and not being able to procure a ladder, got a pole, which reached to the thatch, and having borrowed a rope and a stick, he climbed up the pole, and then ascending by the roof to the chimney, he placed the stick across, and fastening the rope to it, attempted to descend, but finding the flue too narrow, he threw off his clothes, and laying them on the ridge of the house, made a second attempt, and got down by the assistance of the rope; he then opened the door for his companion. While they were in the house there was a heavy thunder-shower, to which Metaclf's clothes were exposed. He attempted to get up again to fetch them, but the pole by which he had ascended was now so wet that he could not climb by it; he was therefore obliged to wait till it dried, when he succeeded in recovering his clothes.

In the year 1732, Metcalf was invited to Harrogate to succeed as fiddler an old man of the name of Morrison, who had played there for seventy years. The old man died in the 102nd year of his age, and played in the year he died. Metcalf was well received by the nobility and gentry, who employed no other fiddler, except a boy, whom he hired as an assistant.

Metcalf now bought a horse, and often ran him for small plates. He kept game-cocks, as he was devotedly fond of cock-fighting. He often hunted, and sometimes went coursing. In the evenings he played at the assemblies.

About the time there was a long room built at the Green Dragon at Harrogate. More music being then wanted, he engaged one Midgeley (one of the Leeds waits) and his son as assistants. Midgeley, senior, being a good performer, was taken into partnership gratis, but the son and Metcalf's former assistant paid five pounds each as premium.

In the year 1735, Francis Barlow, Esq., of Middlethorpe, near York, who kept a pack of hounds, was at Harrogate, and, liking Metcalf, invited him to spend the winter at Middlethorpe, and bring his horse with him. The invitation was gladly accepted, and he went out with Mr. Barlow's hounds twice a week. Having completed a visit of six months at Middlethorpe, he had learnt to walk and ride very readily through most of the streets of York, and as he was riding past the George Inn, in Coney Street, Standish, the landlord, stopped him, calling out, "What haste?" Metcalf told him he was for Knaresborough that night; the landlord replied that there was a gentleman in the house who wanted a guide to Harrogate; adding, "I know you can do that as well as anyone." – "So I can," said he, "but you must not let him know that I am blind, for perhaps he will be afraid to trust me." – "I shall manage that," replied Standish. So going in, he informed the gentleman that he had procured a safe guide. Pleased at this, the gentleman requested Metcalf to come in and take a glass. This, for an obvious reason, the landlord objected to, on the part of Metcalf, but recommended some wine at the door. Metcalf started as soon as the wine was drunk, taking the lead, naturally enough. As they were turning Ousegate corner, a voice shouted out, "SQUIRE BARLOW'S BLIND HUNTSMAN!" But the gentleman had no suspicion that the cry had any reference to his guide. They rode briskly up Micklegate, through the Bar, turned the corner at Holgate, and through Poppleton Field, on to Hessay Moor, and so proceeded forward, going over Skip Bridge. At this time the turnpike was not made between York and Harrogate.

On the north-west of Kirk-Hammerton Moor the road to Knaresborough joined the main road which leads to Borough Bridge by a sudden turn to the left; but Metcalf cleared that without any difficulty. When they came to Allerton-Mauleverer, the stranger asked whose large house that was on the right, and was immediately informed by Metcalf. A little farther on, the road is crossed by the one from Wetherby to Borough Bridge, and proceeds along by the high brick wall of Allerton Park. There was a road leading out of the park opposite to the gate upon the Knaresborough road, which Metcalf was afraid of missing, but the wind being from the east, and he perceiving a blast coming through the park gate, readily turned his horse to the opposite gate, which leads to Knaresborough. Reaching out his hand to open it, and feeling the heel, as it is called, he believed the gate had been changed in the hanging part, as he had not been there for seven months; and backing his horse, exclaimed, "Confounded thee! thou always goes to the gate's heel, instead of the head!" The gentleman observed to him that his horse seemed awkward, and that his own mare was good at coming up to a gate; whereupon Metcalf permitted him to perform this office. Darkness which had now come on, being no obstruction to him, he briskly led the way, resolved that his companion should not again see his face till they got to Harrogate. As they were going through Knaresborough the gentleman proposed a glass of wine, which Metcalf refused, alleging that the horses were hot, and that as they were near their journey's end, it was not worth their while to stop.

Forward they went, and presently some one cried out, "That's Blind Jack!" This, however, was contradicted by another person, who could not clearly distinguish him; and by this means the stranger was kept in the dark as effectually as his guide. They then proceeded over the High Bridge and up Forest Lane, and entered the forest about a mile from Knaresborough. They had now to pass along a narrow causeway which reached about one-third of the way to Harrogate, the forest at that time not being inclosed, and no turnpike being made. Metcalf still kept the lead.

When they had gone a little while upon the forest the gentleman saw a light. He asked what place it was. There were some rocks called Hookston Crags, and near to these the grounds was low and swampy in some places, close by which runs the Leeds road. About this part will-o'-the-wisp used to be commonly seen. Metcalf took it for granted that his companion had seen one of these lights, but for good reason declined asking him whereabouts the light was; and to divert his attention, asked him, "Do you not see two lights – one to the right, the other to the left?" – "No," replied the gentleman, "I see but one – to the right." – "Well, then, sir," said Metcalf, "that is Harrogate." There were then many tracks, but Metcalf made choice of that nearest the fence. By the side of this path, which is very near Harrogate, some larches were planted, and stepping-stones laid for the convenience of foot-passengers. Metcalf got upon this stony path, and the gentleman's horse following, got one of his hind feet jammed between two of the stones. When his horse was freed, he asked, "Is there no other road?" – "Yes," replied Metcalf, "there is another, but it's a mile about"; knowing there was a dirty cart-way, but thinking the stony road preferable to the deep slough of the other, he preferred this rugged path.

On reaching their journey's end, they stopped at the house called the Marquis of Granby, but found that the hostler was gone to bed. Metcalf being very well acquainted with the place, led both the horses into the stable and the hostler soon after appearing, he delivered them into his care, and went into the house to inquire after his fellow-traveller, whom he found comfortably seated over a tankard of negus, in which he pledged his guide. Metcalf took the tankard the first time very nicely, but when attempting to take it the second time, he reached out his hand wide of the mark; however, he soon found it, and drank, and going out again, left the landlord with his companion. "I think, landlord," said the gentleman, "my guide must have drunk a great deal of spirits since we came here." – "Why, my good sir, what makes you think so?" – "Well, I judge so from the appearance of his eyes." – "Eyes! bless you, sir," rejoined the landlord, "do you not know that he is blind?" – "What do you mean?" – "I mean, sir, that he cannot see!" – "Blind! Are you in earnest?" – "Yes, sir; as blind as a stone!" – Come, come, landlord," said the gentleman, "this is too much. Call him in." Metcalf entered. "My friend, are you really blind?" – "Yes, sir; I lost my sight when six years old." – "Had I known that, I would not have ventured with you for a hundred pounds." – "And I, sir," said Metcalf "would not have lost my way for a thousand." Metcalf was rewarded by a present of two guineas, besides a plentiful entertainment the next day at the cost of this gentleman.

In 1736, when the Harrogate season commenced, Metcalf resumed his musical occupation, and was well received at all the inns, where he was always given free quarters for himself and horse.

The Green Dragon at that place was kept by a Mr. Body, who had two nephews with him; and when the hunting season drew near its close, these, with some other young men, expressed a desire for a day's sport; and knowing that Mr. Woodburn, the master of the Knaresborough pack of hounds, had often lent them to Metcalf, they asked Blind Jack to procure for them the pleasure of a run. Metcalf had no doubt but that Mr. Woodburn would grant him this favour, and went, flushed with hope, to Mr. Woodburn, requesting him to lend the pack the next day. This, however, was a favour out of his power to grant, as Mr. Woodburn politely informed him, as he had engaged to meet Mr. Trappes with the hounds next morning upon Scotton Moor, for the purpose of entering some young fox-hounds. Chagrined at this, Metcalf debated with himself whether the disappointment should fall to the lot of Mr. Woodburn's friends or his own, and resolved that it should not be to the latter. He arose the next morning before daybreak, and crossed the High bridge. He took with him an excellent hound of his own, and nipping him by the ears, made him give mouth loudly, himself hallooing at the same time. This device had so good an effect that in a few minutes he had nine couples about him, as the hounds were kept by various people about the shambles, &c., and were suffered to lie unkennelled. Mounting his horse, away he rode with the dogs to Harrogate, where he met his friends ready mounted and in high spirits. Some of them proposed going to Bilton wood, near Knaresborough, but this was opposed by Metcalf, who preferred the moor; in fact, he was apprehensive of being followed by Mr. Woodburn, and wished accordingly to be at some distance from Knaresborough.

Following his advice, they drew the moor at the distance of five miles, where they started a hare, killed her after a fine chase, and immediately put up another. Just at this moment up came Mr. Woodburn, foaming with anger, swearing terribly, and threatening to send Metcalf to the House of Correction.

He swung his whip round his head, intending to horse-whip the rogue, but Metcalf heard the whistle of the lash in the air, and escaped the stroke by making his horse start aside.

Mr. Woodburn then endeavoured to call of his hounds, but Metcalf, knowing the fleetness of his own horse, ventured within speaking, but not within whipping distance of him, and begged that he would permit the dogs to finish the chase, alleging that it would spoil them to take them off, and that he was sure they would (as they actually did) kill in a very short time. Metcalf soon found that Mr. Woodburn's anger had begun to abate; and going nearer to him, he pleaded in excuse, a misunderstanding. The apology was accepted, for Mr. Woodburn, though hot of temper, was very good-natured; and so the affair ended.

Blind Jack became also very skilful at bowls, but he always bargained that he should count three to his adversary's one; and he bribed the jacks to give him hints as to the direction he was to throw, by the inflexion of their voices, lowering their tones in speaking to one another if he flung too much to the right, raising them if he threw too wide on the left.

But what is more singular is, that he was able to distinguish cards by their feel, and that by simply passing his fingers over their surface. By this means he was able to play whist and other games, and beat those opposed to him; by this means realising a little money.

These achievements were far from exhausting his ambition. He aspired to the acquaintance of jockeys, and frequented the York races, where he betted, and was able to make books with men of rank and position, who took an interest in Jack on account of his affliction and the energy of his character.

He commonly rode to the race-ground amongst the crowd, and kept in memory both the winning and losing horses.

Being much in the habit of visiting York in the winter time, a whim would often take him to call for his horse at bed-time, and set out for Knaresborough, regardless of the badness of the roads and the weather, and of all remonstrance from his friends.

About the year 1738, Metcalf having increased his stud, and being aware of the docility of that noble animal the horse, he so tutored his own that whenever he called them by their respective names they would immediately answer him by neighing. This was chiefly accomplished by some discipline at the time of feeding. He could, however, without the help of those responses, select his own horse out of any number.

Having matched one of his horses to run three miles for a wager of some note, and the parties agreeing to ride each his own, they set up posts at certain distances in the forest, marking a course of one mile; having, of course, three miles to go. Great odds were laid against Metcalf, upon the supposition of his inability to keep the course. But Blind Jack was quite equal to the occasion. He procured four dinner-bells, and placed a bell-man at each post. Each man rang in turn, and Metcalf was thus able to run from one post to the next, and know where to turn his horse. By this means he was able to win the race.

A gentleman who was present, named Skelton, then came up, and proposed to Metcalf a small wager, that he could not gallop a horse of his 50 yards, and stop him within 200. This horse was notorious as a runaway, and had baffled the efforts of the best and strongest riders to hold him. Metcalf agreed to the wager on condition that he might choose his ground; but Skelton bargained that there should be neither hedge nor wall on the course, lest his horse should be injured. Metcalf agreed; the stakes were deposited; and knowing that there was a large bog near the old Spa at Harrogate, he mounted at about a distance of 150 yards from it. Having observed the wind, and placed a person who was to sing a song to guide him by the sound, he set off at a full gallop towards the bog, and soon fixed the horse saddle-deep in the mire. He then floundered through the dirt as well as he was able, till he gained a firm footing, when he demanded his wager, which was allotted him by general suffrage. It was with the greatest difficulty, however, that the horse could be extricated. That Metcalf was so well acqainted with the spot was owing to his having about three weeks before relieved a stranger who had got fast in it in the night, and whose cries attracted him.

It was now no unusual thing with him to buy horses with a view to selling them. Happening to meet with a man who had been huntsman to Sir John Kaye, and who had a horse to sell, Metcalf inquired the price of the horse, and asked to try it. Having trotted the horse a mile or two, he returned, and told the owner that the eyes of his nag would soon fail. The man, however, stood firm to his demand of 25 guineas for the horse, alleging that he was beautifully moulded, only six years old, and his action good. Metcalf then followed the man into the stable, and desired him to lay his hand upon the eyes of the horse, and feel their unusual heat; asking, at the same time, how he could, in conscience, demand so great a price for a horse that was going blind. The treaty ended with Metcalf purchasing the horse, bridle, and saddle for £14.

A few days after, as he was riding on his new purchase, he ran against a sign-post upon the common, near a toy-shop, and nearly threw it down. Not discouraged by this, he set off for Ripon to play at an assembly; and passing by a place at Harrogate called the World's-End, he overtook a man going the Ripon road: with him Metcalf laid a wager of sixpenny-worth of liquor that he would get first to an ale-house at some distance. The ground being rough, Metcalf's horse soon fell, and lay for a while on the thigh of his master, when, making an effort to rise, he cut Metcalf's face with one of his fore-shoes. The Rev. Mr. Richardson, coming up at this moment and expressing his concern for the accident, Metcalf told him that nothing had hurt him but the cowardice of his horse, who had "struck him whilst he was down." His instrument, however, suffered so materially, that he was obliged to borrow one to perform on for the night at Ripon, to which place he got without further accident. The assembly over, he set off to return to Harrogate, and arrived there about three in the morning.

He now thought it was time to dispose of his fine horse, whose eyes began to discharge much. After applying the usual remedies of alum blown into the eyes, rowelling in different parts, &c., he found the beast in marketable condition; and knowing that there would soon be a great show of horses without Micklegate Bar at York, he resolved to take the chance of the mart; and setting out the night before put up at the Swan, in Micklegate. The next morning, when the show began, Metcalf's nag attracted the notice of one Carter, a very extensive dealer, who, asking the price, was told twenty-two guineas. Carter then inquired if he was sound, and received for answer, "I have never known him LAME; but I will trot him on this pavement, and if there be any ailment of that sort it will soon appear with my weight." The dealer bade him sixteen guineas, and a little after seventeen; when Metcalf, for well-known reasons, was glad to receive.

In the year 1738 Metcalf attained the age of twenty-one years and the height of six feet one inch and a half, and was remarkably robust withal.

About this time Dr. Chambers of Ripon had a well-made horse with which he used to hunt, but finding that he had become a great stumbler, he exchanged him with a dealer, who took him to Harrogate, and meeting with Metcalf told him he had an excellent hunter to sell at a low price. Metcalf desired to try how the horse leaped, and the owner agreeing, he mounted him, and found that he could, when saddled, leap over any wall or fence the height of himself. The bargain was soon struck, and this happening at the Queen's Head Hotel, several gentlemen who were witnesses of the horse's performance invited Metcalf to accompany them two days after to Belmond Wood, where a pack of hounds were to throw off. These hounds were the joint property of Francis Trappes, Esq., and his brother, of Nidd, near Ripley. A pack superior to this was not to be found in the kingdom.

The wished-for day arriving, Metcalf attended the gentlemen, and the hounds were not long in finding. The fox took away to Plumpton Rocks, but finding all secure there, he made for Stockweld Wood, and found matters in the same state as at Plumpton – he had then run about six miles: he came back and crossed the river Nidd near the old abbey, and went on the east side of Knaresborough to a place called Coney-Garths (where there were earths), near Scriven. Metcalf's horse carried him nobly, pulling hard, and he required proportionate resistance. The wind being high, Metcalf lost his hat, but would not stop to recover it; and coming to Thistle Hill, near Knaresborough, he resolved to cross the river at the Abbey Mill, having often before gone on foot over the dam-stones. When he got to the dam he attended to the noise of the fall as a guide, and ranging his horse in a line with the stones dashed forward for some part of the way; but the stones being slippery with a kind of moss, the horse stumbled, but recovered this and a second blunder; the third time, however, floundering completely, away went horse and rider into the dam. Metcalf had presence of mind to disengage his feet from the stirrups during the descent, but both the horse and himself were immersed over head in water. He then quitted his seat and made for the opposite side, the horse following him. Having secured his nag, he laid himself down on his back and held up his heels to let the water run out of his boots, which done, he quickly remounted and went up a narrower lane which leads to the road betwixt Knaresborough and Wetherby; then through some lanes on the north-east side of Knaresborough, and crossing the Borough Bridge Road, he got to the Coney-Garths, where he found that the whipper-in only had arrived before him.

Here the fox had earthed, as was expected; and the other horsemen (who had gone over the Low Bridge and through the town) after some time came up. They were much surprised at finding Metcalf there, and attributed the soaked condition of himself and horse to profuse sweating; nor were they undeceived till they reached Scriven.

Soon after this, Blind Jack was at Scarborough. As he was walking one day on the sands with a friend, he resolved to take a swim in the sea, his companion agreeing to shout out when he should think he had gone far enough outward; but the other not making a sufficient allowance for the noise of the sea, suffered him to go out of hearing before he shouted, and Metcalf continued swimming until he got out of sight of his friend, who now expected to see him no more. At length Metcalf began to think he must have got out of hearing of his friend, and becoming rather tired he turned on his back to rest himself, his ears being covered with water; but after he had sufficiently rested he turned himself again, and removing the hair of his head from his ears, began to listen, when he thought he heard the breakers beating against the pier which defends the Spa; finding by the noise that he was at a great distance, he increased his efforts, and providentially taking a right direction, he landed in safety, to the immense relief of his friend.

Having an aunt at Whitby, near the Alum Works, he went there, left his horse, and got on board an alum ship bound for London. He arrived at the metropolis, stayed there only a few weeks, played on the violin, and did very well; but meeting so many acquaintances, did not think himself safe. After some time, meeting with a vessel, he returned back again to Whitby; and having a numerous acquaintance at Newcastle, formed at Harrogate, he went thither, and was kindly received by many persons. Amongst the rest was one Councillor Grey, who invited Metcalf to dine with him every day during the time he should stay, which was about a month. One day he said to Metcalf, "You and I are near a size," and brought down a suit of clothes, saying, "I think these will fit you, and are at your service if you please to accept them; they have scarcely been worn; go into the next room and try them on." Metcalf then left Newcastle and went to Sunderland, where he stayed a short time among the sailors; then proceeded to Whitby to his aunt's, with whom he had left his horse, as she was in tolerable circumstances; after that he determined to go to

Knaresborough, and set off in the forenoon, intending to call at Mr. Varley's, as he had been there for six months shortly before. He had company over the moor to Pickering, as he had never been on that road. At Pickering his company left him.

He then went to Malton, which was six miles, though he had never been that road before, but had been at Malton; he got safe there, and continued along the York road. A little from Malton his horse began to tire at a place called Crombeck, where there is a ford dangerous in times of flood. It happened to be a very rainy time, and his horse being weak, he took hold of the bridle-rein to lead him through, not being afraid of the water himself, but fearful of drowning his horse. Having got safe through, her pursued his journey, but his horse being weak, he was under the necessity of leading him part of the road, and walking sometimes up to the boot-tops in dirt.

He soon came to a common called Stockton Moor, about four or five miles from York, where was neither turnpike nor paved causeway at that time, and he had got out of the track and was in great difficulty; but fortunately he heard a cock crow in Stockton, and by turning in the direction whence he heard the call of chanticleer, he got into Stockton. From this place there was a paved causeway all the way to York, upon which he went, now feeling himself safe. He then came down Goodram Gate, crossed Peter Gate, down the Shambles, and through Pavement, over Ouse Bridge, turned into Skelder Gate, and through the Postern, it being in the dead of night, but he wanted no guide, as he knew the places so well; then coming to Middlethorpe, the gates were fast: they were made of wood, with iron spikes at the top, which made it difficult to climb over; but necessity being the mother of invention, he called forth her aid. Metcalf took the bridle from off his horse's head, doubled the rein, and throwing it over one of the spikes of the gate, by that means and the help of a corner of the wall that joined the gate, he got up and climbed over; but when he was at the top his situation was perilous, for if his foot had slipped he would have fallen on the spikes and been impaled. He then opened the gates, and led his horse through, and greatly surprised some women by his appearance, who happened to be up washing. When daylight appeared, the family received him very kindly. He stayed about three weeks, and then returned to Knaresborough, where he met with a north countryman who played on the bagpipes and frequented the houses of many gentlemen in town. He had been in London several times, and he advised Metcalf to take a trip with him, which he did.

By this man Metcalf found out several gentlefolks who were in the habit of visiting Harrogate during the season, and amongst others Colonel Liddell, who resided in King Street, Covent Garden, and who gave him a general invitation to his house. The colonel was member of Parliament for Berwick-upon-Tweed, and lived at Ravensworth Castle, near Newcastle-upon-Tyne; and on his return from London to the North, which generally took place in the month of May, he was accustomed to spend three weeks at Harrogate.

When the winter was over, Metcalf thought he must take a walk out of

London. Accordingly he set out through Kensington, Hammersmith, Colnbrook, Maidenhead, and Reading, in Berkshire; and returned by Windsor and Hampton Court to London in the beginning of May. In his absence, Colonel Liddell had sent to his lodgings to let him know that he was going to Harrogate, and that if agreeable to him he might go down either behind his coach or on the top. Metcalf on his return waited upon the colonel and thanked him, but declined his kind offer, observing that he could with great ease walk as far in a day as he would choose to travel in his coach. The next day at noon the colonel and his suite, consisting of sixteen servants on horseback, set off, Metcalf starting about an hour before them. They were to go by the way of Bugden, and he proceeded as far as Barnet. A little way from Barnet the Bugden and St. Alban's roads part, and he had taken the latter; however, he arrived at Welling, the place where they were to sleep, a little before the colonel, who was surprised at his performance. Metcalf set of again next morning before his friends, and coming to Biggleswade, found the road was crossed with water, there being no bridge at that time. He made a circuitous cast, but found no other way except a footpath, which he was doubtful whether to trust. A person coming up, asked, "What road are you for?" He answered, "For Bugden." "You have had some liquor this morning, I suppose?" said the stranger. "Yes," replied Metcalf, although he had tasted none that day. The stranger then bid him follow, and he would direct him into the highway. Soon after, they came to some sluices with planks laid across, and Metcalf followed by the sound of his guide's feet; then to a gate on one side of the turnpike, which being locked he was told to climb over. Metcalf was struck with the kind attention of his conductor, and taking twopence from his pocket, said, "Here, good fellow, take that, and get thee a pint of beer;" but the other declined it, saying he was welcome. Metcalf, however, pressing the reward upon him, was asked, "Can you see very well?" "Not remarkably well," he replied. "My friend," said the stranger, "I do not mean to tithe thee – I am rector of this parish; and so God bless you, and I wish you a good journey." Metcalf set forward with the parson's benediction, and stopped every night with the colonel. On coming to Wetherby, he arrived at the inn before him, as usual, and told the landlord of his approach, who asked him by what means he had become acquainted with that, and was informed by him how he had preceded the colonel the whole week, this being Saturday, and they had left town on Monday noon. The colonel arriving, ordered Metcalf into his room, and proposed halting till Monday, but Metcalf replied, "With your leave, sir, I shall go to Harrogate to-night, and meet you there on Monday." So he set off for Knaresborough that night, and met the colonel at Harrogate on Monday, as he had said.

Metcalf became now in great request as a performer at Ripon assembly, which was resorted to by many families of distinction, such as Sir Walter Blacket of Newby; Sir John Wray, Sir R. Graham, Squire Rhodes, Squire Aislaby of Studley, and many others. When he played alone, it was usual with him after the assembly to set off for Harrogate or Knaresborough; but when he had an assistant he remained all night at Ripon to keep him company, his partner being afraid to ride in the dark.

Finding himself worth £15 (a larger sum than he ever had before), and a main of cocks having being made in the neighbourhood, he became a party, and lost two-thirds of his whole fortune. The remaining £5 he laid out on a horse which was to run at York a few days later; and had the good fortune to win the last wager. Metcalf still followed cock-fighting, cards, and racing, but continued to play at the assemblies; but his profession interfered with his sports, and he cast about in his mind how to obtain an independence. Now it fell out that about this time a Miss Benson, daughter of the host of the Royal Oak was about to be married to a young man whom Metcalf was convinced she did not like. It was a match made up by the parents, and there was no affection in it – at least on her side. Blind Jack had some reason to think that the fair lady was not insensible to him, and he hastened to Harrogate, and hung about the Royal Oak till he had an opportunity of speaking to the damsel, who was to be married the very next day. Metcalf used his most urgent persuasion with the girl to elope with him that night, and obtained from her a tardy consent. It was arranged that she should put a lighted candle in the window when ready to run away, and Metcalf engaged a friend to look out for the candle for him. This having been settled, the lady went into the house, and in a short time was followed by Metcalf, who was warmly received by the supposed bridegroom and company.

The tankard went briskly round with "Success to the intended couple!" in which toast, it may be readily believed, Metcalf joined most cordially.

Having stayed till it was near dark, he thought it time for putting business into proper train. Going then to the public-house known by the name of the World's End, he inquired for the hostler, whom he knew to be a steady fellow; and after obtaining from this man a promise either to serve him in an affair of moment in which he was engaged, or keep the secret, he related the particulars of his assignation and the intended elopement, to forward which he desired him have his master's mare, which he knew would carry two. This agreed on, he requested the further service of meeting him at Ross's Library at ten o'clock. A whistle was to be given by the first who got there, as a signal. They met pretty punctually, and Metcalf asked if he saw a star, meaning the lighted candle. After half-an-hour's delay the signal-light appeared. They then approached the house, and left the horses at a little distance, not choosing to venture into the court-yard, which was paved. On the door being opened by the lady, he asked her if she was ready, and she replied in the affirmative. He advised her, however, to pack up a dress or two, as she probably might not see her mother again for some time. She had about twenty gowns at that time, and a new pillion and cloth. Metcalf asked her for it. "Oh, dear," she said, "it is in the other house; but we must have it." She then went to the window and called up her sister, who let her in. The pillion and cloth were in the room where the intended bridegroom slept, and on his seeing her enter, she said, "I will take this and brush it, that it may be ready in the morning." – "That's well thought on, my dear," said he. She then went down, and all three hastened to the horses. Metcalf mounted her behind his friend, then got upon his own horse, and away they went. At that time it was not a matter of so much difficulty to get married as it is at present, and they had only the trouble of riding twelve miles, and a fee to pay, without any calling of banns requiring a delay of three weeks.

Metcalf left his bride at a friend's house within five miles of Harrogate, and came to the Queen's Head to perform the usual service of playing his violin during the breakfast half-hour. In the meantime Mrs. Benson and her other daughter began to prepare for breakfast, and observing that Dolly lay very long in bed, her mother desired that she might be called; but her usual bed-fellow declaring that she had not slept with her, she was ordered to seek her in some of the other rooms. This was done, but in vain. They then took it for granted that she had gone out early to take a morning ride with Mr. Dickenson (the intended bridegroom), but he could give no account of her. All her friends now began to be seriously alarmed, and a person from the Oak came and informed Metcalf of all that had happened there that morning.

Metcalf listened seriously to the news, and then composedly said, "You need not be alarmed. I MARRIED HER since you saw me last night!"

He then sent a message through the brother of his Dolly to the father and mother, to the effect that he asked their pardon. He acknowledged that he was far below them in circumstances, but his affection for their daughter was sincere, and he promised that he would make them the best amends in his power by affectionate treatment of his wife.

It is hardly to be supposed that they were mollified by this assurance.

Metcalf took a small house at Knaresborough. It was a matter of wonder that Miss Benson should have preferred a blind man to Dickenson, she being as handsome a woman as any in the country. A lady having asked her why she had refused so many good offers for Blind Jack, she answered, "Because I could not be happy without him." And being more particularly questioned, she replied, "His actions are so singular, and his spirit so manly and enterprising, that I could not help liking him."

Metcalf continued going to Harrogate as usual, and one day determined to pay a visit to his mother-in-law. He mounted his horse, and riding up to the kitchen-door called for a pint of wine. There were then only women in the house, who were afraid to serve him, and they all ran upstairs in a fright. He then rode into the kitchen through the house, and out at the hall-door, no one molesting him.

He afterwards went to demand his wife's clothes, but was refused; on a second application, however, he succeeded. His wife having brought him a boy, and some respectable people being the sponsors, they employed their good offices to heal the breach between the families, and were fortunately successful. On the birth of a daughter (the second child) Mrs. Benson herself was godmother, and presented Metcalf with twenty guineas.

He continued to play at Harrogate in the season; and set up a four-wheel chaise and a one-horse chair for public accommodation, there having been nothing of the kind there before. He kept these vehicles two summers, when the innkeepers, beginning to run their own, he gave them up, as he also did racing and hunting; but still wanting employment, he bought horses, and went to the coast for fish, which he took to Leeds and Manchester; and so indefatigable was he that he would frequently walk for two nights and a day with little or no rest; for as a family was coming on he was eager for business as he had been for diversion, keeping up his spirits, and blessed with good health.

Going from Knaresborough to Leeds in a snowstorm, and crossing a brook, the ice gave way under one of his horses, and he was under the necessity of unloading to get him out; but the horse soon as free ran back to Knaresborough, leaving him with two panniers of fish and three other loaded horses in the midst of a snowstorm at night. After much difficulty, however, he divided the weight amongst the others, and pursuing his journey, arrived at Leeds by break of day.

Once passing through Halifax, he stopped at an inn called the Broad Stone. The landlord's son, and some others who frequented Harrogate, seeing Metcalf come in, and having often heard of his exploits, signified a wish to play at cards with him; he agreed, and accordingly they sent for a pack, but before playing he asked to feel them over. The man of the house being his friend, he could depend upon his honour in preventing deception. They began to play, and Metcalf beat four of them in turn, playing only for liquor. Not satisfied with this, some of the company proposed playing for money, and when engaged at shilling whist, Metcalf won 15s. The losing party then proposed to play double or quit, but Metcalf declined playing for more than half-a-guinea points; till at last, yielding to much importunity, he got engaged for guineas, and, favoured by fortune, won, ten, and a shilling for liquor each game, which completely cleared the loser of his cash, who took up the cards and went out, but shortly returned with eight guineas more. Metcalf's friend examined the cards to see if they were not marked, and finding all fair, they went on again, until those eight pieces followed the other ten. They then drank freely at Metcalf's cost, he being now in circumstances to treat. About ten o'clock at night he took his leave, saying he must be at Knaresborough in the morning, having sent his horses before. On his way he crossed the river Wharfe, about a mile below Poole; the water being high, his horse swam, and he got safe home. Thus ended his pursuits as a fishmonger, the profit being small and his fatigue very considerable.

From the period of his discontinuing the business of fishmonger Metcalf continued to attend Harrogate as a player on the violin, in the long room, until the commencement of the rebellion in 1745.

The alarm which took place was great; and loyalty to the House of Hanover, and preparations against the Jacobites, were general in the county of York.

Amongst the many instances which mark this, none were more striking than the conduct of William Thornton of Thornville, near Knaresborough, for he determined to raise a company of soldiers at his own expense, and went to Knaresborough about the 1st October, 1745, where he sent for our blind hero to his inn, and asked him if he knew of any brave fellows who were likely to make spirited soldiers. Jack having satisfied his patron on this head, he was appointed assistant to a sargeant already procured, with orders to begin recruiting the next day.

Such was their success that in two days only they enlisted 140 men at 5s each, their allowance being 1s. per day; out of whom the captain drafted sixty-four, the number of privates he wanted. Soon after, he brought them to Thornville, where he ordered every other day a fat ox to be killed for their entertainment, and gave them beer seven years old, expressing great pleasure at its being reserved for so good a purpose.

He now began to sound the company as to their attachment to the cause and to himself. "My lads!" said he, "you are going to form a part of a ring-fence to the finest estate in the world! The king's army is on its march northward, and I have confidence that all of you are willing to join them." They replied, enthusiastic for the whole ox a day and the seven-year-old beer, "We will follow you to the world's end!"

All matters being adjusted, the company was drawn up, and amongst them BLIND JACK cut no small figure, being near six feet two inches high, and, like his companions, dressed in blue and buff, with a large gold-laced hat. Jack played a march, and off the company moved for Boroughbridge to join General Wade's army, which was there.

On reaching Newcastle, by order of General Wade they were united with Pulteney's regiment, which having suffered much in some late actions, was thought unduly weak. Captain Thornton gave orders for tents for his men and a marquee for himself. He pitched them on Newcastle Moor, and served out a pair of blankets to each tent. On the first night of their encampment the snow fell six inches.

After stopping there for about a week, the General received intelligence of the motions of the Jacobite army, and gave orders to march by break of day for Hexham in three columns, wishing to intercept it upon the west road, as their route seemed to be for England that way. The tents were instantly struck, but the Swiss troops in the van not being willing to move at so early an hour, it was half-past ten before they left the ground, and the snow by that time was extremely deep. The troops were often three or four hours in marching a mile, the pioneers having to cut through some of the drifts, level some of the obstructions, and fill up several ditches, to make a passage for the artillery and baggage.

About ten at night they arrived at Ovington, the place marked out for them, with straw to rest on; but the ground was frozen so hard that but few of the tent-pins would enter in, and in those few tents which were pitched the men lay upon one another, greatly fatigued with their march, it having been fifteen hours from the time of their striking their tents till their arrival at this place, although the distance was only seven miles.

The next day they reached Hexham, where they halted. On Monday night about ten o'clock the army was put in motion by a false alarm. After stopping there about three days, General Wade returned to Newcastle to catch the post-road leading to Yorkshire, and immediately began his march for Yorkshire by way of Pierse Bridge, Catterick, and Boroughbridge; and continuing his route southward, encamped his men on Clifford Moor, where they halted a few days, and then moved to ground between Ferrybridge and Knottingley. The Scottish army had now penetrated southward as far as Derby; but the General having heard that they had received a check from the Duke of Cumberland, sent General Oglethorpe with 1000 horse towards Manchester, either to harass the enemy in their retreat, or to join the Duke's forces; and retired himself with the remainder, by Wakefield-Outwood and Leeds, to Newcastle.

In the meantime the Duke came up with the army of Prince Charles Edward at Clifton, on the borders of Westmorland. Lord George Murray occupied the town, and the Highlanders were fortified behind hedges and a ditch.

The Duke coming upon the open moor after sunset, gave orders for 300 dragoons to dismount and advance to the brink of the ditch; the rebels then fired upon them from behind the hedges; they returned the fire, and fell a few paces back. The Highlanders mistaking this for flight, rushed over the ditch, but meeting a warmer reception than they expected, were glad to retreat, and continued their route to Penrith, and from thence to Carlisle, where they left part of their army.

His Royal Highness thought it advisable to reduce this place; and on its surrender he returned to London. General Wade continued his march for the North, dismissing all the foreigners from his army; and General Hawley, on coming from London to take the command, was joined by some regiments which had been withdrawn from Flanders. They marched to Edinburgh, and from thence to Falkirk, and pitched their tents on the north-east side of the town on the 16th January; the Highland army being at Torwood, about midway between Falkirk and Stirling, and about three miles from the English camp, they could easily see each other's camp light. The English army lay all night on their arms in expectation of being attacked, but the van and picket-guards came in on the morning of the 17th, having observed no motions in the hostile camp which showed any signs of an attack, although they were as near as safety would permit. Soon after, the enemy were observed to move some of their flags from Torwood towards Stirling, which made the English suppose that they were retreating; but this motion was a feint to deceive them. However, upon this the soldiers were ordered to pile their arms and take some refreshment; and although Lord Kilmarnock was in the army of Prince Charles Edward, General Hawley went to breakfast with Lady Kilmarnock at Callander House. The enemy in the meantime stole a march down a valley northward, unperceived; but just before the army discovered them, they were seen by a person, who ran into the camp exclaiming, "Gentlemen! what are you about? The Highlanders will be upon you!" On which some of the officers said, "Seize that rascal; he is spreading a false alarm!'' – ''Will you believe your own eyes?'' said the man; and at that moment the line of Highlanders was seen fringing the high ground on Falkirk Moor.

It is unnecessary here to relate the details of the engagement of Falkirk, so graphically described by Sir Walter Scott in ''Waverley,'' resulting in a momentary gleam of hope to the adherents of Prince Charles Edward, and in as brief a discouragement to English. Captain Thornton lost twenty of his men, together with his lieutenant and ensign, who were taken prisoners. The captain was in a house when the English were surprised, and hearing the bagpipes at the door, he ran up-stairs, and hid in a room behind the door. One of the Highlanders ran in, looked round, but not seeing him, called out, ''None of the rascals are here.''

The woman of the house having seen the captain go up-stairs, went to him soon after, and opening a closet door, entreated him to enter, which he did; she then brought a dresser and placed dishes, &c., upon it, which prevented all appearance of a door in that place; and fortunately there was no bed in the room. About ten minutes after he had been fixed in his new quarters a great number of people, consisting chiefly of Highland officers, amongst whom was Secretary Murray, took possession of the apartment, which being large, they proposed making use of for business during their stay.

In the meantime Metcalf had escaped the Highlanders. Knowing that two of his master's horses had been left at a widow's house a short distance from the town, he made his way to the place with intent to secure them. This woman had in the morning expressed great seeming loyalty to King George; but when Metcalf returned in the evening, the wind had changed: she now extolled Prince Charles, and said, ''The defeat of George's folk was a just judgment.''

Metcalf went into the stable and found the horses, saddled them, and was leading out the first, when he was surrounded by a few stragglers of the Highland army. ''We must have the beast,'' said they; but Metcalf refusing to give him up, they said one to another, ''Shoot him!'' On hearing two of them cock their pieces, he asked, ''What do you want with him?'' – They answered that they wanted him for the Prince. – ''If so, you must have him,'' replied he. They took him, and immediately went off. Metcalf then brought out the other, but as he was about to mount, the captain's coachman (whose name was Snowden), joined him, and Metcalf inquiring of him the fate of his master, was answered that he had not seen him for some time. This induced Metcalf to think that the worst had befallen him. They then thought it advisable to attempt falling in with the rear of the army, but before they had proceeded many yards their horse sank up to the saddle-girths in a bog; however, being strong, and plunging out, they mounted again, and soon joined the army as they had wished; when, on making diligent inquiry after their captain, they were told that he was left behind. Snowden thereupon returned as far as he could with safety, but without gaining any intelligence, and Metcalf walked on with the army.

They arrived at Linlithgow, where they halted, and the next day marched to Edinburgh. There the mob and the lower orders of people were very free in their expressions, and some of the higher also spoke out warmly in favour of Prince Charles, making no secret of their wishes and hopes that "the King should have his own again."

The next morning as many of Captain Thornton's men as had escaped being taken prisoners (about forty-eight in number) assembled; and none of them knowing what had become of the Captain, they supposed him to have shared the fate of many other brave men who had fallen in the action. There was therefore no more ox and beer to sustain their loyalty. The disappearance also of two other officers and twenty of their men greatly dispirited them, and to this was added the suspension of their regular pay. This induced some of them to apply to Metcalf for a supply in order to carry them home; but this he refused, in part, no doubt, because he had not the means of paying them.

The headquarters of the army were now at Edinburgh, the staff being located in Holyrood Palace. The superior officers sent for Metcalf, thinking it singular that a person deprived of sight should have entered the army. One of the officers belonging to the dragoons who retreated from Falkirk, speaking ironically of Thornton's men, asked Jack how he got off the field of battle. Metcalf answered, "I found it very easy to follow by the sound of the dragoon horses, they made such a clatter over the stones." This reply turned the laugh against the officer, who coloured with anger and shame. Colonel Cockayne then asked how he durst venture into the service, blind as he was. To which he replied "that had he possessed a pair of good eyes, he would never have come there to have risked the loss of them by gunpowder." Then making his obeisance he withdrew.

He now determined upon a journey to Falkirk in search of his captain; but this being attended with difficulty, he applied to a Knaresborough man who lived at Edinburgh, and was of the party of Prince Charles Edward, telling him that he wished to be a musician to the gallant young Prince, as he found it was all over with the English. The man informed him that they had a spy, an Irishman, going to the Prince, and that he might travel with him. This he agreed to do, and they started together; but on coming up to the English out-sentries they were stopped. Metcalf inquired for the captain, and informed him of the real cause of his journey. By him he was kindly advised to lay aside his dangerous project; but as he still persisted, he was allowed to proceed with the spy, and arrived at Linlithgow, where they stayed all night. They met with several women who had been plundering, and were then on their return to Edinburgh; and the spy instructed them how to avoid the English sentries. Metcalf was very careful to examine the clothes they had got, making it appear he wanted to purchase some, thinking that by chance he might meet with some of his captain's, and so ascertain if he were dead. One of the women sent a token by Metcalf to her husband, who was Lord George Murray's cook. This woman's guide was a horse-dealer, who soon became acquainted with Metcalf, having frequented the fairs in Yorkshire, and at this time by some means had got introduced to the heads of both armies, and obtained a pass and orders from each to press horses. This man's fate was remarkable; for going into Stirling, where the English army lay, he found that orders were given to let no strangers pass without an examination. He said that he had a protection from General Huske. Being ordered to produce it, he had the misfortune to take that out of his pocket which he had got from the Pretender; and when informed of his mistake instantly produced the other. But too late! for he was tied up by the neck to a lamp-post and hung.

A short time before Metcalf and the spy had got clear away from Linlithgow, some of the vanguard of the rebels came in and called for whiskey; and it was supposed that they dropped there a silver-mounted pistol, which on their setting out the spy picked up and offered to Metcalf. He refused it, saying he thought it not advisable to have fire-arms about him, as he expected to be searched. So they pursued their journeys, and presently fell in with the rebel out-guard, several of whom accosted Metcalf, and as all seemed well, they were allowed to pass, and arrived at Falkirk, where Metcalf inquired for Lord George Murray's cook to deliver his present, and was afterwards introduced to and conversed with Lord George Murray, Secretary Murray, and other gentlemen. Lord George Murray gave him part of a glass of wine, an article at that time of great rarity, for, as the rebels had been there three times, and the English twice, they had almost swept the cupboard clean of crumbs.

Whilst conversing with them he was very cautious, knowing that his life was in danger if the real purpose of his journey became known.

He then made his way towards the market-place, where a number of Highlanders were assembled. This was on Wednesday, the 22nd; but it happened that his master had left the place that morning about four hours before his arrival.

We must now return to Captain Thornton, whom we left on Friday in the closet, in close neighbourhood to the Highland chiefs, who every day transacted business in the room. The quartermasters of the Jacobite army having taken the house, and given the woman to whom it belonged a small apartment at the back, it made Captain Thornton's position very critical; but every night she took care to carry him such provisions as she could convey through a crevice at the bottom of the door, and this she did for fear of alarming those who slept in the adjoining rooms. The closet was only a yard and a half square, and the captain's clothes being wet when he entered, made his situation the more uncomfortable, as he had got a severe cold, and sometimes could not forbear coughing even when the rebels were in the room. Once in particular, hearing a cough, they said one to another, "What is that?" But one of them answered that it was somebody in another room, not in the least suspecting that one of their enemies lay hid so near.

On Monday night the woman of the house went to the door to carry provisions as usual, when the captain said to her, "I am determined to come out, let the consequence be what it may; for I will not die like a dog in this hole," But she begged that he would bear this confinement until the next night, and she would adopt some plan to effect his escape. She accordingly consulted an old carpenter who was true to the Hanoverian cause, and he came the following night when the room was vacant, removed the dresser, and liberated the captain. They proceeded downstairs in the dark to the woman's apartment, where she made tea whilst the carpenter and captain concerted their plan of operation. They dressed him in a plaid and brogues, and put on him a black wig. The captain had only ten guineas about him (having left his cash with his lieutenant, Mr. Crofts), eight of which he gave to the woman who had so faithfully preserved him, and two to the carpenter; who, to secrete them, put them into his mouth along with his tobacco, fearful of a search by the Highlanders, who would have suspected him had they found more than a shilling.

Everything being ready, they set out, the captain, with a bag of tools, following his supposed master. On coming into the crowd, the old carpenter looked about and was rather dismayed, for although in disguise, the captain did not look like a common workman. This made the old man dread discovery, so he called out to him: "Come alang, ye filthy loon; ye have had half a bannock and a mutchkin of drink in your wame: we shall be o'er late for our day's wark." Whether this artifice served him or not is uncertain; but they got safe through the throng, and leaving the high road, pursued their journey across the country. Having come to a rising ground, the captain took a view of Falkirk Moor, and said, "Yonder's the place where such a sad piece of work was made last Friday." The old man at the same time looking the other way saw about 300 Highlanders, who had been on plunder, coming down a lane which led from Callander House (Lord Kilmarnock's seat) into the main road; and being desirous of passing the end of this lane before they came up, in order to avoid them, said, "We shall have a worse piece of wark of it than we had on Friday if ye do not hasten your pace," and begged the captain to come forward, which he did; but walking briskly up a hill, he suddenly stopped, and said, "I am very sick." However they gained their point, and passed the Highlanders; for had they come up with them, the captain's speech or appearance might have led to suspicion, and he would have been shot or led back to Falkirk as a prisoner. On going two miles farther, they arrived at a house belonging to a friend of the carpenter's, and which had been plundered. There the old man got an egg, but not being able to find a pan to boil it in, he roasted it in peat ashes, and gave it to the captain to put in his wame or stomach. Proceeding a few miles farther, they arrived at another house, where they procured a horse for the captain. He arrived at the English outposts, and making himself known, was permitted to pass, and reached Edinburgh in safety.

To return to Metcalf, whom we left at Falkirk, and whose dress was a plaid waistcoat laced with gold, which he had borrowed of a friend at Edinburgh, together with a blue regimental coat faced with buff. Jack told the Highlanders, in answer to their inquiries, that he had been fiddling for the English officers, and that they had given him that coat, which had belonged to a man who was killed; and also that his intention was to serve in the same capacity with Prince Charles. But a person coming up who had seen Jack at Harrogate, said, "That fellow ought to be taken up, for there is something more than common in his proceedings;" on which Metcalf was taken to the guard-room and searched for letters, but none were found, he having only a pack of cards in his pocket, which they split, to see if they contained any writing in the folds. Finding nothing, he was put into a loft in the roof of the building, along with a dragoon and some other prisoners, and there for three days they were suffered to remain in confinement, exposed to severe cold.

Metcalf and his fellow-prisoners were brought out at the end of this time, and tried by a court-martial. Metcalf was acquitted, and had permission given to go to the Prince; but as he asked to borrow a clean shirt they inquired where his own was. He said at Linlithgow, but that he durst not go there on account of George's fellows. They then informed him he might safely go there along with the Irish spy. He knew that his companion had letters for the Highlanders' friends at Edinburgh, but had no intention to pass the English sentries. Metcalf therefore amused him with assurances that he had £10 at Edinburgh, for which he should have no occasion if he joined the Prince, and that he would give his friend a share of it. The spy on hearing this became very desirous of his company to Edinburgh, wishing to finger the money, and proposed going across the country; but Metcalf said he could pass the English sentries by saying he was going to Captain Thornton. They then proceeded, and after going two miles they met an officer who was reconnoitring, and he knowing Metcalf, told him that his master was arrived safely at Edinburgh. On leaving the officer the spy accosted him with, "So, then, you ARE going to him." "No!" said Jack, "nor to any such fellows." They then passed the sentry, as Metcalf proposed, and arrived at Edinburgh, where they parted, but promised to meet the next evening at nine o'clock. Jack went directly to his captain, who rejoiced at so unexpected a meeting. Metcalf told him that he had given him a great deal of trouble, adding that he thought people might come home from market without being fetched. The captain smiled and said, "What is to be done, for I have neither money nor clothes, having left all behind at Falkirk; but I have bills upon the road to the amount of £300?" This proved fortunate; for had they been a few days sooner, these also might have been lost. The reason of the delay was that all letters directed to Scotland were at this time sent to London to be examined at the General Post-Office. Metcalf told the captain that he could get him some money, but this the other thought impossible. However, he went to a friend and obtained £30. Tailors were immediately set to work, and next morning the captain was enabled to visit his brother officers at Holyrood.

The army remained quartered at Edinburgh, while part of the rebels were in Falkirk, and another part at Stirling, where they raised several batteries, and besieged Stirling Castle.

The Duke of Cumberland arrived at Edinburgh on the 30th of January, 1746; and two days afterwards marched at the head of the army towards Falkirk, Prince Charles' army leaving it a little time before. Captain Thornton visited the Duke often, and his Royal Highness took particular notice of Metcalf, speaking to him several times on the march. On the arrival of the army at Linlithgow, intelligence was received that the rebels were marching towards them to give them battle; upon which the army was drawn up in order, and the Duke rode through the lines, and addressed the men as follows: – "If there be any who think themselves in a bad cause, or are afraid to engage the enemy, thinking they may fight against any of their relations, let them now turn out, receive pardon, and go about their business without any further question." On the conclusion of this speech, the whole army gave three hearty cheers. But the intelligence proving false, they proceeded to Falkirk, and continued their journey to Stirling, Perth, Montrose, Brechin, and Aberdeen, where they halted. The army of the Prince was encamped at Strathbogie.

At Aberdeen the Duke gave a ball to the ladies, and personally solicited Captain Thornton for his fiddler, there being at that time no music in the army except Colonel Howard's (the Old Buffs), which was wind music, and the performers, who were Germans, were unaccustomed to country dances. As the Prince's army was only twenty miles distant, no invitations were sent until five o'clock, though the ball was to begin at six. Twenty-five couples danced for eight hours, and his Royal Highness made one of the party, and several times as he passed Metcalf, who stood on a chair to play, shouted, "Thornton, play up!" But Jack needed no exhortation, for he was well practised and better inclined.

Next morning the Duke sent him two guineas; but as he was not permitted to take money, he informed his captain, who said, as it was the Duke's money, he might take it, but observed that he should give his Royal Highness's servants a treat (he had only three servants with him – viz., his gentleman, cook, and groom). So the next night two of them paid Metcalf a visit, and a merry party they made, the captain ordering them plenty of refreshments.

In a little time they proceeded on their march, and engaged the gallant army of the Prince on Culloden Moor. The battle ended in the total rout of the army of the young "Pretender," and the somewhat severe treatment of his soldiers by the "Butcher" Duke.

The English prisoners were all liberated. Three of Captain Thornton's men had died in prison; the rest returned home.

The rebellion having been completely suppressed and peace restored, Captain Thornton returned home, accompanied by Metcalf, who had the happiness to find his faithful partner and children in good health.

Blind Jack being now at liberty to choose his occupation, attended Harrogate as usual; but having in the course of his Scotch expedition kept his eyes open (if we may use such an expression of a blind man), he had become acquainted with various articles manufactured in that country, and judging that some of them might find a market in England, he repaired in the spring to Scotland, and supplied himself with various articles in cotton and worsted, especially Aberdeen stockings. For all these articles he found a ready sale at the houses of gentlemen in the county of York; and being personally known to most of the families, was everywhere kindly received. He was never at a loss to know among one thousand articles what each had cost him, as he had a method of marking them which enabled him to distinguish them by the feel. It was also customary with him to buy horses for sale in Scotland, bringing back galloways in return. He was an admirable judge of horses by running his hands over them.

He also engaged pretty deeply in contraband trade, the profits of which at that time were so considerable as to make it worth while running the risk. Once, having received a pressing letter from Newcastle-upon-Tyne requiring his speedy attendance, he set out on horseback from Knaresborough at three in the morning, and got into Newcastle the same evening about six o'clock, a distance of nearly seventy-four miles, and did not feel fatigued.

Having received some packages, he employed a few soldiers to convey them to a carrier, judging that men of their description were least liable to suspicion. After sending off his goods, he stayed two nights with some relations, and then set out for home. He had with him about a hundred-weight of tea, cased over with tow, and tightly corded up; this he put into a wallet, which he laid across the saddle.

Coming to Chester-le-Street (about half-way between Newcastle and Durham), he met at the inn an exciseman, who knew him as soon as he had dismounted, and asked him what he had got there. Metcalf answered, "It is some tow and line for my aunt, who lives a few miles distant. I wish she was far enough, for giving me the trouble to fetch it." The officer said to him, "Bring it in"; he replied, "I am only here for a few minutes; it may as well remain on the horsing-stone." By this seeming indifference about his packet he removed suspicion from the mind of the exciseman, who assisted in replacing it across the saddle.

Once having disposed of a string of horses, he bought with the produce a quantity of rum, brandy, and tea, to the amount of £200, put them on board a vessel for Leith, and travelled overland on foot to meet the vessel at that port. He had about thirty miles to walk, and carried near five stone weight of goods, which he did not choose to put on shipboard. At Leith he had the mortification to wait six weeks without receiving any tidings of the vessel, which many supposed to have been lost, there having been a storm in the interval. The distress of mind resulting from this induced him to say, "If she is lost I wish I had been in her, for she had all my property on board." Soon after, however, the ship got into Leith harbour. He then went on board, and set sail for Newcastle; but another storm arising, the mate was washed overboard, the main-sail carried away, and the ship driven near the coast of Norway. Despair now became general, the prospect of going to the bottom seemed almost certain. Metcalf had now no wish to go to the bottom with his property, and vowed he would give all his fortune to touch dry earth again. But the wind changing, hope began to return, and the captain put about for the Scotch coast, intending to make Aberbrothock. A signal of distress was put up, but the sea ran so high that no boat could venture out with a pilot. He then stood in for the harbour, but struck against the pier end, owing to the unmanageable state of the vessel from the loss of her main-sail; she narrowly escaped being bulged, but having got to the back of the pier, was towed round into the harbour with nearly five feet of water in her hold.

As the vessel stood in need of repairs, Metcalf put his goods on board another, and went in her to Newcastle. There he met with an acquaintance, and thinking the fellow trustworthy, over his cups informed him that he had got 400 gallons of gin and brandy for which he had a permit, and about thirty gallons for which he had none, and which he wanted to land. In a quarter of an hour he found that the man whom he had taken for a friend had gone down the quayside and given information of what he knew, and all the goods were seized and brought on shore. Metcalf imagined that none were seizable but the small part for which he had not obtained a permit; but was soon undeceived, the whole being liable to seizure as not agreeing with the specified quantity.

He then repaired to the Custom-house and applied to Mr. Sunderland, the collector. This gentleman knew Metcalf, whom he had seen at Harrogate; he received him very kindly, but informed him that it was not in his power to serve him, the captors being the Excise people, and not of his department. He, however, suggested that some good might result from an application to Alderman Pelreth, with whom Metcalf was acquainted, and who was intimate with the collector of the Excise. The alderman gave him a letter to the collector, representing that the bearer had bought 400 gallons of spirits at the Custom-house at Aberdeen, and that the extra quantity was for the purpose of treating the sailors and other friends, as well as for sea-stock for himself. At first the collector told him that nothing could be done for him until he should write up to the Board, and receive an answer; but Metcalf remonstrating on the inconvenience of the delay, and the other reconsidering the letter, he agreed to come down to the quay at four o'clock in the afternoon, which he accordingly did, and released everything without any expense.

A short time after, the regiment called "The Queen's Bays" were raised; they were quartered at Knaresborough and the adjacent towns; but after a short stay they were ordered to the North. The country people seemed unwilling to supply carriages for the baggage, the King's allowance being but ninepence a mile per ton: that of the county, one shilling in the West Riding, and fifteenpence in the North Riding. Metcalf having two waggons, was desirous to try this new business; and to make sure of the job, got the soldiers to press his two carriages, which were accordingly loaded, and he attended them to Durham himself. Previous to loading, however, the country people, who knew the advantage of carrying for the army, and who had kept back in hopes of an advance in the price, came forward with their waggons in opposition to Metcalf; but they were now too late – Metcalf had secured the job.

On arriving at Durham, he met Bland's dragoons on their march from the North to York; they loaded his waggons again for Northallerton, and would willingly have engaged them to York; but this he was obliged to decline, having promised to bring twenty-three wool-packs to Knaresborough. He was just six days in performing this journey; and cleared, with eight horses and the one he rode, as much as £20.

Some horses belonging to the Queen's Bays, stationed at Durham, were to be sold, and Metcalf, hearing of the sale, set off from Knaresborough only the day before, and arrived there in time. Amongst the horses to be sold was a grey one, belonging to one of the drums. The man who had the charge of him not having been sufficiently careful in trimming him, had burnt him severely, which caused a swelling. Had his careless conduct been known to his superiors he would have been punished for it; upon that account the matter was hushed up. Metcalf, however, having been apprised of the circumstances from a farrier whom he had got to know, determined to purchase him, judging that the horse would be sold cheap. He was not mistaken. He bought him for very little, and realised a good profit out of him shortly afterwards.

In the year 1754 Metcalf commenced a new business. He set up a stage-coach between York and Knaresborough, and conducted it himself, twice a week in the summer season, and once in the winter; and this business, together with the occasional conveyance of army baggage, employed him until his first contract for making roads, which suiting him better, he disposed of his draught and interest in the road.

An Act of Parliament having been obtained to make a turnpike from Harrogate to Boroughbridge, a person of the name of Ostler, of Farnham, two miles from Knaresborough, was appointed surveyor. Metcalf being in company with him, agreed to make about three miles of it, between Minskip and Ferrensby. The materials were to be procured from one gravel-pit for the whole length. He therefore provided deal boards and erected a temporary house at the pit, took twelve horses to the place, fixed racks and mangers, and hired a house for his men at Minskip, distant about three-quarters of a mile. He often walked from Knaresborough in the morning, with four or five stone-weight of meat on his shoulders, and joined his men by six o'clock. By his attention and diligence he completed the work much sooner than was expected, to the entire satisfaction of the surveyor and trustees.

During his leisure hours he studied measurement in a way of his own, and when certain of the girth and length of any piece of timber, he was able to reduce its true contents to feet and inches, and would bring the dimensions of any building into yards and feet.

About the time that this road was finished the building of a bridge was advertised to be contracted for at Boroughbridge, and a number of gentlemen met there for that purpose at the Crown Inn. Metcalf, amongst others, went also. The masons varied considerably in their estimates. Ostler, the surveyor of the roads, was appointed to survey the bridge, and Metcalf told him that he wished to undertake it, though he had never done anything of the kind before.

On this the surveyor acquainted the gentlemen with what Metcalf proposed; when he was sent for and asked what he knew about a bridge. He told them that he could readily describe it, if they would take the trouble of writing down his plan, which was as follows: – "The span of the arch 18 feet, being a semicircle, makes 27; the arch-stones must be a foot deep, which, if multiplied by 27, will be 486; and the basis will be 72 feet more. For the arch, it will require good backing; for which purpose there are proper stones in the old Roman wall at Aldborough, which may be brought, if you please to give directions to that effect." The gentlemen were surprised at his readiness, and agreed with him for building the bridge. The persons who had given in their estimates were much offended; and as the stone was to be procured from Renton, a sale quarry belonging to one of the masons who was there, he was unwilling to sell any to Metcalf; upon which he went to Farnham, and found good stones which the lime-burners had left (being too strong for their purpose), got them dressed at the place for a trifle, conveyed them to Boroughbridge, and having men to take them off the carts, set them, and completed the arch in one day.

Soon after, there was a mile and a half of turnpike road to be made between Knaresborough Bridge and Harrogate, for which Metcalf also agreed. Going one day over a place covered with grass, he told his men that he thought it different from the ground adjoining, and would have them try for stone or gravel, which they immediately did, and found an old causeway, supposed to have been made in the time of the Romans, which afforded many materials for the new road. Between the forest lane-head and Knaresborough Bridge there was a bog in a low piece of ground. The surveyor thought it impossible to make a road over it, but Metcalf assured him he could accomplish it. The other then told him that if so he should be paid as if he had carried the road round the bog. Jack set about it, cast the road up, and covered it with whin and ling, and made it as good as any part he had undertaken. He received for his contract about £400. He afterwards contracted for making five miles of road between Harrogate and Harewood Bridge, and received for it £1200. For a mile and half through part of Chapeltown to Leeds, and for lengthening the arch of Sheepscar Bridge, he received £400.

The following are some of his other contracts: – Four miles of the road between Skipton and Colne, and two miles on the Burnley Road. Two miles of the road through Broughton to Marton, and two miles more through Addingham and over part of Rombalds Moor, for all which he received £1350. Four miles between Mill Bridge and Halifax, and five miles between Wakefield and Chickingley Beck, near Dewsbury; and received for the same £1200. Three miles and a half between Hag Bridge and Pontefract, and one mile and a half on the Doncaster Road, from Crafton, through Foldby. For the road from Wakefield to Pontefract, Doncaster, and Halifax, he received £6400. From Blackmoor foot to Marsden, and from thence to Standish foot; also from Lupset

Gate through Horbury; and also three miles from Standish to Thurton Clough; from Sir John Kaye's seat to Huddersfield; and thence to Longroyd Bridge toll-bar, in the course of which were several bridges, the whole distance about twenty-one miles, for which he received £4500.

In the building of bridges, where the foundations were bad, he laid on a sufficient thickness of ling (where it could be got), otherwise straw; he next laid planks five inches thick, with square mortices cut through, and driving in a number of piles, made the foundations secure. He then laid springs for the arches upon the planks, which caused all to settle regularly. And though he built many arches of different sizes, none ever fell. He also undertook to build houses, amongst which was one belonging to Mr. Marmaduke Hebden, near Huddersfield, nine yards wide, twenty-three long, and twenty-one feet from the foundation to the square of the building, with twenty chimneys.

Metcalf having now made up his mind to follow building and road-making, finding it remunerative, contracted for and executed at various times a great many roads.

About the year 1781 Metcalf, hearing how beneficial the cotton business was to all that were engaged in it, resolved to have a share in that also; he accordingly purchased the necessary machinery, but the scheme failed, as a time came when no yarn could be sold without loss; therefore he gave up that business. In 1789 he contracted for making several pieces of road in Lancashire, between Bury and Heslington, and another part from Heslington to Accrington; and also a branch from that to Blackburn, the work of two summers, for which he received £3500. In 1791 he returned into Yorkshire, and began to speculate in buying and selling hay, measuring the stacks with his arms, and having learnt the height, he could soon tell the number of square yards contained in the whole.

Having gone to York in the first day of 1795, he set out on January 9th to walk to Green-Hammerton, on his way to Thornville Royal, and accomplished the distance, which was ten miles, in three hours and a half. He slept that night at Thornville Royal, and next day walked to Knaresborough, January 10th, the birthday of Sir Thomas Slingsby's eldest son, which was kept with great rejoicings.

Thence he went to Spofforth, where he resided with his daughter, after the death of his wife in 1778. There he died on the 27th April, 1810, in the full possession of his faculties, aged ninety-three. He was buried in Spofforth churchyard.

At the time of his death his descendants were four children, twenty grandchildren, and ninety great and great-great grandchildren.

"PEG PENNYWORTH."

MARGARET WHARTON, an unmarried lady of great wealth and ancient family, was one of the Yorkshire oddities of last century.

She belonged to the family of the Whartons of Skelton Castle, in Cleveland, and possessed a fortune of £200,000, of which, with rare liberality, she made her nephew a present of £100,000. Her charities were liberal, but always private, and if she heard that a recipient of her bounty had disclosed the good deed, that person never received another penny from her.

She was a short, stout lady, dressed fashionably, had an aristocratic air, and liked to be respected as rich and of good family.

For some time she resided at York, and visited Scarborough in the season, where she was well known on account of her eccentricites. She used to send for "a pennyworth of strawberries" or "a pennyworth of cream" at a time, and pay down her penny, as she had an aversion to tradesmen's bills. From this she obtained the name of "Peg Pennyworth," which stuck to her through life. An incident occurred at Scarborough in which she displayed her dislike to public charities. She was solicited by some gentlemen to give a subscription to a charity on behalf of which they were making a collection. Peg pulled out her purse with an ominous frown, and turned out its contents into her palm. This was in or about 1774, when light guineas were in disgrace. She deliberately selected from among the coins the lightest guinea she could find, and handed it to the gentleman.

The celebrated Foote is said to have drawn her character in a farce. When informed of this she exclaimed, with a smile, "I will see it acted, as I live." She did, and expressed her satisfaction that the character in the play did her justice.

She frequently catered for herself, making her own purchases, and taking them home in her carriage. Once, having purchased some eels, she put them in her pocket, entered her coach, and called on a lady friend and invited her to come out with her for an airing.

The warmth of Peg's pocket revived the seemingly dead eels, and they began to wriggle out to enjoy a little fresh air. The lady who was sitting beside Peg, happening to look down, saw what she thought was a serpent writhing into her lap, and several hideous heads breaking out of the side of Mistress Margaret Wharton. She uttered an awful shrièk, bounded to her feet, pulled the checkstring, and cried, "Madam! madam! you are swarming with adders! Coachman, stop! Let me out! Let me out!"

Mistress Wharton coolly looked at the eels, now escaping rapidly from her pocket, gathered them up, and shoved them into her reticule, saying, "I protest, madam, it is only my eels come to life. Sit you down again, and don't be frightened."

One day at Scarborough she had ordered a large meat-pie to be baked for dinner. It was a very large one – to serve for herself, some visitors, and all the servants. When it was made she ordered the footman to take it to the bakehouse, but he declined, saying that it was not his place, neither did it comport with his dignity, to be seen in Scarborough stalking through the streets in plush and tags, bearing a huge meat-pie.

Mistress Margaret then ordered the coachman to take it, but he declined.

"Bring out the carriage, then!" said Peg Pennyworth. The horses were harnessed; the coachman put on his powdered wig and mounted the box; the footman took his place behind; and Mistress Margaret Wharton, bearing the meat-pie, sat in state in the carriage. "Drive to the bake-house."

So the coachman whipped his horses, and the meat-pie was carried thus to the baker's. An hour or two later the carriage was ordered out again, the coachman remounted the box, the footman took his stand behind, and the lady drove to the bakehouse to fetch her pie, which she carried back thus to her house. "Now," said she to the coachman, "you have kept your place, which is to drive; and you," turning to the footman, "have kept yours, which is to wait; and now we shall all have some of the pie."

Mistress Wharton had a visiting acquaintance with a lady, a clergyman's wife, in York. On the death of her husband, the widow retired with her four daughters to Thirsk, and she invited Peg Pennyworth to visit her.

To her dismay, one day up drove Mistress Wharton in her carriage, with coachman, footman, and lady's maid. The widow, whose means were not very ample, endured having all these poeple quartered on her for a month, but at the expiration of that time she was obliged to hint to the nephew of her guest that "the pressure on her means was rather greater than she could bear."

"Let my aunt have her way," said Mr. Wharton. "I will pay you two hundred a year during her life, and one hundred during your own, should you survive her."

Mistress Margaret Wharton never left the house of the widow, but died there after some years, in the one hundred and third year of her age, in 1791. The annuity was regularly paid to the widow lady to the day of her death.

❋ ❋ ❋

PETER BARKER,

THE BLIND JOINER OF HAMPSTHWAITE.

PETER BARKER was born on July 10th, 1808. At the age of four he was deprived of sight by an inflammation of the eyes, and ever afterwards he was—

> "dark, amid the blaze of noon,
> Irrevocably dark; total eclipse,
> Without all hope of day."

The loss of his sight caused Peter from an early age to cultivate music, and he became a skilful performer on the violin; and as he grew up to manhood he frequented the village feats, dances, and merry-makings all round the country, as a performer on that instrument. This led him into habits of intemperance. But he had a strong will, a tender conscience, and seeing that he was sinking in his own respect and in that of others, he determined to abandon his musical profession.

But he must earn his livelihood; and he determined to become a joiner. He fell to work to make a chair, succeeded in the first attempt, and for the rest of his life followed carpenting as his profession. He handled his tools with all the dexterity of a practised workman; his shop was always in order, the tools in their proper position in the rack, or in his hands. The only peculiarity about his instruments was in the foot-rule he used for marking his measurements, the lines on which were marked by small pins, of different numbers, to indicate the different feet on the rule. The idea of having his rule thus marked was suggested by a lady who interested herself in his welfare. She wrote to a manufacturer of carpenters' rules in London, to inquire if such a thing could be had as a rule with raised lines and figures; the answer was that no such rules were made. Failing to procure an article of this kind, she suggested the making of the measurements on it with pins; and this was carried into effect.

The articles made by this blind workman were firm and substantial, the joints even and close, and the polish smooth. It is said that a cabinet-maker at Leeds, having heard reports of the blind joiner's skill, procured a chair he had made, and showed it to the workmen in his shop, asking them their opinion of the chair. After examining it, they said that they thought there was nothing particular about the chair, only it was a thoroughly well-made, serviceable one. "So it is," said the master; "but – will you believe it? – the man who made it never saw it: he was blind from a child." Their indifference was at once turned into amazement.'

The writer of a memoir of Peter Barker[1] says:—

"We have frequently seen him at work, and were it not from the more frequent handling of the articles operated on, and the nearness of his fingers to the edge of the chisel or saw, there was nothing apparently to distinguish his manner from that of an ordinary workman. In 1868 we found him at work in the church, repairing the seats, and watched him for some time before he was conscious of the presence of any one. He showed us what he had done – lowered the fronts of both the pulpit and reading-desk, the one twenty inches, the other a foot: brought forward a pew some three feet, and refronted it with panels of old carved oak, which he asserted was very difficult to work over again; showed us a piece of carving which he, in conjunction with the church-warden, had only discovered the day before, and which was upwards of 200 years old; led the way into the belfry, giving a word of advice to be careful in ascending the old rickety stairs; showed the clock, which he had under his care to keep clean and in going order. At this point, while seated on a bench, he gave us a narrative of his first acquaintance with the clock, which we give in his own words as nearly as we can remember: – [2] "You see, our clock is yan o' these aud fashion'd hand-made 'uns, not made exact and true by machinery as they are now, but ivvery wheel cut an' filed by hand. Aud Snow, a notified clock-maker 'at lived up aboon abit here, had the managing of her a lang time, at so much a year. He used to come just at t' time when his year was up, give t' aud clock a fether full o' oil, tak his brass, and there was no mair on him till t' next year. At last she gat as she wadn't gang at all; she wad naither turn pointers nor strike. T' foaks i' t' toon were sadly dissatisfied; they neither knew when to get up nor gang to bed, as they had done afore, when t' clock was all reet. T' church-maister sent for t' clock-maker, and he come an' come ageean, an' fizzled and faff'd aboot her, but nivver did her a farthing's worth o' good. At last he was forced to give her up as a bad job; she was fairly worn out, an' she wad nivver be no better till she was mended with a new un; and that's aboon twenty year sin, an' t' aud clock's here yet. Then Johnny Gill, another clever fellow, took her under hands, and she lick'd him as fairly as she'd deean aud Snow. I was i' t' church by mysel one day, I hardly know what aboot, when it com' into my heead 'at I would try my hand at her; I nivver had deean nowt o' t' sort; but if ye nivver try, ye nivver can dea (do) nowt. So t' first thing I did was to give her a reet good feelin' all ower her; an' then, heving settled all her parts fairly i' my mind, I fell to work and took her to pieces, bit by bit, got all t' works out of her, and cleaned her all ower reet soundly, particularly t' pivots, and then gav 'em all a sup o' nice oil; then I put her together ageean; efter a few trials I got her all reet, got her started – she strake an' kept time like a good un.

[1] Published by T. Thorpe, Pately Bridge, 1873.

[2] The strong provincial dialect is somewhat modified in this, or it would be unintelligible except to Yorkshire readers.

Efter I finish'd I com' doon, an' into th' church garth, and wha did I meet there but Mr. Shann, our vicar at that time, and just as I was meeting him t' clock strake ageean. 'What's that, Peter?' he says. I says, 'It's t' clock, sir!' He says ageean, 'What does this mean, Peter?' I says, 'It meeans t' time o' day when t' clock strikes.' He began o' laughing, and said, 'You're a queer fellow, Peter, I mean who made the clock strike?' 'Oh,' I says, 'I've deean that mysel, sir. I've been at her a goodish bit to-day, an' I think I've gotten her put all reet at last.' 'Well done, Peter, you're a clever fellow,' he says. 'But you sha'n't do all this for nothing. I shall let the churchwardens know what you have done. You must have some reward.' 'Varry weel, sir,' I says, and so we parted. And he was as good as his word. When t' churchmaisters met, he tell'd 'em all aboot it, and they allowed me four shillings for my job; and I was to have ten shillings a year for keeping her ganning ivvery year efter.''

In the month of July, 1865, the clock did not strike correctly. As Peter told the tale himself: – ''I was i' t' shop when I heard her at it, two or three times. I stood it as lang as I could; at last I banged down my teeals (tools), and says to mysel', 'I'll mak thee either strake reet, or I'll mak thee as that thou'll nivver strike ageean.'' Away I went, spent an hour over her, gat her reet, and she's kept reet ever sin'.''

His biographer says: – ''Once on a visit to Peter's cottage, we found a window had been recently inserted, according to his statement, to make the fireside more lightsome – Peter having been mason, joiner, and glazier himself. In short, he appeared to be able to do any kind of work that he had the desire or the will to do. He was an expert in the art of netting – fabricating articles in that line from the common cabbage net to the curtains which adorn the windows of the stately drawing-room. As a vocalist he sang bass in the church on Sundays. He was also one of the bell-ringers; and during the winter months the curfew bell is rung at Hampswaite at eight o'clock every evening. When it was Peter's turn to ring he took a lighted lanthorn with him – not for the purpose of seeing others, but that others might see him.

''He always fattened a pig in the winter season, and had a method of measurement of his own for ascertaining how much weight the pig had gained every week; and to such measurement and calculation the pig was weekly subjected until he attained the proper bulk and weight. Peter generally bought his pig himself, and for that purpose attended the market at Knaresborough, where the bargain was cause of much amusement to the onlookers. When the pig was pointed out which was thought likely, the seller had to seize the same, and hold it still as possible, until Peter had felt it over and ascertained its *points*, and passed his judgment on its feeding qualities.''

Peter learned to read with is fingers in 1853, and was given a New Testament with embossed letters.

He was very fond of children, and would play tunes to them on his fiddle at his shop door of a summer evening, whilst they danced and sang. He had made this fiddle himself, as well as the case in which he kept it.

So delicate was Peter's touch that he was able to tell the hour on a watch by opening the case and running his fingers lightly over the face.

Peter in his youth had a romantic courtship, and married a wife. She presented him with a son, born in 1846; and died on June 3rd, 1862. The boy, who was his father's constant companion and delight, died the following year, on Jan. 19th, 1863, leaving the poor blind joiner's house completely desolate.

After a few weeks' illness, Peter died in his cottage, near the churchyard gate, on February 18th, 1873, at the age of sixty-five.

THE WHITE HOUSE

On the road between Raskelfe and Easingwold stood in 1623, and stands still, a lonely inn called "The White House."

The wide, brown, heathery moor called Pill-Moor then extended to the roots of the Hambledon hills; on a slight rising ground above the marshes stood here and there a farm or cottage; and here and there a portion of the soil had been enclosed. To this day a large portion of the moor remains untilled, and is a favourite resort of botanists, who find there several varieties of gentian and orchis, rare else-where. Originally it stretched from Borough Bridge to the Hambledons, intersected by the streams flowing into the Ouse, patched here and there with pools of water.

In the White House lived a man called Ralph Raynard, and his sister. Ralph paid his addresses to a fine-looking young woman, dark-eyed, dark-haired, who lived at Thornton Bridge, at the Red House, where the road from Brafferton or Tollerton crossed the Ouse to Topcliffe and Ripon. The old house, lonely, surrounded by trees, with traces of a moat or pond, in spring full of yellow flags, stands to this day, almost deserted. The girl was poor, and a good match was of the first advantage to her; she was at the time in service at the Red House, and thither Ralph came to visit her.

But, for some cause unknown, they quarrelled, an estrangement ensued, and Ralph came no more across Thornton Bridge.

At the same time a yeoman named Fletcher, living at Moor House, in the parish of Raskelfe, had cast his eyes on the comely young woman, and he took advantage of the rupture between the lovers to step in and offer his hand to the damsel. He was at once accepted, in a fit of resentment against Ralph Raynard, and the marriage rapidly followed; so that she soon found herself the wife of a man whom she did not love, and some miles nearer the White House, where lived Ralph, whom she did love, than when she had resided at Thornton Bridge.

The resentment she had felt died away; an explanation followed when too late. There was a scene – despair on both sides, and resentment entertained by both Ralph Raynard and Mrs. Fletcher against the unfortunate yeoman who stood between them and perfect union and happiness.

On market-day, when Mrs. Fletcher ambled on her nag into Easingwold, she invariably halted at the White House, when the hostler, one Mark Dunn, a beetle-browed, uncouth fellow from Huby, received and held her horse as she dismounted and entered the inn. Ralph, the host, was always there, and received Mrs. Fletcher with an affection which dissatisfied his sister, a woman of sense, who saw that this cherishing of an old passion could lead to no good. When Mark Dunn disappeared for hours at a time, she shrewdly suspected that he was sent on messages to Raskelfe.

More than once she interfered and rebuked Ralph, her brother, warning him of the dangerous consequences of thus encouraging the attachment of a woman now bound to another man by the most sacred ties. With an oath he bade her mind her own business, and not interfere with him.

Fletcher could not but be aware that his wife did not love him; whispers reached him that she met her old sweetheart when he was from home; that her nag was seen standing an unreasonable time outside the door of the White House. He caught Mark Dunn one evening prowling in his orchard, and he fell on him with a stick. The ungainly fellow howled with pain, and swore revenge.

Fletcher became gloomy, neglected his affairs, and began to fall into difficulties. He had been sincerely, passionately attached to the dark-eyed, handsome girl he had brought to his home. He had done his utmost to render her happy, and now she was making his home miserable, destroying the former serenity of his spirits.

He was obliged to go one day on business to Easingwold. He would not return till late. His wife knew it. Something troubled his mind. A presentiment of evil which he could not shake off hung over him, and he wrote on a sheet of paper—

"If I should be missing, or suddenly wanted be,
  Mark Ralph Raynard, Mark Dunn, and mark my wife for me,"

directed it to his sister, and on reaching Easingwold, posted it.

No sooner was he gone than Mrs. Fletcher mounted her horse and rode to the White House. She asked to see Raynard, and he walked by her side some way back to Raskelfe. There they parted; and Raynard was next observed in close conversation with his hostler, Mark Dunn.

It was May-Day. In the sweet spring evening Fletcher was returning on foot from Easingwold, when he came to Daunay Bridge, where at that time a road branched off from the highway from the North to York, and traversing the Lund, led to Raskelfe. As he crossed the bridge he stood still for a moment, and looked up at the stars, just appearing. Next moment Raynard and Dunn were upon him; they had sprung from behind the bridge, and he was flung over it into the water. The stream is narrow and not deep, so that, once recovered from the shock, he could have easily crawled out. But the murderers leaped into the water after him. Mrs. Fletcher, with a long sack over her shoulder, ran out from the shadow of a bush where she had been concealed, and they held the farmer under water, the two men grasping his throat, his wife retaining his feet in the sack, into which she thrust them, till his struggles ceased, and he was, or was supposed to be, dead.

The body was then thrust into the sack which Mrs. Fletcher had brought for the purpose, and the three guilty ones assisted in carrying or dragging the body along the road towards the White House. They were alarmed once; the clatter of a horse's hoofs was heard, and they concealed themselves by the road-side. The horseman passed, they emerged from their place of hiding, and continued their course.

As they drew near to the inn a streak of light from the inn-door showed that it was open. They heard voices. The horseman had called for something to drink, and it was brought to him without his dismounting. Then Miss Raynard was heard calling, "Ralph! Ralph!" She wondered, perhaps, at his long absence, or wanted him for some purpose in the house.

No answer was returned. Raynard, Dunn, and Mrs. Fletcher lifted the body over the low hedge into Raynard's croft or garden, and buried it in a place where the ground had been disturbed that day by his having stubbed up an old root. They carefully covered the body with earth, and Raynard sowed mustard-seed over the place.

It was thought prudent that Mrs. Fletcher and Raynard should not meet after this.

People wondered what had become of Fletcher; but knowing that he was somewhat embarrased in his circumstances, they readily accepted the statement of his wife – that he had gone out of the way to avoid having a writ served on him.

Thus matters stood till the 7th July, when Ralph Raynard rode to Topcliffe fair. It was a bright sunny day. He passed the Moor House, but did not stay there; crossed Thornton Bridge, went before the Red House, where he had so often visited and spent such happy hours with the woman who was now his accomplice in crime, along by Cundall to Topcliffe.

He dismounted at the inn there – the Angel, an old-fashioned house near the dilapidated market-cross. He led his horse out of the yard into the stable. The sun glared without; within it was dark. As he was removing the bridle from his horse, suddenly he saw standing before him the spirit of Fletcher, pale, with a phosphoric light playing about him, pointing to him, and saying, "O Ralph, Ralph! repent. Vengeance is at hand!" In an agony of horror he fled out of the stable. In the daylight without he recovered composure, and endeavoured to believe that he had been a victim to delusion. He thought he must buy some present for the woman, love for whom had led him to the commission of murder. He went to one of the stalls to buy some trinket – a chain of imitation coral beads. "How does it look on the neck?" he asked, extending it to the keeper of the stall. Then he looked up and saw a ghastly figure opposite – the dead man with the coral round his neck, knotted under his ear, and his head on one side, the eyes wide open, with a blaze in the eyes, and heard him say: "How like you a red streak round the neck such as this? I will put one round the throat of my wife; and you shall wear one too!"

Sick and faint, he hastened back to the inn, and called for beer. Towards evening he rode home. He saw as he came towards the Carr, where there is a dense clump of trees, a figure looking at him. It was deliberately getting out of a sack, and shaking and wringing water out of its clothes. With a scream of terror Raynard plunged his spurs into the horse's flanks, and galloped past Cundall, home. As he crossed Thornton Bridge he closed his eyes, but when he opened them again he saw the well-known figure of the dead man walking before him so fast that his horses could not catch him up. The ghost trailed the sack after it, and left a luminous track on the road. When it reached a point at a little distance from the White House – the very spot where Raynard, Mrs. Fletcher, and Mark Dunn had turned aside with the body – the spectre strode across the heather, leaped the low hedge, and melted, apparently, into the ground, where now a rich, green crop of mustard was growing.

"You're back earlier than I thought," said the sister of Ralph Raynard. "I reckon thou'st not been stopping this time at Moor House?"

Raynard said nothing, except "I'm ill."

"Ah," said his sister, "I've gotten thee a nice bit o' supper ready, with a beautiful dish o' salad."

And she laid the cloth, and placed upon it a plate of fresh-cut *mustard!*

Raynard's face grew rigid and white.

"What is the matter?" asked his sister.

Opposite him, on the settle, sat the dead man, pointing to the salad.

Ralph sprang up, drew his sister away, and told her all.

She, poor woman, horror-struck, ran off at once to Sir William Sheffield, a justice of peace, residing at Raskelfe Park. The three guilty parties were apprehended and taken to York, where, on July 28th, 1623, all three were hung.

When they had been cut down, the bodies were removed and conveyed in a waggon to the White House, the hang-man seated by the driver in front. There is a little rise not far from the inn, commanding the spot where the murder was committed, and the green mustard-bed where the body of Fletcher had been hidden, but which had been removed and buried in Raskelfe churchard. On this hill a gibbet had been erected, and there the three bodies were hung, with their faces towards the dismal flat and the gurgling stream where the murdered man had been drowned. There they hung, blown about by the autumn storms, screeched over by the ravens and magpies, baked by the summer sun, their bare scalps capped with cakes of snow in the cold winter, till they dropped upon the ground, and then the bones were buried and the gallows cut down.

About eighty years ago the plough was drawn over Gallows Hill, when a quantity of bones were unearthed by the share. They were the bones of Raynard, Dunn, and Mrs. Fletcher. The hill to this day bears its ill-omened name, and people mutter about Raskelfe the doggerel lines—

> "A wooden church, a wooden steeple,
> Rascally church, and rascally[1] people."

[1] Raskelfe is commonly called Rascall.

JEMMY HIRST;

AN ODDITY.[1]

JEMMY was born at Rawcliffe, in the West Riding, on October 12th, 1738. His father was a respectable substantial farmer, without great brilliancy of parts, but with the usual Yorkshire shrewdness.

The boy soon began to exhibit originality; mischievousness was mistaken by a fond mother for genius, and he was destined for the Church. He was sent accordingly to a boarding-school, to a clergyman, at the age of eight, to acquire the rudiments of the necessary education.

But at school Jemmy's genius took an altogether perverse turn. He was always first in the playground and last in class; a leader in mischief, a laggard in study. Finding his master's spectacles on the desk one day, Jemmy unscrewed them, and removed the glasses. When the Principal came in, he gravely took up the spectacles and put them on. Finding them dim, he removed them. When he was seen demurely to wipe where the glasses had been, and then, with his fingers through the rims, to hold them up to his eyes to see what was the matter, the whole school burst out laughing. The pedagogue demanded the name of the culprit. Jemmy had not the honesty or courage to proclaim himself the author of the trick, and the whole school was whipped accordingly. On the morning of the 1st April, early, a big boy in his dormitory sent Jemmy to the master, expecting that he would knock at his bedroom door, wake him, and get a thrashing for his pains. Jemmy turned out of bed and went outside the door, waited a minute, and then came into the dormitory again. "Ah! Tom, thou'rt in for it. Thou mun go at once to Lovell for having made an April fool of him and me." The boy, believing this, went to the master's door, knocked him up, and got well thrashed for his pains. "You will know in future what is meant by the biter being bit," said Jemmy, when the boy returned, crying. "There's an old fable about the viper biting the file and breaking his teeth. Perhaps you can understand the moral of it now."

The Principal kept an old sow. Jemmy used to get on her back, tie a piece of

[1]"The Life and Adventures of J. Hirst." Hepworth, Knottingly (n.d.) Another Life published at Pontefract.

twine – ''band'' a Yorkshire boy would call it – to the ring in her snout, run a nail through the heel of his boot to act as spur, and gallop the old sow round the yard. This was often performed with impunity, but not always. The master saw him from his window one morning as he was shaving, and rushed down with a horse-whip in his hand. Jemmy was careering joyously round and round the yard when a crack of the lash across his back dislodged him. He was fed next day on bread and water as a punishment.

One night Jemmy and some of his schoolmates got out of the house with intent to rob an orchard. But one of the day scholars had overheard the boarders planning the raid, and he informed the farmer whose orchard it was purposed to rob, and he was on the look-out for the young rogues. When they arrived he suffered one of them – it was Jemmy – to climb an apple-tree without molestation, but then he rushed forth from his hiding-place and laid about him with a carter's whip with hearty good-will. The boys fled in all directions, except Jemmy, who escaped further up the tree, and there remained, unable, like a squirrel, to leap from bough to bough, and so escape. The farmer went under the tree and shouted to him, ''Come down, you young rascal! I'll strap thee!''

''Nay,'' answered Jemmy, ''dost see any green in my eye? It's like I should come down to get a whipping, isn't it?'' And he began leisurely to eat some of the apples, and pelt the farmer with others. The man, highly irate, began to climb the tree after him. Jem remained composedly eating till the farmer was within reach of him, and then he drew a cornet of pepper from his pocket and dusted it into the eyes of his pursuer. The man, half-blinded, desisted from his attempts to catch the boy, in his efforts to clear his eyes, and Jemmy split past him down the tree and escaped. Next day the farmer came to the school to complain, and Jemmy received thirty strokes on his back with the birch. ''Ah!'' said Jemmy, ''thou'st made my back tingle, and I'll make thine smart.'' So he got a darning-needle, and stuck it in the master's hair-bottomed chair in such a way that when anyone sat down the needle would protrude through the cushion, but would recede on the person's rising again.

At school hour the master came in, and seated himself in his chair with his usual gravity. But suddenly up he bounded like a rocket; then turned and examined the cushion, very red in the face. The cushion seemed all right when he felt it with his hand, so he sat himself down on it again, but this time much more leisurely. No sooner, however, was his weight on it than up came the needle again, and with it up bounded the master.

''Please, sir,'' said Jemmy, affecting simplicity, ''was there a thorn in the seat? If so, thou'd better run two or three times round t' school yard; I did so yesterday to work t' birch buds out o' my flesh.''

Jemmy had one day tied two cats together by their hind legs and thrown them over a rail, when the master, who had been watching him from an upper window, made his appearance on the scene, horsewhip in hand, and belaboured Jemmy severely. But little Hirst always retaliated in some way. The master

used to walk up and down in the evening in the yard behind the school. He
wore a foxy wig. Jemmy one evening went into the study where Mr. Lovell
kept his fishing tackle, for he was fond of angling. The window was open;
Jemmy cast the hook, as for a fish, and caught the little fox-coloured wig. Then
leaving the rod in the window, and the head of hair dangling above the master's
reach, he ran down into the school. The Principal was therefore obliged to go
upstairs with bald head to his study to recover his wig. This final act of
insubordination was too much for Mr. Lovell – it touched him in his tenderest
point; and he wrote to Mr. Hirst to request him to remove the unmanageable
boy from his school.

He was fourteen years old when his father took him away, and was little
advanced in his learning. Every prospect of him going into the Church was
abandoned, but what trade or profession he was qualified for was as yet
undecided. His father wanted to put him to school again, but Jemmy so steadily
and doggedly persisted in his refusal to go to another, that his indulgent father
ceased to press it. The boy showed no inclination for farming, and no
persuasion of his father could induce him to take a farming implement in his
hands to work with. His chief pleasure consisted in teaching pigs and calves to
jump.

Mr. Hirst had a friend at Rawcliffe, a tanner, and this friend persuaded Mr.
Hirst to bind Jemmy apprentice to him; and as the boy showed no
disinclination to the trade, he was bound to the tanner for seven years.

The tanner had a daughter called Mary, a year younger than Jemmy, and a
tender friendship grew up between the young people: Jemmy was softened and
civilised by the gentle influence of the girl; he took willingly to the trade,
beacame settled, lost his mischievous propensies, and promised to turn out a
respectable member of society. An incident occurred three years after he had
entered the tanner's house which tended to cement this attachment closer.
Mary went one Saturday to spend the day with an aunt living at Barnsley.
Jemmy ferried her over the river in a boat belonging to the tanner, and promised
to fetch her in the evening. Accordingly, towards nightfall, he crossed the river,
and made his boat fast to a stake, and then walked to Barnsley to meet the
young girl. Mary met him with her usual smile, and tripped by his side to the
boat, but in stepping into it her foot slipped, and she was swept down by the
current. Jemmy instantly leaped overboard, swam after her, overtook her
before she sank, and supporting her with one arm, succeeded in bringing her
ashore, where several persons who had witnessed the accident were assembled
to assist and receive her.

Mary's parents showed Jemmy much gratitude for his courageous conduct in
saving her life, and the girl clung to him with intense affection; whilst Jemmy,
who seemed to think he had acquired some right over her by his having saved
her life, was never happy unless he was by her side. They were always together.
She would steal in to do her needlework in the place where he was engaged in
his trade, and when work was over they were together walking in the lanes and
fields.

But in the midst of this happiness a stroke fell on them which for ever altered the tenor of Jemmy's life. Mary fell ill with small-pox. The lad watched by her bedside night and day, giving her medicine, making up her pillow, tending her with agonising heart, utterly forgetful of himself, fearing no risk of infection, heedless of taking his natural rest. The whole time of her illness he never slept, and could scarcely be induced to leave her side for his meals.

On the fifth day she died. The blow was more than Jemmy could bear, and he was prostrated with brain-fever.

That the poor boy had naturally very deep feelings is evident from his having, some few years before, been laid up with fever when his mother died. Hearing of her death whilst he was at school, he became ill and was removed home, where it was some time before he got over the shock. Mary had taken the place in his vacant heart formerly occupied by his mother, and with years the strength of his feelings had increased. Consequently the loss of Mary affected him even more than that of his mother.

In his brain fever he raved incessantly of the poor dead girl, and for several weeks his life was despaired of. By degrees he slowly recovered; but for some time it was feared that his reason was gone. At the end of six or seven months he was able to take a little exercise without attendance; but as will be seen, he never wholly recovered the blow, and his conduct thenceforth was so eccentric that there can be no doubt his brain was affected.

He left the tanner's, abandoned the trade, and returned to his father's house, where he idled, preying on his fancies – one day in mad, exuberant spirits, the next overwhelmed with despondency.

When aged five-and-twenty he took a fancy to a fine bull-calf belonging to his father, which he called "Jupiter," and he began to train it to perform various tricks, and to break it to bear the saddle. Jupiter bore the bridle patiently enough, but plunged and tossed his horns when the saddle was placed on his back. Jemmy next ventured to mount his back. The young bull stood for a minute or two, as his father said, "right down stagnated," and then began to plunge and kick. Jemmy held fast, and Jupiter, finding he could not thus dislodge his rider, set off, tearing across the paddock towards a thick quickset hedge at the bottom. But instead of leaping it, as Jemmy expected, the bull ran against the fence, and precipitated his rider over the hedge into the ditch on the further side. Jemmy was unhurt, except for a few scratches and some rents in his garments, and patches of mud, and picking himself up, raced after Jupiter, nothing daunted, caught him, and remounted him, mastered the beast. After this he rode Jupiter daily, to the great amusement of people generally, especially when he trotted into Snaith on market-days on the back of the now docile bull.

On the death of his father he was left about £1000. The farm he gave up, having no taste for agriculture, and he took a house on the bank of the river, not far from his old master's the tanner. The house had a few acres of land attached to it, which he cultivated. The old housekeeper, who had known him since a child, followed him to his new home; and in his stables was a stall for Jupiter.

He began to speculate in corn, flax, and potatoes, and having considerable natural shrewdness underlying his eccentric manners, he managed to realise enough to support himself comfortably. He invested £4000 in consols, and had £2000 lying at interest in a neighbouring bank. He rode out with Lord Beaumont's foxhounds, always on Jupiter, who was trained to jump as well as to run. When he was seen coming up on the bull, Lord Beaumont would turn to those with him at the meet and say, "Well, gentlemen, if we are not destined to find game to-day, we may be sure of sport."

His dress was as extraordinary as his mount, for he wore a broad-brimmed hat of lambskin, fully nine feet in circumference; his waistcoat was like Joseph's coat of many colours, made of patchwork; his breeches were of listings of various colours, plaited together by his house-keeper; and he wore yellow boots.

Though Jupiter could keep up with the foxhunters for a few miles, his powers of endurance were not so great as those of a horse, and he began to lag. Lord Beaumont would pass Jemmy, and say, "Come, Mr. Hirst, you will not be in at the death."

"No; but I shall at the dinner," was Jemmy's dry reply. Lord Beaumont always took the hint and invited him to Carlton House to the hunting dinner.

His Lordship had a nephew visiting him on one occasion, a London exquisite, who thought he could amuse himself at Jemmy's expense. One day at the meet this young man said to Captain Bolton, "Let us quiz the old fellow." – "By all means," answered the captain; "but take care that you do not get the worst of it."

When Jemmy came up, the young dandy, bowing to him on his saddle, said, "I wish you a good morning, Joseph."

"My name isn't Joseph," answered Jemmy.

"Oh, I beg pardon. I mistook you by your coat and waistcoat for that patriarch."

"Young man," said Jemmy, with perfect composure, "'t win't do to judge by appearances. As I wor-a-coming up, says I to mysen, 'You're a gentleman.' When I gotten a bit closer, says I, 'Nay, he's a dandy.' And now that I heard thee voice, I knows thou'rt nowt but a jackass."

Jemmy was out with the hounds one day, along with Lord Wharncliffe and Lord Beaumont and several of the gentry of the neighbourhood. It was agreed amongst them unknown to Jemmy, that he should be let into a scrape, if possible. Accordingly, after the start, Lord Wharncliffe kept near him, and led him into a field surrounded by a low, thick hedge – low enough for Jupiter to clear without any trouble. On the other side of the hedge in one place there was a drinking-pond for the cattle, five or six feet deep, and full of water at the time. Lord Wharncliffe kept close by Jemmy, and edged towards where the pond was; and then, putting spurs to his horse, he leaped the fence, and Jemmy did the same to Jupiter, and clearing the hedge in gallant style, came splashing into the water, and rolled off Jupiter.

Lord Wharncliffe, when he saw Jemmy fairly in the middle of the pond, turned back, and alighted, in order to assist him out of the water. He found him half blinded with mud and dirt, trying to scramble out, his clothes completely saturated. Jemmy managed to get out without assistance, but it was some time before their united efforts could extricate Jupiter.

Lord Beaumont offered Jemmy a change of clothes if he would go to his house, but he would not hear of the proposal, declaring he would see the day's sport over first; and so they rode on together towards the rest of the party, who were halted near Rawcliffe Wood. The fox had been caught after a short run, and the huntsman were already beating after another.

Jemmy was greeted with a general titter. Captain Bolton laughed out, and said, "Why, Jemmy, you've been fishing, not hunting. What have you caught?"

Jemmy looked hard at him – he was in no good humour after his plunge – and said, "I reckon there's a flat fish I know of that I'll catch some day."

"Why, Jemmy," said Lord Wharncliffe, laughing, "I saw you catch a flounder."

"Ha! Ha!" said the captain, "that's good! You've taken the shine out of your smart clothes to-day, Jemmy."

"A little water will give it back to them," answered Hirst, sulkily.

"Jemmy," asked Captain Bolton, "did you think you were drowning in the wash-tub? Did you say your prayers in it?"

"No," answered Jemmy, angrily, "I didn't; but what I was doing then was wishing I'd got a contemptible puppy named Bolton in the pond with me, that I might kick his breech."

Jemmy soon saw that he had been the victim of a planned trick, and he determined to have his revenge. "I know very well that Lord Wharncliffe led me o' purpose into t' pond – I could see't by his manner; but I'll be even wi' him."

He did not carry his purpose into execution at once, lest he should arouse suspicion, but about a month afterwards, when in company with Lord Wharncliffe, he adroitly let drop that he had seen a number of snipe on Rawcliffe moor. This moor, now enclosed, was then a wide, open common, full of marshy places, and with here and there bogs covered with a little green moss, deep holes full of peat water, not to be discerned except by those who were well acquainted with them and the treacherousness of their bright green covering. Lord Wharncliffe, Captain Bolton, and some others, made up a party to shoot on the common the following day, and met Jemmy, who undertook to show them where the snipe most congregated.

They had a good day's sport, and when it fell dusk were returning home, Jemmy beside Lord Wharncliffe, whom he engaged in conversation, and Captain Bolton, with his gun over his shoulder, immediately behind, joining in the conversation at intervals. Jemmy led the way direct to one of these bog-holes, and on reaching the patch of moss adroitly slipped on one side, and let

Lord Wharncliffe and Captain Bolton walk straight into it. The moss at once yielded, and both sank to their breasts, and only kept their heads above water by spreading out their arms on the moss. In this condition they were perfectly helpless. To struggle was to endanger their lives, for if the web of moss were torn, they must infallibly sink beneath it.

Jemmy looked at them from the firm ground with a malicious grin.

"Ha, ha! captain," said he, laughingly; "art thou saying thy prayers in yond wash-tub?"

"Go to the devil!" roared Captain Bolton.

"Nay," answered Jemmy, "thou'rt going to him as fast as thou can, unless I pull thee out."

He held out his gun to Lord Wharncliffe, and assisted him from the hole. "There, my lord, now you have tit for tat."

"Well, Mr. Hirst, I shall take care how I play with edged tools again. But I think it is too bad of you to punish Captain Bolton as well as me."

"Why, my lord, he seemed to enjoy the horse-pond so much that I thowt I'd let him taste the bog-pit. I've no doubt it gives him a deal o' pleasure."

"You old scarecrow!" said the captain, angrily. "I've a great mind to shoot you."

As he was helping Captain Bolton out with his gun he said drily, "Sure it's a rare funny sight to see a queer sole angling for a flat fish."

The immersed man little enjoyed the jokes at his expense, and he swore at Jemmy. "Ah!" said that oddity, "I don't think thou'rt a fish worth catching. Shall I fling him in again, my lord? He's nowt but what folks would call a little common-place."

Jemmy's old housekeeper died, and he supplied her place by a strange creature, nearly as great an oddity as himself, called Sarah, who for many years had kept house for a rag-and-bone dealer at Howden, but who at his death had returned to Rawcliffe, her native place, and was living with her brother there when Jemmy engaged her.

Having made money by his speculations in corn and potatoes, he resolved to retire from business. He invested £4000 in the funds and £2000 in the bank, and lived on the interest. He was now forty-five years old.

An inactive life, however, did not suit him, so he turned his mind to mechanics, and made several curious contrivances, some useful. He constructed a windmill to thrash corn, but for this purpose it did not answer, though it served for cutting up straw and chopping turnips.

His next contrivance was a carriage, the body of which was made of wickerwork. It cost him a year's constant application to finish it, and when completed it was calculated to cause a sensation. It was a huge palanquin, with a top like an exaggerated Chinaman's hat, supported on four iron rods, which were screwed into the shafts, the shafts running the whole length of the carriage, and resting on springs connected with the axle of the wheels. The sides and back of the carriage were made of wickerwork matting. The axle-case was faced with a clock dial with numbers, and hands connected with a piece of ingenious mechanism, afterwards perfected and patented by another person, which told the distance the carriage had gone by measuring the number of rotations made by the wheels.

Jemmy used for his hunting-suit a lambskin hat, a rabbit-skin jacket, a waistcoat made of the skins of drakes' necks with the feathers on, a pair of list breeches, yellow, blue, black, and red, stockings of red and white worsted, and yellow boots. His best room was furnished as curiously as his person. Instead of pictures, the walls were hung round with bits of old iron and coils of rope; in one place an old frying-pan, in another a rusty sword, a piece of a chair, or a jug.

One evening, after a day's sport, he invited the party to join him for a social evening, and the offer was eagerly accepted, as every one was curious to see the interior of his house. He gave them a very fair entertainment, and amused them all the evening with his jokes. Immediately over Lord Wharncliffe's head was suspended a pair of horse's blinkers.

"Do you wear these?" asked a Mr. Sadler who was present.

"No, sir, I do not; I keep them for donkeys of a peculiar make, who stand on their hind legs and ask impertinant questions."

"What do you mean?' asked the young man, reddening. "Is that intended as a personal remark?"

"Draw your own inferences," answered Jemmy, knocking the ashes out of his pipe.

The young man was so offended that he demanded satisfaction for the insult. The company tried hard to pacify him, but in vain. Jemmy then whispered in Lord Wharncliffe's ear, and the latter immediately rose from the table, and said, "Now, gentlemen, Mr. Hirst is quite willing to give Mr. Sadler that satisfaction he desires. He has requested my services as second. I have granted his wish. As soon as Mr. Sadler can arrange with any gentleman to act as his second, I shall be happy to arrange preliminaries with him."

Mr. Sadler having chosen a second, the belligerents were desired to leave the room for a few moments until arrangements had been made for the duel.

As they left the room Lord Wharncliffe whispered in the ear of one of the party, "Follow Mr. Sadler into the other room, and take a bottle of wine with you; get him to drink as much as possible, and we will manage to make the affair end in fun."

The gentleman did as desired. Then Lord Wharncliffe and Jemmy, slipping in by another door, proceeded to dress up a dummy that was in a closet hard by in Jemmy's clothes.

Mr. Sadler was then told that all was ready, and he returned into the room rather the worse for the liquor he had drunk.

The pistol was put into his hand, and he was stationed opposite the dummy, which with outstretched arm pointed a pistol at him. The signal was given, and Mr. Sadler fired; then Jemmy, who was secreted in a closet hard by, pulled a string, and the dummy fell with a heavy thud upon the floor.

Mr. Sadler, who thought he had killed his antagonist, was sobered instantly, and was filled with remorse and fear. He rushed to the dead man and then towards the door, then back to the corpse to see if life were quite extinct. Then only, to his great relief, he found that the supposed dead man was made of wood. The company burst into a roar of laughter, and when he had sufficently recovered from his bewilderment he joined heartily in the mirth raised at his own expense. Jemmy, emerging from his place of concealment, apologised for the offence he had given, and both shook hands. The carouse was renewed with fresh vigour, and the sun had risen an hour before the party broke up, and its members unsteadily wended their way homewards.

Jemmy had bought a litter of pigs, and entertained the idea of teaching them to act as setters in his shooting expeditions, and therefore spent a considerable time every day in training them. There were only two that he could make anything of. But he never could induce them to desist from grunting. It was impossible to make them control their emotions sufficiently to keep quiet, and this inveterate habit of course spoiled them as setters.

When the litter was about six months old, one of the little pigs discovered his potato garden, and that by putting its snout under the lowest bar of the gate it could lift the gate so that the latch was disengaged from the catch, and the gate swung open; by this means the pig was able to get to the roots. Hirst saw the pig do this several times, and he determined to stop the little game. He therefore ground the blade of a scythe, and fixed it, with the sharp edge downwards, to the lower bar.

Shortly after, Jemmy saw the pig go to the gate, but in lifting it off the hasp the scythe-blade cut the end of the snout off. Jemmy burst out laughing, and called his old housekeeper to see the fun; but old Sarah was more compassionate than her master, and begged him to kill the pig and put it out of its pain.

The carriage did not altogether satisfy Jemmy; he therefore enlarged it to double its former size. He made it so that, when necessary, he could have a bed in it; and then he bought Andalusian mules to draw it, and with them he drove to Pontefract and Doncaster races, which he attended every year, and created no small sensation along the roads and on the course. Bear and bull baiting were favourite pastimes with him, as was also cock-fighting. He kept two bulls and a bear for this purpose. He used to call the bear Nicholas. It was a large savage animal, and was always kept muzzled at home.

One morning, after it had been baited and had destroyed four dogs, he took it something to eat, but it would not touch the meat. "Ah! thou'rt sulky; then I mun gi'e thee a taste o' t' whip." So saying, he struck the bear over the muzzle with a hunting-whip he carried in his hand.

He had no sooner done so than the bear sprang upon him, seized him, and began to hug him. Jemmy roared for help, and a favourite dog rushed to his assistance and seized Bruin by the ear. The bear let go Jemmy to defend itself against the dog, and Jemmy, who had the breath nearly squeezed out of him, managed to crawl beyond the reach of the beast. The dog seeing his master safe, laid himself down by him, facing the bear, to guard him from further attacks. Sarah found her master half-an-hour after on the ground, unable to rise, and in great pain. She raised him, assisted him to the house, and put him to bed. He was confined for three weeks by the injuries he had received.

A few weeks after his recovery he attended Pontefract races in his carriage, drawn by four splendid mules, and no one on the course could keep up with him when he put the mules to their speed. Sir John Ramsden was in a carriage drawn by two fine bays, of which he was not a little proud, and he challenged Jemmy to a trial of speed round the course. Off they started, Sir John taking the lead for a short time, but Jemmy's mules, with their light carriage, soon overtook Sir John's bays, and came in a hundred yards before them. It was the most popular race run that year on the Pontefract course.

He also constructed for himself a pair of wings, and by an ingenious contrivance was able to spread the feathers. But his attempt to fly from the mast-top of a boat in the Humber failed. He fell into the water, and was drawn out covered with mud, amidst the laughter of a crowd which had assembled to witness his flight.

Jemmy's eccentricities had reached the ears of King George III, and he expressed a desire to see him. Lord Beaumont promised to do his best to persuade Hirst to come to town, but at the same time he told the King that if Jemmy took it into his head to decline the invitation, no power on earth could move him.

Accordingly, Lord Beaumont wrote to Jemmy, stating his Majesty's wish to see him, and urging him to come as soon as possible. At the end of the week Lord Beaumont received the following reply: –

"MY LORD, – I hve received thy letter stating his Majesty's wish to see me. What does his Majesty wish to see me for? I'm nothing related to him, and I owe him nothing that I know of; so I can't conceive what he wants with me. I suspect thou hast been telling him what queer clothes I wear, and such like. Well, thou may tell his Majesty that I am very busy now training an otter to fish; but I'll contrive to come in the course of a month or so, as I should like to see London."

Lord Beaumont showed Jemmy's letter to George III., who laughed when he read it, and said, "He seems to think more of seeing London than of the honour of introduction to royalty."

Jemmy spent a month in getting ready for his journey to London; he had an entirely new suit made – a new lambskin hat of the old dimensions, an otter-skin coat lined with red flannel and turned up with scarlet cloth, a waistcoat of the skins of drakes' necks, list breeches, red and white striped stockings, and shoes with large silver buckles on them. His carriage was repainted in the most lively colours; and when all was ready he adjured Sarah to look well after his favourites during his absence, and then drove off at a slashing pace, drawn by his four Andalusians.

He created a sensation in every town and village he passed through. People turned out of their shops and houses to see him.

He put up at Doncaster at the King's Head Inn. The hostler there exhibited Jemmy's carriage and mules at a penny charge for admission, and realised something handsome thereby. The landlord also reaped a good harvest, for the inn was crowded as long as Jemmy stayed there.

Jemmy reached London in three days. Lord Beaumont's butler had been sent some time before to Tottenham, with orders to wait there till Mr. Hirst made his appearance and then to conduct him to his Lordship's town residence.

On Jemmy arriving at Tottenham, the butler informed him of his lordship's orders, and then rode off before him to show the way. The news spread through London, and the streets were crowded, so that the carriage could hardly make its way through the numbers of people whom the report of the arrival of an eccentric Yorkshireman on a visit to the King had drawn together. Jemmy, who was immensely conceited, was greatly delighted with this ovation. On reaching Lord Beaumont's house he was welcomed by his Lordship with great cordiality; and after lunch was driven out in Lord Beaumont's carriage to see the sights of London. The King was informed of Jemmy's arrival, and his Majesty expressed his wish that Jemmy should be presented to him on the morrow. Lord Beaumont vainly endeavoured to press on the strange fellow the obligations of the Court ceremonial. "D——— your forms and ceremonies!" said he, impatiently. "If the King don't like my ways, he must let it alone. I did not seek his acquaintance – he must take me as I am. I am a plain Yorkshireman, and if the King asks me a question in a plain manner, I shall answer him in a plain way, so that he or anybody else may understand. I can do no more."

Lord Beaumont saw it was in vain to press him further in the matter, and therefore left him to follow his own course.

On the following morning, Jemmy set out in his wicker-work carriage, in all the glory of drakes' necks, lambs' wool, and otter skins turned up with scarlet, to visit the King. But if the streets were crowded the day before, on this occasion they were crammed, for the news had spread that Jemmy was going in state to Court.

Lord Beaumont and a couple of Horse Guards accompanied the carriage, and with difficulty made a passage for Jemmy; and all along the streets the windows were filled with heads.

When Jemmy alighted he was conducted by Lord Beaumont into an ante-chamber, to await the King's pleasure. The Duke of Devonshire was also waiting there for an audience with His Majesty, and on seeing this extraordinary fellow enter, he burst into a fit of uncontrollable laughter, and exclaimed, "'Pon my honour! what a scarecrow. Why, Beaumont, where did you pick up that ridiculous object? Why have you brought such a merry-andrew here?'' Jemmy listened patiently for a moment only to the Duke's exclamations and laughter, and then seizing a tumbler of water that stood on the sideboard, he dashed it in the Duke's face, exclaiming that the poor man was in hysterics: he ran to the Duke, loosed his cravat, pulled his nose, and shook him, pretending that he was using his best endeavours to bring him round from his fit.

At that moment a messenger came to announce that his Majesty wished to see Lord Beaumont and Mr. Hirst; so Jemmy was ushered into the royal presence. But instead of kneeling and kissing the hand that was extended to him in silence, he caught it and gave it a hearty shake, saying, ''Eh! I'm glad to see thee such a plain owd chap. If thou ever comes to Rawcliffe, step in and give me a visit. I can give thee some rare good wine, or a sup of brandy and water at ony time.''

The court was convulsed with laughter, and King George III. could hardly contain himself. However, he did not laugh out openely, but with courtesy maintained his gravity, and asked Jemmy how he liked London. ''I like it weel enow,'' answered the oddity; ''but I hadn't ony idea afore yesterday and to-day there were sae mony fools in it.''

''Indeed!'' said the King; ''you pay us a very poor compliment, Mr. Hirst. I did not know that we were so badly off for wisdom in London. Perhaps that is an article in such demand in Yorkshire that there is none to spare for cockneys.''

''Why, I'll thee how it were,'' said Jemmy. ''When I come into t' town yesterday, and to thy house to-day, the streets were full o' crowds of folks gathered as thick as owt to see me, just a cause I happ'd to be dressed different frae other folk; and as I were waiting out yonder i' t' fore-chamber, there were one o' thy sarvants burst out laughing at me; but I reckon I spoiled his ruffled shirt for him and punished his impertinence.''

The King asked an explanation of Lord Beaumont, and when he had heard what Jemmy had done to the Duke of Devonshire, the King laughed heartily.

''Did you think to find London streets paved with gold?'' asked the King.

''Mebbe I did,'' answered Jemmy; ''but I've found out I was mista'en. It's nowt but a mucky place, after all.''

''A Yorkshire bite,'' said his Majesty.

''Aye,'' answered Jemmy, ''but I'm no a bite for thee.''

After some further conversation the King and his attendants descended to look at Jemmy's carriage, and he showed the clock for marking the distance he travelled; the King was interested with this, and praised it as an ingenious contrivance. Jemmy then showed him the place he had made for the reception of his wine when he travelled, but which was then empty. His Majesty immediately ordered it to be filled with bottles from the royal cellar.

As Jemmy was taking leave of the King he heard a young nobleman say to another, ''What an old fool that is to wear such a hat; it is three times as large as is necessary.''

Jemmy turned sharply upon him and said: "I'll tell thee what, young chap, folks don't always have things aboot 'em that's necessary, or his Majesty could dispense varry weel wi' thee."

Lord Beaumont gave an entertainment at which Jemmy was present, and danced with a niece of his host. He danced very well, and was very popular; all the evening he was surrounded by a knot of young ladies and gentlemen who did their best to draw him out. But it was dangerous game, for those who attempted to play jokes on him generally got the worst of it. A young man present asked Jemmy to procure him a suit of clothes like his own, as he wanted them to attend a masquerade in. Jemmy asked in what character he wished to appear.

"Oh, as a clown, of course," was the answer.

"Nay, then," said Jemmy, "thou'st nowt to do but go just as thou art; nobbudy 'll mistake thee for owt else."

"You have got your answer," said Lord Beaumont's niece, laughing; "I hope you are satisfied with it."

During his stay in London, Jemmy visited the Court of Chancery, and whilst Lord Beaumont was talking to a friend, a barrister in wig and gown passing by stopped, and staring at Jemmy, said, "Holloa, my man, what lunatic asylum have you escaped from, eh?"

"Bless me!" exclaimed Jemmy, catching Lord Beaumont's arm; "sithere, yonder's an owd woman i' her night-dress that'st tummled out o' bed into an ink-pot, and is crawling aboot. Let's get a mop and clean her."

After spending a week in the metropolis, he returned home much delighted with his visit, which furnished him with topics of conversation for a long time.

Sarah, his old housekeeper, falling ill, and being unable to work, Jemmy engaged the services of a young woman from Snaith to wait upon him, and she so accomodated herself to Jemmy's whims, that she soon became a great favourite with him. He would not, however, allow followers about the house; and as Mary had a sweetheart, the meetings between them had to be carried on surreptitiously.

However, one day whilst Jemmy was hunting, his bull tripped in jumping a fence, and fell, with Jemmy's leg under him, which was broken with compound fracture.

This invalided him for some while. He had a block-tackle fixed to a hook in the ceiling of the room, and a sling made for his leg to rest in, fastened to the lower end, and whenever he wished to alter the position of his leg, he hoisted it up or let it down with the tackle.

During his illness the restraint of his observant eye was off Mary, and the sweetheart had opportunities of visiting her. One night, when Jemmy was somewhat recovered, he was sitting in the corner of his garden enjoying a pipe of tobacco, when he saw a man jump over the wall into the garden and make his way to the kitchen window, then rap with his fingers against the glass. Mary came out to him, and they spent some time in conversation together, and when they parted he promised to return and see her the following night.

Jemmy heard every word that had been said, and he sat chuckling to himself, and muttered, "So thou'lt come again to-morrow night, wilt thou? I'll learn thee to come poaching on my preserves."

Next morning, very early, Jemmy rose and dug a hole, four or five feet deep and six or seven feet long, just under that part of the garden wall where the sweetheart had clambered over the night before, and covered it all over with thin laths and brown paper, and then sprinkled mould over it, so that it had all the appearance of solid earth. A small stream of water ran through his garden into the river. Jemmy cut a small grip from it to the hole he had dug, and filled the hole with water; then choked the grip up and went into his house, laughing to himself at what would probably happen that night.

Stationing himself at nightfall in the garden where he could not be seen, he had not long to wait before he saw a head rising above the wall, then the body of a man, and in another moment the expectant lover had cleared the wall, and dropped on the covering of the pitfall. The laths and brown paper yielded to his weight, and he plunged up to his neck in water. The unfortunate young man screamed with fright, and Jemmy and Mary rushed to the spot.

"Holloa, my man! what's the matter? What art a' doing i' yond water-pit? Hast a' come to steal my apples and pears?"

Then turning to Mary, he asked if she knew him. The poor girl hesitated, but at last confessed that the young man was her sweetheart. "Well, then," said Jemmy, "help him out and get him into t' house, and let us change his clothes, for I reckon he's all over muck."

The young man was brought in dripping like a water-rat.

"Now, then," said Jemmy, "thou mun have a dry suit. Which wilt a' have – a pair o' my list breeches and rabbit-skin coat, or my old housekeeper's peticoats and gown?"

The young man ungallantly chose the former, thinking if he must be made ridiculous before the eyes of Mary, he would be less so in male than female attire. Jemmy gave him a glass of hot brandy-and-water, kept him talking by the kitchen fire till his clothes were dried, and then dismissed him with permission to come to the house openly, and visit Mary as often as he liked. The young fellow became in time a great favourite with the old man, and when he married Mary, Jemmy gave him £50 to start life with.

Jemmy took it into his head to make himself a coffin, for he said he was getting old, and did not know how soon he might require one, and therefore it was best to be ready. It took him a month to construct it. It had folding-doors instead of a lid, and two panes of glass in each door; and he fitted the inside with shelves for a cupboard, saying that he might as well turn it to some use whilst he was alive, and then fixed it upright in the corner of his sitting-room. Twelve months after, he had a second coffin made on the same model, but better, and with some improvements, by a joiner at Snaith, which cost him £12. "He always wished people to believe that he made it himself; but this was not the case, for the person that made it declared to us that Jemmy enjoined him not to divulge who had made it during his lifetime."[1] Inside the coffin he placed a handle connected with a bell outside, so that, as he said, if he wanted anything when in his grave – shaving water, sherry, or his boots – he would ring the bell for his servant to bring them to him.

He bought a sloop, which he called "The Bull," and made a voyage in her once as far as Boston; but he was so sick during the passage that he could never after be persuaded to set foot on her again. "Nay, nay," said he, "a yard of dry land is worth a mile of water."

Otter-hunting on the marshes between Rawcliffe and Goole was one of his favourite pastimes. He kept a small pack of otter-hounds for the purpose.

One day, when out with three dogs, near where Tunbridge House now stands, the dogs started an otter and gave him chase. He made for a drain, and there being plenty of water in it, he dived several times. The dogs followed him in the water, and Jemmy ran along the edge waiting for him. When the otter came out close to him, Jemmy struck at him, but missed his aim and fell, owing to the mud being slippery. The otter immediately seized him by the leg, and succeeded in dragging him into the water before the hounds could come to his assistance. A favourite dog, named Sancho, dived, and seizing the otter by the throat, forced it to release Jemmy's leg, and he reached the bank greatly shaken and exhausted. He fortunately wore that day a thick pair of leather boots, which prevented the teeth of the otter from cutting his flesh. The other dogs had dived to the assistance of Sancho, and they brought the otter to the bank, where Jemmy clubbed it. It was the largest otter that he had ever caught, and he had the skin tanned. He kept it for two or three years, and then made a present of it to a hair-dresser who used to attend and shave him.

As he was returning one night about eight o'clock from Howden, where he had been to the bank to draw some money, he was attacked by a couple of footpads, who probably knew where he had been. One seized the bridle of his bull, and the other took hold of Jemmy's arm and demanded his money. Jemmy suddenly drew a pistol from his pocket and fired it – according to his own account – full in the man's face, then struck spurs into the bull and galloped home. After getting assistance, he returned to the place where he had been stopped, but could find no trace of the persons who had attempted to rob him.

With the assistance of the captain of his sloop, Jemmy rigged some sails to his carriage, and after a few trials of the new contrivance in the lanes about Rawcliffe, he set off one day to Pontefract with all sail set. Having a fair wind he went at a dashing speed. When he reached the town every one turned out to see the wonderful ship that sailed on dry land.

But when Jemmy reached the first cross-street a puff of wind caught him sideways, upset the carriage, and flung Jemmy through the window of a draper's shop, smashing several panes.

[1] "Life and Adventures of James Hirst," Knottingley : Hepworth (n.d.)

The crowd that followed speedily righted the carriage and extricated Jemmy, who paid for the damage he had done, and led the way to the nearest tavern, where he treated the whole crowd with ale. This bounty naturally elicited great enthusiasm, which exhibited itself in prolonged cheers, to Jemmy's great delight, for he was one of the most conceited of men.

The authorities having intimated to him that he would not be allowed to sail back through the streets, the crowd yoked themselves to the carriage, and drew him triumphantly out of the town, and would have dragged him half way to Rawcliffe had not a favourable wind sprung up, when Jemmy spread his sails again, and was blown out of sight of the crowd with expedition. He reached home without any further mishap.

A friend writes to me: – "I remember Jemmy Hirst well coming to Doncaster races in his wretched turn-out, and with a bag of nuts, which he always brought with him for a scramble. He was not a very reputable individual, and must have been, I fancy, half-witted. He was wont to issue flash notes on the 'Bank of Rawcliffe,' meaning the river bank, for five farthings; and as these bore a great resemblance to the notes issued by a banking firm in Doncaster, he was able to deceive many people with them."

Among other accomplishments, Jemmy played the fiddle tolerably well. In winter he would collect all the boys and girls of Rawcliffe at his house in the evenings, once a week at least, when he would play the fiddle for them to dance to. At nine o'clock punctually he rang a bell and dismissed them. He never would allow them to remain a minute longer. They were sent away with buns, simnel-cake, or apples.

On another evening of the week he would have all the old women to tea, but he would allow no men in to have tea with him on these occasions. They were invited to come in later, and then dancing and singing began, which continued till nine, when he would dismiss them with a glass of rum or gin each.

On the evenings that he wished the children to come he blew a horn thrice at his door, and six blasts of the horn assembled the old people.

In his old age, Jemmy was frequently laid up with gout, when he amused himself with the composition of doggerel verses, mostly about himself. They were contemptible productions, but his vanity made him suppose that he was a poet. He got these rhymes printed, and sold them for a penny to his numerous visitors, and as sometimes on a Sunday he had three or four hundred people to see him, he realised a good sum – enough to keep him for the week – from this source.

But besides selling his verses, Jemmy used to make money by showing his coffin to visitors. He would induce them to enter the largest one, which was contrived to close upon any one inside, and hold him fast as a prisoner till released from the outside. No one once within was suffered to escape without payment – men were charged a penny, women one of their garters. In this way Jemmy accumulated hundreds of garters, which he tied to his chair. They were of all sorts, from a piece of silk down to a bit of whip-cord. He used to say that he could always tell a woman's character by her garter.

His old housekeeper, Sarah, after a tedious illness, died, and then Jemmy would not suffer any one to attend him except the wife of the captain of his sloop, "The Bull," who used to live in the house with him when her husband was at sea. All his pets were sold off, except a fox which he called Charley, that was chained in the back-yard; and his pointer pigs were converted into bacon and eaten.

During the last few years of his life Jemmy was confined a great deal within doors, and the neighbouring gentry used very often to visit him for the sake of old times; but he never would tolerate a visit from a clergyman. He had no religion whatever, and very little morality either. No one ever saw him inside a church or chapel, or got him to enter on religious conversation.

He was visited one day when he was visibly declining by Lord and Lady Wharncliffe; and the latter, on his swearing at the twinges of his gout, gently reproved him, pained to see how utterly indifferent he seemed to the future. "Mr. Hirst," said her Ladyship, "you should not swear; you really ought to make some preparation for death."

"Haven't I, my lady?" asked Jemmy. "I've had my coffin made these ten years."

It was in vain that Lady Wharncliffe endeavoured to get him into a serious turn; he turned off all her remarks with a bantering reply.

Jemmy was subject to temporary fits of insanity, in one of which he stripped himself stark naked and ran all round Rawcliffe. Fortunately it was night, so that there were not many people abroad; but he nearly frightened one young fellow out of his wits as he came bounding upon him in the moonlight, round a corner. The cries of this man brought people to his assistance, and they ran after Jemmy and caught him as he was stepping into a boat with the purpose of ferrying himself across the river, his mind in this disordered condition returning to the event of his youth, when he rowed across to meet his poor Mary. They brought him, not without trouble, to his house, and put him to bed. What made it the more remarkable was, that he had been confined to his bed all day with gout, and could scarcely move a limb.

Jemmy died on October 29th, 1829, at the age of ninety-one. By his will he left £12 to be given to twelve old maids for carrying him to his grave, £5 for a bagpiper from Aberdeen to play before him alternately with a fiddler to whom he also bequeathed £5, as he was borne to the churchyard.

The executors had some trouble in carrying out his wishes. The rector of Rawcliffe protested against the music being played on the occasion; but eventually a compromise was effected, and the piper was alone allowed to head the funeral to church, playing sacred music. Sacred music on a Scottish bagpipe!

Long before the funeral started for the church hundreds of spectators had collected in front of the house. Everything being in readiness, the procession moved off – the neighbouring gentry and farmers on horseback, followed by the piper; next came the coffin, carried by six of the old maids and two men, the other six of the old maids bearing the pall. The piper played a psalm tune; but as soon as ever the funeral was over, the fiddler met the piper at the church gates, and they struck up the tune of "'"Owre the hills and far awa'," followed by the crowd to Jemmy's late residence, where they received their money and were dismissed.

THE TRAGEDY OF BENINGBROUGH HALL.

IN 1670, Beningbrough Hall, a fine Elizabethan red-brick mansion, stood in a park near the junction of the Ouse and Nidd. The old house had been pulled down, and replaced by an edifice neat and commodious, as the guide-books would say, and we need say no more.

In 1670 Beningbrough Hall belonged to a Roman Catholic family of the name of Earle. Mr. Earle, the proprietor, was in somewhat embarrassed circumstances, and was mixed up with some of the plots then rife. He was much away from the Hall – generally in London; but the house was full of servants, under the control of a steward, Philip Laurie, and a housekeeper, named Marian – a comely woman, just passing into middle age.

One day, when Laurie was absent, two gentlemen arrived at the Hall, cloaked, with their hats drawn over their eyes, and were admitted by Marian. One of these was Mr. Earle himself, anxious to escape recognition. Who the other was did not transpire. After some conversation with the housekeeper, Marian summoned the servants into the hall, and ordered them immediately to collect and pack the plate and pictures – everything that was of value and readily moveable. Mr. Earle did not show himself – he remained in the housekeeper's room; but his companion appeared, and announced that he and Marian were acting under the authority of Mr. Earle, and he read them a letter from that gentleman requiring the removal of his valuable property as the housekeeper should direct.

The servants were much surprised; but as it was known that their master was in difficulties, and as some suspicion seems to have entered their heads that he was engaged in a plot, their wonder died away; they diligently discharged their duty, and everything was speedily collected and stowed away in leather bags or wooden boxes in the hall. The housekeeper then dismissed the servants, and she and the stranger conveyed the articles packed up into her room.

Where were they next to be conveyed to, so as to be readily removed? Mr. Earle expected a warrant for his arrest on the charge of high treason, and the confiscation of all his property. He was therefore desirous to remove all he could in time to escape to France.

To avoid observation, it was advisable that his valuables should be secreted somewhere near, but not in the house. Marian then, with some hesitation, told the master that an attachment subsisted between her and the gamekeeper, a man named Martin Giles; that she could rely on his not divulging the secret, and trust him with the custody of the plate, &c., till it suited the convenience of Mr. Earle to take them away. She was accordingly despatched to the gamekeeper's cottage, and he was brought to the Hall, and as much of the secret confided to him as could not well be retained. He promised most frankly to do what was desired of him, and as he was a Roman Catholic, Mr. Earle felt satisfied that he could trust him not to betray a master who professed the same faith.

When Philip Laurie returned he found to his surprise that the house had been stripped of everything precious. He was extremely incensed, and in an angry interview with Marian charged her with having told tales of him to her master, and so of having lost him the confidence of Mr. Earle. She did not deny that she mistrusted his honesty, unhappily recalled a circumstance he thought she knew nothing of, and took occasion to give him "a bit of her mind"; but she protested that she had not spoken on the subject to her master.

Philip Laurie asked where the property was removed to. She refused to tell him. He swore he would know. He did not trust her story. The house had been plundered; the opportunity had been taken when he was absent, and Marian was privy to a robbery.

After violent words on both sides they parted. As he left the room the steward turned, fixing his eyes, blazing with deadly hate, upon the housekeeper, and muttered a few inarticulate words.

It was not long before Laurie suspected or discovered where the valuables were secreted.

Chance had thrown in his way a labourer of bad character named William Vasey, a poacher and a reputed thief. Laurie walked through the park to the cottage of this miscreant, and it was resolved between them that the housekeeper should be murdered, and then that the lodge of the gamekeeper should be robbed.

In the evening Marian was taking her accustomed walk along a beech avenue beside the Ouse. It was evening, and the red evening sky was reflected in the water, which looked like a streak of blood. The rooks were cawing and wheeling about the tree-tops, settling for the night.

A white owl that lived in the ivy that covered the north side of the house floated, ghostlike, through the gathering darkness. Marian in her white cap walked quietly in the avenue. She was a Roman Catholic, and was reciting her beads. Laurie knew that she was accustomed every evening to retire into this walk to say her rosary.

At one point a beech-tree had been blown over, and had left a gap to the west, through which the faint reflection of the evening sky fell, leaving the shadows beyond it in deeper gloom. For some unaccountable reason, as Marian came to this gap, instead of passing it and continuing her walk, she stood still, and then turned. A second time she walked the avenue and came to this gap. A mysterious repugnance to advance caused her to hesitate and halt.

Thinking that this was an unreasonable feeling, she walked on a couple of steps, and then stood still, turned round, and looked at the spot where the sun had gone down.

At that moment Vasey sprang from behind a tree, and thrust Marian over the brink. With a shriek she sank.

Next morning the body was found, a part of the rosary clenched in her hand, and the other portion was discovered caught in the stump of the broken beech. Prints of a man's boots in the mud showed that Marian had not died by accidentally falling into the water.

Suspicion of the guilt of the murder fell upon Martin Giles, the gamekeeper. Laurie was in the Hall the whole time, and therefore no one supposed him implicated in the commission of the crime. The gamekeeper had behaved mysteriously for the last day or two. He had avoided his usual friends; he had been seen privately conversing with the housekeeper. Only Marian and he knew that their master had been in the house; his presence had been concealed from the other servants, who only saw his companion. The removal of the valuables to the house of Giles had been accomplished by the two gentlemen with the assistance of the gamekeeper alone. After the valuables had been taken away, the two gentlemen in disguise had ridden off.

The servants, who had noticed that there was some mystery to which Giles and Marian were privy, thought that the keeper had killed the poor woman out of dread lest she should prove an untrustworthy depositary of the secret, whatever it was. It was known also that the lovers had been accustomed to meet in the beech avenue, the place where the murder had been committed.

Whilst the tide of popular indignation ran strong against the unfortunate gamekeeper, Laurie and Vasey resolved on committing the robbery – before also Mr. Earle and his companion had found means to remove the property entrusted to his custody.

At midnight Vasey and the steward went to the gamekeeper's cottage. Laurie was to remain outside, and the other ruffian to enter and rob the house. They thought that Martin Giles was sure to be asleep; but they were mistaken. The man had been sincerely attached to poor Marian, and lay tossing in bed, wondering who could have murdered her, and vainly racking his brain to discover some clue which could guide him to a solution of the mystery. As he thus lay, he thought he heard a slight sound downstairs. But the wind was blowing, and the trees roaring in the blast; the little diamond panes in the latticed windows clattered, and the keeper thought nothing of it.

Presently, however, he heard the latch of his door gently raised, and in the darkness he just distinguished the figure of a man entering the room. He immediately jumped out of bed, but was felled to the ground. As he struggled to rise he was again struck down, and for the moment was stunned. But he recovered consciousness almost immediately. He had fallen upon a sheep net, which lay in a heap on the floor. He quietly gathered up the net in his hands, sprang to his feet, and flinging the net over the murderer, entangled his arms so that he could not extricate himself.

He wrenched the bludgeon out of his hand, and struck him over the head with it, so that he measured his length insensible, on the floor.

Had Martin only known that this ruffian had been the murderer of her who had been dearer to him than anyone else in the world, there is no doubt the blow would have fallen heavier, and would have spared the hangman his trouble.

Giles then threw open his window and fired off his gun, to alarm the inmates of the Hall.

In a few minutes the servants made their appearance, amongt them Philip Laurie, with a ghastly face. A sign passed between him and Vasey, and he recovered some of his composure. The captured ruffian had assured him he would not betray his accomplice.

Vasey was taken into custody, and on the following day was removed to York Castle, where he was committed for burglary with intent to commit murder.

When Mr. and Mrs. Earle heard of what had taken place, the latter came with the utmost speed into Yorkshire. Mr. Earle, fearing arrest for treasonable practices, did not venture to do so.

Laurie's conduct had already excited suspicion. He had not been seen issuing from the Hall on the night of the attempted robbery with the other servants, and was found on the spot fully dressed, and that not in his usual costume, but one which looked as if intended for a disguise.

Mrs. Earle sent for him to her boudoir, and dismissed him from her service. As yet there was not charge sufficiently established against him to warrant her committing him to custody; but she added, Vasey had declared his full intention to confess before his execution.

Laurie, a desparate man, flung himself on his knees, and implored his mistress not to send him away; or if, as he heard, she was about to escape with Mr. Earle to France, would she allow him to accompany them?

She indignantly thrust the wretch from her. He started to his feet, drew a pistol from his coat-pocket, and presented it at her head. She struck up his hand, and the contents of the pistol shivered the glasses of a chandelier that hung in the room. He rushed out of the room, ran to his own apartment, put another pistol to his forehead, and blew his brains out.

Vasey now confessed everything, and was executed at the Tyburn, outside Micklegate Bar, at York, on August 18th, 1670.

It is said that at night a pale, female figure is seen to steal along the bank of the Ouse, where the avenue stood in olden time, and to disappear in the churchyard of Newton, which adjoins the park, where Marian was buried.

A YORKSHIRE BUTCHER.

THE subject of this memoir has been dead but a few years, and therefore I do not give his name, lest it should cause annoyance to his relatives. He was a tall, red-faced, jovial man, with a merry twinkle in his small eyes; a man who could tell a good story with incomparable drollery, and withal was the gentlest, kindest-hearted man, who would never wound the most sensitive feelings by ridicule. He had a splendid bass voice, and sang in the church choir; his knowledge of music was not inconsiderable, and for some time he was choirmaster, and performed a feat few other men have been able to accomplish – he was able to keep the discordant elements of a choir in harmony. His inimitable tact, unvarying good nature, and readiness to humour the most self-consequential of the performers, made him vastly popular with them, and prevented or healed those jars which are proverbial among professed votaries of harmony.

This worthy butcher thus narrated his courtship:—

"It's a queer thing, sir, hoo things turns oot sometimes. Noo it war a queer thing hoo I chanced to get wed. I war at Leeds once, and I'd na mair thowts aboot marrying na mair 'an nowt; and I war just going doon t' street, tha knaws, sir, when I met wi' my wife – that's her 'at's my wife noo, tha knaws. I'd kenned her afore, a piece back; soa shoo comes oop to me, an' shoo ses, 'Why James, lad, is that thee?' – 'Aye,' I ses, 'it is awever.' – 'Weel, James,' ses she, 'what's ta doing wi' thysen noo?' – 'Why,' I ses, 'I's joost getten me a new hoose.' Soa wi' that she ses, 'Then I lay, James, if tha's getting a new hoose, tha'll be wanting a hoosekeeper.' Soa I ses to 'er, ses I, 'Tha ma' coom and be t' wife if ta likes; tha mawn't be t' hoosekeeper, tha knaws, but tha ma' coom and be t' wife.' And soa shoo ses, 'I ain't partikler. I don't mind if I do.' So we never had na mair to do aboot t' job."

I asked him if he ever had found occasion to regret such an expeditious way of settling the matter. He shook his head and said, "Noa, sir, niver. Shoo's made a rare good wife. But shoo's her mawgrums a' times. But what women ain't got 'em? They've all on 'em maggots i' their heads or tempers. Tha sees, sir, when a bone were took out o' t' side o' Adam, to mak wife for 'm, 't were hot weather, an' a blue-bottle settled on t' rib. When shoo's i' her tantrums ses I to her, 'Ma dear,' ses I, 'I wish thy great-great-grand ancestress hed chanced ta be made i' winter.'"

153

When he was married he took his wife on a trip to Bolton, and spent a week on his honeymoon tour. As soon as he was returned home, the first thing he did was to put his wife into the scales and weigh her. Then the butcher took out his account-book, and divided the expenses of the marriage and wedding-tour by the weight of the wife. "Eh! lass!" said he, "thou'st cost me fourteen pence ha'penny a pound. Thou'st the dearest piece o' meat that iver I bought."

He had a baromoter. The glass stood at set-fair, and for a whole week the rain had been pouring down. On the eighth day the glass was still telling the same tale, and the rain was still falling. Our friend lost his patience, and holding the barometer up to the window he said, "Sithere, lass! thou'st been telling lees. Dost thou see how it's pouring? I'll teach thee to tell lees again!" And he smashed the glass.

He was laid up with gout. The doctor had tried all sorts of medicines, but nothing seemed to profit him. At last the medical man said, "Try smoking. I daresay smoking would do you a deal of good."

"Ah," said the wife, "it's possible it might. But thou seest, doctor, chimleys is made so narrow nowadays that one cannot hang un up i' t' reek (smoke) as one did wi' one's bacon i' bygone days."

His wife was dying. She was long ill, and during her sickness was always exclaiming, "Eh! I'm boun' to dee. It win't be long afore I dee. I shan't be long here" – and the like. Our jolly butcher heard these exclamations day after day, and said nothing. At last he got a little impatient over them, and said one day, as she was exclaiming as usual, "O dear! I'm goin' to dee!" – "Why lass, thou'st said that ower and ower again a mony times. Why doan't thou set a time, and stick to it?"

On another occasion his wife slightly varied the tune to "Eh! the poor bairns! What will become o' t' bairns when I dee? Who will mind t' bairns when their mother is dead?"

"Never thee trouble thy head about that," said her husband; "go on wi' thy deein'. I'll mind t' bairns."

He was going to York with his son, a boy of eighteen. He took a ticket for himself and a half-one for the boy. When the train drew near to York, the ticket-collector came round, and exclaimed at this half-ticket, "Where's the child?"

"Here," said the butcher, pointing to the tall, awkward youth.

"What do you mean?" asked the indignant ticket-collector. "He ain't a child; he's a young man!"

"Ah! so he is, now," answered the butcher; "but that's thy fault, not mine. I know when we got in at Wakefield he were nobbut a bairn; but tha'st been going so confounded slow that he's growed sin' we started!"

Many years ago, on a rare occasion, James took a glass too much. It was the last time such a misfortune took place with him. His clergyman was obliged to speak to him about it, and in doing so said – "You know, James, beasts do not get drunk."

"There's a deal o' things belonging to all things," answered the worthy butcher, who never suffered himself to be cornered. "If a horse were o' one side o' a pond, and another on t' other side, and t' first horse ses t' other, 'Jim I look towards ye!' and t' other ses to the first, 'Thank y' kindly, Tom; I catches your eye.' And the first horse ses again, 'Tha'll tak' another sup, lad, and drink ma health'; the second will be sewer to say, 'I will, and I'll drink to lots o' your healths.' Why, sir, them two horses will be nobbin to one another iver so long. Lor bless ye! them two horses win't part till they's as drunk as Christians."

James at one time was not well off. He had a brother whom we will call Tom, who had some money.

Now James happened to hear that his brother was very ill, and as they had not latterly been very good friends, he was afraid lest, if Tom died, he would not leave him his money.

So he immediately set off to his brother's house, and on his arrival found him ill in bed. He went up to the room in which his brother lay, and began – "Weel, Tommy, an' hoo art a'?"

"Oah, James!" said Tom, "I'se vara bad. I thinks I's boun' to dee."

"Eh!" said James, "well, mebbee tha'lt outlive me, Tommy; I nobbut feels vara middlin mysen. I hain't felt weel for a long while, and I war just thinking, Tommy, o' sending to Mr. Smith, t' lawyer, to mak' me a bit o' a will, tha knaws. Hast a' made *thy* will, Tommy?"

"Noa," said Tom, "I hain't; but I was thinking wi' thee, James, o' sending for Lawyer Smith. Noo, who wast a' thinking o' making thy heir, James?"

"Weel, tha knaws, Tommy," said James, "mebbe thou and me hain't lately been vara particklers; but I war thinking it ever owt ta be, 'Let bygones be bygones'; and soa I was thinking o' leaving my bit o' brass to thee. Noo, Tommy, hoo wast a' thinking o' leaving thy money?"

"Why," said Tommy, "as thou'st been sa good as leave thy money ta me, I think it wadn't be reet if I didn't do t' same by thee, and leave thee my brass."

"Weel," said James, "I think thou couldn't do better; and soa let's send for Mr. Smith to mak' our wills, and I think mebbe, Tommy. *thou'd better ha' thy will made fust*."

So these two men sent for the lawyer to make their wills. Tommy's was made first, and a very few days after he died. His money then came to James, who in reality was not ill in the least, but had only pretended to be so.

One of James the butchers' sayings I well remember. He was addressing a young man who was courting a girl, and was very hot and eager in his pursuit of her.

"I'll gi'e thee a bit o' advice, Joa: Don't bother to shuttle a happle-tree to get t' fruit; tak' it easy; wait, and t' apples will fall into thy lap o' their selves. Don't go coursing over hedges and threw ditches after rabbits; wait a bit, and t' rabbits 'all come into thy springes without trouble. Don't take on running after t' lasses; take it easy, and thou'lt find, Joa, lad, that t' lasses will run after thee."

At one time James rented some land of a neighbouring gentleman of large fortune and estates who was well known for his hospitality. James was invited with other tenants to dine on Court day at the Hall, and dinner was served up in the best style. On his return home to his wife, he gave her an account of it. "Eh! Phoebe, but it wad ha' capped owt. There were beef and mutton, and chickens and game, and ivery thing one could think of. I's sewer I were fair an' bet wi' it all; but what bet ma moast o' all were 'at we'd ivery one on us a small loaf lapped up i' a clout."

Liqueurs were handed round after dinner. Our good friend took his little glass of the, to him, unknown tipple, and after drinking it off at one gulp, and considering a while, turned round to the waiter and said, "John, bring us some o' this 'ere i' a moog."

At a club dinner, a wedding breakfast, or a funeral lunch, James was overflowing with anecdotes. He was generally the hero of his stories; but I do not believe that they all in reality happened to himself. The stories often told against the principal actor in them, and therefore he may have thought it legitimate to appropriate to himself tales which made him appear in a ludicrous light.

I can remember only a few of these stories.

"It was one night in November last that I and my wife Phoebe was sitting tawking i' t' house. It were a dark night, as black as Warren's best. Now I mun tell thee that our Rachel Anne – that's our grown-up daughter – were at that age when they mostly likes to ha' a sweetheart, Shoo'd gotten a young man. I don't like to name names, but as we're all friends here, I don't mind saying he were a downright blackguard. It were old Greenwood's son, tha knaws; t' lad as were locked up by t' police for boiling a cat. Well, Rachel Anne were mad after him, and nother her mother nor I liked it. We were nicely put out, I promise you.

"To go on with my tale. Phoebe and I were sitting by t' fire, when all at once I ses to my old woman, 'Phoebe, lass, where's Rachel Anne? Shoo's not at home, I reckon.'

"'Nay, James, lad,' said she, 'shoo's at a confirmation class.'

"'At a confirmation!' said I, and I whistled. 'I thowt confirmation was ower.'

"'Ah! I dunnow sure; but that's what shoo said.'

"'Is owd Greenwood's son, Jim, going to confirmation class too?'

"'I cannot tell,' shoo said.

"'No more can I,' said I; 'but I'd like to know?'

"'So should I,' said she.

"'Win't thee look out o' chamber window and see if there's a leet i' t' school?' said I. So my owd woman went upstairs and looked, and when shoo came doun, 'No, there ain't,' said she.

"'I thowt not,' said I.

"Well, we sat by t' fire some while, and then my owd lass went into back kitchen to get a bit o' supper ready. Shoo hadn't been there long afore shoo come back and said, 'James, lad!'

"'Ah!' says I; 'what's up?'

"'Why, this,' says she; 'there's summun i' t' back yard.'

"'How dost a' know?' says I.

"Says she, 'I heard 'em taukin'; and there's a lanthorn there.'

"'There's impidence!' says I. 'Who is they?'

"'I think Rachel Anne is one,' says Phoebe.

"'And Jim Greenwood is t' other,' says I; 'and I'm glad on't.'

"'Why?' says Phoebe.

"'Lass,' says I, 'I'll pay yond chap out, I will. I'll go out by t' front door, and I'll come on him, and I'll let him know what I think of him, coming arter our Rachel Anne. And when I've gotten howd on him, I'll hollow. Then do thou run o' t' back door, and I'll howd him tight, and thou can poise him behind as much as thou like. Since we've been man and wife these fourteen year,' says I, 'we've taken our pleasure in common,' says I. 'We've been to Hollingworth Lake together,' says I. 'And we've been to Southport together,' says I. 'And wunce we've went together to t' exhibition i' Wakefield together. So,' says I, 'we'll ha' the kicking, and the shuttling, and the rumpling up o' yond lad o' Greenwood's together. O glory!' And then I run out o' t' front door as wick as a scoprill,[1] and came shirking round towards t' back door i' t' yard. Well, t' night were dark, but I could see there were some folks there, and I could see the glint o' a lanthorn, and t' leet from t' back kitchen window came on a bit o gownd, and I know'd it belonged to Rachel Anne.

"'Drat him!' said I to mysen, 'what is lasses coming to next, when they brings their young men under the noses o' their parents wot can't abear them?'

"So I came sloping up along the wall till I was quite near. Will you believe it? – her young man, that's owd Greenwood's lad Jim, was sitting as easy as owt i' a chair.

"'Oh, you charmer!' says Rachel Anne. I heard her voice. I know'd it were she. 'You're near perfect noo!'

"'Oh lawk!' thinks I, 'there's no accounting for tastes.' Jim he ain't ower much o' a beauty, I promise thee. He's gotten a cast i' one o' his eyes, and when he washes his face he's gotten a black stock on; and when he don't why, then he's all o' a muck , face and neck alike.

"'Can I get thee owt?' says Rachel Anne, as shameless as owt. 'Ah! tha wants a pair o' boots. I reckon father's gotten an owd pair he win't miss. I'll get them for thee.' Then sudden, as she was going away to t' back door, she turns and says, 'My! he ain't got no pipe. I mun get him one o' father's.'

"'Oh, ye abandoned profligate!' groaned I, 'robbing thy parents to bestow all on this owdacious waggabone! But I'll be even wi' thee! I'll let my fine gentleman know the looks o' my back-yard! I'll let un ha' a taste o' my baccy! I'll let un know the feel o' my boots!'

"'Father's breeches fit un rare!' said Rachel Anne.

---

[1] As lively as a teetotum.

"Well, now! if that warn't too much. I yelled –

"'Ah! ye dirty waggabone! Thou stealing rascal! Thou cock-eyed ragga-muffin!' And I wor upon him in no time. I caught un by t' neck and shook un furious. I wor nigh brussen wi' rage. He were fair down capped, and said nowt. But, as you'll see presently, he were gathering up his rage for a reglar outburst. He were nigh brussen too.

"'Well,' says I, 'wot is't a doing here? I knows! Thou'rt arter my Rachel Anne. Well. Tha'lt never marry my daughter if I can help it. I'll never own thee wi' thy ugly face for a son-in-law. I win't run the chance o' cock-eye i' my grand-children. If my dowter will ha' thee, I'll disown her; I win't speak to her again.' Then I shook him. 'Take that,' says I gave him a blow o' the fist on his nose, and I reckon I flattened it in. 'Dost a' like it?' says I. 'Take another taste – a little stimulant will do thee good.' Then I kicked un off t' chair, and dragged him up, and shook, and shook, and shook him till I were all of a muck wi' sweat. So I hollered to my Phoebe. 'Phoebe, lass! come and poise un i' t' rear. I'll hold un i' position.' Well, she came out, and she gave him a crack.

"'Now,' says I, 'I'd like to look i' thy ugly face and take stock o' t' damages. I've done thy beauty. Phoebe, lass! give me t' candle.' Shoo went t' lanthorn, and browt out t' candle and gave it to me.

"Jim Greenwood hung all limp, like old clothes i' my hand, and never spoke. But I didn't know what fire and fury was in him then. He wor just one o' them chaps as endures what you may say and do up to a certain point, but when that point is passed, then – Lor'!'

"I took t' candle from my owd woman – that's my wife, I mean, tha mun know – and I held it afore me. Lor-a-mussy, I were flayed! I let go hold, and let t' candle tumble on Jim – that's owd Greenwood's son, tha knows – and I stood shakin' i' all my limbs. I'd smashed his nose right in; I'd broken t' bridge and knocked it in, and there weren't nowt on it remaining. And his eyes – Lor'! I hadn't time to think, for I had passed t' point, and t' chap couldn't stan' no more. I'd let t' candle fall on him, and set him on fire. Folks don't over much like being set fire to – lestways owd Greenwood's son didn't; for he did blaze, and bang, and fizz, and snap, and crackle away! He reglar exploded, he did! I stood in a sort o' maze Like – I were dazed. Phoebe screamed. And then came a great haw-haw from my boys, who were all there. I could see 'em now by t' leet o' t' burning sweetheart. 'Lor', father!' said Rachel Anne, as innocent as owt, *What hast a' been doing to our Guy Fawkes?*'

"Well, sir, will you believe it? – it was nowt but a Guy Fawkes full o' straw and squibs and crackers 'at I'd involuntarily set on fire."

This story was told, scarcely above a breath, during a missionary meeting, whilst a colonial bishop was addressing us. James did not laugh himself – was as grave as was proper on the occasion; but his little eyes twinkled roguishly, and those who could hear the whispered tale with difficulty restrained their laughter.

"I think I can tell you summut as happened to my brother Tommy," said

James, after we had sung "From Greenland's icy mountains," and were walking at a judicious distance from the colonial bishop. "Well, my brother Tom were a rare bird to drink. He'd been to t' Horse and Jockey one day, and had supped enough beer for once, and when he came out about half after ten, he warn't ower clear as to t' direction he sud go. Howm'ever, he took t' loin (lane) all right. Presently there come some one along t' road. 'Now,' thowt he, 'I mun keep clear o' he, or he'll run hissel' again' me, and knock me down.' T' mooin were up, just settin', and castin' shadows; so he made a great roundabout to avoid lurching again' t' man as were comin' along; but seeing his shadow, ma brother mistook that for t' man, and thowt t' shadow had cast t' feller. So he tried to step ower t' chap and avoid t' shadow. As tha mun see, he came wi' a crack again' t' chap.

"'Ye druffen rascal,' said he, giving ma brother a bang on t' lugs (ears) as made his head spin.

"'It's thy fault,' said Tom. 'What dost a' mean by having a standing-up shadow and solid too?'

"The chap gives him another crack and tumbles him down. When ma brother got up again he went on his road again, saying to hissel', 'I winna go blundering again' no more shadows to-night if I see anybody coming.' Just then he thowt he saw another chap; so to get out o' his way he turned into a field by a gate to let un pass. Now, ma brother had a little too much beer in his head; soa when he got into t' field he couldn't get out again. He rambled round and round, and t' mooin went down.

"'Weel,' ses he, 'I don't care; I'll sleep where I am.' And he ligs him down on t' ground. He hadn't been long asleep afore he wakened wi' cold. T' dews o' neet came falling on him and wetted him, and his teeth were chattering; so then he opened his eyes. And what dost a' think he seed? Why, standing above him were a hawful form as black as a crow. His legs was crooked, his arms was spread, and Tom could see claws on his fingers. His face were like nowt earthly; and he had bristling hair, and great horns like a coo. Tom could see t' glint o' his wicked een fixed on him.

"Weel, now, Tommas weren't that sort o' chap exackly as might flatter hissen angels 'ud come after him out o' heaven; so the thowt came on him it were t' owd chap come to fetch his soul to t' other place.

"Tom lay quite still. He thowt t' owd chap mebbe would let un lig a while if he shammed sleep. He wouldn't be so unmannerly as to wake un up for the purpose o' takin' him away. Tha knaws t' owd chap war' a gem'man once, tho' he's fallen a bit sin'. Yet what's born i' t' bone comes out i' t' flesh – leastwise so Tom thowt.

"Soa Tom lay quiet. But presently he thowt he felt t' owd chap's fingers feeling in his pocket for four and two-pence he'd gotten aboot him somewhere. Soa Tom turned round sudden on him and ses, 'Tha mun tak ma soul if tha's boun' to do soa; but I'll trouble thee to let t' four and twopence aloan.'

"Ah! he war' a deep one war' t' owd chap. As sharp as owt, when Tom turned on un, he were standing up stiff and unconcerned, and looking t' other way.

"Nah, as Tom had spoken, 't warn't no use his pretending any more to be asleep. So he thowt, 'What am I to do next? Tha mun do more wi' traycle than tha can wi' brimstone. I'll soap un down a bit.'

"Then Tom opens his eyes and looks at un and ses, 'Owt fresh?' But he wouldn't answer and reveal the mysteries o' his shop.

"So Tom ses, ses he, 'I reckon tha'st coom a rare long way, and it's thirsty work walking, or flying, or travelling by train, or whichever way tha hast comed. And,' ses he, 'I tak it vara civil o' thee to come for me. There's ma owd woman grummles if shoo's to come for ma to t' Horse and Jockey, and that's half a mile from my home. And mebbe tha's comed for me five thousand mile. It's vara civil. It's not like a north countryman that,' ses he. 'We are outspoken folk, and there ain't much civility among us, but hard rubs. But I won't be outdone by a south countryman i' civility. I daresay tha'rt dry. Tha'll stop a bit, and I'll fetch thee a sup o' home-brewed beer.'

"Soa Tom gets up on his feet, and away he goes as wick as a scoprell, and gets home, and dashes in at t' door. There were Sarah Anne, his wife, as red as a turkey-cock, and swollen fit to brussen wi' he getting home so late.

"But Tommy he out wi' it at once. 'Sarah Anne, lass! run and get a jug o' beer and a mug, and off wi' thee as fast as tha' can to t' owd chap – he's waiting for thee.' He thowt, tha knaws, to get t' owd chap to tak t' wife instead of he. But Sarah Anne she up wi' her fist and knocked him down as flat as ginger-beer as he had t' cork out a fortnight. 'Ah, James,' ses ma brother to me, 'I've tried to send ma owd woman to t'owd chap, but shoo winna go. Tha mun tak' a horse to t' water, but tha canna mak' un drink.'

"Weel, next morning ma brother Tom hoo went to look at t' place where he was i' t' neet, and there he see'd t' owd chap still. . . . But by day leet – what dost a' think? – he was nowt but a flaycrow (scarecrow)."

THE ONE-POUND NOTE.[1]

SAMUEL SUTCLIFFE lived at Hebden Hay, or Hawden Hole, about a quarter of a mile west of Newbridge, nearly at the bottom of the steep slope which descends from Whitehill Nook to the river Hebden. The house is still standing, easy to be recognised by its whitewash and by the yew-tree which grows between the door and the path leading to Upper Hepton and Tommy Rocky's. Beside the farmhouse there is under the same roof a cottage at the east end. In the field at the west end, and below the house, stretching down to the stream, were formerly some mounds, where it was said that the Heptonstall people during the plague buried their dead. Crabtree says (p.15): "Of that dreadful epidemic, the plague, one hundred and seventeen persons are said to have died at Heptonstall in 1631, several of whom were buried at home, but all entered in the register there." In the old barn near the house, pulled down a few years ago, since 1817, an old man cut his throat. The yew-tree is no inapt symbol of the melancholy associations of this secluded spot – a cemetery, a suicide, and a murder.

Samuel Sutcliffe, commonly called Sammy o' Kattie's, lived there to the age of eighty, a bachelor. He was a manufacturer of worsted pieces, and for several years farmed the small farm. The only person living with him was his nephew, William Sutcliffe. On Saturdays, sometimes the uncle, sometimes the nephew, attended Halifax market; sometimes both. On Saturdays, towards evening, the old man might have been seen crossing the old bridge at Hebden Bridge, and calling at the "Hole in the Wall" to take a single glass of ale and hear the news, while he gave himself a very brief rest after his walk from Halifax, before

[1] The circumstances of the murder and the discovery of the murderer were collected with great care by the brother of a friend of the author, now dead, and were communicated by him to the *Hebden Bridge Chronicle* in 1856. The papers of the compiler have been kindly sent to the author, and placed at his disposal. The facts of this extraordinary story were collected partly from individuals now surviving, who lived in the neighbourhood at the time, especially from one who was a principal witness at the trial at York, and partly from documents. Of the latter the principal are a good report of the trial given in the *Leeds Mercury* of Saturday, March 22nd, 1817, and a confession by the condemned parties drawn up in the usual style of confessions, and printed at Leeds for the purpose of being hawked about the streets. The *Manchester Mercury* of Tuesday, March 18th, 1817, gives a short account of the trial and condemnation of the prisoners, and concludes with a confession of the principal prisoner; being a long verbatim extract from the confession printed at Leeds for sale by hawkers. One of the official books belonging to Heptonstall church contains a copy of the charge of the judge to the jury at York, taken verbatim from the *Leeds Marcury* of March 22nd.

163

passing on. He was a stout, active man for his age; sober, steady, and industrious; and by economy, but without penuriousness, had saved a considerable sum of money. The cottage adjoining Sammy's dwelling was inhabited by a weaver named William Greenwood.

For five or six years the nephew, William Sutcliffe, had carried on a little business in the fustian trade on his own account; and for two years he had the take of the farm, on which he kept a couple of cows. His business led him to travel into Lancashire, Craven, and even Westmoreland. His journeys were taken three times a year: he started on Monday morning, and returned usually on Friday evening, sometimes on Saturday. He left Hawden Hole on one of these journeys on Monday, February 3rd, 1817, and was this time expected home on the Thursday night following, but circumstances prevented his return till the Saturday.

The name of the murderer was Michael Pickles, commonly designated "Old Mike." He lived at Northwell, near Heptonstall, on the road leading from Heptonstall by Newbridge to Haworth. His cottage, since pulled down, was of one storey: it contained two rooms – one towards the valley and the township of Wadsworth, into which the door entered, formed the dwelling or "house;" the other, trenching back into the hill-side, was called the "shop," and contained the looms. Some portion of the walls of the shop are still visible. Approached from the road, Old Mike's cottage stood a little below and a little beyond the principal house now standing at Northwell. A small garden was attached, in the walls of which are still to be seen the recesses which contained Mike's bee-hives. The plump-looking navel-wort, possibly introduced by him, may be seen peeping from crevices in the walls. Like Hawden Hole, Northwell has also its characteristic tree. The sombre Scotch pine which stands prominently forward in front of Northwell is in the corner of Mike's garden, and is said to have been planted by him. He lived at this cottage fifteen years. His age was forty-one. He is described as a strong, broad-set, but not a tall man, with rather dark hair, pale, cadaverous face, no whiskers, and large rolling eyes. He was left-handed, his hands being very large: he often made exhibition of the power of his left hand in grasping and crushing anything placed within it, in which exploit he surpassed all competitors. He had a very large, flat foot; his knees inclined very much inwards. He had the reputation of being "double-jointed," whatever may be meant by that term. His occupation was sometimes that of weaving at Northwell, sometimes of gardening for his neighbours, but more frequently that of an out-door labourer in dry-walling, and especially in constructing, of large stones, what is called "weiring," for preventing the river-edge from encroaching on the neighbouring fields; for which his great strength qualified him. He had the reputation of being light-fingered. In dressing the gardens of his neighbours he not unfrequently helped himself to some of the contents. His house was generally very well supplied with milk in summer, which was considered to have been obtained by milking the cows in the fields. Above all, he had the reputation of stealing bee-hives, to which the fact of his being a bee-keeper was a sort of cover. As a gentleman was one night riding along the "Needless Road" when not quite dark, he and his horse were suddenly startled, on coming in view of the steep field stretching from that road up to Northwell, by the sight of a strange figure moving slowly and heavily up the field: it was Mike with his not uncommon night burden, a hive of bees on his head. Another gentleman, stopping late at Kebcote Inn because of the rain, saw Mike and a companion take shelter there about half an hour after midnight, the former being loaded with the customary "hive-piche" on his head. In the floor of his house, under the bed, he had excavated a secret hiding-place for stolen goods, covered by a moveable flag-stone. The paving before his door had been raised by the earth taken from this so-called "cave." Notwithstanding these dishonest practices, Mike made a considerable profession of religion. He was a joined member at Birchcliffe Chapel, having with his wife, received adult baptism. Whether he was originally sincere in his profession and afterwards fell away, is more than doubtful when we consider that, notwithstanding his mal-practices, he continued to make great religious profession. In conversation he would expound at large the doctrines of Christianity. To approach him with the view of holding short discourse with him on general topics while he was gardening for you, was to incur the risk of a sermon from him. He fetched milk from old Sammy's at Hawden Hole, and was in the habit of sitting and conversing with him, not unfrequently of reading to him during the long evenings. They had been acquainted many years.

Mike's accomplice was John Greenwood, a weaver, a tallish, slender man, aged twenty-nine years, with lightish hair, whose features gave the impression of a weak and undecided, rather than a depraved and wicked disposition. His characteristic want of firmness rendered him the easy dupe of any deeper adept in villany who might throw temptation into his way. It is believed that he would not have been connected with the murder but for the persuasion of Mike. His character does not appear to have lain under any suspicion, although, as his confession afterwards showed, he was already addicted to dishonest practices. He and Mike married sisters. He lived in a cottage attached to a remote farm in Wadsworth called Bog-eggs, above Old Town, a little below the moorland prominence called Tomtitiman from which so noble a prospect of this district may be obtained. His cottage, now unoccupied, forms the upper part of the building at Bog-eggs, being contiguous to the farm-house.

On Thursday, the 6th of February, 1817, "Joan o' t' Bog-eggs" went over to Northwell to try to obtain some money from Old Mike, saying that he was "pinned." Times were very hard just now, and doubtless there was much suffering among the poor. Flour was selling at eight shillings per stone, and meal at four and sixpence to five shillings. Old Mike said that he had no money, but that he knew of a place where they could get some. This was just the sort of temptation in which Joan's (John's) weak principles were likely to fail; and Mike was exactly the sort of man to attempt to turn Joan's infirmities to his own advantage. Mike's plausible speech soon prevailed over Joan's scruples; and it was agreed that that night they should sally forth and rob Old Sammy.

On Thursday evening, February 6th, 1817, "Old Mike" and "Joan o' t' Bog-eggs" were sitting by Old Mike's fireside at Northwell. The night was wearing late, and the family had been sometime in bed. It was clearly understood between Mike and Joan, that after waiting till the hour was sufficiently advanced, they should sally out and rob "Sammy o' Kattie's." The hour agreed upon was midnight. Mike was smoking his pipe, and thinking over the circumstances of the intended burglary. Simple, unthinking Joan had fallen asleep under the influence of the warm fire. A length the clock struck twelve, and Mike aroused his companion, saying, "Come, it's time to be going." They took with them Mike's gun, and left the house, proceeding towards Whitehill Nook, along a field called Adcock, which is to the left of and above the public road leading to Whitehill Nook. They then travelled down the steep rough wood to Hawden Hole. Thrice Joan's heart failed him as he thought of the possible consequences to them both of the meditated robbery. Reassured by Mike's argument, he proceeded to Old Sammy's. Half-past twelve was the hour for the moon to rise; but the night was cloudy, though without rain. Arrived at the house, Joan was placed as sentry before the door, with the gun in his hand, and directed to shoot any person who should offer interruption. Mike, perfectly familiar with the premises, took out a window at the west end of the house. There was more than one window at that end. He took out the larger one, being that nearest to the river. He then entered the house, and undid the door, and opened it. Besides a lock, the door was also fastened by a stout wooden bar placed across it, with the ends inserted in holes in the masonry. Coming out of the house through the now opened door, he fastened the door of William Greenwood, the neighbouring cottager, by placing the wooden bar across the doorway, and fastening the latch to the bar with string. Probably they both entered Sammy's cottage. Mike mounted the stairs into the room where Old Sammy was sleeping alone. About a month before, the old man had bought a small oak box, in which he placed such of his papers and documents as were of value, and most of his money. The box was placed in a bucket which stood in one corner of his bedroom. Mike secured this bucket, with its contents. Three cotton pieces and four warps were also taken from the bedroom: the pieces were marked by William Greenwood. A cloth-coat, and a pair of shoes belonging to William Sutcliffe, which wanted soling, were also taken, and a new shirt of Sammy's.

But old men sleep lightly. Before these things were secured and got away, Sammy awoke. Sitting up in bed to listen, he heard footsteps in the house. He endeavoured to alarm his neighbour in the adjoining cottage, and called out "William! William! William!" Fearful of being disturbed or detected, Mike approached the bed and seized his old friend and companion by the throat with his terrible left hand. Gripping him as in a vice, he held him down; nor did he quit his grasp till the spark of life was extinguished.

William Greenwood was disturbed during the night. He fancied he heard a noise in Sammy's house, but could not be sure. He called out, but received no answer. He conjectured that the old man might be talking in his sleep; at any rate, he took no more notice of the matter, and fell asleep again. The wind was very strong, and roared terrible in the yew-tree. Probably the noise which he heard was Sammy's voice calling out "William" the third and last time. The silence which ensued was, as Mr. Hardy eloquently described it at York, "the silence of death."

I have a short document drawn up at Halifax for the satisfaction of William Sutcliffe, on the 17th or 18th of February, 1817, that he might possess some account of the manner of his uncle's last struggles, in which is recorded the substance of what Mike confessed on the subject at Halifax, February 17th. It is as follows: – "The further examination of William Sutcliffe, of Hawden Hole, in Heptonstall, who saith that on Monday, the 17th day of February, 1817, Michael Pickles, the prisoner, told this examinant that after he had entered the dwelling-house of his late uncle, Samuel Sutcliffe, and had go into the bedroom, the said Samuel Sutcliffe rose up on the bed and called out, 'William! William! William!' on which the said Michael Pickles seized the said Samuel Sutcliffe by the throat, and heard no more from him, except that he sobbed, as it was soon over with him, and he bore very little. And saith that the cause of his asking the question of the said Michael Pickles as to his uncle's death was to know what his said uncle said previous to his death, and if he suffered much."

Mike now descended the stairs, and greatly alarmed his companion by telling him he was afraid he had killed Sammy. Leaving the bucket outside the house, they made off to Northwell with their booty – the cotton pieces, the warps, the shoes, the cloth-coat, the shirt, and, above all, the oak box with its contents.

Having arrived at Northwell, Mike deposited the cotton pieces and warps in the hiding-place under the flag-stone. Joan took the shoes. The oak box they at once burnt to prevent detection, but preserved the contents. Mike told his wife he was afraid he had killed Sammy, and she began to cry. He also charged Joan to keep it a secret, even from his wife, for his revealing it would cause them both to be hanged. In dividing the money Joan contrived to take advantage of his more crafty companion; for he pocketed one note unknown to Mike. Mike's "Confession" says respecting the remaining notes – "John Greenwood took the guinea-note, and gave me the two Bank of England notes, and I gave him nine shillings and sixpence in silver, which made it equal – one pound ten shillings and sixpence each."

William Sutcliffe in his evidence at York said that on going from home on Monday, February 3rd, "he left his uncle four one-pound notes and some silver, to pay wages with in his absence. His uncle had also some notes of his own; among others, one of Mytholm Bank, which had been issued without the signature of Turner, Bent, and Co. It was No. 63. His attention had been called to this note on the 1st February (the preceeding Saturday); his uncle had brought it down-stairs in an old book: there were also in this book another pound-note and a guinea-note" – in all seven notes. William Sutcliffe on his return said that Sammy's three notes were pinned in a ready reckoner. Now, on examining the house the following morning, among some loose papers in the window down-stairs, there were found three one-pound notes which had escaped the notice of the robbers. These three which were left being added to the four which Mike and Joan took away, made seven notes. It would seem that Sammy had separated one of William's four notes from the remaining three; that this note he had placed in his box up-stairs with the three notes belonging to himself; and that thus his three notes and one of William's were taken away, while three of William's notes had been left in the pocket-book in the window down-stairs. The note which Joan appropriated to himself, unknown to Mike, was the unsigned Mytholm note. Had this note fallen into Mike's hands, he would probably have observed the danger arising from the circumstance, and destroyed the note; but the ignorant and unsuspecting Joan was not aware of the danger.

There was at this time a set of men in the Cragg valley who went by a bad name. In order to shift the suspicion of the murder and robbery from himself and Mike, Joan, on his way home to Bog-eggs, instead of crossing the valley at Foster Mill, travelled down towards Mytholmroyd, and crossing the Calder at Carr Bridge, threw down the papers and documents obtained from Sammy's box at Carr Green, hoping thereby to induce suspicion that some of the Cragg band were the robbers and murderers.

And now for the events of the following morning. During the week Sammy had paid some money for work to a man named James Greenwood, of Lobbmill; but a balance of four shillings was left unpaid. Before daylight on Friday morning James Greenwood presented himself at Sammy's door, having come for his four shillings. He was surprised to find the door wide open. This excited his fears that some mischief had taken place during the night. He knocked at William Greenwood's door, stated the suspicious circumstance, and desired him to come out. On attempting to do so, he found that the door would not open. James Greenwood then discovered (it was still dark) that the door was fastened by means of the wooden bar. It was now ascertained that Sammy's house had been entered by robbers through the window, and that he lay lifeless in his bed. His mouth was full of blood, and some had run out upon the bed-clothes. The empty bucket was found outside the door. William Greenwood, who had seen Sammy at half-past ten the night before in good health, looked for the cotton pieces which he had taken in the previous day, but they were gone. He observed one footstep leading to the window which had been removed. It was the mark of a bare foot.

There was great consternation in the neighbourhood as soon as the murder was known. Mr. Thomas Dineley, surgeon, of Hebden Bridge, was called in. He gave his opinion that the deceased died of strangulation. It is commonly said that he also pronounced Sammy to have been strangled by a left-handed person; but some persons very likely to know most of the facts have no remembrance of this circumstance.

The papers and documents were found at Carr Green early in the morning by Olive Heyhirst, who was going to fetch milk.

Several persons expressed to each other their suspicions that Old Mike was the criminal. A woman met him in Northwell Lane on Friday morning. He said, "Have you heard that Old Sammy's murdered?" She replied, "If he is, it's thee that's done it."

Mike afterwards confessed that the day after the murder he could neither eat, drink, nor sleep, and was always uneasy wherever he was. On Friday evening he went to Heptonstall to be shaved. He was in such a state of restless agitation that the barber had much difficulty in fulfilling his office, and when Mike was gone out, the barber said to some bystanders, "Yon's the man that's murdered Sammy."

William Sutcliffe, the nephew, returned from his journey on Saturday afternoon. A messenger had been sent to expedite his return; but he was not able to get back more than a couple of hours earlier than he would otherwise have done. He now privately made known to several neighbours, and among others to Mr. John Sutcliffe, of The Lee, that among the missing property there was an unsigned Mytholm note. It had been entered by Mr. Barker, the clerk to Turner, Bent, and Co., but was not signed by them. Having been pinned in the ready reckoner, it would show the marks of pin-holes. At that time several firms near Hebden Bridge issued private notes of various values. Messrs. Turner, Bent, and Co. issued both guinea and one-pound notes, printed in black ink. Messrs. Rawden of Callis Mill, issued both guinea-notes and five-shilling cards, printed in blue ink, and therefore called "blue-backs." Mr. John Sutcliffe, of the Lee, issued cards, value three shillings and sixpence, printed red. Mr. Edmondson issued seven-shilling notes. Mr. Richard Chatburn, of sprutts, issued three and sixpenny cards. Mr. Robert Sutcliffe, of New Shop, put out five-shilling notes. Silver was very scarce just then; the smooth shillings which had been current were being called in by Government, and stamped ones were being issued instead.

Monday, February 10th, Mike attended service at Birchcliffe Chapel. The minister, Mr. Hollinrake, during his sermon made some strong remarks about the murder. His text was Matthew xxiv., 43 – "But know this, that if the goodman of the house had known in what watch the thief would come, he would have watched, and would not have suffered his house to be broken up." This smote Mike's conscience so severely that he afterwards declared that, if any one had looked him earnestly in the face, he might have discovered that he was the man. An inquest was held at Heptonstall; and poor old Sammy's remains were interred at Heptonstall church. Standing outside the churchyard, at the east end, near the street, you may read his epitaph through the rails: – "In memory of Samuel Sutcliffe, of Hebden Hay, in Heptonstall, who died February 7, 1817, aged eighty-one years."

John Greenwood had a brother living at Luddenden, named William. John went to him, and gave the unsigned note into his hand. He then received the note back again from his brother. This farce was enacted between them to enable John to give an evasive answer to anyone who should make troublesome inquiries as to how he became possessed of the note. John now went to the house of Thomas Greenwood, of Birchcliffe, and completed the purchase of a clock from him, giving him in payment the unsigned note, with some other money. Another version of the story is that given by William Greenwood, the brother, at York, viz., that "John Greenwood came to his father's house on Tuesday, February 11th, and on going home, desired William to 'go agatards' with him; when he told him that he had bought a clock of Thomas Greenwood that came to forty-two shillings; that he would give him a note which the witness was to give to Thomas Greenwood on John's account, and say that he had lent it to John. This William did; but he then began to think that John had not come by the note in an honest manner."

A woman named Betty Wadsworth, having an illegitimate child, had been disowned by her relatives, and was now living "afore t' friend" at Rawholme with another William Greenwood, commonly known by the name of "Will o' t' shop." She possessed a chest of drawers, which, to raise money, she disposed of to Thomas Greenwood, of Birchcliffe, who in payment handed over to her the unsigned note on Tuesday, February 11th. The same evening she went to the shop of John Hoyle, of Woodend, to buy groceries, and offered the unsigned note in payment. Hoyle refused to receive it, seeing it was unsigned. She took it back to Rawholme. Wednesday morning, the 12th, she sent it up to Thomas Greenwood by Sarah, wife of "Will o' t' shop," complaining that he had paid her a note which was not genuine. Now this Thomas Greenwood[1] was a weaver for Mr. John Sutcliffe, of The Lee; and on the day before Tuesday he had received from Mr. John Sutcliffe, for wages, a Halifax Bank note. Not being able

---

[1]Greenwood is probably the most prevalent name in the neighbourhood. Out of 755 entries in a public register in the neighbourhood, the name Greenwood occurs 48 times, Helliwell 34, Sutcliffe 33, Cockcroft 18, Smith 18, Akroyd 15, Crabtree 15, Mitchell 14, Stansfield 13, Uttley 13, Horsfall 12, Midgley 12, Gibson 11, Taylor 11, Pickles 9, Fielden 9. Gill 9, &c. We may here remark on the prevalence of patronymic names, which sometimes are really useful, however inelegant, in a district where the same names recur so frequently. Thus "John o' Abbie's" and "Joan o' Jim's" were the ordinary names of two individuals who were each legally designated John Stansfield. By how many useful variations is the name John Sutcliffe represented! To strangers this practice is the more puzzling from the frequent use of abbreviations, such as Eam, Tham, Lol, Abbie, Jooas, Kit (or Katie), Joan, Tim, and Tum; for Edmund, Nathaniel, Lawrence, Abraham, Joseph, Catherine, John, Timothy, Thomas. There was formerly a "Jimmie, o' Jamie, o' James, o'th Jumps." "George o'my Gronny's" and "Will o' Nobody's" are bold specimens of what may be done by the principle in question carried out with a little licence. Not unfrequently, also, people are named from their residences, as "John up th' steps," and "Old Ann o' th' Hinging Royd." Bye-names also becone sometimes attached as if they were real family surnames. If it were not personal, many singular instances might be given. Persons are frequently unable, without some consideration, to recognise the legal names of their neighbours. Upon the hillside at Jumps, near Todmorden, I once asked a little girl who was her father. "Will o' th' Jumps," she replied. "And who's Will o' th' Jumps?" I again inquired. "He's Ailse o' th' Jumps, fellie," replied the girl; and I doubt whether she had any idea whatever of her legal surname.

to read, he was not aware whether the rejected note was that which he had received from William Greenwood, of Luddenden, or from Mr. John Sutcliffe. Doubting whether he should be able to get a good note from John or William Greenwood in exchange for it, he decided to try The Lee first, and hope for a successful issue of the experiment. He went immediately to The Lee, and found in the warehouse Mr. Richard Aked, who was learning the business with Mr. Sutcliffe. To him he gave the note, saying that Mr. Sutcliffe must have given him an unsigned note by mistake the day before. Mr. Aked took the note to Mr. Sutcliffe, who was breakfasting. He at once saw this note was the key to the discovery of Sammy's murderer. He sent for some constables, and meanwhile learned from Thomas Grenwood that the note had come from "Joan o' t' Bog-eggs." James Wilson, the constable, sizer, of Hebden Bridge Lanes, soon made his appearance, and with him three others – viz., George Hargreaves, John o' Paul's (Greenwood), and John Uttley, commonly called John Clerk, being the clerk of Heptonstall church. Mr. John Sutcliffe and Thomas Greenwood accompany the officers to Bog-eggs, and Joan is apprehended. He declares that the note was paid to him by his brother William. Joan is therefore set at liberty, and William is apprehended at Luddenden, and taken to Halifax in proper custody the same day. He is brought before Thomas Horton, Esq., J.P., at the justice-room, Copper Street. He refuses to give any account of the note, being afraid of criminating his brother, till Friday, February 14th. On that day William Greenwood confesses the hoax as to the passing of the note from Joan to him, and back again. The same day Joan is re-apprehended, and declares before Mr. Horton that he received the unsigned note from Old Mike. William Greenwood is set at liberty. Old Mike is looked for, but cannot be found, his wife stating that he is gone off seeking for work.

Sunday February 16th, Mike is apprehended at his brother's at Cowside, near Blackshaw Head. He is kept in custody at an inn in Heptonstall for the night. He declared to the Rev. J. Charnock, who visited him, "I am as innocent as you are; I am as innocent as a child unborn."

Monday morning, February 17th, Mike was taken to Halifax, before Justice Horton, with many other persons who had by this time been apprehended on suspicion. (Some had already been brought before Mr. Horton at Halifax. As many as sixteen or seventeen persons in all were taken up. Some of these confessed other crimes, being, however, unconnected with this murder, as of stealing meal and flour, and a gun from Handganroyd Mill, sheep-stealing, &c. I believe that one or two persons were convicted of sheep-stealing. The rest escaped, partly from the unwillingness of the parties robbed to prosecute.) Mike is confronted with Joan, and denies Joan's accusation. Joan contradicts himself by some blunder as to the day of the week and day in the month when he went to Old Mike's to borrow money. Hereupon Mike appears to be cleared, and is set at liberty. Joan's father comes to Joan, and entreats him, if he knows anything about the robbery, to confess it. At length he yields to this persuasion, and unreservedly confesses all about both the robbery and the murder. John

Uttley, the constable, is in court, and having a horse at the inn, he volunteers to pursue Old Mike on his way back to Heptonstall. He overtakes him in King's Cross Lane, walking quickly homewards, and eating "sweet parkin." Uttley calls out, "You must come back with me." Mike, off his guard, asks, "What! has he been telling something?" Uttley brings him quietly back to the magistrates' room. Mike no longer denies the crimes of murder and burglary. When he and Joan were confronted by each other there occurred such a scene of crimination and recrimination that it was found necessary to place Joan in the cell (or cellar) until the minutes of Joan's confession had been read over to Mike. After Mike had confessed many circumstances connected with the affair, the prisoners exchanged places, and the minutes of Mike's confession were read over to Joan. Both were now consigned to their cells.

Tuesday, February 18th, the prisoners were again before Mr. Horton, but nothing new was elicited. They were this day committed to York Castle. The same day James Wilson, the constable, searched Mike's house for the third time. His evidence at York is that "he found, concealed under a flag, under the bed, three fustian pieces and four warps, and some other articles, and above the fireplace a gun. The cotton pieces were identified by William Greenwood, Sammy's neighbour, who had taken them into the house of the deceased and marked them; the other articles were identified by William Sutcliffe."

The *Leeds Mercury* of Saturday, Feb. 22nd, says that on Wednesday, the 13th, the two prisoners passed through that town, strongly ironed, on their way to York Castle.

The trial took place at York Castle on Friday, March 14th, 1817. The prisoners were arraigned on an indictment of murdering Samuel Sutcliffe, and also on an indictment of burglary. Both admitted the burglary; both denied the murder. By the recommendation of the judge they pleaded "Not guilty" to both indictments. No fewer than 22 witnesses were taken to York, including all the individuals whose names have been given above; with Mr. William Sutcliffe, of Heptonstall, who made Sammy's writings; Mr. John Barker and Mr. Jas. Bent, of Mytholm, and Mr. Henry Sutcliffe, of Pendle Forest, &c. Mr. Hardy, in a very eloquent and perspicious opening, stated the facts of the case. The names of the witnesses whose evidence is given in the *Leeds Mercury* (Saturday, March 22, 1817), are William Sutcliffe, William Greenwood (the neighbouring cottager), Thomas Dyneley, Betty Wadsworth, John Hoyle, Sarah Greenwood, Thomas Greenwood, William Greenwood, of Luddenden, Thomas Horton Esq., Olive Heyhirst, John Thomas, of Midgley, and James Wilson. John Thomas "was a shoemaker, and received a pair of shoes from the prisoner, John Greenwood, on the 8th of February, which he delivered to the constable, and which, being produced in court, were identified by William Sutcliffe as the shoes which he had left in the house" when he went on his journey. The other witnesses gave evidence agreeing in most particulars with the facts stated above.

The remainder of the proceedings at York we give in the words of the *Leeds*

Mercury of Saturday, March 22nd, 1817. "The prisoners being called upon for their defence, Michael Pickles said – John Greenwood came to my house and said he was pinned, and asked me to go with him to Sammy's, of Hawden Hole, which I did, and he took the gun with him. When we got to the old man's house, we got in at the window, and we both went into the chamber where the old man was. He started up in bed when he heard us, and we both ran away, I never touched the man.

"John Greenwood said – The robbery was proposed by Michael Pickles, for I did not know that there was such a house – I had never been there in my life. When we got to the house, Pickles went in at the window, but I stayed at the outside. I was never in the biggin' at all, but stood at the shop-end all the time, and Pickles brought out all the goods to me that he had taken out of the biggin.' He then told me that he had taken the old man by the neck, and was afraid he had killed him; and I said, 'Surely thou hast not hurt the old man?' Michael Pickles gave me the gun to carry, but I tied my handkerchief in two knots over the lock, for fear I should do some mischief with it. When we got back to Pickles' house, he told his wife he was afraid he had killed the old man; and his wife began to cry. Pickles charged me that I should keep it a secret from everyone, even from my wife, for if I told I should be hanged.

"Three witnesses were called. Two of them spoke favourably of the character of John Greenwood. The third stated that he had a wife and three children, but that he did not know much about his character.

"His Lordship, in his charge to the jury, stated that where two or more persons were jointly engaged in the commission of any burglary or other felonious act, and one of the party killed a person in furtherance of their common object, every one of the party would in law be guilty of the crime of murder. And it was necessary, continued his Lordship, for the safety of society, that it should be so, that associations in guilt might be as much as possible prevented. If indeed an individual of any such party should put a person to death to gratify his own private revenge, and not for the furtherance of their common object, in that case he alone would be answerable for the murder. His Lordship explained that this furtherance comprises all acts done to prevent or overpower resistance and to prevent discovery. Applying this rule to the case before them, his Lordship said that if the jury were satisfied that both the prisoners had gone to the house of the deceased for the purpose of committing a robbery, and that one of them, to prevent any alarm or discovery, had by violence occasioned the death of the deceased, it would be murder in them both, though one of the prisoners should not have been within the house at the time, and should have given no consent to the murderous deed, or even have known of its being committed. That a burglary had been committed in the house was too evident to admit of a doubt. It also appears from all the circumstances of the case that the death of Samuel Sutcliffe had been produced by strangulation, and it was admitted by Pickles that he had seized him by the throat, and that when he quitted his grasp he had reason to suppose he was dead. If the jury were satisfied of these facts, and further thought that Michael Pickles had committed this violence, not from any personal enmity (of which there was not the least proof), but with a view to prevent alarm and secure the accomplishment of their design of robbing the house, it would be the duty of the jury to find both the prisoners guilty.

"The jury turned round in the box for a moment, and then pronounced against both prisoners the fatal verdict of 'Guilty.' His Lordship proceeded, after a most solemn and affecting address, to pass the sentence of the law, which was, that they were both of them to be hung by the neck on Monday until they were dead, and that their bodies should be delivered to the surgeons for dissection.

"John Greenwood fell on his knees, begging for mercy, and protesting his innocence of the murder.

"It is understood that since his conviction he has acknowledged to the chaplain that he was in the house, and stood at the foot of the steps with the gun.

"The sentence of the law was carried into execution on Monday, March 17th, a few minutes after eleven o'clock, and their bodies, after being suspended the usual time, were delivered to the surgeons for dissection. The body of Pickles has been sent to the Dispensary at Halifax."

MR. WIKES, OF LEASEHOLME.[1]

THE living of Leaseholme, in the North Riding of Yorkshire, was held by three successive generations of the Wikeses for upwards of a century; all of whom were men of literary talents, popular preachers, great oddities – but much given to the bottle. The first of the Wikes family who held the living was a gentleman who had been captain in the army in the reign of Charles I., and had fought for the unfortunate monarch throughout the civil war. In one of the battles he received a wound in his leg, which incapacitated him from further active service, and the death of the king and the supremacy of Cromwell prevented him from looking to Government for promotion.

But on the Restoration Mr. Wikes cast about for some berth in which he might spend his declining years in ease and comfort. The living of Leaseholme fell vacant, and he applied for it, remembering how his old friend the sea-captain, Lyons, had obtained the bishopric of York from Queen Elizabeth.

Captain Wikes was ordained by the Archbishop of York, and given the living he solicited, King Charles II being glad to reward an old soldier of his father, who had shared his misfortunes, thus economically to himself.

Mr. Wikes also held the incumbency of Ellerburn, near Leaseholme, and took service in the morning at Leaseholme, and in the afternoon at Ellerburn, or *vice versa*.

One year, when the 30th of January fell on a Sunday, Mr. Wikes marched off to Ellerburn for morning service, with a pathetic sermon on the martyrdom of his royal master in his pocket; but on his arrival at the place he found the clerk and sexton near the churchyard, with a short pole in their hands, watching a domestic quarrel that was going forward on the opposite side of the beck that flows through the village. The parson asked why the church was empty and his subordinates were not in their places. The clerk pointed accross the beck, and bade Parson Wikes "look and see a woman combing her husband's head with a three-legged stool."

Mr. Wikes at once plunged over the brook, and striking the husband with the fist, tore the furious pair asunder, shouting, "Be quiet, you brute!" to the husband, and "Hold your tongue, you vixen!" to the woman. Both fell on him, and he had hard work in defending himself from husband and wife. In the fray that ensued the yells of the parson – "Peace, you monster! Have done,

[1] "Anecdotes and Manners of a few Ancient and Modern Oddities." York, 1806.

termagant! Hands off, you coward! Retire, virago!'' – were mingled with the abuse and blows of the disputants, till the absurdity of the whole scene burst upon them all, as the crowd of delighted parishioners and neighbours gathered in a circle about them, and they fell back laughing, and shook hands all round.

But matters did not end here. When husband and wife disagree, and a third party interferes, according to local custom, all three are doomed to ''ride the stang,'' whilst the people shout and caper around the victims, chanting, as they beat frying-pans and blow horns—

> ''Rub-a-dub, dub-a-dub, ran-a-tan-tang,
> It's neither what you say nor I say, but I ride the stang.''

The parishioners insisted on the immemorial custom being complied with, and Parson Wikes was made to sit astride on the short pole the clerk and sexton had prepared; two others were provided for the belligerent husband and wife; and the whole village prepared to march in procession with them. But though the parson sat complacently on his pole, the husband and wife refused to submit to the ignominious custom, and he armed himself with the pitch-fork, she with the poker, and begun to defend themselves against the villagers. Parson Wikes was carried to the scene of conflict, and the clerk and sexton, in their eagerness to join in the struggle, dropped him into the beck. Then the villagers rushed upon him, swearing that he was shirking his duty of riding the stang, and he had to stand up to his middle in the water, and fight them off. Armed with the stick, which he whirled about him in single-stick fashion, he rattled their heads and arms with it to such good purpose that he was able to beat a retreat into the church, where he rapidly vested himself in his surplice, and placed the sanctity of the place and garb between him and his opponents.

The crowd now poured into the church, and Parson Wikes proceeded with the service, leaving a trail of water up and down the chancel as he paced to the alter and thence to the pulpit. Having prefaced his sermon with an announcement that he took in good part the disorderly conduct and undignified treatment he had met with, he preached them a moving sermon on the merits of Charles the Martyr, and the ingratitude of the people of England to such a virtuous monarch, and wound up with – ''Let those who feel the consequence of such a misfortune deplore with me upon this melancholy oaccasion; but if there be any among you (and I make no doubt there are) who may have secretly wished for this event, they have now got their desire, and may the devil do them good with it.'' After which he made the best of his way home to his rectory, and endeavoured to counteract the effects of his dipping by moistening his clay within with hot punch.

THE REV. MR. CARTER,

PARSON PUBLICAN.

I CANNOT do better than extract verbatim the following account from a curious book entitled "Anecdotes and Manners of a Few Ancient and Modern Oddities, interspersed with Deductive Inferences and Occasional Observations, tending to reclaim some Interlocutory Foibles which often occur in the Common Intercourses of Society." York, 1806:—

"The Rev. Mr. Carter, when curate of Lastingham, had a very large family, with only a small income to support them, and therefore often had recourse to many innocent alternatives to augment it; and as the best of men have their enemies – too often more than the worst – he was represented to the archdeacon by an invidious neighbour as a very disorderly character, particularly by keeping a public-house, with the consequences resulting from it.

"The archdeacon was a very humane, worthy, good man, who had imbibed the principles not only of a parson, but of a divine, and therefore treated such calumniating insinuations against his subordinate brethren with that contempt which would accrue to the satisfaction and advantage of such as listen to a set of sycophantic tattlers culled from the refuse of society. Besides, the improbability of a malevolent story generally renders it more current by increasing the scandal; and the world, like the pious S. Austin, believes some things because they are impossible. However, he considered that not only the conduct of the inferior clergy claimed his attention, but also to have some idea how far their subsistence was compatible with the sanctity of their functions; therefore, at the ensuing visitation, when the business of the day was over, he, in a very delicate and candid manner, interrogated Mr. Carter as to his means of supporting so numerous a family – ever thinking of this admirable hint to charity, that the more a person wants, the less will do him good – which was answered, as related to me by one well acquainted with the parties, in nearly the following words:—

"'I have a wife and thirteen children, and with a stipend of £20 per annum, increased only by a few trifling surplice fees. I will not impose upon your understanding by attempting to advance any argument to show the impossibility of us all being supported from my church preferment. But I am fortunate enough to live in a neighbourhood where there are many rivulets which abound with fish, and being particularly partial to angling, I am frequently so successful as to catch more than my family can consume while good, of which I make presents to the neighbouring gentry, all of whom are so generously grateful as to requite me with something else of seldom less value than two or three-fold. This is not at all. My wife keeps a public-house, and as my parish is so wide that some of my parishioners have to come from ten to fifteen miles to church, you will readily allow that some refreshment before they return must occasionally be necessary, and when can they have it more properly than when their journey is half performed? Now, sir, from your general knowledge of the world, I make no doubt but you are well assured that the most general topics in conversation at public-houses are politics and religion, with which ninety-nine out of one hundred of those who participate in the general clamour are totally unacquainted; and that perpetually ringing in the ears of a pastor who has the welfare and happiness of his flock at heart, must be no small mortification. To divert their attention from these foibles over their cups, I take down my violin and play them a few tunes, which gives me an opportunity of seeing that they get no more liquor than necessary for refreshment; and if the young people propose a dance, I seldom answer in the negative; nevertheless, when I announce time for return, they are ever ready to obey my commands, and generally with the donation of a sixpence they shake hands with my children, and bid God bless them. Thus my parishioners enjoy a triple advantage, being instructed, fed, and amused at the same time. Moreover, this method of spending their Sundays is so congenial with their inclinations, that they are imperceptibly led along the paths of piety and morality; whereas, in all probability, the most exalted discourses, followed with no variety but heavenly contemplations, would pass like the sounds of harmony over an ear incapable of discerning the distinction of sounds. It is this true sense of religion that has rendered my whole life so remarkably cheerful as it has been, to the great offence of superstitious and enthusiastic religionists. For why should priests be always grave? Is it so sad to be a parson? Cheerfulness, even gaiety, is consonant with every species of virtue and practice of religion, and I think it inconsistent only with impiety and vice. The ways of heaven are pleasantness. Let "O be joyful" be the Christian's psalm, and leave to the sad Indian to incant the devil with tears and screeches. Now, to corroborate my remarks upon cheerfulness as conductive to contemtment, I will by leave solicit so much of your indulgence as to hear the following extract from the works of an eminent divine of the Established Church: – The Thirty-Nine Articles are incomplete without a fortieth precept enjoining cheerfulness; or you may let the number stand as it does at present, provided you expunge the thirteenth article, and place that heavenly maxim in the room of it. Might not the Archbishop of Cashel have been a sound divine though he added the arch-stanza about Broglio to the old Irish ballad in praise of Moll Roe? Or did the Bishop (not the Earl) of Rochester's poems on the man-like properties of a lady's fan ever impeach his orthodoxy in the least?'

"Here the archdeacon very candidly acknowledged the propriety of Mr. Carter's arguments in defence of his conduct, and complimented him on his discernment in using the most convenient vehicle for instruction; observing that, although he might deviate a little from the plans generally advised for the accomplishment of that purpose, yet it bore no less authority than the celebrated Dr. Young who wrote a play ('The Brothers') for the propagation of the Gospel, the profits of which he consecrated to the Society for Propagating the Gospel in Foreign Parts."

JOB SENIOR,

THE HERMIT OF RUMBOLD'S MOOR.[1]

Job's mother was Ann Senior of Beckfoot, near Ilkley; he was an illegitimate child. His father, a man named Hacksworth, left him a little money when he died. Job grew up a spruce, active young man, very strong, and not devoid of good looks. He was employed as a labourer by the farmers round Ilkley; but afterwards went to live at Whitkirk, near Leeds. He there fell into disorderly ways, drank, and became careless in his dress and dirty in his habits. Yet he was a good workman, and when he returned to Ilkley he was readily engaged by the farmers to plough, mow, and reap for them. He was a good fence-waller, and being a man of prodigious strength, is said to have used very hard stones for the purpose, and when days were short he was frequently seen walling by candlelight. Some of his walls are still pointed out, and the large stones he lifted elicit surprise. In winter he employed himself in wool-combing at a place called The Castle, near Ilkley. It is related of him that he once laid himself down on the combing-shed floor, and that some of his fellow-workmen chalked out his figure on the floor. By this outline he used to cut his shirts, the material being coarse harden, sewed with strong hemp-string.

Job was at one time an hostler in the village, and a person who knew him well at the time says that at this period his dissipated habits made him the subject of many a practical joke.

He was afterwards employed by the farmers at Burley Woodhead; but as he became old and infirm, and troubled with rheumatism, he could not work as formerly, but did what he could, making no stipulations for wages, but asking only for his board, and that his employers should pay him whatever extra they thought his labour entitled him to receive.

About this time he became acquainted with a widow named Mary Barret, who lived in a cottage near Coldstone Beck, on the edge of Rumbold's Moor. The widow had a little garden and a paddock which, together with the cottage, had been left her by her husband, who had taken the land from the common and built the cottage on it. Job thought if he could secure the hand of the widow the house and land would be his for life. So one day he paid her a visit.

"The Hermit of Rumbold's Moor." Bingley: Harrison (n.d.)

"I'll tell ye what I've been thinking," said Job Senior.

"What hast a' been thinking on then, Job? Out wi' it, lad," said the widow.

"Well, I've been thinking thou'st getting ou'd, and thou lives all by thy sen i' this house. And I'm a young man" – (he was about sixty) – – "and I lives all by my sen by yond crag. Why should not thou and me make it agreeable to live together?"

"Dost a' mean that I'm to take thee as a lodger?" asked Mary Barret.

"Nay, nay, lass!" answered Job; "I mean we'd better goa to t' kirk together and be wed."

"I reckon I'm ower ou'd for that," said the widow. She was in her eightieth year.

"I doan't know if tha be ou'd," said Job; "but I knows vary weel thou'rt bonny."

No woman's heart, not even in her eightieth year, is proof against flattery, and the fair Mary blushed and yielded to the blooming Job, and married they were.

"It's an easy gotten penny by the light o' the moon," said Job, looking over his domain.

Mrs. Senior did not long survive her second marriage. She had a long sickness, and Job was kind to her in it. "It's cou'd, Job," she said to her husband one evening when he returned from his work on the moor. "It's cou'd i' this bed, and I cannot feel t' warmth o' t' fire."

"Thou shalt be warm, ou'd lass, if I can fashion it," said Job. "But as I cannot bring t' fire nigher thee, I mun bring thee nigher to t' fire." So he pulled up a couple of flags in the floor besides the hearth, dug a pit, and made the old woman's bed in this premature grave, so that she could be close to the fire and comfortable, and if she wanted a cup of tea, could put out her hand and take the pot from the hearth.

"Eh, Job!" said old Mary another day, "I think I'd like summut good to eat afore I dies."

"Ah!" answered her husband; "then I'll get thee a rare good morsel, that'll set thee up on thy legs again, ou'd lass."

So he bought a pound of bacon, roasted it, caught the melted fat in a large iron spoon, and ladled it down his wife's throat.

"It's rare good now, isn't it!" exclaimed the husband, as the old woman gulped it down. "Open the trap and I'll teem (pour) down some more."

The old woman lay back in her hole and groaned. "I'm boun' to die!" she said.

"Nay, lass! take another spoonful first."

But the poor creature was dead. Job looked at her disconsolately for a minute, and whilst doing so the fat of the frying bacon fell into the fire and blazed up. "Eh! but I mustn't waste the fat," said Job. "If t' ou'd lass cannot take it, why, I mun eat it myself. Ah! it's varry good; but it's hot. I reckon 't were too hot for her ou'd insides."

Job now thought that the house, garden, and paddock were his own; but he was mistaken. The family of Barret, the first husband of Mary, claimed it and took possession of the field. Job clung desperately to the cottage and the potato-garth. One evening when he returned from his work he found that the cottage had been pulled to pieces. He had hidden some money in the walls, and this was either lost or stolen. His rage and disappointment completely disturbed his brain, and from that time forward he lived in a miserable hovel he erected for himself out of the ruins of the house, in idleness and squalor.

His hut was like a dog-kennel; to enter it he was obliged to creep on hands and knees. Within it was only large enough for him to lie down in and turn himself about: it was thatched, and provided with a rude door, but no window. The garden had contained fruit trees; but these he stubbed up, and instead planted the whole garth with potatoes. He made large, unsightly ridges, and put in a great quantity of seed, always for the following year when his gathered his crop in autumn. In one corner of his garth was a peat fire where he roasted his potatoes. His custom was, when eating, to sit with one leg on each side of the fire of peat, his little bag of oatmeal before him; then with his staff he poked the potatoes out of the embers, peeled them with his dirty fingers, rolled them in his meal bag, and then ate them. He always drank his water warm.

"Do you drink your water warm, Job!" asked a visitor.

"Yes," replied the hermit, "I reckon I does."

"And your butter-milk too?"

"Aye, aye. Sithere." And he poked two stone bottles out from the embers. "I do it to clear my voice," said the hermit. "Now thou shalt hear my four voices." He then got up, set his face to the crag, and began a wonderful performance of four voices – treble, alto, tenor, and bass. He said he had picked up his "four voices" by listening to the choir in Leeds parish church. He usually sang sacred hymns, such as "While shepherds watched their flocks by night," "Christians, awake," and the Old Hundredth. He went about the country in winter, singing in four parts for money, and his performance was sufficiently remarkable for him to be brought to perform in public at the theatre at Leeds, and in the Headingly Gardens and the Woolsorters' Gardens at Bradford, where he stayed for weeks at a time. He would sleep in any outbuilding or blacksmith's shop; indeed, he was so dirty that few people would like to have given him a bed in their houses.

He used to walk leaning on two rough sticks, wearing a pair of heavy wooden clogs on his feet, stuffed with hay, his legs bandaged with straw. His coat was of many colours and much patched; his trousers were to match. He wore no braces, but kept his trousers in position with a hempen belt, part of an old horse-girth, which he buckled round his body. A bag on his back was fastened at the front to his belt. His head was adorned with a hat of the most antique shape, without a brim, and stitched together with hemp-string.

The condition of his skin, which had not seen water for years, need not be described. His hair, once jetty black, now hung in heavy clotted locks on his shoulders. His eyebrows were black and prominent; his eyes low-set and watery. He wore a coarse beard, grizzled with age, and very dirty. From his hat depended a tobacco-pipe, hung by a string.

"Never," he would say to his visitors, "never take to nowt, but whenever you can get a penny, felt (hide) it, and let nobody know about it, and then they cannot get it from you. Get all the brass ye can, and as soon as ye can buy a bit o' grund like this o' mine, ye see, set it with potatoes, and it'll keep ye. There'll be a peck or two spare; ye can sell them, and so ha' brass. Are ye married?" said the hermit to a young man who went to see him.

"No," answered the visitor.

"Then ye are right there, young chap. Keep so. If ye get a wife, ye'll see shoo'll be coming on wi' a family, and then that'll take all your brass. I' th' first place, ye'll want a house and furniture, and then there'll be rent and taxes, and your wife'll be always wanting summat for hersen or the bairns. And besides, just look how more flour ye'll want, and sugar, and soap, and candles. And look how mony more potatoes ye'll want for them all to eat. Eh! but they're the animals 'at eats brass. They say that maggots eats cheese, and weevils eats clothes, and mice eats corn; but wife and bairns eats brass, and it's t' brass as gets cheese, and clothes, and corn. Nay, lad! have nowt to do wi' them soort o' cattle. And then – if th' wife takes to bonnets and gowns, ye're ruined directly. Nay, nay, grund is better nor a wife, and potatoes nor bairns. If ye want to save your brass and snap up a bit o' grund, ye munna be married."

Job's end came as he was on one of his single rounds. It Is thought that some youngsters drugged his drink, in prank, at Silsden, and the consequences were a violent attack of English cholera. He got back to Ilkley, and crept into a barn belonging to the White Sheaf Inn; but the landlord seeing that his end was near, sent for the parish authorities, and he was moved to the Carlton workhouse, as he belonged to Burley. He died in the course of a few days, at the age of seventy-seven, and was buried in Burley churchyard, near Otley.

NANCY NICHOLSON,

THE TERMAGANT.

Mrs. NANCY NICHOLSON[1] was born at Drax, in the county of York, on the 3rd day of May, 1785, and was the only child of the Rev. John Jackson, vicar of Drax, by his second wife. Mr. Jackson had a son by a former marriage, but he was taken by his mother's relatives into Cumberland; consequently the daughter, Nancy, was the only child at home, and from her infancy was indulged to a fault, and suffered to grow up without restraint, so that she soon became a terror to the other children in the school of which her father was master.[2]

It is curious that the child of a schoolmaster should have been suffered to grow to womanhood almost wholly without education; but such was the case. The following extract from a letter written by her when aged sixty-four shows how miserably her education had been neglected: – "Dear Mrs. Wilson, – Your letter just came in time as I whas thinking of letting my land but if John Harrison will come and we can a gree I ceep it on if not I shall let it Mr. Totton of Howden whants it and Taylors of Asselby also I Ceep all land and Hosses while I see him pray send him word to Come this week as I must have my Patays up and also my stakes wants thrashing."

Having naturally a certain amount of shrewdness, it was mistaken for talent, and low cunning for genius. Being indulged in every way, her headstrong will became intolerant of the smallest restraint. She played with the boys of the school, and acquired from them the coarsest language, and throughout her life never learned, indeed never attempted, to control her tongue.

When Miss Jackson was about twenty years old, the Rev. John Nicholson, a young man from Cumberland, came to Drax to assist Mr. Jackson in his school. He was at that time a well-disposed, gentlemanly young fellow, who gave promise of being a scholar and of use in his generation. But Miss Jackson, who was not without charms of person, was the ill-omened star that was to blight his life. Living in the house of her father, he was brought in daily contact with her, and she exerted some sort of fascination upon him. If two young

[1] "The Life of Mrs Nancy Nicholson, who died August 6th, 1854." Howden : W. Small. 1855.

[2] The Free Grammar School at Drax, where twelve boys are boarded and educated from a fund left for the purpose.

people are brought much together, they are sure to form an attachment, and it was so in this case. Nancy concealed her evil disposition from the usher, and laid herself out to catch him.

Mr. Nicholson could not be blind to the fact that Miss Jackson was entitled to property on the death of her parents, and it is probable enough that to a needy young clergyman without interest, the chance of making himself master of a competence may have had more to do with his paying his addresses to Miss Jackson than love.

In the year 1810 Mr. Jackson died, and perhaps this event decided Mr. Nicholson to offer his hand to Nancy. He was at once accepted, and the interest of her friends secured for him immediately the vacant situation of master of the Grammar School. Shortly after the marriage he also became vicar of Drax.

Mr. and Mrs. Nicholson were married at Drax Church in October, 1811, and she then became undisputed mistress of the establishment. Her harsh and tyrannical disposition had now free scope to develop, and the first to feel it was the mother who had encouraged her as a child. The widow was soon obliged to leave the house, where her daughter made it impossible for her to live in comfort and tranquillity. The servants would not stay; no fresh ones could be induced to enter the house under such a mistress. She was therefore obliged to do all the work of the school-house herself, making the unhappy boarders help her in cleaning the house and in washing clothes. The poor boys were scantily fed, and otherwise miserably provided for.

Four gentlemen, including Lord Downe, were trustees of the Grammar School at Drax, and made visits of inspection regularly every quarter. Nancy was always prepared for these occasions. She had a clean cloth on the table, a plentiful dinner provided, and a dumpling set before each boy. But she took care to impress on each boarder that the one who left the largest amount of dumpling on his plate would receive a reward, and he should receive a hiding who emptied his plate. "And," said Mrs. Nicholson, "let any boy beware how he looks sad or dissatisfied."

When these quarterly visits took place in the cold weather, she had a large fire lighted in the school-room, round which she assembled the boys, and when the trustees came in, she would address them with – "Well, gentlemen, and you, my lord, you see how saucy these boys are; scarce one of them has eaten his dumpling. And capital dumplings they are, my lord and gentlemen!"

When Mr. and Mrs. Nicholson had been married about three years they took an orphan niece of Mr. Nicholson's from Cumberland to provide for, and to this child for several years she behaved with the greatest cruelty, until at length Mrs. Nicholson's mother took compassion on the child, and removed it to her own house. However, when Mrs. Nicholson considered her niece capable of working, she insisted on her return, making her do the work of a servant, and subjecting her to the harshest treatment. The work was heavy, as she kept two or three cows, besides pigs and poultry.

The schoolboys were compelled to collect her eggs, and she caused them to rob the neighbours to obtain a greater number. These depredations were not unknown to the neighbours, but they good-naturedly excused the boys, as they knew they were urged to them by Mrs. Nicholson. She gave the boys a penny a score for all the eggs they could bring. She would then say, "Now, boys, I have such nice apples; I will give you a good pennyworth of apples for your penny; do have a pennyworth." The boys durst not object, and bought the apples. But still she was not satisfied, but would say, "Come, I will play you a game at push-pin for your apples, and I daresay you will win." However, as may be supposed, they never were suffered to win, so that she obtained eggs, penny, apples, and pins also. She committed various other depredations on the property of her neighbours, such as taking coals, corn, goslings – and, in short, anything that came within her reach. One Sunday morning, while the neighbours were at church, she made some of the boys assist her in stealing a hen and fourteen chickens. These she confined in a brick oven till the following morning, when she took them to Selby and disposed of them in the market.

For many years she regularly attended Selby market with her butter, which more than once was seized and taken from her for being light weight. She employed the boys in collecting rags, old iron, &c., all of which she took to Selby, because she could obtain a better price there than at home. It was in vain that Mr. Nicholson remonstrated with her on the disgrace her conduct brought upon him; she only replied in abusive language.

On Sunday morning she was always remarkably late in her attendance at church, generally entering in the middle of the service, and her appearance was like anything but that which became a vicar's wife, and formed a strange contrast to that of her husband, who retained his care to appear like a gentlemen, in clean and well-brushed clothes, and with scrupulously white cravat.

Nancy was neither clean nor well-dressed. For many years she would not afford herself a new bonnet, until at length her mother, utterly ashamed of her appearance, bought one for her. But Mrs. Jackson made her give up the old bonnet before she received the new one, being convinced, if she had the chance, that Nancy would put the new one away and continue to wear the old one.

Mr. and Mrs. Nicholson continued in the school-house several years, during which time they amassed a considerable sum of money, with which they bought lots of property in the parish, Mrs. Nicholson always contriving to have her name inserted in the deeds as well as Mr. Nicholson's, so that he could not deprive her of her life-interest. One field which they purchased at Carlton she had conveyed to her own use and disposal. This caused great dissension between them when discovered by Mr. Nicholson.

At length the trustees were obliged to interfere in behalf of the school. They did so with the utmost reluctance. All respected and pitied Mr. Nicholson, who was a good Christian and a gentleman, and was prepared to discharge his duty conscientiously. But it was impossible for him to control his wife, and make her treat the boarders with ordinary humanity. She was a genuine Mrs. Squeers; but he was a very different sort of person to the Yorkshire school-master of "Nicholas Nickleby."

The trustees were obliged to insist on an investigation. It was conducted with the greatest consideration for the feelings of Mr. Nicholson; but the investigation ended in the school being taken from him.

"Oh, Nancy, Nancy!" Mr. Nicholson would repeat, "you have disgraced me terribly!"

The humiliations he was obliged to undergo broke his spirit, and his self-respect, which had battled against adverse circumstances, gradually gave way. She used the most insulting language to him, not only in private, but in public, making the most odious insinuations, and bringing the scarlet spot of shame to his cheek. The unfortunate man was made to drink to the dregs the cup of degradation.

At last, maddened beyond self-control, he beat her with his horse-whip. A friend, whose house was situated a mile from that of the Nicholson's has told me that his father has often heard at that distance the screams of rage uttered by Nancy when in a passion with her husband. Their quarrels became the gossip and scandal of Drax. Mr. Nicholson, at last, driven of an evening from his home, would visit farmers, or sometimes the public-house, and forget his humiliation in the society of his inferiors. On these occasions he sometimes took too much.

When they lost the school-house the Nicholsons built a new house for themselves on some ground they had purchased at a place called Newland, near Drax, where Mrs. Nicholson had full opportunity for keeping cows, pigs, and poultry, her favourite occupation. But having no family, she would not be at the expense of a servant, and soon gave herself up to sloth and dirt, both in her person and house.

She would rarely admit any visitors, and if Mr. Nicholson occasionally ventured to invite a friend, she would either offend the guest at the time (unless she saw her way to gaining some advantage by him), or revenge herself on Mr. Nicholson after his departure. And if Mr. Nicholson absented himself from the house without her consent, she always upbraided him on his return with the vilest language, attributing to his neighbours or tenants to evil motives.

The following extract from the correspondence of a young lady from Cumberland, a cousin of Mrs. Nicholson's, who was staying a few months at Drax in the year 1837, gives a lively picture of her mode of life at that period:—

"One evening after my tea my sister and I proposed, as we frequently did, to walk out as far as Newland, to see Mr. and Mrs. Nicholson. It was a delightful evening, and a pleasant walk we had. Chatting over bygone times and talking about our future prospects, we soon arrived at the little gate, through which we entered the back grounds belonging to the house, and passed on into the kitchen, where we found Mr. and Mrs. Nicholson seated by the little window which looks out upon the road. As soon as we had got seated and the usual salutations were over, Mrs. Nicholson (who, bye-the-bye, I must confess, however little to my credit, was my cousin) began with saying, 'Well, Miss H——n, there is going to be a confirmation at Selby to-morrow, and Mr. Nicholson will have to go with the young people; what do you say, will you go with him? You have never been at Selby, and it will be a nice opportunity.' 'I certainly would like it very much,' I replied, 'if you are going also. But how are we to go?' 'By Langrick Ferry,' said Mr. Nicholson. 'We must be up there by nine o'clock and meet the packet. You can be up by that time?' 'And who do you think is going to pay a shilling a-piece to go by the packet? Not I, nor you either,' said Mrs. Nicholson, in an angry tone. 'And as for Mary Anne, she has more sense than to waste her money in that way.' I replied by saying, 'Oh, a shilling is not much; and as there is no other conveyance by which we can get, we have no alternative, as we cannot possibly walk it.' – 'No,' said she, 'we cannot walk it, but there is a man who has a cart, and I am sure if we could get a dozen to go he would take us at threepence a-piece. There's plenty of lasses and lads who are going to be confirmed would be glad of the chance. Why, you see, we should make three ourselves, and Mr. Nicholson can speak to some of them. The man can put the shelvings on, and we'll go rarely.' 'Who do you mean will go?' said the clergyman. 'Do you think that I will go to Selby in a waggon, or Miss H——n either? No, you shall not bring me to that. You have made me give up my horse and gig long since; but, go as you will yourself, I and Miss H – n will take the packet.' At this his amiable wife got into such a rage, and went on at such a rate, that to make matters up I was glad to give my consent to go with her in the waggon, and Mr. Nicholson said he would ask one of the churchwardens to take him in his gig. This pacified her, and as we rose to take our departure, she said she would see the man about the cart, and I was to mind and be ready at nine o'clock, when they would call for me with it. However, I could not bear the idea of the neighbours around seeing a great waggon filled with country rustics stopping at our front door for me to go with them, so I told her I would come to their house by that time, and we would go direct from there. But she was afraid I wanted to get off going, and it was not without extorting a faithful promise from me that I would not disappoint her that I succeeded in obtaining consent at last.

"The morning came, chill and gloomy, and I rose, hoping it was going to rain, that I might make that an excuse for not going. So I made myself ready, and taking an umbrella, set off for Newland. I had proceeded as far as a turn there is in the road, when I heard such a shouting and hurrahing that I stopped to see from whence it proceeded. I had not long to look, for turning the corner, the wagon appeared in sight, with about fourteen or fifteen young people in it of both sexes, and Mrs. Nicholson in the centre, laughing and shouting as loud as the rest. She soon saw me, and bawled out, 'Oh, yonder is Miss H——n coming! Stop the cart! – Stop the cart!' By this time I had come up to them, but was trembling with shame at the idea of going with them, and I felt vexed at the predicament I was in. At length I said, 'I think the cart is so full there is no room for me, as the rain is already falling, I would rather not go. So do not disturb yourselves, for I will walk back as quick as possible.' 'Oh, it's not going to be much rain, and you shall come,' replied Mrs. Nicholson; 'so make room for her, lasses. There, Betty, you can sit on the edge of the shelves, and Polly can take your place. Now, Miss H——n, jump in, and let us be off.' It was in vain that I made every excuse I could think of. She appealed to them all, and they joined her, until I was forced to consent, and off we drove. I felt thankful that it was raining a little as we passed through the village, so I put up my umbrella to screen myself from view, pretending that my clothes would get wet and spoiled.

"On we went, and after we had got through Drax the young people and she indulged themselves in conversation such as I had never heard before, and strove in vain to get me to join them, or laugh at their low and obscene discourse. Mrs. Nicholson at length said, 'Come, lasses can't you raise a song? We'll get her to laugh just now, I warrant us.' They then inquired of her what they must sing, and she told them three or four songs, all of which they sang with all their might, and she every now and then asking me how I liked it. At last she said, 'Give us some sea songs; she comes from a seaport town, and will maybe like them better.' So, first one and then another was sung, but with no better success. At length I saw a gig coming fast after us, and begged them to give over till it got past. They all looked, and said it was Mr. Nicholson. 'Oh, sing away! Don't give over. Let them see how we are enjoying ourselves. Don't stop for him,' said Mrs. Nicholson. 'Come, go on – go on! – 'No,' replied some of the young people, 'we won't sing while Mr. Nicholson is going past. Wait awhile.'

"Oh, how glad was I that they kept quiet while the gig was passing, although she was urging them to sing all the time.

"Many other carriages passed us on the road, and they sang and shouted loudly without regarding them; but I did not feel so mortified as I should have done had I not been a stranger whom they could not know.

"At length we arrived at Selby, and I begged that I might be allowed to get out at the entrance to the town. But no. She declared I should not till we arrived at the inn where the cart would put up; and I was obliged to submit. On reaching the inn many were the people that stood looking at us as we alighted. I got out almost the first, and Mrs. Nicholson was the last. I had then an opportunity of seeing her costume in full. There she stood, dressed in an old dirty print gown, so straight that it was like a sack around her, and over her shoulders was thrown an old scarlet cloak, very short, with three small capes, the largest of which did not reach down to her waist. Then the bonnet is beyond description, and the cap beneath, with one plain muslin border that had not been ironed, and sadly soiled. These, with a pair of great dirty shoes that looked fit for a ploughman, over a pair of coarse black, or rather brown, worsted stockings, which her short petticoats displayed to full advantage, completed her attire. And thus, with a great, square, butter basket hanging over her arm, stood like some gipsy woman the wife of the Rev. Mr. Nicholson.

"We then went to the inn, where Mr. Nicholson and all the other clergymen were to meet the children, from whence they would proceed to church, each at the head of his own flock. We found Mr. Nicholson in a room upstairs with some other clergymen. To these he introduced me as his cousin, but none of them appeared to notice Mrs. Nicholson. At last she said, 'Come, Mr. Nicholson, we have business at the bank, and we will have time enough to get it done before you have to walk to church.' And bidding me come with them also, she proceeded downstairs, and left the inn. Mr. Nicholson was dressed in his gown and bands, and no one who was not acquainted with them would have thought for a moment that she was his wife. However, she trotted on before us with her basket, and, I daresay, we were neither of us sorry that she did so. When we reached the bank Mr. Nicholson's business was soon settled, and then she said he had better go on to the children, or he would be too late. 'Come, then, Miss H——n,' said Mr. Nicholson, 'she can meet us at the church.' I replied, 'I had better wait for her.' (I had been told that she was jealous of almost every female that he spoke to, so I feared if I went with him she might abuse me about it another time.) But though I declined going with him till I was ashamed, she insisted that I should go. Accordingly we left her, and went again to the inn. The procession was just walking off when Mr. Nicholson requested me to take his arm, and we walked before the children of his flock to the church. At the entrance we separated. He desired me to go upstairs into the gallery, as he would have to remain below with the children. I was shown into a pew in the gallery, and viewed the imposing and solemn sight with reverential feelings. I thought, how much it was to be feared, many were there that knew not what they did. I thought of our journey to Selby; and then I wondered why Mrs. Nicholson was not coming. Often and often did I look to the entrance behind me to catch a glimpse of the bouncing dame in the old red cloak. (She was then very stout, being upwards of seventeen stones in weight.) At length the service was concluded. I hurried down as fast as possible, and, without waiting for Mr. Nicholson, went out to seek her. After having sought for some time, I spied her in a spirit-shop. She saw me at the same time, and called to me to go in. She seemed quite in good humour, and asked where Mr. Nicholson was. I replied I had left him in the church, having come out to seek her, as I wondered she had not come according to promise. She said she had been doing business all the time, but when she had ordered some spirits here she had done, and would then go with me to the inn, as it was time to be starting for home.

"When we got again to the inn, and into the room where we had been before, she inquired for Mr. Nicholson, and was told he was in another room. She said, 'I suppose he is tipsy; show me where he is.' The waiter went out, and she followed him, desiring me to wait until her return. In a short time she came back, saying, 'Aye, he is yonder, tipsy enough. He has been dining and drinking wine with a set of them, and now he is laid upon a sofa, and I cannot get him to stir. It will have cost him a fine deal; but he won't tell me anything, and what is worse, I can't get his money from him, and he has a large sum in his pocket. I expect the cart will be here presently, and they won't wait for me. I suppose I must go, but if I leave him, he'll be robbed. I never can walk home, and besides, I shall have my three pence to pay. So I suppose I must go. Oh, Mary Anne, do you go and speak to him, and see if he will come. The gentleman with whom he came has gone for his gig, and if he won't go with him, and we leave him, he will be robbed, and perhaps murdered.'

"'Well,' I replied, 'I'll go and see; but if he won't move for you, I don't expect he will for me. But, see there is the waggon with its live load at the door. For my part I would rather walk all the way than go in that horrid thing.'

"She went out, and I followed her down a short passage, at the end of which we entered another room, where one or two gentlemen were sitting. We found Mr. Nicholson lying on a sofa. I went up to him and said, 'Come, Mr. Nicholson, won't you go home? The cart is at the door waiting for Mrs. Nicholson, and she is quite distressed that you would not speak to her.' He replied that he would go directly the gig was ready. She then came forward and said, 'Give me your money, or you will lose or spend it.'

"'No,' he replied, 'I won't; you shall not have it. Go away, I do not want you here.'

"'Well, then,' said she, 'may Miss H——n stop with you?'

"'Yes,' he replied, 'I shall be glad of her company.'

"'No,' I said, 'I cannot stop, for I intend walking home, and it is time I was going.'

"'Oh, you must not leave him,' said Mrs. Nicholson. 'He will get more to drink, and Mr.——will not get him home. He will be as stupid as a mule if he gets any more drink; so, there's a dear good girl, do stay with him, and don't let him get any more drink, and mind and watch that nobody robs him, and see that he does not lose his bands. Now,' she said, addressing him, 'mind you do as Mary Anne wishes you.'

"'Yes; certainly,' he replied.

"'But,' I said, 'I shall have a long walk; so I must go directly.'

"'No,' said Mr. Nicholson, 'you had better come with us. I am sure that Mr.——, the churchwarden, will be glad to accommodate you with a seat in his gig. I will go and ask him.'

"'You'll get more drink if you go,' said Mrs. Nicholson; 'he is in the parlour below, and I'll go and ask him myself. So promise me, Mary Anne, that you won't leave him, and then I'll be content.'

"Just then the gentleman himself entered the room, and Mr. Nicholson asked him if he could take this young lady also. He said he could, with the greatest of pleasure. Mrs. Nicholson was delighted with this arrangement. She charged me again not to leave him, and then hurried away, and got into the cart, where the driver was grumbling at having to wait so long.

"Mr. Nicholson, Mr.——, and myself had a pleasant chat until the gig drove up. We were soon wheeling along the road, and overtook the waggon a short distance from the town, Mrs. Nicholson bawling out as we passed – 'Mind, Mary Anne, and take care of him; don't let him out of your sight till I come.'''

About this time they bought some more land, and, as usual, Mrs. Nicholson wanted to have it secured to herself, but her husband positively refused to hear of it. On the morning when he was going to order the writings she endeavoured to gain her point by a little coaxing. As she assisted him on with his coat she said, "Come, Johnny, honey, I'll give you a glass of gin for fear you get cold. It is such a cold morning." And when she gave it to him she added, "Now, Johnny, honey, you'll get these deeds made the same as the others?" "No, Nancy," he replied, "I shall not indeed. I have been deceived by you too often." This led to a torrent of abuse, before which Mr. Nicholson fled. He went to Howden to order the writings, from which, however, he excluded her name, an offence which she never forgave him, and the loss of that land after Mr. Nicholson's death was a constant subject of regret.

A small orchard was attached to one of their houses at Drax, and at the end of the building was a plum-tree. Mrs. Nicholson frequently cast a long eye on the plums, and as she was not on the best terms with the person who occupied the premises, she determined, as the tree was not within the orchard fence, that she would have the plums for herself. Accordingly, by alternate scolding and coaxing, she prevailed on Mr. Nicholson to go with her early one morning to assist in pulling the plums. When they arrived at the place she said – "Now, Johnny, honey, you'll be like to get into the tree." He told her the consequence of the act, and endeavoured to dissuade her from the attempt, but in vain. She insisted on his climbing; to this he at length consented, and commenced pulling the plums, which Mrs. Nicholson received in her apron. While they were thus engaged the tenant discovered them, and assembled several other people as witnesses. He then ordered Mr. Nicholson out of the tree, and afterwards summoned him before a magistrate for stealing the plums.

Mr. Nicholson felt keenly the disgraceful position in which he had placed himself by wielding to his wife's solicitations, and upbraided her bitterly, declaring that he should die of shame if he had to appear before a magistrate. Mrs. Nicholson advised him to feign himself ill, and undertook to appear in his stead. Accordingly, Mrs. Nicholson set out, and met at Langrick Ferry with the constable and witness, when the constable inquired for Mr. Nicholson. She informed him he was so poorly he would not be able to walk. The constable said he would get a horse for him, for come he must. Having procured a horse, he went to Mr. Nicholson's, who, finding he had no means of escape, determined to go and endeavour to come to some arrangement with his tenant when he arrived at the ferry.

Having proposed to settle the affair amicably, the tenant assured Mr. Nicholson that he felt no resentment against him; and if he would pay £5 for expenses, he would proceed no further. The money was paid, and the affair settled, but much to the vexation of Mrs. Nicholson. The tenant, however, generously proposed to spend the five pounds, stating that he only wanted protection, not profit. He accordingly ordered supper for all present, and spent the remainder in drink. Mrs. Nicholson sulked for some time, but at length joined the party, considering that she might as well get all she could out of the £5 as let them enjoy it without her.

After Mr. Nicholson refused to let his wife's name appear in the deeds for the property he purchased, she saved up a considerable sum of money unknown to her husband, and with it bought some property at Rawcliffe. The deeds for this property she ordered to be made in her mother's name, and thus revenged herself on Mr. Nicholson for excluding her name from his deeds. Mr. Nicholson often said it was his money which bought it, and they had frequent altercations about it.

Her disposition for avarice seems to have increased, if possible, with her years. Her mother frequently declared it was impossible for anyone to live with her, and that although Nancy was her only child, she (her mother) would rather spend her declining years in the Union than in the house with her.

In the year 1842 Mrs. Jackson died, leaving Mrs. Nicholson the whole of her property for her own disposal, over which he, her husband, notwithstanding the marriage, could have no control. After her mother's death she at once resolved to keep a separate purse, being determined that Mr. Nicholson should not squander her money by his extravagance. She told him she would not ask him for anything but the egg, butter, and fruit money, just to provide groceries, &c., and she would superintend his house for her meat without any wage. But Mr. Nicholson had to provide a servant, and he was bound to pay for coals, taxes, butcher's meat, drink, and extras of all kinds, without touching the profits of the dairy. She would never let him have a single penny without insisting on its return, but she was by no means scrupulous about helping herself from his pockets when she had an opportunity, and if he missed anything, she always persisted that he had lost it.

As soon as she had got matters settled after her mother's death, she wrote to a cousin in Dublin, desiring him to come over and divide the land, which, up to this time, had been a joint estate. But previous to his coming, Mrs. Nicholson took care to pay a visit to the person who occupied the greatest portion of the land. She got him to show her all over the property, and point out to her where the best land was situated, promising as he was an old tenant that he should never be disturbed. Having obtained all the information she could, she took advantage of her cousin, who was ignorant of the different qualities of the soil, and she took care that no person should have an opportunity of telling him till it was too late to retract. When he came over to Yorkshire to accomodate her by dividing the land, she laid her plans, and partly by promises if he gratified her in letting her have such and such portions in her allotment, and partly by threats of disinheriting him if he refused, she succeeded in getting nearly all the best land laid to her share, and left him only the same quantity of the inferior quality.

At the same time that the cousin from Dublin was at Drax, another cousin, a widow from Cumberland, happened to arrive on some business of her own. Mrs. Nicholson conceived the project of getting this widow to come and live in Yorkshire, doubtless thinking she would be able to make her useful, and, besides, she had a house unoccupied at Drax, and thought she might find in this cousin an eligible tenant. These circumstances induced her to behave with tolerable civility to her visitors for a short time, but her temper was so irritable that they could not speak freely in her presence.

Her cousins had agreed to depart from Yorkshire together, and travel in company as far as Liverpool, and the day of their departure was fixed, much to the satisfaction of all parties, for she sorely grudged the expense of providing for them, and, as may well be believed, they did not find themselves particularly comfortable at Drax.

Mrs. Nicholson had living with her at this time a great-niece of Mr. Nicholson's, who was acting in place of the servant whom she had discharged in a fit of jealousy.

The young girl had striven all she could, along with Mr. Nicholson, to make the visitors comfortable, and generally contrived during the day to have some eatables deposited where she could have free access to them at night when they went to bed, so that while Mrs. Nicholson was enjoying her supper in the dairy, her visitors, thanks to the young girl's kindness, were quietly enjoying themselves upstairs in their bedrooms.

Mr. Nicholson, during the visit of these friends of Mrs. Nicholson's, had behaved with the utmost kindness and cordiality towards them. On Monday evening previous to their departure (which was fixed for Wednesday), as they were together walking in the orchard, Mr. Nicholson directed their attention towards some fine geese. "Yes," he repeated, as his visitors admired them, "they are fine ones, and we will have one killed and roasted for to-morrow's dinner, as it may be a long time before we shall all have an opportunity of dining together again." "No," exclaimed Mrs. Nicholson, "we will not; they are not your geese, they are mine; and I intend to send them to Selby market where I shall get four and sixpence a-piece for them." "Well, if they are yours," replied Mr. Nicholson, "you will surely not refuse to have one of them taken as a treat for your friends the last day they will be here." "Yes, but I will, though," replied she. "You care nothing about a goose, do you?" said she, addressing herself to them. Of course they answered "No." "But," said Mr. Nicholson, "we must have one; and if you will not give a paltry goose as a treat to your friends, I will buy one from you, for I am determined we shall have it." "Well, then," she replied, "I will sell you one for five shillings." "No," he answered; "you said you would get four and sixpence at the market, and I will give you no more." After much altercation and debate, it was at length agreed that he should have a goose for four and sixpence, but he refused to pay the money without a receipt, for he knew if he did not get one she would swear that he had not paid for it. At last a receipt was written out and duly signed, and deposited by Mr. Nicholson in his pocket-book. The evening passed away pleasantly enough, and the visitors retired to rest not a little amused at the bargain which had been made between the husband and wife. Very different, however, were the sentiments they experienced for the two individuals; for the husband they could not help feeling both pity and esteem, but for the wife they felt nothing but disgust.

In the morning a scene ensued which it is difficult to describe. The visitors were awakened by loud quarrelling and angry and bitter words. They arose and went downstairs, and found Mr. and Mrs. Nicholson almost at blows. It was supposed that Mrs. Nicholson, after they had all retired for the night, crept into her husband's room when she had been assured he was asleep (for at this time, and long previous, they had occupied separate apartments), and taking the pocket-book out of his pocket stole therefrom the receipt for the goose; she then replaced the pocket-book, and went quietly to bed. In the morning Mr. Nicholson rose early to have the goose killed and dressed in good time, and it was ready for the spit when Mrs. Nicholson came down-stairs. When she saw it, she was in a furious rage. She stormed and raved. and swore she would have Mr. Nicholson taken up for theft. Just then her cousins came down-stairs and endeavoured to make peace, but in vain. She declared she would have him taken up, for the goose was hers, and he had stolen it.

"How can you say so," he replied, "when I have your own receipt showing that I paid you for it?"

"You are a liar!" she replied. "You did not pay for it. You have no receipt. You have killed my goose; but I will have you taken up, I will."

"Did you ever hear such a woman?" said Mr. Nicholson, appealing to the company. "Is she not enough to drive a man mad? You all saw me pay for the goose last night, and I can produce the receipt she gave me for it.'

"You can't! You can't! I never gave you one, and you shall pay me for the goose yet. Show the receipt if you have it, you thief!"

Mr. Nicholson took out his pocket-book immediately, thinking to silence her; but the receipt was gone. Finding it had been abstracted from his pocket-book, he was very much enraged, and accused her of having taken it. But she did not care for that, and after some more angry recrimination, Mr. Nicholson, for the sake of peace, and to prevent the company from being any longer annoyed by their disagreement, consented to pay for the goose a second time, and it was then roasted for dinner.

After dinner was over she suddenly declared her intention of going to Cumberland to see some property she had there, and also to visit her half-brother and his children, whom she had not seen for many years. Another inducement was her fear that her cousin would not return to settle in Yorkshire unless she accompanied her on her journey to Cumberland, when she would have an opportunity of continually urging her to do so. She also thought she could travel cheaper in her cousin's company than alone, for she always managed to lean pretty heavily on her companions.

The plan which the other friends had formed of travelling as far as Liverpool together was prevented by this fresh arrangement, and one of the cousins was placed in a dilemma by a little act of kindness on the part of the niece, who had hidden in her box a few fine pears as a remembrance for the children in Cumberland. Now, Mrs. Nicholson had declared that she would not take any box or trunk with her, and desired her cousin to bring down her trunk to see if room could be made for the few things she would require during her absence from home. No time was therefore to be lost in removing the pears, which the niece slyly effected by transferring them to her pocket whilst her aunt was looking in another direction. Had Mrs. Nicholson seen the pears in the box, she would have had cousins, niece, and all indicted together for stealing them.

On the Wednesday morning her cousin from Dublin, with his wife and daughter, took their departure, heartily glad to leave their inhospitable relative.

Mrs. Nicholson immediately commenced preparing for her journey, giving a particular charge to her niece not to let Mr. Nicholson get possession of the butter or apple money during her absence, and to keep close watch over him that he did not get drunk. Previous to her departure, Mr. Nicholson asked her to bring back with her into Yorkshire his sister, who was decrepit and destitute, and dependent on him for her support. She agreed to the proposal, remarking if he would keep her he could do it cheaper at home. But before she would undertake to bring the old lady she required a promise in writing from Mr. Nicholson that he would refund all travelling expenses incurred on his sister's account; remarking to her cousin that she would charge him plenty, for she was not going to be at the trouble of bringing the old woman for nothing; and she thought if she proved good for anything, she might make her take the place of a servant, if the niece left her, as she often threatened to do.

Taking all these things into consideration, she promised to bring her sister-in-law with her when she returned from Cumberland. And now, all other things being arranged, she began to contrive the most economical way of making the journey. She proposed to take the packet for York at Langrick Ferry. She could walk the distance very well, but as her cousin had a trunk she advised her to hire a cart, which would take them all, for it would cost as much if she sent the trunk itself. Accordingly, a cart was procured, they bade farewell to Mr. Nicholson, and proceeded on their journey. They got safe on board the packet, and nothing particular occurred until they arrived in York, about three o'clock in the afternoon, when Mrs. Nicholson told her cousin that she knew a respectable house in Lendal where they could lodge cheap. Upon proceeding there they found very comfortable accommodation, and the cousin was much relieved by finding that the landlady perfectly understood Mrs. Nicholson's character.

At this time Mrs. Nicholson's dress consisted of an old mourning print dress, very thin and faded, and so scanty for her corpulent figure that it was scarcely sufficient to cover her under-garments, which were of corresponding description. Over her shoulders was an old black or rather brown stuff shawl, bound round the edge with what had once been black crepe; her bonnet was an old fancy straw, trimmed with black ribbon; a cap to correspond; a large yellow silk handkerchief round her neck, and a large printed apron tied before her, completed her travelling attire. In the trunk was deposited a black, stuff dress. This, along with the shawl she wore, had been bought for her by her mother thirteen years before, as mourning for an aunt, and it had also served as mourning for her mother, for whom she was then wearing it. In addition to the gown, there was a black apron, an old vest, and an old dimity skirt, which formed the whole of her wardrobe. However, the idea of these treasures being in the trunk made her very anxious about its safety in the various stages of their journey. After they had had taken some refreshment, Mrs. Nicholson said they must now consider which would be the cheapest way of getting into Cumberland. It would never do to go by train. She knew there were fly waggons travelling from York to various places, and they must try and find them out.

Being, however, informed that the fly waggons had ceased travelling since all goods were forwarded by train, it occurred to her that perhaps she might get conveyed cheaper by luggage train. Accordingly she went to the railway station, and applied at the offices of Pickford and other carriers, telling them of her wish to travel by the fly waggons, but as they were superseded by the luggage trains, she thought they might take passengers along with the goods in the same way as was formerly done by the waggons. The clerks and porters told her they could not do anything of the sort; there were regular passenger trains, and she could not go by any other. She said she could scarcely afford to travel in that way, and begged to be allowed to go with the goods. But her labour was in vain, and much to the satisfaction of her thoroughly-ashamed companion, she was obliged to relinquish her hopes, and return to her lodgings, fatigued, dispirited, and abusing everybody she had met with.

On the following morning she reluctantly consented to take the train as far as Northallerton. When she arrived there several hours were spent in similar fruitless attempts to procure a conveyance to Darlington. Finding her efforts were useless, she began to consider that the expense of lodgings would be incurred if they remained there much longer, and she then determined to take the last train at night for Darlington, at which station they arrived about ten o'clock. Proceeding towards the town, they inquired where they could get a decent private lodging, and were directed to an old couple, with whom they spent the night and next day till the conveyance they had chosen was ready to depart.

They found the waggon was very heavily loaded, having among other things several very long fir planks. There was some difficulty in getting Mrs. Nicholson mounted, but at length she got squeezed in, and reclining herself on the planks, endeavoured to compose herself to sleep. But what with the jolting of the waggon and the confined space into which she was squeezed being insufficient for her huge person, her limbs became completely cramped; and this, with the excessive closeness of the place, for the waggon was covered with canvas, made Mrs. Nicholson ill. Reaching out her arms in the dark, she seized her companion by the hair, and exclaimed, "Oh, I am dying! Oh, do get the man to stop! Oh, do, or I shall die in this confounded waggon." In vain did her companion beg she would relinquish her hold of her hair, telling her if she did not release her she could not get to the front of the waggon to make the man hear. The only reply was, "Oh, I am dying! Get a knife out of your pocket and cut the cover open." At length her companion succeeded in disengaging herself from Mrs. Nicholson's grasp, and scrambling over the various packages in the waggon, attracted the attention of the waggoner, who immediately stopped his horses, and did all in his power to render the situation of the travellers a little more comfortable. They arrived at Barnard Castle about nine in the morning. Here the driver said they would remain until noon, and then proceed to Brough.

Mrs. Nicholson told the landlady of the house where the waggon stopped how ill she had been on the road; that she could not afford to travel by a better conveyance; that she could not take any refreshment except a cup of tea, and that she had plenty of eatables with her in her basket. The kind landlady looked at her as if she sincerely pitied her, and said, "Well, never mind, you shall have a kettle boiled, and you shall make yourself comfortable. I will charge you nothing for it." She then showed the travellers into a neat little room, and said she hoped when Mrs. Nicholson had taken some tea, and had a little rest on the sofa, she would be able to proceed on her journey as soon as the waggon was ready.

They arrived in safety at Brough, intending to proceed on their journey next morning. But in the morning she was very ill. She had been little accustomed to exercise for some time before, and the long and toilsome journey in the waggon had been too much for her.

A day or two recruited her strength, and with the recovery of health, she forgot her dislike to the waggon, for they next proceeded by carrier's cart by Appleby to Penrith. But here she declared her intention of finishing her journey on foot, for what with lodgings and what with travelling expenses, she said it was going to cost as much as if they had proceeded direct by railway. The trunk was accordingly re-directed, to be left at Coldbeck, in Cumberland, till called for, and given in charge of the carrier, with many injunctions from Mrs. Nicholson to be careful of it, as it contained many things of consequence.

When they reached the little inn at Blencow the landlady eyed them suspiciously from head to foot,

The landlady, being unable to accomodate them, sent a domestic to inquire for lodgings, but returned unsuccessful, for a company of Sappers and Miners who were then in that neighbourhood occupied every place which was available in the little village.

Mrs. Nicholson declared her intention of remaining, repeatedly asserting that the landlady was compelled to accommodate them. But the landlady appeared to be anxious to get rid of them, and said she could not be compelled to accommodate more travellers than the size of the house would afford.

Fortunately Mrs. Nicholson remembered having an old acquaintance in the place, and from him a light cart was obtained to convey the travellers to Southernby, where Mrs. Nicholson's tenant, Mr. Ralph, resided. Here they remained a day or two, and were treated most hospitably.

Mr. Ralph conveyed them in his own cart to Park End, near Coldbeck, where Mrs. Nicholson's brother and family resided. The travellers received a hearty welcome and the kindest treatment. On the day after their arrival at Park End, at Mrs. Nicholson's request, her nephew proceeded to Coldbeck to inquire after the trunk. He brought the trunk back with him, and informed them that it had been carried by mistake to another person of the same name, who had opened it, but finding it was not hers, she had fastened it up again as well as she could, and said the owner would find all right inside. "Oh, my apron, my good black apron, I am sure it will be gone," exclaimed Mrs. Nicholson; "I wish I had never put anything into your nasty trunk. My good skirts, too, if they are gone I'll make them pay dearly for them." The trunk was soon examined, and fortunately her precious things were all safe, so that peace was soon restored.

They remained at Park End about a week, and but for the restraint her presence always inflicted on those connected with her, the kindness they received would have made the visit delightful.

Mrs. Nicholson's nephew took his aunt and her cousin to the place where Mr. Nicholson's sister resided. She explained to the persons who had the care of her the arrangement which Mr. Nicholson had made for her future custody, and desired them to be in readiness to convey her to Whitehaven when she was sent for. Both the old woman and the person she lived with, who was a niece of Mr. Nicholson's, seemed much affected at the thought of parting with each other; but the idea of joining her dear brother seemed to console the old lady. Alas! she little knew the cheerless home that awaited her.

When they had arranged this business, they returned to Park End. Her nephew then took her to visit another lady, an old acquaintance of Mr. Nicholson's, between whom it appeared a rather close intimacy had subsisted previous to Mr. Nicholson's removal to Yorkshire. They received as usual a very kind reception, and an invitation to remain.

Many sheep are kept in that part of Cumberland, and this was the period for the annual clipping. At this season they make a kind of feast with what is called there "butter sopps." Mrs. S——, the lady of the house where they were staying, presented Mrs. Nicholson with some of the butter sopps in a basin, requesting her to take them to Mr. Nicholson as a present from her, jocosely remarking that she would like to be within hearing when he was eating them. Mrs. Nicholson accepted the butter sopps, and promised to deliver the message.

Part of old Miss Nicholson's furniture was sold, and arrangements were made for removing the remainder to Yorkshire. Then Mrs. Nicholson and the old lady started. It happened that part of the furniture of Miss Nicholson had been bought by parties from Whitehaven, and a cart was engaged next day to convey a sofa and a clock to the abode of the purchaser. Mrs. Nicholson persuaded her cousin to proceed in this cart to Whitehaven, at which place her other sister resided. This lady was the companion of Mrs. Nicholson when she went to Selby confirmation, and wrote the lively account of her visit which appears in this memoir. Mrs. Nicholson's notable plan of travelling in the cart with the sofa and clock was adopted. The sofa was placed lengthways on the cart, so that the two passengers when seated thereon travelled sideways. The clock-case lay behind, with a basket containing the works placed on the top. They proceeded along pretty well until they were near a town named Distington, through which they had to pass, when by some means the works of the clock began to strike like a bell ringing, nor could their efforts to stop it avail. With every roll of the cart it went tingle, tingle, tingle, until the people began to look out of their houses as they passed. "Come and look," said they; "here is such a fat woman mounted on a sofa, and they are ringing a bell and going to show her."

This exasperated Nancy Nicholson to the utmost. She swore at the urchins that ran by the side of the cart, and the more furious she grew the more provoking did they become.

When they arrived at their cousin's house at Whitehaven the servants were struck with amazement at her great size, and exclaimed, "However shall we get her off the cart? We shall be forced to take her to the warehouse and bouse her out with the crane." However, they managed to assist her down without the aid of the crane, and she was very soon made so comfortable that she forgot the vexation of her journey through Distington.

Mrs. Nicholson, old Miss Nicholson, and a cousin who was travelling with them, and to whom the reader is indebted for the details of the journey, were hospitably received by the cousin at Whitehaven.

Mrs. Nicholson appears to have been still fearful that her companion would not return with her, and therefore determined to take her departure by the packet which left Whitehaven on Saturday for Liverpool, and her cousin arranged to accompany her. They had been informed that the packet would start at two o'clock in the afternoon, but just as they were sitting down to dinner a gentleman called to say the packet was then making ready. Immediately all was bustle and confusion. It was necessary to convey down the vessel not only the luggage, but Mr. Nicholson's sister also, who was unable to walk. The dinner was left untasted, but the kind cousin at whose house they had been staying placed the meat and vegetables in a basket, and sent it after them, saying they must dine when they got on board.

All their friends assembled on the pier from which the packet sailed, and the sad farewell was followed by many prayers for her who had been lured away from her friends and home by what they considered the specious promises of Mrs. Nicholson.

The travelling party now comprised Mrs. Nicholson, her sister-in-law (who was quite decrepit, and could scarcely walk even with the assistance of sticks), the cousin who had accompanied her throughout the journey, and her two children.

Soon after the packet left Whitehaven, it commenced blowing pretty strong, and many of the passengers were very sick; amongst the rest, Mrs. Nicholson and her cousin.

When the passengers left Whitehaven they expected to reach Liverpool by midnight, when they would have been able to take the first train in the morning for Manchester. The wind had caused some delay, and unfortunately the packet had run against a loaded schooner, which had carried away one of her paddles, and in consequence the remainder of the voyage was performed without the aid of steam.

It was late in the forenoon when our travellers arrived in Liverpool, and having procured a cab, as Miss Nicholson could not walk, they proceeded at once to the railway station in Lime Street. To their dismay they found the station closed, and on inquiry were informed that it would not be open again for some hours. They were now in an awkward dilemma, for Mrs. Nicholson declared her intention of remaining in the street until the doors were opened, for she could not think of being at the trouble and expense of removing her sister-in-law backwards and forwards in vain.

Her cousin urged her to go to the nearest public-house, as it would be disgraceful to remain at the doors of a railway station for such a length of time on the Sabbath-day. Her cousin felt herself degraded, as she had both friends and relations in Liverpool, and was fearful of being recognised. But entreaties and expostulations were all in vain. Mrs. Nicholson seated herself and her sister-in-law on the baggage, and took out the mutton and potatoes, declaring herself right hungry, and they would have their dinners. Mrs. Nicholson shared out the mutton and potatoes, settled herself down with the dish on her knees, and commenced her dinner most vigorously, declaring the meat was very good. Heartily glad was the cousin when the doors opened; in a few minutes they obtained their tickets, and were soon on their way to Manchester. On their arrival they alighted from the train, not being certain that they could proceed any further that night, and their movements being very slow, the train started off again before they got fresh tickets. After the train had departed and the crowd dispersed, the party proceeded to the waiting-room to consult about procuring lodgings for the night, when Mrs. Nicholson settled the point by declaring she would not leave the station. They were still in the midst of their discussion when some of the company's servants entered the waiting-room, and curtly informed them it was necessary to depart, as the last train had gone, and they wanted to close the station. But Mrs. Nicholson told them the train had gone off and left them, as that old woman, pointing to her sister-in-law, was unable to walk; and if she was removed from the station that night they would not be able to get her there again in time for the morning train. They replied that there was an hotel close to the doors of the station where they might all be accommodated, and being so near, the old woman could be brought to the train in the morning without much difficulty. "Oh," replied Mrs. Nicholson, "do, if you please, my good man, let us remain here; we would rather remain here than go anywhere else. We will give you a trifle to let us stop where we are, for we cannot afford to pay for our beds. But we will give you something if you will let us stop here; we can sleep on the long settle." "Well, poor woman," replied the kind-hearted man, evidently touched with pity, "I cannot give you leave to stay, neither can I accept anything from you; but I will acquaint the master, and see what I can do for you." He accordingly departed, and in a little time returned, saying it was quite contrary to their rules to permit anyone to remain in the station all night. However, as their case was so pitiful, and they had missed the train, they would be allowed to remain till morning. He then kindly offered to make a fire, which, however, Mrs. Nicholson declined, but thanked him heartily for his kindness. She said if he would only permit the gaslight to remain burning, it would be all they would require. He granted her request, and very kindly bade them good-night, and shut the door.

The travellers then endeavoured to compose themselves to rest, Mrs. Nicholson exulting in her success in obtaining leave to remain at the station, whereby they would save the expense of lodgings. Fortunately a pair of pillows belonging to the cousin were corded on the top of one of their trunks. They were accidentally omitted when the other portion of her furniture was packed off, and they now proved extremely useful. The cords were speedily untied, and Mrs. Nicholson and her sister-in-law each took a pillow, and laid down on the edge of the long seats of the waiting-room. Her cousin and her children, with the help of sundry bundles, followed their example, and wrapping themselves in shawls and cloaks, were soon settled down, and prepared for a sound sleep after the fatigues of the day.

On the following morning they took tickets for Selby, where they arrived safely without any further adventures, and returned to Drax in the evening by the carrier's cart, after having been absent from home about a month.

Mr. Nicholson received his poor old sister very kindly.

Mr. Nicholson's niece left a few weeks after her aunt returned from Cumberland, after which time Mrs. Nicholson treated the poor sister-in-law with the greatest cruelty, compelling her to walk without the assistance of her sticks, although she was scarcely able to totter along.

It will be readily imagined that under these circumstances matters became worse in Mr. Nicholson's house.

It was about the end of November, 1844, that husband and wife had a violent quarrel, which ended in a mutual agreement to separate.

Mrs. Nicholson's intention was to take up her abode in a house belonging to her at Drax, which was next door but one to that occupied by her cousin, and at that time unoccupied, and thither she moved with such furniture as Mr. Nicholson would spare her. A series of miserable squabbles ensued, an account of which is given in full in the chapbook from which this notice is taken, but which we will spare our readers.

The final quarrel took place in 1845, when Mr. Nicholson beat his wife, in the house where she lived. He never from that day visited her again, or would suffer her to re-enter his doors. Indeed, they never again met.

She remained at Newland some time, and then moved to Asselby. The first change she made there was to turn out of his farm the tenant who had given her so much information previous to the division of the land with her Dublin cousin, by means of which she had obtained the best land. For the purpose of gaining this information she had made her tenant a promise that he should never be disturbed. He reminded her of her promise, but she had made her plan, and cared neither for his entreaties nor for her promise. He was compelled to leave the farm at the termination of his tenancy, which was the Lady-day following her final separation from her husband.

She persuaded her cousin to come and live with her at Asselby, promising her if she would do so that she would leave her all her property. The cousin, although to do so was extremely inconvenient, and certainly most unpleasant, agreed on these terms to do what she wished.

Poor Mr. Nicholson had bought an accordion, which he amused himself in the long evenings with playing. On a summer night he sat out under the trees and practised on his instrument. Nancy was highly exasperated when she heard this. It was done, she concluded, out of malice, to exhibit to the whole parish that he was indifferent to his loss, and could be supremely happy without his wife.

"And I can be happy too," said Nancy, and she launched out in the extravagance of an organ. She could not play it, but she could pull out all the stops, bang her fist on the notes, and let the roar of the instrument proclaim to the neighbourhood through the open windows that she too was merry.

But not satisfied with this, she determined to be revenged on her husband by obtaining, if possible, his inhibition. She resolved on bringing Mr. Nicholson's intemperance under the notice of the Archbishop, yet so ingeniously did she lay her plans, that when the investigation took place, the part she had taken in it did not transpire.

It appears that Mr. Nicholson had a dispute with a tenant at Drax about giving up possession of his premises at a certain time, and this tenant called on Mrs. Nicholson at Asselby, requesting her to be a witness as to the time of his entering into possession, when she instigated him to write to the Archbishop of York and give a full account of Mr. Nicholson's various acts of intemperance, with a full detail of all the circumstances in his conduct which were likely to degrade him in the eyes of the Archbishop.

Mrs. Nicholson then caused letters to be written to the Archbishop, complaining that Mr. Nicholson had beat her, and caused her to be turned away without a home. This brought about a correspondence between the Archbishop and Mrs. Nicholson, but, contrary to her hopes, it ended in the Archbishop advising Mrs. Nicholson to consult a solicitor on the subject.

The investigation caused Mr. Nicholson's suspension from preaching for two years, which event gave Mrs. Nicholson great satisfaction. She wrote several letters to him from Asselby, in some of which she abused him, and in others expressed a wish to be again reconciled, but she never received any reply.

Being now in comparative tranquility with all around her, she was at a loss for an object on which to employ her ever active brain, when one day, as she was reading over the advertisements in the newspaper, she suddenly exclaimed, "I am tired of doing nothing, and I think it is a sin to be idle. To be sure I have what will keep me, and somebody after me, but I would rather be employed. I will try to obtain a housekeeper's situation. I know there are many who would be glad to have such a person as me, if it was only to take care of things for them." It Is probable that no one else would be of the same opinion, but from that time she searched the advertisements in the newspapers with an interest truly ridiculous. Week after week passed, but nothing appeared which was likely to suit her.

At length an advertisement appeared for a cook and housekeeper wanted for a single gentleman. The address was copied, and a letter written, describing her as a clergyman's daughter, &c. It was read over several times by Mrs. Nicholson previous to its being deposited in the post-office, and the reply was anxiously looked for. At length it arrived, when it appeared that the advertiser was a highly respectable physician residing at Thirsk, and he appointed a time for meeting Mrs. Nicholson at the Railway Hotel at York.

Mrs. Nicholson immediately considered herself engaged, and as she expected to leave Asselby for some time, she made great preparations for securing her apartments and the property they contained, locking and marking every drawer and cupboard, so that she might know if anyone meddled with them during her absence.

She had then to consider what clothing would be necessary for this important occasion. She thought it probable that she would be expected to dress rather smartly in her new situation, and accordingly packed up in a band-box an old-fashioned black silk pelisse, lined in front with yellow; a pink muslin gown which she had got soon after her marriage, and which was consequently too small for her at this time; her never-failing black stuff gown for occasional use; and a light shawl. These formed her wardrobe and filled the band-box, which was then tied up in a large old shawl. She then packed a few articles in a reticule basket covered with a piece of old blue print. This she secured with a padlock passed through the lid of the basket and the willows at the top which were left uncovered by the print.

In vain her friends tried to persuade her not to take her clothes with her, as it was doubtful if she would get the situation. She appeared to think that it was impossible, because she was determined to go, let the place be what it might, never seeming to think the other side would refuse. She was then entreated to dress herself as tidily as possible, but she would only go her own way. So she arrayed herself in an old print gown, very much soiled, the indispensable apron, a woollen plaid shawl, a cap very much crushed, and a bonnet little better.

The day appointed for meeting the gentleman at York was wet and stormy, but Mrs. Nicholson resolutely faced the storm, and taking the packet at the ferry, arrived in safety at York. She then set off to walk to the hotel, but by the time she reached the end of Skeldergate she was pretty well fatigued with her great bundle and basket, and her shoes were covered with mud, her bonnet blown back off her face, and her hair hanging about in disorder.

She was in this state when she arrived at the hotel, and inquired if Mr.——from Thirsk was there. She was immediately shown into his presence. On entering the room she made a low curtsey, placed her bundle on the floor, and sat down on the nearest chair, almost overcome.

The gentleman approached from the other end of the room, which was a large one, and looking at her for about a minute, he inquired, ''Were you wanting me?''

''Yes, sir,'' she replied. ''I suppose you are Mr.——, from Thirsk?''

''I am,'' said the gentleman.

''Oh, then,'' said she, ''I am Mrs. Nicholson who wrote to you about your situation as cook and housekeeper.''

The gentleman, who appeared rather nervous, immediately replied, ''Oh, dear me – you Mrs. Nicholson! – you the person who wrote to me! I understood——''

Here his sentence was left unfinished, and he commenced again, ''Oh, my good woman, it must be some mistake. Are you the person who wrote to me?''

''Yes, sir,'' she replied; ''and I assure you I will take all possible care of anything intrusted to me.''

''Oh, dear!'' said he, ''you are not at all the kind of person that I require. I have hitherto had my sister to superintend my house, but she is going to travel in Italy, and I want a person qualified to supply her place.''

''Oh,'' answered Mrs. Nicholson, ''I can do that. I have been used to manage a family of fifteen, and I am sure I can do all you require.''

''Oh, dear, no!'' again retorted the gentleman, who began to look upon her with some degree of apprehension. ''I assure you, you are not the sort of person I want. There must have been some mistake, my good woman – you really will not do for me.'' So saying, he retreated towards the other end of the room.

Mrs. Nicholson began to feel disappointment, but resolved to try again. Once more advancing towards him, said she, ''Well, sir, I am very sorry you think so. However, I have no objections to travel, and if your sister should want a companion——''

Here the gentleman interrupted her, saying, ''My good woman, no such thing, I assure you. You really will not do at all. There has evidently been some mistake, for had I known before, I need not have troubled you.''

''Well, indeed,'' said Mrs. Nicholson, ''it has been a great deal of trouble, for I have come all the way on purpose, and have brought my clothes with me.''

The gentleman involuntarily cast his eye first at the great bundle and then at the speaker, and observed he was really sorry, though he could not be answerable for her actions, but if she desired, he would order her some refreshment.

However, she declined, and took her departure, murmuring something about her disappointment and the trouble she had been at.

Week after week rolled on, and she was still pondering over a situation, when her attention was again attracted by an advertisement for a housekeeper. Application was made, and an answer duly returned, informing her that her services would be required to manage a large establishment. Her wages would be thirty pounds per annum, and she would have the control of all the female servants, except the lady's maid and the governess. The others she would have power to engage and discharge at her own discretion. She was requested to go over immediately to meet the lady and gentleman at their own house.

Mrs. Nicholson was delighted with these proposals, and already fancied herself at the head of the establishment. She immediately began to calculate how much money she could save out of her wages, and the various perquisites which she considered would be within her reach, and she then rejoiced that she had not obtained the old bachelor's situation at Thirsk.

As this situation promised to be one of importance, she thought it would be necessary to take most of her smart clothes, but after mature consideration she made up her mind to take precisely the same as she had taken to York. The band-box had not been unpacked since her former journey, so that she had only the covered basket to fill, and she was then ready to start.

The letter she had received directed her to a beautiful mansion near Skipton in Craven. As it was necessary to be there as early as possible, she was obliged to travel by rail. When she arrived at the station at Skipton, she inquired the way to A——, and after a weary walk, at length reached the entrance to the grounds surrounding the Hall. After proceeding a few yards along the avenue, she sat down to arrange her dress, and then took a survey of the place. From the spot which she occupied she could obtain a slight glimpse of the building. "Why," she exclaimed, "this is much finer than K—— Hall; I shall have a grander place than him." After resting a short time she proceeded to a door, and slightly tapping at it, retired a few steps. It was speedily opened by a female domestic, who inquired of Mrs. Nicholson what she wanted. She replied by asking if Mrs.—— was at home. The girl having answered in the affirmative, she requested her to be so kind as to inform the lady that Mrs, Nicholson had arrived.

"Oh, certainly," replied the girl; and eyeing her from head to foot, she asked, "are you Mrs. Nicholson?"

"Yes," replied Mrs. Nicholson, "and I have just arrived by the train."

The girl then invited her to walk in, and she was shown into a small sitting-room. In passing along she saw that the house was very extensive, and the apartments so numerous and so grand that she would not be able to stop there. She had just made up her mind that the place was too grand for her, when the door opened and a lady entered. Mrs. Nicholson arose and curtsied, but was full of confusion, and unable to utter a word. The lady requested her to sit down, and informed her that Mrs.—— would be with her in a few minutes.

"What," answered Mrs. Nicholson, "are not you Mrs.——?"

"Oh, no," replied she; "I am her maid."

"I suppose Mrs.—— is expecting me?" said Mrs. Nicholson.

"Oh, yes," replied the maid; "she sent the carriage to the railway station to meet the train, and bring you here. But it returned some time since. The groom said he made inquiries, but could not hear of a passenger likely to be the new housekeeper."

During this speech the lady's maid appeared to be examining Mrs. Nicholson's dress most minutely.

In a short time the lady herself appeared, and the maid withdrew, but Mrs. Nicholson had both seen and heard sufficient to prevent her from feeling the least desire to remain. She therefore at once said to the lady, "Oh, ma'am, I am sorry I have come here, for I could never stay in this great place."

The lady replied, "Well, Mrs. Nicholson, I am sorry likewise, for I was really in hopes I had met with an excellent housekeeper. However, as you see it yourself, I shall be spared the necessity of wounding your feelings."

The lady then repeated what the maid had told her about sending the carriage to the railway station, but Mrs. Nicholson appeared quite incapable of entering into conversation. The lady evidently observed her confusion, and behaved with the utmost kindness and condescension. She remarked that night was coming on; therefore if Mrs. Nicholson would remain till morning, she would give orders for her accommodation.

Mrs. Nicholson decided not to remain, and she also declined taking any refreshments, but she expressed a desire to see some of the rooms in the Hall. The lady readily granted her wish, and showed her through the splendid apartments herself. She again expressed her sorrow a mistake, as expressed it, had occurred, and Mrs. Nicholson replied that she was sorry too, for the journey had been a great expense to her, but she hoped the lady would give her something towards it.

The lady smiled at her request, and gave her a few shillings, remarking that she had now paid for advertising for a housekeeper.

Mrs. Nicholson humbly thanked her, and took her departure, amidst the half-suppressed titters of the servants, who had assembled to witness her exit.

These events were seldom referred to afterwards, and Mrs. Nicholson thenceforth rested satisfied without seeking another situation, but continued steadily her usual mode of living and amassing money.

In the beginning of the year 1850, having heard that Mr. Nicholson was dangerously ill, she felt anxious to see him, but first caused the question to be put to him if he wished to see her, when he expressed the greatest abhorrence at the idea, and declared that he never wished to see her more. He died on the 8th February following.

At the invitation of the executors she attended the funeral. She was dressed in her never-failing black stuff gown, and a white Tuscan bonnet which she bought soon after she separated from her husband. The bonnet was trimmed for the funeral with a narrow black gauze ribbon.

Mr. Nicholson left a will wherein he provided for his poor old sister for life, with remainder to a niece in Northamptonshire. His household furniture and effects were to be sold. Of course he could not prevent Mrs. Nicholson from having a life interest in any property referred to in the deeds in which her name was inserted.

When the sale of the furniture was advertised, Mrs. Nicholson determined to go over to Newland and take possession of the house. Her cousin was invited to accompany her. She was much troubled at the thought of the sale, for the things had formerly been hers, and she seemed to feel great pain at parting with them in that way. At length she declared, as she could not keep them herself, she would endeavour to prevent anybody else from enjoying them. She then broke the glass over the clock face, and with a penknife cut slits in the carpets and haircloth covering of the sofa. These were not visible at the time of the sale, but would undoubtedly appear when brought into use.

The sale took place on the Saturday, and it was late in the evening when it was concluded. Several friends invited Mrs. Nicholson to their homes, but she refused to leave the house. Two bedsteads and a crimson sofa were left, which the purchasers could not conveniently remove that evening, and which Mrs. Nicholson gladly allowed to remain, as they were likely to be useful to her. She had previously observed a large bundle in the garden, which had evidently been overlooked by the auctioneer and his assistants. This she contrived to conceal in the cellar until all the company had retired, when she brought it forth, and found it to contain an excellent pair of blankets and a good quilt, which enabled the pair to make their quarters rather more comfortable. She also found in the cellar a barrel containing a considerable quantity of ale, with which she nearly filled an old kettle, and having boiled it over a fire made of sticks and old wood, she drank the greater part of the kettleful at her supper, and was soon as fast asleep in her new-found blankets, laid on the bare bedstead, as if she had been on a bed of down.

When morning arrived, the house, as might be expected, presented a very desolate appearance. The cold was intense, but Mrs. Nicholson resolutely refused every invitation to leave it. She and her cousin found plenty of sticks and wood, with which they kept up a tolerable fire, and having drunk some more boiled ale, Nancy commenced a thorough inspection of the house. She found some old lumber which had not been worth selling, and in one of the chambers a good heap of barley. Into this chamber she removed all the lumber, together with all those pots and pans, whether broken or sound, a quantity of doctors' bottles, and every piece of wood about the place which was not then required for their fire.

Having only a life interest in the house, she determined to remove the fixtures. She pulled the shelves out of the cupboard, tore down the banisters at the top of the stairs, took the lock off the parlour door and the rollers from the windows, and deposited them in the chamber with the lumber and the barley. When night again drew on she had all arranged to her satisfaction. Again she boiled her kettleful of ale, and again slept soundly in her blankets as on the previous night.

Early on Monday morning she deposited in the chamber the blankets, the quilt, and the old kettle, and having securely locked the door and placed a private mark upon it she might know if an entrance had been attempted, she waited anxiously until the owner of the bedsteads and sofa arrived and took them away. She then secured the house by nailing down the windows, &c., and taking the path across the fields, once more returned to Asselby.

Almost immediately after she arrived at home, she was informed by the niece whose husband was tenant of the farm, that, owing to heavy rent and other circumstances, their affairs had become embarrassed. Mrs. Nicholson had always promised to be a friend to them, and they now offered to give all up to her, hoping by that means to secure a continuance of her friendship. But she suddenly took offence at something or other, and seized upon all they possessed, which was immediately advertised to be sold by auction, and her niece and family left the house the same evening.

There was then no one left about the premises but herself, and as she could not bear to be alone, she again entreated her cousin to remain with her for a time.

The sale of her niece's stock and furniture proceeded. At the conclusion, the villagers, to whom she had always been an object of dislike, made a large straw effigy, and paraded it up and down the place. They then set fire to it in front of her window and saluted her with songs, hisses, and execrations.

The sight of the fire thoroughly alarmed her, and throwing open the window she screamed and swore like a mad woman. She sent for a constable and shouted for help. No one appeared to interfere on her behalf, but when the effigy had ceased burning, the crowd dispersed of their own accord.

Nancy Nicholson was so offended at having been burnt in effigy that she determined to leave Asselby, and as she had again a house at liberty at Drax, she moved her furniture into it, and persuaded her cousin to accompany her.

About six weeks after the death of her husband, an elderly gentleman began to pay his addresses to Mrs. Nicholson. A second suitor speedily followed, and shortly afterwards a third. This bevy of suitors had a wonderful effect on the old lady, and she began to pay great attention to her dress and personal appearance. She purchased within one week three new gowns, all of which she had made up with flounces; she got also a new bonnet, and had several caps newly trimmed. She then brought from her stores several rings, not one of which was gold except her marriage ring, and with these she adorned her fingers. An hour or more she would spend every morning in rubbing her rings, and in oiling and dressing her hair, taking great pains to set herself off to the best advantage, assuming all the giddy flirting airs of a girl of sixteen. There is little doubt she would have married a second time, but feared parting with her money, and it is thought that none of her suitors were particularly anxious to take her without it.

About this time she began to attend the Roman Catholic chapel at Howden, and shortly after was received into the Roman Church by baptism; and at that time she certainly appeared to have more devotional feeling than she ever displayed either before or afterwards. But on being applied to for a small donation towards the new church then in course of erection at Howden, she speedily withdrew from the Roman communion, remarking that she had a good pew in the parish church, to which she could go without expense whenever she felt disposed, and she would, too, in spite of every one.

Mrs. Nicholson could never get a servant to live with her for any length of time, her filthy habits being past endurance. She endeavoured to do without assistance, but finding that impossible, she prevailed on her cousin to come once a week to help her to clean up a little. She had her bed in the room down-stairs where she lived, and her chambers were not swept for months previous to her death. If her cousin offered to clean up-stairs, she would reply that it was of no consequence, for no one went up but herself. He cousin received no payment for her attendance, although she found her own provisions, relying entirely on Mrs. Nicholson's oft-repeated promise that she should be rewarded in her will. Her weekly attendance was continued until about the beginning of July, 1854, when Mrs. Nicholson engaged a daughter of the niece before mentioned, to go three times a week. She also found her own provisions, but had wages for her labour. The cousin, at Mrs. Nicholson's request, still went occasionally.

Soon after this Mrs. Nicholson became very ill, but was without medical advice until the 4th August, making her words good in that respect, that she would never have another doctor until the last extremity. On that day she allowed one to be sent for, and on the following day she gave instructions for her will to be made. She bequeathed the farm and house she occupied, with all her furniture and money in the bank, to the niece before mentioned. She left another farm to the cousin in Ireland, who had been defrauded when they separated their land. She left £1500 to the son of a half-cousin by her mother's side, residing in Cumberland. But the great bulk of her property was left to her half-nephew mentioned in the account of her visit to Cumberland.

Although both the medical gentlemen and the solicitor very kindly urged her to remember the cousin who had so constantly attended upon her, without having hitherto received the slightest recompense or reward for her trouble and expense, she refused to leave her anything.

About a fortnight before her death she wished for some wine, and sent for a bottle of the best that could be procured. The wine was brought, and she was informed the price was four shillings, which caused her great dissatisfaction. She accused the person who brought it with extravagance in paying so much, and with folly in not ascertaining what would be allowed for the bottle when empty.

She then ordered a five-gallon barrel of ale, all of which she consumed in the week previous to her death. Hearing from the doctor that she could not live long, she was dreadfully afraid of dying before she had finished the barrel, and so not have all she could out of her money. As she had not been accustomed to drink fermented liquors for some years before, there is no doubt she must have been half-stupefied with beer during the last week of her existence.

She signed her will on Sunday morning, August 6th, 1854, and died the evening of the same day.

THE WOODEN BELL OF RIPON.

NEAR the railway station at Ripon is a quaint block of old almshouses, with an ancient chapel dedicated to St. Mary Magdalen, of grey stoke, backed by a grove of elms. The little chapel contains some curious wood carving, the original stone altar, and a large oak chest in which reposes a solitary curiosity – a wooden bell, painted grey-green. The chapel is fortunately unrestored, left in its picturesque antiquity to moulder away. Any one who had seen the chapel of Barden Tower some years ago, and what it has become under the hand of the restorer, will know what it is to be grateful that a venerable relic of antiquity has not been furbished up to suit modern taste. That St. Mary Magdalen's would have fallen into bad hands had it been given over to restoration may be judged by the hideous new chapel which the authorities have recently erected close to the almshouses.

By that wooden bell in the oak chest hangs a tale.

In the time of our grandfathers, Dr. W——, was Dean of Ripon, a divine of the old port-wine-drinking school.

Now St. Mary Magdalen's chapel was no longer used. By the ancient endowment there was to be a resident chaplain and daily service in the little church, which the inmates of the almshouses were expected to attend. But the chaplaincy and it emoluments were usually held by one of the canons of the Minster. The stipend went into his pocket; the duties were neglected. If the old almsfolk wished to pray to God daily, they might totter three-quarters of a mile up to the Minster.

Dean W——, took on himself the chaplaincy; that is, he appropriated to the stocking of his cellar the money bequeathed to the almonership of the Magdalen Hospital.

But his cellar fell low. The Dean wanted money; his credit with the wine-merchants was as low as his cellar. How was money to be raised?

One day he had the bell of the Magdalen Chapel removed from the gable in which it had hung for many centuries, and had hung silent for many years.

The bell was supposed to have gone to the founders; and the money paid for it to the wine-merchant; anyhow, soon after, a hamper of fine crusted port arrived at the Deanery.

But Ripon people, though long-suffering, could not quite endure the "robbing of the churches." Murmurs were heard; the Dean was remonstrated with. He puffed out, turning as red as a turkey-cock—

"Well, well! the bell shall go back again."

And sure enough next week the bell was seen once more hanging in the gable of St. Mary Magdalen's chapel as of yore.

The Ripon people were content. The bell was never rung, but to that they were accustomed. Who cared whether the old goodies in the hospital were ministered or not? It was no affair of theirs if the founder's wishes were set at nought, and the walls of the Magdalen never sounded with the voice of prayer.

But next spring, as on many a former one, the swallows built their nests among the eaves, and found a place about the altar of God's deserted house, as they had done in the days of the Psalmist. When nesting-time came, some boys began climbing about the roofs in quest of eggs.

One of them, seeing a rope dangling from the bell, caught it and began to pull, when, to his amazement, the bell uttered no sound. He crept under it. There was no clapper; and what was more, it hardly looked hollow. His curiosity was excited, and he climbed up to it, and discovered that the bell was only a piece of deal turned, and painted the colour of bell metal!

The story sounded further than ever had the old bell; and for very shame the Dean was obliged to take it down, and hide it in the chest of the Magdalen chapel.

Autumn came round. The Dean had notable espalliers in his garden. His trees were too attractive to the urchins of Ripon to escape visits. This highly incensed the Dean; and one night, hearing the boys at his apple-trees, he rushed, stick-in-hand, upon them. One he caught by the scruff of his neck. The others fled over the wall.

"Oh, you young ruffian! you audacious young scoundrel!" roared the Dean; "where do you think thieves will go to hereafter? What do you think will happen to them here?"

"Please, sir! please, sir!——"

"Hold your wicked tongue, you rascal!" thundered the Dean, whistling his cudgel round his head, "I shall thrash you unmercifully now, and lock you up in the black-hole to-night, and take you to the magistrate to-morrow, and have you sent to prison. And then, if you go on with your stealing, sir! you will go – there!" And the Dean progged with his stick in the direction of the centre of the globe.

Then he shook the boy furiously – "one, two," bang came the stick down.

"Please, mercy, Mr. Dean; spare me!"

"Spare you, sir! no – three."

"But please, Mr. Dean, *my father made the wooden bell for you.*"

"Go along, you rascal," gasped the Dean, relaxing his hold, and rushing back into his house.

In 1877 the Dean of Ripon (Dr. Freemantle) wrote to me relative to this matter: – "My attention has been directed to an anecdote told by you in your book called 'Yorkshire Oddities' of the late Dean W——. I have made it my business to ascertain the correctness of the story, but as it has excited a good deal of feeling in the minds of some of the old residents here. We have found a bell which was sent from the Deanery at least 40 years ago, and which has been in the crypt of the Cathedral ever since. It is exactly the same size as the wooden bell, which we have recovered from a heap of cinders." So Dean W—— did not sell the bell after all!

OLD JOHN MEALY-FACE

OLD JOHN M——[1], a character in his way, and a celebrity in his very little circle, was born in the parish of Topcliffe, near Thirsk, on February 20th, 1784.

He was thrice married. His first and second wives I did not know; the third he married March 29th, 1838. She was afflicted with paralysis of her legs during a great part of her later life. She was a charming old woman – religious, amiable, and a general favourite with her neighbours.

Old John had sharp features, an eagle nose, and a prominent chin. He wore drab corduroy breeches and blue stockings. He shaved all the hair off his face. The nickname he bore in the village, where he resided on his small farm, was "Mealy-Face." He obtained it by this means: John was a close-fisted old man who stinted himself, and his wife above all, in every possible way, for he dearly loved money. He did not allow his wife enough food, and she, poor thing, was wont, when he was out for the day at market or at fair, to bake herself a loaf from which she could cut a hunch when hungry.

Her husband found this out, and was very wroth. When he went to market he pressed his face down in the flour at the top of the bin, and on his return put his face back in the depressions, to make sure that the flour had not been disturbed.

The old man was not without dry humour. The story is told of him that a clergyman called on him one day to say he was about to leave his present sphere of work, "the Lord having called him to work in another vineyard."

"Then," said Old Mealy-Face, "I lay you get a better wage."

"Yes," answered the clergyman, "it is a better living by a hundred-a-year."

"Heh! I thowt seah (so)," said John, dryly; "else the Lord mud ha' called while (till) he'd been hoarse, and ye'd niver ha' heeard."

An excursionist met him on Whitson Scar, on the Hambledons. The traveller had come from Thirsk, hoping to see the glorious view stretching to Pendle Hill, in Lancashire. But a fog came on and obscured the scene. The gentleman coming upon John, who had been to Helmsley on some business or other, accosted him in an off-hand manner:

"Hey, gaffer! there's a fine view from here, ain't there, on fine days?"

"Aye, sur, it might be worse."

"One can see a long way, I'm told."

[1] I suppress the name, as the old man died but lately.

"I reckon one may if one's got eyes."

"Now tell me, gaffer, can one see as far as America, do you think?"

"One can see a deel furder," answered John.

"You don't mean to say so?"

"Eh, but I do. One can see t'moon from Whitson on a moonshiney neet."

Old John had a famous pear-tree in his garden. Two years running his pears were stolen, and no doubt were sold in Thirsk market, without John being a penny the richer. The old man grimly awaited the thief as the fruit ripened in the following autumn, sitting nightly in his window, gun in hand.

One dark night, just before market-day, he heard someone at his tree. He took careful aim at the spot whence the sound proceeded, fired, and a scream told him his bullet had taken effect. In fact, he had hit the thief in the thigh; but the ball had fortunately penetrated the flesh, and broken no bone.

The pear-stealer was caught, and on the first opportunity brought before the magistrates at Thirsk. The presiding magistrate – I think it was Sir John Galway, but am not certain – deemed it advisable to caution John M—— against too free use of his gun.

"You know, my good friend, that a gun loaded with a bullet might have killed the man who stole your pears."

"Ah, it might, and it would, but t'gun snecked (kicked) as I were blazin' wi' it."

"If the gun had not 'snecked', as you call it, the bullet would probably have gone into the poor fellow's heart and killed him dead."

"I'll tak' care it deean't sneck again," said Old John, who had no scruples against shooting a pear-stealer.

Whilst in the parish of Topcliffe I am constrained to relate an anecdote illustrative of Yorkshire shrewdness, though unconnected with Mealy-Face.

An old woman – Molly Jakes, we will call her – died, or was thought to have died, and was buried by the parish. A few days after the funeral the vicar was talking to the sexton, when the latter said, drawing the back of his hand across his nose, "Ye thowt old Molly Jakes were dead, sur?"

"Dead, dead! bless my soul! of course she was."

"Well, mebbe she is neah (now)."

"What do you mean? speak, for heaven's sake!"

"Nay, sur, it's nowt! Only I thowt efer I'd thrown the mould in as I heard her movin' and grum'ling under t' greand (ground)."

"You dug her up at once, man?"

"Nay," said the sexton, "I know two o' that," casting a knowing look at the parson. "T' parish paid one burying: who was to pay for digging her up and putting her in ageean, if she died once maire? Besides," said the sexton, drawing his hand back again across his nose, "Old Molly cost t' parish hef-a-croon a week when she war wick (alive). Noo she's felted (hidden) under t' greeand, she costs nowt. If I'd dug her up and she lived ever seah (so) long, what would ha't' rate-payers 'a said teah (to) me?"

John M——, once, when I was in his house, told me a curious tale about himself. He was riding one night to Thirsk, when he suddenly saw passing him a radiant boy on a white horse. There was no sound of footfall as he drew nigh. Old John was first aware of the approach of the mysterious rider by seeing the shadow of himself and his horse flung before him on the high-road. Thinking there might be a carriage with lamps, he was not alarmed till by the shortening of the shadow he knew that the light must be near him, and then he was surprised to hear no sound. He thereupon turned in his saddle, and at the same moment the radiant boy passed him. He was a child of about eleven, with a bright, fresh face.

"Had he any clothes on, and if so, what were they like?" I asked. But John was unable to tell me. His astonishment was so great that he took no notice of particulars.

The boy rode on till he came to a gate which led into a field. He stopped as if to open the gate, rode through, and all was instantly dark.

"I'm an owd customer," said John when he presented himself to be married the third time; "soa, vicar, I hope ye'll do t' job cheap. Strike off two-thirds, as it's the third wife."

John Mealy-Face died at the age of eighty-four, and was buried at Topcliffe on November 5th, 1868.

THE BOGART OF HELLEN-POT.

A TALE OF THE YORKSHIRE MOORS.[1]

I took the opportunity last autumn, just before the break up of the weather, of shaking off the dust of shoddy-mills, and getting a whiff of air, unadulterated with smoke, in a run among the Yorkshire moors for the better part of a week. I spent the night at Bolton, and slept soundly, after a ramble through the beautiful Wharfedale, and an examination of the Strid, where the river gushes through a rift in the rock so narrow that it is supposed possible to stride across it, though I never heard of any man venturesome enough to make the attempt. A friend accompanied me, a Mr. Keene, and on the following day we ascended the valley of the Wharfe to Arncliffe, visiting on the way the picturesque ruin called Barden Tower, and the magnificent hanging crags at Kilnsea.

At Arncliffe, a quaint moor village, my companion fell lame, and was unable to accompany me next day on a mapless ramble in search of whatsoever was picturesque and wild. It was a glorious day, the sky pure and blue, the air elastic, the heather and fern twinkling with dew. It was really very hard for poor Keene to spend ten hours alone in a dismal little country inn, without either a book or a newspaper, whilst I was brushing through the heather, scrambling limestone scaurs, and exploring ravines, inhaling at every breath life and health and ozone. But it served him right. What was the fellow thinking of when he put on a pair of new boots for his walking expedition? He looked wistfully after me out of the parlour window, and called to me to be back for a dinner-tea at seven, adding that he hoped his feet would be better in the afternoon, and then he would stroll to meet me.

Leaving Arncliffe, and noticing a bright, fretful little stream, dashing through a broken and beautiful cleft in the hills, I took a sheep-track above it, and determined on following its course. In a few minutes I seemed to have left civilisation behind me entirely. The great expanse of moorland which opened before, the utter absence of all signs of cultivation, the wild rocky pile of the Hard Flask on one side and of Fountains Fell on the other, gave the scene a savage grandeur which one hardly expects to find in England. The little beck moaned far away below me out of sight, the wind soughed pleasantly among

[1] Contributed by me to *Once a Week*, March, 1867.

the heather, and the curlew, which I constantly started, rose with a melancholy pipe and flew away to the grey scars on the side of Fountains Fell.

Being of the geological persuasion, I usually carry about with me a hammer and a small sack or pouch, which I sling round my neck, for the conveyance of specimens. I revelled in these limestone hills, spending hour after hour chipping off fragments of rock, and breaking them up to extract fossils. I hardly knew whither I rambled, but I certainly got into Silverdale, for I lunched on my bread and cheese with Penigent towering above me on the west, and beyond it rose the glorious pile of Ingleborough. I ascended Penigent, the height of which is 2270 feet, and watched the sunset from the top. Then I followed the precedent of the illustrious King of France who, having marched to the top of a hill, marched down again. But I was quite out in my geography. Now, with the map before me, I see that my ideas as to the direction in which Arncliffe lay were entirely wrong. My walk during the day had been of such a zig-zag nature that I had lost my compass points, and had made no landmarks. The consequence naturally was, that I had descended Penigent on the wrong side, and then instinctively perceiving I was in the wrong, I did a foolish thing – I struck off from my line of course at right angles. It would have been better for me to have retraced my steps up the mountain-side, and taken bearings again whilst there was still a little light; but instead of doing so, I involved myself more and more in confusion, and at last, as it became dark, I was utterly ignorant of where I was, and which was the direction in which my face was turned.

Under such circumstances a man is tempted to allow himself to be that which in a brighter hour he would repudiate – a fool. I remember mentally expressing my conviction that I was an idiot, and indignantly asking myself how I could have thought of setting out on a walk in an unknown country without map or compass? My exasperation with self was by no means allayed when I tripped over a stone and fell my length in a sludgy patch of swamp. At the same time I became conscious of a growing pain in my vitals, and was sensible of a vacuum in that region of the body which is situated beneath the lower buttons of the waistcoat; and a vacuum is what nature is well known to abhor. There was a dinner-tea spread for me in the inn at Arncliffe: chickens and ham I knew had been promised; trout I naturally anticipated would prove part of the fare in a famous fishing district; veal cutlets perhaps, and mashed potatoes. Heavens! and I not there. I know I groaned at the thought, for the sound as it issued from my lips startled me. As I walked on with drooping head, those veal cutlets and mashed potatoes rose up before me tauntingly. I am a man of resolution, and finding that the vision only aggravated matters, I beat the veal cutlets down; yet, when they vanished, a new phantom rose to distress me. During the day I had examined on the slopes of Coska, Fountains, and Penigent several of those curious pots which are peculiar to the Yorkshire limestone moors. These pots, as they are called, are natural wells, hideous circular gaping holes opening perpendicularly into the bowels of the mountain.

In rainy weather the tiny rills which descend the fells precipitate themselves into these black gulfs and disappear. Far down at the bottom of the mountain the streams bubble out again from low-browed caverns. Some of these pots are many hundred feet deep; some are supposed by the vulgar to be unfathomable, for certainly their bottoms have not been sounded yet, and a stone dropped falls and falls, each rebound becoming fainter, but the ear catches no final splash.

Now, the number of these frightful holes I had stumbled upon during the day made me fear lest in the darkness I should come upon one, and tumble down it without hope of ever coming up alive, or indeed of my bones receiving Christian burial. It was now in vain for me to endeavour to revive the dream of veal cutlets in order to obliterate the hideous image of these pots; the pots maintained the day, and haunted me till – till I suddenly became conscious of some one walking rapidly after me, endeavouring apparently to overtake me. The conviction came upon me with relief, and I stood still, eagerly awaiting the individual, expecting at length to be put in the right direction. The stars gave light enough for me to discern the figure as that of a man, but I could scarcely discover more. His walk was strange, a wriggle and duck accompanying each step, the reason being, as I ascertained on his coming alongside of me, that he was a cripple in both legs.

"Good evening, friend," said I; "I'm a stranger lost on the moor: can you direct me towards Arncliffe?"

"On, on with me," was the answer, and the hand was waved as though pointing forward.

"Dark night this," I said.

"Darker below," he muttered, as though to himself; "darker, darker, darker,"

"Shall we have a bit of moon, think you, presently?"

He made no answer, and I turned to look at him.

There was something in the way he walked which made me uneasy. When he took a step with his right foot he worked his body round facing me, and then his head jogged on to his left shoulder and reclined upon it. When he stepped out with his left foot his body revolved so that his back was presented to me, and the head was jerked on to the right shoulder. I noticed that he never held his head upright; sometimes it dropped on his breast, and once I saw it drop backwards. The impression forced itself on me that just thus would a man walk who had his neck and legs broken, if by any means the possibility were afforded him to attempt a promenade.

"How far to Arncliffe?" I asked, but he vouchsafed no answer. I tried another question or two, but could obtain no reply. I lost my temper, and laid my hand on his shoulder to draw his attention to what I was inquiring, but with a wriggle he glided from under my hand, and hobbled on before me.

I had no resource but to follow him. He kept ahead of me, and seemed determined not to enter into conversation; yet I offered him half-a-crown if he would give me the information I desired to obtain.

I was puzzled with my strange companion, and felt somewhat uneasy. I felt that he was a bit "uncanny," both in his appearance and in his manner.

Presently we came near water, as I judged by the sound, which was that of a beck murmuring among stones. On went my conductor, following the water-course, and so rapidly that I had difficulty in keeping up with him. When he leaped on a stone or scrambled up a turf-hummock, so as to stand against the horizon, where a feeble light still lingered, I could distinguish the horrible contours of his body, and the sight invariably heightened my uneasiness.

Suddenly I missed him!

I called – but there was no reply! I stood still and listened, but heard nothing save the bubbling of the stream, and, far, far away, the to-whoo of an owl.

Noiselessly a bat fluttered past me, coming instantaneously out of the blackness of the night, and vanishing back into it as instantaneously.

"I say, you fellow!" hallooed I to the vanishing guide.

"You fellow!" answered the scaurs of Penigent, in a lower key.

"To-whoo," faintly called the owl.

"What do you mean by deserting me like this?" I roared.

"Like this," muttered the echo. "To-whoo," responded the owl.

"I must follow the beck," I said; "that will lead me to the river, and the river will guide me to some habitation of living man."

"Living man," growled the echo. "To-woo," sang the owl.

I stumbled over the water-worn stones, and splashed into water. My ankles were scarified, my shins bruised; I narrowly escaped breaking my bones as I fell again and again. I did not dare leave the stream, lest I should lose my way.

Then a nightjar began to hiss from among the rocks, and the stream to dash along more wildly. The banks rose higher, and I seemed to be walking through a railway cutting. I looked up, and saw the rugged outline of rock and furze on the eastern bank, and on top of a huge block stood a distorted human figure. It was that of my strange companion.

Down the slope he came with wriggle and jump; he came straight towards me, spread out his arms – in a moment they were clasped round me, and I was lifted from my feet. I was so astonished that I made no resistance at first, and it was only after he had taken a dozen steps with me, and I heard the splash of the beck falling into what must be a pot, and saw the black yawning hole open before me, and felt the man bending as though about to leap down it with me in his arms, that I tore my right arm lose, caught at a young rowan-tree which leaned over the gulf.

At the same moment there flashed before my eyes the light of a lanthorn, the flame small and yellow, yet sufficient to illumine the face of the bearer – a young woman, the countenance wondrously beautiful, but full of woe unutterable.

The lanthorn passed across the open mouth of the pot. The moment it became visible the arms which held me were unclasped, and I saw the man sink down the abyss, with the light reflected from his upturned face. He went down it, not with a whizz as a falling stone, but slowly as a man might sink in water. Thus I was well able to observe his blanched face and wide dilated eyes fixed with horror on the lanthorn flame.

Having recovered my feet, naturally my first impulse was to run up the bank, and get as far as possible from the ugly well into which I might have been precipitated. My next was to look round for the young woman who bore the light. I could see the lanthorn at some little distance, but I could not distinguish the bearer.

I called to her; she lifted the light till her hand came within its radiance. The small white hand beckoned me to follow.

I ran to catch her up, but the faster I pursued, the swifter glided the flame before me. Evidently the bearer did not desire to be overtaken. When I stopped, she stopped; when I advanced, she moved onwards; always keeping the same distance ahead of me. So we must have proceeded for a couple of miles, when suddenly the light went out, and at the same instant I became conscious of a small farm-house lying before me.

In less time than it takes me to write this I had entered the enclosure which surrounded it, had rapped hastily at the door. A gaunt moorland farmer opened it, and looked at me with surprise.

"Can you let me have shelter for a litle while, and then a guide to Arncliffe?" I asked. "I have lost my way, and have met with a strange adventure, which has somewhat shaken my nerves."

"Sit here; come here; sit thee down there," he said, pointing to the ingle corner with the stem of his pipe, and then closing and bolting the door, he stalked over to the opposite corner and sat down on a rocking-chair. He eyed me musingly, and smoked steadily without making any remark. After having puffed away for ten minutes, he shouted at the top of his voice:

"Gi'e him a glass of ale, lass."

"A'm boune to, lad," replied a voice from the back-kitchen: and looking over my shoulder, I noticed that there was a woman in the little lean-to back room, "fettling up" by the light of a rush-candle.

"Thou'rt none boune to Arncliffe to-neet?" said the man, slowly withdrawing his pipe from his mouth.

"I am, if you will direct me," I replied, "for I have a friend there who is expecting me, and who will be sorely put out at my non-appearance earlier."

"Humph!"

He smoked for ten minutes more, and then said:

"And what brought thee to this road?"

"I will tell you," I replied; and then proceeded to relate what had happened to me. As soon as I mentioned the strange companion I had met with—

"It's t' Boggart, lass!" called the farmer to his wife, "he's gotten agait misleading folk again."

When I spoke of the flash of light before which the man had quailed, and which had revealed the face of a woman, pale and sad, bending over it—

"Weel done, Peggy!" roared the farmer; "'tis no but Peggy wi' t' lanthorn, lass," – again to his wife.

"She's a good 'un," responded the lady from the kitchen.

"Who are the Boggart and Peggy?" I asked; "they seem to be intimate acquaintance of yours."

The great Yorkshireman did not answer, but whiffed away, with his dreamy eyes fixed on the fire.

"So t' Boggart thowt to ha' hugged thee down Pothoile!"

Then he laughed. "I reckon," mused he again, "I reckon he were a bit flayed to see Peggy come anent him that road!"

"I wish," said I, "that you would tell me all about him and her."

"So I will, lad, bi'm bye, if thou'rt boune to Arncliffe to-neet." He looked up at me. "We can gi' thee a bed if thou likes: it's no but a poor one, but it's none so bad – eh, lass?" The last two words were shouted to his wife.

"Ay, ay," she replied from the kitchen.

"Thank you very kindly," said I; "if it were not for my friend at Arncliffe, I would accept your offer with alacrity; but as it happens, I *must* return there to-night."

"Gi'e us a leet, lass!" called the man, knocking the ashes from his pipe, rising, and taking down a lanthorn.

The good woman lighted the candle for him, and the great Yorkshireman shut the lanthorn door, took up his cap, and said to me—

"Now, if thou'rt boune to come, come on."

I rose and followed him. He led the way, and as we walked towards Arncliffe he told me the following tale:—

"Some hundred years ago there lived a young woman in a cottage near Kettlewell. A strange man came into the neighbourhood, gained her affections, and married her. They settled at the little farm in which my guide now resided. They had not lived a twelvemonth together before the constables entered the house one evening, and took the man up on the charge of bigamy. He had a wife and family living at Bolton, in Lancashire. As they were carrying him off, he broke from them and fled over the moors, and was never retaken. By some it was supposed that he had escaped to America, but by others that he had fallen into one of the Pots and had perished. His poor second wife, heart-broken, wandered all that night searching for him, and was found dead on the side of Penigent next morning. And they say," added my guide, in a low voice, "that she seeks him still; and when she's gotten him she'll tak' him before the throne of God to be sentenced for having ruined her happiness, and been the cause of her death. That's why he's so flayed (afraid) of meeting wi' she, and sma' blame to him."

"So you think the wretched man perished in one of the pots?"

"I reckon he did. And he'll never have his rest till his bones are laid i' t' churchyard, and that'll never be."

"Farmer," said I, after a pause, "have you plenty of rope about your house?"

He grunted an assent.

"Then I will descend the pot to-morrow."

I am sorry to state here that my companion was so completely thrown off his balance by this announcement that he swore.

"Shall you have time to assist me?" I asked.

"I'm none particular thronged," he replied.

"Some additional help will be needed," I continued; "if you have a workman or two disposed to earn a day's wage by being useful to me, bid them be ready with all that is requisite at the mouth of the pot to-morrow."

"Aye! if we can addle us a bit brass that road," responded the farmer, "we're t' chaps for thee. But I reckon thou'rt no but making gam' of me."

"I am not, indeed," I replied; "get plenty of rope ready, and a stout pole laid across the mouth of the hole, and I will go down to-morrow."

I was as good as my word. Keene accompanied me next day to the little farm, and there we found half-a-dozen men with ropes and windlass ready to assist in the exploit.

As the sun was shining, I felt no fear whatsoever, and I laughed and chatted whilst a belt was strapped round my waist, another under my arms, and the cord passed beneath them. Before descending I took up my geological bag and slung it round my neck; I also picked up my hammer.

"You may be sure I shall find some magnificent stalactites down there," said I.

"Are you ready?" asked Keene.

I sat on the edge of the gulf under the mountain ash to which I had clung for life the night before. I directed my eyes downwards, and saw the little stream lose itself in spray after a leap or two. How awfully black the abyss seemed! "Now then!" I slipped down, and the windlass was slowly unwound. Click, click, click! I heard each sound of the crank as it descended. The air about me was cold and damp. Beautiful ferns and mosses flourished on every ledge; presently, however, I got beyond the fern zone. I was in darkness. The spray of the falling stream was so finely comminuted that it was more like the mist than spray. The walls of the pot were green with lichen, and now I was below the region of mosses. Here, on a little patch of moist *Marchanta polymorpha*, I found a poor butterfly, the common meadow brown. It had probably fluttered some way down the chasm in the giddiness of the moment, its wings had been clogged with spray, and it had been carried lower and lower till at last it had alighted, dripping and chilled, without hope of seeing sunlight again, on a small ledge covered with lichen. I rescued the poor insect, and put it inside my hat. I began to swing like a pendulum, and at one time had some difficulty in preventing myself from striking the rocky sides.

I could not see the walls now; I could not hear the click of the windlass. All below was perfectly black; not a sign of a bottom; but white terraces, covered with stalagmite, gleamed up round the well-like ribs, catching a little light from above. With my hammer I broke off a large mass of deposit formed by the droppings of water largely impregnated with lime. It whizzed down, but still I heard no final splash. I shouted – only faintly, as the pressure on my lungs from the belt prevented my using my voice to its full extent – but the whole well seemed alive with echoes. I tried to turn my head and look up at the sky, but I was unable. The darkness and chill began to tell upon me, and an agonising cramp contracted my legs. However I managed to place my feet upon a ledge, and stand up. Those working the windlass, feeling that the strain was off the rope, let out no more. When the cramp left me, I cast myself off again, and dropped below the ledge. After a while I began to hear a sound of falling water, and in a few minutes passed an opening in the side of the pit, out of which gushed an underground stream, and precipitated itself down the chasm.

Now I became conscious of a broad ledge of rock, extending considerably out into the well, and contracting its size; something lay upon it – fragments of broken stalactites and stalagmites, I fancied – what they were I could not distinguish, especially as at the same moment I saw them I perceived something black rising towards me. In one second I saw the face of the Boggart flash up at me full of hideous triumph, and I felt the grip of his arms about my waist. Next moment I lost all consciousness.

When I came to myself I was lying in the sunshine on the slope above the pot – Hellen or Hull-pot is its name – with Keene and the farmer bending anxiously over me.

"I'm all right," said I, in a low voice; and in a couple of minutes I was sufficiently recovered to sit up.

I took off my hat, and away flew the butterfly I had rescued, oblivious of the hours of darkness and misery it had passed through.

"Did you reach the bottom?" asked Keene. I shook my head.

"We let out all the rope we had," said my friend, "and then we pulled up again, and found you at the end in a dead faint. I see you have not been idle," he added, lifting my geological bag. "Full of stalactites, I suppose," and as he shook it the contents rattled.

"No," said I, "I put nothing into it."

"Then how comes it filled?" he asked. "Why, halloo! what have we here?" and he emptied out of it a heap of human bones and a shattered skull. *How* they got into the sack I shall never know. The remains were very old, and were encrusted with stalagmite. They lie now in Horton churchyard. I believe the Boggart has not been seen since.

.   .   .   .

For a considerable time during our walk from Malham Tarn to Settle I had been silent. Keene could endure it no longer, and at last exclaimed, "Really this is intolerable! You have been in a brown study for the last half-hour without speaking a word. A penny for your thoughts!"

"To tell you the truth," I replied, "I have been thinking over what might have happened if you had fallen lame at Arncliffe, *if* I had gone on a geological walk without you, and had lost my way on Penigent, and had fallen in with a Boggart, who tried to precipitate me down a pot, and if I had been rescued by an *ignus fatuus*, and had finally descended the pot and brought up the Boggart's bones!"

Mr Keene stared at me with amazement. I then related to him what I have just related to you, good reader, and I concluded with the observation: "All this, you know, *might* have happened, but unfortunately it *didn't*. You have had my thoughts, so hand me your penny."

JONATHAN MARTIN,

THE INCENDIARY OF YORK MINSTER.[1]

JONATHAN MARTIN was not a native of Yorkshire, but as it was in Yorkshire that he lived part of his time, and as his name is inseparably connected with the glorious Minster at York, which he partially burnt, he claims our notice in this volume.

He was born, according to his own account, at Hexham, in Northumberland, in 1782, of poor but honest parents, and by them, at a suitable age, was put apprentice to a tanner. He appears to have served his apprenticeship with steadiness, and on its expiration, when he was in his twenty-second year, he removed to London, intending to travel. Soon after his arrival in the metropolis, as he was one day viewing the Monument, a man accosted him, and inquired if he wanted a situation. Martin told him he wished to go abroad, on which the man replied that he could suit him exactly, as a gentleman of his acquaintance had a son on board a frigate on the Indian station, who wanted a person of Martin's description, and would give him thirty-two shillings per month, besides his chance of prize-money.

Martin eagerly accepted this offer. But he soon found that he was in the hands of a press-gang; and he was sent to the Nore, where he was placed on board the Hercules, 74 guns, which formed a part of the expedition against Copenhagen in 1804 under Lord Nelson. After the surrender of the Danish fleet he was drafted into one of the prizes, an 84-gun ship, which, with a squadron of seven other vessels, was ordered to proceed to Lisbon to blockade the Russian fleet in the Tagus, in order to prevent it from falling into the hands of the French. These ships were taken by the British, and were brought to England.

The next affair Martin mentions in his biography as having been engaged in was in assisting to bring off the troops from Corunna in January, 1809. He says, setting sail from Vigo Bay—

"We reached Corunna in one day, and then approached the shore: the numerous carcases of dead horses, all floating in the bay, showed us the toil our

[1] Authorities for this memoir: – "A Full and Authentic Report of the Trial of Jonathan Martin for setting fire to York Minster; with an Account of the Life of the Lunatic." York: Bellerby, 1829. His own Life, written by himself, 1828, 1829. "York Castle in the Nineteenth Century; being an Account of the Principal Offences Committed in Yorkshire from the year 1800." By L.T. Rede. Leeds, 1829.

army had suffered. We could plainly see the French and English camps from our ships, each occupying a hill very near to the other. We made every exertion to get close in, to cover the embarkation of our troops, who were sadly annoyed by the fire from the French artillery on the heights. Our ships replied to the French as well as the heavy sea then setting would allow. By great exertion the whole embarkation was completed. They then directed their batteries against our transports, who had to slip their cables, and stand out of the reach of their guns. During this scene of confusion and terror several boats were sunk by the fire of the enemy and some by the violence of the sea. Our vessels presented an awful spectacle, from the number and condition of the wounded, who occupied our cockpit, cable tier, every spare place on board, and whose misery was rendered greater by the tempest which arose, and prevented that attention being paid to them which their situation required: a great number perished solely on this account. During the gale five transports were lost, from which only few lives could be saved, owing to the state of the weather and the rocky nature of the coast.''

Having landed the wounded man in England, the ship on board which Martin was sailed for Lisbon. Of his adventures at sea Martin tells several remarkable incidents; but they are many of them connected with dreams, and if not wilful falsehoods, are most probably misrepresentations. Of such probably is what he relates as occuring whilst he was in Lisbon. He says that whilst in the Tagus the whole crew went on shore except himself, a young negro, and the captain's wife and daughter. The black, knowing the captain had a quantity of gold in his chest, proposed to Martin to murder the ladies, and take a boat and escape with it – to India, Martin says. To this he refused to accede, and ultimately succeeded in persuading the Indian (African?) to abandon his dreadful intention. About this time, he says—

''I began to see my lost and ruined state as a sinner, and to cry to God for mercy and salvation, hoping He would spare me to return to my native land, when I would join myself to the people of God. But alas! my vows, often repeated, were as often broken. Notwithstanding, the Lord heard my prayers, and restored me to my parents as safe and well as when I left them. My deliverance from on board a man-of-war was extraordinary, but the Lord having given me favour in the sight of the whole crew, when all hands were piped to breakfast, a boat appointed for the purpose was brought under our bows, and the soldiers formed a circle on the forecastle of the ship, to prevent the sentry seeing what was going forward; I dropped into the boat and got ashore, and remained in safety at the water-man's house until our ship sailed. I entered on board a transport going to Egypt for corn for our troops then lying at Messina. When I arrived in Egypt, I was filled with delight on beholding the place where our blessed Lord took refuge from the rage of Herod; and where the wisdom of Joseph (directed by Almighty God) saved the land of Egypt and his own father's house from the effects of the seven years' famine, of which I had so often read. A wide range of buildings was pointed out to me by the Turks, which they said formerly held the grain preserved by Joseph. Reflecting on these things, led me to review my mis-spent life, and to see how often God had preserved me in many dangers, and how ill I had requited Him; so that my thoughts troubled me sore, and I resolved anew to amend my life. I began to be comforted by reflecting that He preserved me for wise purposes, and that I should live to praise Him. Blessed be the name of the Lord, I was not disappointed."

A Mr. Nicoll, a native of Peterhead, who was formerly in the navy, and was a messmate with Martin in two vessels, of which one was the "Hercules," says—

"I remember Martin well, and sailed with him first about 1803. He was always skittish. We used to say that he was fitter for a parson than a sailor; nicknamed him Parson Saxe. He was often sulky and idle. He did not pray much, but was inclined to argue on religious subjects; he said he had a light that we had not, and that he held meetings in his dreams. He told extraordinary and unaccountable tales; but," said Mr. Nicoll, "they have gone from me, as I treated them as fudge and palaver." Mr. Nicoll adds that Martin was jolly as any at one time, and would drink and dance and be merry as the rest; at another time he would weep bitterly. Some were angry with him, others ridiculed him; "but I," said Mr. Nicoll, "thought him more rogue than fool. I remember his saying that a book was shot from his hands at Cadiz, and that he considered it a warning from heaven. Some one told him he should have been otherwise employed than in reading at such a time; in reply to which he abused the person who rebuked him. It was my opinion that he shammed a good deal for a sulk. He was particularly fond of viewing and conversing about the celestial bodies, but had a dread of any one pointing to a star,[1] and would not believe that they were other worlds; and, indeed, grew quite angry at such an assertion. I have often said such things as a scot (jest), to draw him on, and he has abused me. He was hale enough, but used to complain of weakness, and, I as I thought, sham sick."

A Greenwich pensioner, who served with him, says:— "I knew Jonathan twenty-three years ago and upwards; he was a good sailor, but had fits of melancholy, and then would talk of dying and a future state. I have often told him that our days were fixed, and he blamed me for saying so. I remember somebody larking in the top, and he, Martin, fell, catching the hair of the sailor in his way; he actually tore off a portion of his scalp; he saved himself by clinging to the cross-tree. He quarrelled with and fought a man named Dobson, who died in Greenwich Hospital some years since. They sat across a bench and fought. Martin was beaten. He was laughed into this quarrel."

Martin gives the following account of his escape:—

"Being on the main yard, and losing my balance, I found myself falling; there seemed nothing to save me from being dashed to pieces. The loose end of the tracing line, about an inch thick, was hanging near me. I got it round

---

[1] In Yorkshire this prejudice exists strongly. A Yorkshireman once pulled down my hands as I pointed to the Great Bear, saying that if I pointed to a star I should be struck dead – it was a sin.

my left hand, and grasping it with my right, the swing of the rope, together with my weight, threw me overboard, and I remained suspended by an arm, within a few feet of the sea, until my shipmates came to my assistance; and I praised God that I received no material injury, except in my arm being a little wrenched by my weight. Again, falling by accident out of a gun-port, my shipmates succeeded in rescuing me when not able to help myself. And being on the top-gallant-yard, the topping-lift broke, and the end I was on went down like the end of a beam. In my fall I grappled with the backstay, and brought myself up, and landed on the cross-trees. Thus the Almighty preserved me from death when there was no other hope – the height from the deck being about eighty feet.''

He relates also to the following circumstance, which was corroborated by a Greenwich pensioner:—

"After I was appointed to the gunners' crew, when on our voyage to Cadiz, the gunners' yeoman, who had charge of the stores and all the powder, shot himself through the head in the store-room, where there were upwards of five hundred barrels of gunpowder, and joining the place where all oakum and old ropes lay. When the report of the pistol was heard in that place, the consternation became general throughout the ship's company, as an explosion was to be dreaded. Some were for making to the boats; others, more desperate, were for leaping overboard, expecting the ship to blow up every moment. In the midst of the panic produced, I and four of my shipmates ran below, rushed into the store-room amidst the smoke, and soon extinguished the little fire produced by the wadding of the pistol, and then we discovered the body of the unfortunate man lying bleeding, his brains literally strewed over the floor. Thus did God put in our hearts to risk our lives, and by that means save our ship's company, six hundred in number, from an awful death.''

"Martin,'' says one of the Greenwich pensioners, "went with a boat's crew to get water. In crossing some buoys he fell in; the accident was not perceived, but we at length missed him; when we got him out he was all but gone. He said we had conspired against him, but God had delivered him. I remember this, for Dobson threatened to thrash him if he repeated it. Martin was punished for drunkenness, and bore it in a very cowardly manner. When he was in the mortar-boat he sang psalms, but when we were afterwards very near wrecked, he was as cool or cooler than any one on board. He fell overboard whilst assisting in hooking a shark, but was picked up almost immediately. He got hurt in falling, and would never assist in the hooking again. We had many sick and dying aboard, and the sharks often followed in our wake: we burnt bricks and covered them with tarpaulin, &c., fixing a hook in the brick; this fish would swallow. Martin was very active in this, until his accident. After that he said, 'The Lord was vexed at the guile.' He hated the Catholics.''

Another pensioner, who corroborated a portion of the foregoing, added: "Martin was much noticed by the officers; but he told them many falsehoods, and at last was generally disliked. He was at one time in such favour with his superiors, that two men were punished for cutting the slings of his hammock whilst he was asleep, which is generally passed over as a joke; but he pretended to have been hurt with the fall. When angered, he would swear as much as anyone, and sometimes immediately afterwards would cry and pray. His dreams and stories would have filled a book. I saw him years afterwards at Portsmouth. Never knew that he had deserted; he was continually amongst the crews of the King's ships. Went to London with him, and he talked a good deal about religion when at Portsmouth, but lived very loosely in London.[1] Martin told me a veriety of his adventures – that he was nearly murdered by the Algerines, &c., &c., but that he was marvellously delivered, and that God had told him in his dreams to quit the sea. He had a good deal of prize-money to receive, but there was a delay in his getting it. The day he was to have it finally, he was to meet at Rotherhithe; he never came, and from that time (1810) I never saw nor heard of him.''

Martin does not tell us how long he remained in the transport service; but when he was paid off, he proceeded to Newcastle to visit his parents, in 1810; and then went to work with Mr. Page, a farmer at Norton, in Durham.

"Here," he observes, "commenced that series of trials which almost obliterated the remembrance of my former difficulties, and which, were they not well-known to many now living, might appear to border on romance.'' In reading his life, however, we can find no traces of "trials" which were not brought upon himself; and there is very little of the "romantic" about them. A few months after his residence at Norton he married, and became the father of a son.

"I had him baptised Richard,'' he says. "I was deterred from giving him my own name on account of the sins of my youth, as I conceived if I did, the Lord might take him away.'' Not long after, he dreamed that his mother came to see him, and told him he would be hanged; and his dream produced a strong impression upon his mind.

His thoughts became more directed than before to religious matters, but not without "manifold backslidings," as he himself confessed.

At Yarm, in Yorkshire, four miles from Norton, where he lived, was a Methodist chapel, and he used to attend church at Norton in the morning, and chapel at Yarm in the evening. One Sunday morning he received the Holy Communion in the church at Norton, and in the evening he was at a love-feast at the Wesleyan chapel.[1] This was his first formal reception into full membership with the Methodist body. He had obtained, as he calls it, "perfect

---

[1] Neither Mr. Nicoll nor the other pensioner assert that Martin was guilty of a loose life. Perhaps this was only on the occasion of his visiting London with the sailor who mentions it. Mr. Nicoll says Martin was a moral man.

[1] As an instance of Martin's carelessness of expression, I may say that he relates in his own biography that he attended the love-feast at Yarm half-an-hour after Communion at the church at Norton. Yarm is four miles from Norton. This mistake arose from the Life being written from his dictation by a second, who wrote half-an-hour per afternoon.

liberty". He was converted, a new being, emancipated from obedience to the law, being justified by faith only.

He now began to feel strongly against the Church of England, which taught the necessity of obedience to the moral law even to those who walked in the Spirit. The laxity of the clergy in going to parties, balls, and plays, offended him.

"I knew also that I was not authorised by law to interfere with the Establishment. I betook myself to fasting and prayer, earnestly seeking direction of the Lord how I should proceed in this matter. I dreamed on Friday night that a man held out to me a piece of honeycomb, of which I did eat, and felt refreshed, and concluded this a gift divine. I felt greatly encouraged. On Saturday I gave away most of my working clothes among my shopmates, having fully resolved to confess to my Lord and Saviour the next day before the congregation; not doubting but the step I was about to take would lead me into trouble. I spent that night chiefly in prayer, for strength to perform the task I had undertaken – of warning people of their dangerous state by their carnal security; the necessity of repentance and regeneration, by the operation of the Spirit; and finally of their having the witness of the Holy Ghost that their sins were blotted out through faith in a crucified Saviour."

He accordingly entered the church with the clerk early in the morning, and whilst the latter went to ring the bell, Martin secreted himself in the pulpit, and remained hidden there till the end of the prayers, when he suddenly stood up, and gave forth as his text, St. Mark iv. 21-23, and began to preach, with violent gesticulations. He was at once removed by the churchwardens and constable, but was allowed to remain in the church, though dislodged from the pulpit.

About this time he was favoured, or deluded, with the following vision:—

"I dreamed that I was called to the city gates of London, and beheld the inhabitants tearing each other's flesh in the most horrible manner, and I heard a voice speak to me – 'In one day this city shall be burnt to the ground.' And I was taken by the Spirit of the banks of a river, and I commenced digging the earth, and cast up several sharp-edged weapons, in particular a large axe, stained with human blood. I took hold of it, and that instant there appeared, as I thought, St. James, and I struck off his head at one blow, and awoke out of my sleep. This strange concern opprest me in the spirit, and I said, 'This is no other than Popery and persecution are intending to come forward amongst true Christians. Oh! England, beware of Popery!"

Martin now began to write letters to the clergy and other members of the Church, "entreating them, as they valued their souls, to amend their lives, and flee to the blood of sprinkling for mercy and pardon." His conduct seems to have been so improper, so marked by a "zeal not according to knowledge," that he was expelled from the Methodist Society; and he complains that his religious friends were afraid to own him – he was left alone in the world; and, to add to his troubles, he lost his employment. He then went to Whitby and worked for a few weeks, but soon returned to Norton, and from thence went to Bishop Auckland, where he obtained employment; and determined once more to attempt exhorting the people in the church. He was, however, taken out by a constable; and then he began that practice which he appears never afterwards to have abandoned, of posting papers on the church doors, as a warning to the clergy and congregation. The following is a copy of one of these singular productions:—

"Oh! hear the word of the Lord, you clergymen, for the mighty sword is expanded over your guilty heads; now shall you come to a complete dissolution; now shall your candlesticks be completely overthrown; now shall your blindness come to the light, and your shame before all people, for the Lord will not suffer you to deceive the work of His hands any longer. Oh! prepare yourselves to meet your God, you double-hearted sinners; cry aloud for mercy, and now shall my God make bare His arms and conquer the devil, your great master, for the monster of hell shall be completely overthrown, and you and him shall not deceive the nations any longer, for now shall God be worshipped in spirit and truth; now you shall and must throw away your little books you carry into the pulpits to deceive the people with; you now preach for wine and gluttonous living, and not for precious souls – will you not get your portion with the rich man in hell if you do not repent and find mercy?

JONATHAN MARTIN,
"Your sincere friend."

Martin continued for some time attending church, and disturbing the service by his groans and exclamations of assent to, or dissent from, what was enunciated from the pulpit. At Bishop Auckland one day he heard the preacher declare that no man could be absolutely certain that his sins were forgiven, and his happiness hereafter was assured, till he had put off mortality, and his eyes were opened in the light of eternity. This was too much for Martin to bear. He says:—

"The bitterness of my soul constrained me to call out – 'Thou hast no business in that pulpit, thou whitened sepulchre, thou deceiver of the people, how canst thou escape the damnation of hell?' I was determined to address the people on the following Sunday, and tell them the state they must be in under such a ministry, and of the justness of that God who will judge the world in righteousness. John Bunyan admonished his hearers to an upright and strict life, being assured if this were neglected they were void of religion, and Popery would again spread through England. Like poor John Bunyan, I was pulled out of the place as soon as I began to speak. The clergy man employed an attorney to write against me, and I was apprehended as a vagabond; and they wanted my master to swear that I was deranged. My master objected thereto, stating that I had been with him seven months, and had been a faithful servant. He inquired of my master and several neighbours at Norton if they were not afraid of me, but was answered in the negative."

Martin mentions here that his wife had become a great enemy to him since he joined the Methodists; that she wanted him to leave them, and vowed to God that, unless he deserted them, she would disown him as a husband; and "from that period to the day of her death, eight years, she kept her world, but his firmness was not shaken."

"About this time the Bishop (I think of Lincoln) was to hold a confirmation at Stockton, for the Bishop of Durham. I had heard that he was a good man, and that numbers attended his visitation. I was glad to hear so good a report of him, and concluded that if he were really so good a man and so eminent a Christian, he would not fear death, and resolved to try his faith by pretending to shoot him. I had been in Newcastle to see my brother, and recollecting he had an old pistol, I asked and obtained it, and brought it home with me. On my arrival, my wife, observing the pistol, inquired what I wanted with it. I replied with a smile that I got it to shoot the Bishop. I laid it down carelessly, determined, if she should remove it, and I should receive no encouragement by a dream, I would proceed no further in the matter. When I got up in the morning the pistol was not to be found, and there, as I thought, the matter dropped; but some officious person hearing of it, told the clergyman of Norton, and he laid a complaint before the magistrate against me. A vestry meeting was then called, to which I was summoned. My previous interference with the church was urged against me, and so much was I tormented with questions on the subject, before I went to the vestry, and while there, that I was considerably agitated and off my guard. However, the reverend gentleman was little better tempered than myself, and showed a degree of rancour that I did not expect. I was asked if I had a pistol to shoot the Bishop with; to which I replied, 'that I did not mean to injure the man, although I considered they all deserved shooting, being blind leaders of the blind; consequently both must fall into the ditch.' I was then suffered to depart, but was next day taken into custody, and brought before the meeting of justices at Stockton, and examined very harshly. They asked me, if I had found the pistol, would I really have shot the Bishop? I replied, 'It depended upon circumstances – I would ask him some questions out of the Creed, and if he did not answer me satisfactorily as to his conversion, and the evidence of the Spirit, he must be branded as a deceiver of the people.' For this I was sentenced to be confined in a mad-house for life, but glory be to God, they could not keep me an hour longer than my Lord and Saviour thought fit. I felt as happy under this trial, in the assurance of Jesus' love, as if I had been going to a place."

He was at first confined in a lunatic asylum at West Auckland, but was afterwards removed to a similar establishment at Gateshead. His afflictions then and subsequently he relates thus:—

"I had not for a long time seen my wife and child, as during the time I was so rigorously confined they had been denied admittance. My poor wife had long been labouring under heavy affliction, having a cancer in her breast. When I began to work they were allowed to come and see me, and my wife at parting said – 'Farewell, Jonathan, look to Jesus; pray for me; may God bless you; my strength is failing, and I feel that I shall not be able to come any more.' She spoke prophetically, for we met no more. A short time after, she took to her bed, from which she never rose. My readers may judge of my grief to think that my poor wife was a-dying, at no great distance, and when she requested to see me, even in custody and in chains, the keeper was so unfeeling as to refuse her dying request. She afterwards sent my son (little more than seven years old), hoping that his youth, innocence, and distress might soften their hearts, but his appeal was unheeded. She sent him again with her dying love to me, and the keeper's wife shut the door in his face, and the child was suffered to return weeping to his mother. His supplication, as I afterwards heard, would have melted any heart, crying, 'What will become of me? My mother is dying, and my father is shut up in a mad-house, where I am not so much as allowed to see him.''

It must be remembered that Martin's account of things is not to be trusted in all particulars. At the same time it is certain that asylums were not conducted at that period with humanity and judgment.

Mrs. Orton, the keeper's wife alluded to, was examined at the trial of Martin, ten years later. She said: "When Martin was with me I thought him a really insane person. He would sit on the floor with two cross-sticks as if he was fiddling, either singing hymns or whistling. I have known him fast four days – and say it was God Almighty's orders – in imitation of Christ fasting forty days on the Mount. He was often under restraint, and was bad to manage.''

He succeeded in making his escape from the asylum[1] on the 17th of June, 1820, but was caught at Norton and brought back. On the 1st of July, 1820, he made his escape again by rubbing the rivets of his irons with freestone, which he managed to secrete in his room. He broke through the ceiling, got into a garret, and escaped through the tiles upon the roof. He thence descended cautiously and safely to the ground; and thus ended his captivity of three years.

With great difficulty – still with the rings of his chains on his ankles – he reached the house of Mr. Kell, an intimate friend, of the same way of thinking, at Cadlaw Hill. Mr. Kell freed him from the remains of his fetters – "the degrading emblem of slavery,'' as Jonathan termed them. Mr. Kell was a distant relation of Martin on his mother's side; and he remained there a fortnight, till his strength was recruited, when he left him, designing to proceed to an uncle's, a distance of sixteen miles, to assist him to get in his hay harvest. However, before he reached his uncle's house, he was met by his cousin, who told him that Orton, the keeper, with a constable, had been there in search of him: he therefore escaped as fast as he could to Glasgow, where another uncle resided; and he reached it in safety. From Glasgow he went to Edinburgh; and was in that city at the rejoicings on account of the coronation of George IV.

---

[1] Nicholson, the keeper of the Gateshead Asylum before the Ortons, said at the trial: "Martin was under my care eleven or twelve months. He conversed very rationally. I should not have thought him fit for a lunatic asylum.''

Martin stopped at Edinburgh only one day, being anxious to see his wife; and on returning to Norton he found his wife still alive, but in the last stage.

After remaining three weeks with his friend Mr. Kell, he determined to go to London to be near his brothers, one of whom was the celebrated imaginative painter so well known by his wonderful pictures, "The Eve of the Deluge," "The Plains of Heaven," &c.

His friend having furnished him with money, he left Darlington for London on the 1st August, 1820, exactly a month after he had made his escape. He went, however, no farther than Boroughbridge, where, on September 8th, he received a letter informing him of his wife's death, and of his having had his house robbed of money and goods to the amount of £24. He gives a pitiable account of the last illness and the distress of his poor wife:—

"I learned afterwards that my dear wife had to go through great tribulation. There was a woman allowed one shilling and sixpence per week to wait on her, but she always locked her in at night, without any attendant but the poor child to wait on his wretched mother; until my sister, hearing of their condition, came and took him away with her. So greatly neglected was he, that there was none to cut the bread for him; and when my sister came to see them he had the loaf picked out, as if eaten by mice, not being able to cut it himself. In this pitiable condition my poor boy sat up several nights with his mother, to hold the drink to her when she became too weak to do it for herself."

He then went to Hull, where he began to preach to his mates in the tannery where he worked. "I was moved to speak to them of their drunken lives, what would be the consequence if they did not repent. One or two of them, more wicked than the rest, got above me with a bucket of bullock's blood, which they heaved over me; but that did not move me from my stand: then they tried water. Then the devil put it into their minds to heave wet skins in my face, and that did not make me quit my stand until the hour was up."

Notwithstanding these checks, which in Jonathan's description strongly reminded the reader of the sufferings of Mawworm, he continued his exhortations in and out of the shop, and if we are to believe his own account, two hundred persons were converted by him.

From Hull he was driven by this treatment by his carnally-minded shopmates, and went to Norton, where his old master, Mr. Page, having obtained the consent of the magistrates that Martin should not again be consigned to the asylum, employed him as a tanner. But he soon after (in 1822) removed to Darlington, where he also worked at his trade, and spent his evenings in preaching to and praying with those who would hear him. He boasts that through his labours in seven weeks "two hundred precious souls were set at liberty." He remained at Darlington apparently till 1827, and here he pretends to have had some remarkable visions.

"I should inform my readers how I was taken to the seaside in a vision, and beheld a countless army of men arising from the waves. As I stood gazing thereon a man advanced towards me, and said, 'Where shall we find bread for so great a multitude?' He quickly answered, 'Where they can.' They then advanced with great fury, and covered, as it were, the whole earth, and I thought England fled before them. This dream made great impression on my mind after I came to Darlington, and I determined to make known the things that will befall England, unless we all turn to the Lord with full purpose of heart, for I dreamed of a great battle between Newcastle and Scotland; and again, that the son of Bonaparte came and conversed with me, and having a musket, said he would shoot through the door of an Englishman. He tried three times, and the third was successful.

"I then left him, and was soon overtaken by some baggage waggons; all those French fired their muskets in the air. I was taken prisoner, and they shut me up with the Word of God and a Wesley hymn-book in my hand. In the prison the sun shone upon me with all its splendour, and I rejoiced to see the mercy of God towards me."

He then burst out into the following denunciation against clergymen:—

"Deceive not yourselves, oh, you clergymen, for my dream has been doubled, for you will have to fly to the mountains to hide yourselves from your enemies, for the son of Bonaparte has a second time appeared to me. The first time he stood before me, he stood with a firelock in his hand, and said to me, I will shoot through the door of an Englishman. The first time he tried to present, but he was too weak, but willing to avenge the death of his father, though but a child. The second time he levelled the firelock, but could not stand the force of powder. The third time he levelled and fired, and hit his mark, and said, I will shoot through the door of an Englishman. The second dream was like unto the first: he broke through the door, and demolished the house before me with great dexterity and art. The youth appeared before me with a beautiful countenance, with a light complexion, and light curled hair; and as he passed before me through the door, I held out my hand, and he shook hands with me. I have the honour of shaking hands with the son of Bonaparte, though I have not seen his father, and he vanished out of my sight. He came from Denmark to reside in England. O England! prepare for war, and to meet a hot reception; for as you surprised the Danes at Copenhagen, so will the son of Bonaparte surprise you and reign in England, and come off victoriously. The thing is certain, and will come to pass. You must not think the time long, for the youth will soon be ready to act the part of his father, and do valiantly; for he shall be a scourge to the wicked clergymen of England."

At Darlington he was wont to declare that prayer-books had been the means of sending many souls to hell. He then wore a coat and boots of seal-skin, with the hairy side outwards. Afterwards he procured an ass, which he rode upon, to be more like Christ; and he used to preach to a society of Oddfellows at the High Cross at Darlingon. His son Richard he put with a pedlar Jew, as his assistant; and when remonstrated with, said that his reason was that little Dick might labour at the conversion of the Jews. He was a good workman.

"I came to Lincoln on one Saturday in September, 1827, and on the following

Sunday went to view the Cathedral, as I was a stranger in the town. I heard the voice of singing close by the Cathedral; I drew near, and as I stood listening, a young man, a Methodist, opened the door and invited me in. Three violent young men (for piety), Sunday-school teachers, pressed me hard to join them to assist them in instructing the rising generation, and pray to God would give a blessing to their labours. I told them I would as well as God would teach me. We had not been long together before the Lord put it in our minds to hold a short prayer-meeting, that God would own our feeble efforts, and bless the children. Whilst I was at prayer it was impressed on my mind to pray that the Lord would fill the large Cathedral full of converted clergymen, and that He would distribute them amongst all the churches of Great Britain, that blind guides and the devil might not deceive the people any longer. I was fervent in prayer, and that prayer disturbed the devil out of his den. A public-house being next door, the landlady and her company came into the room whilst I was on my knees, the landlady afraid of losing her company, and, as it were, hell broke loose upon me. The devil fiercely attacked me, but I stood to my arms: the powers of the bottomless pit could not make me rise from my knees until I had prayed for my enemies; then I arose and gave out a hymn to conclude the meeting. When the landlady could not turn us out, then she engaged her wicked company to attack me. They surrounded me, and flew upon me like fiery serpents from hell, gnashing their teeth, and crying out: 'Out with him, head first! Break his neck over the stones!' But I alighted on my feet, and the devil was conquered.''

At Lincoln, where Martin worked for a man named Weatherall, he compiled and printed his biography; two editions were soon disposed of, and he printed a third edition in 1828, of five thousand copies. A friend and fellow-believer wrote his biography from his dictation, and it underwent some sort of supervision, for Martin was wholly ignorant of spelling, and had little idea of constructing a grammatical sentence.

By hawking his little book about the country, and by quartering occasionally in the houses of those who were willing to extend their hospitality to him account of his gifts and prayer and the Word, he contrived to make a decent living. He frequented the Methodist chapel at Lincoln, and received his card of membership from the minister there. In 1828 he got acquainted with a young woman, twenty years his junior, named Maria Hodson, who lived at Boston. Martin visited her there, and they were married in Boston parish church. Shortly after the marriage they came together to York, on the day after Christmas-day, 1828, and obtained lodgings in the house of a shoemaker named William Lawn, No. 60, Aldwark.

During his stay in York he employed himself in vending his books, and was well known in the city from wearing a glazed, broad-brimmed, low-crowned hat, and a singular black leather cape, which came down to his elbows, with a square patch of fur sewn on the back, and extending from one corner to the other. At York he attended the Methodist meeting, but sometimes was with the Primitives, or Ranters. When he had any vacant time, he spent it in reading either the Bible or his hymn-book. On Sunday afternoon he was wont to go to the Minster, and on the 6th of January the following letter was found tied to one of the iron gates of the Minster choir; it was fastened by a shoe-maker's waxed thread, but was not directed. A verger, however, took it down and gave it to one of the canons or minor canons, who, however, thought it too absurd to deserve notice. The following is a verbatim copy of it:—

"York, Janrey the 5 – 1829.
"Hear the word of Lord, Oh you Dark and Lost Clergymen.
"Repent and cry for marcey for know is the day of vangens and your Cumplet Destruction is at Hand for the Lord will not suffer you and the Deveal and your blind Hellish Docktren to dseve the works of His Hands no longer.
"Oh, you Desevears will not milleons of the mighty and Rich men of the Earth have to Curs the Day that ever they gat under your blind Docktren know to be a shamd of your selvs and wepe for your Bottls of Wine and your downey Beds will be taken away from you I warn you to repent in the name of Jesuse and believe he is able on Earth to forgeve Sines, for there is no repenting in the greave Oh you blind Gydes are you not like the man that bilt his Hous upon the Sands when the Thunder starmes of Gods Heavey vangens lites upon your Gildrys Heads a way gos your sandey Foundaytons and you to the deepest pet of Hell re Serve the Curses of millions that your blind Doctrens has Decevd and to reseve Gods Heve Curs and the Ward pronounst Depart you Carsit blind Gides in to the Hotist plase of Hell to be tormented with the Deveal and all his Eanguls for Ever and Ever.
"Jona. Martin, a frind of the Sun of Boneypart Must Conclude By warning you again Oh Repent repent He will soon be able to act.

"the part of his Father
"Derect for Jonathan Martin
"Aldwark No. 60"

Another epistle was also found, on Wednesday, the 21st of January, by a sailor from Hull, who being at York, visited the Cathedral in company with his wife. When walking along the western aisle he saw on the ground near a pillar, a small packet, which he had the curiosity to open. It was tied with a shoemaker's waxed thread, covered with old matting, and contained a stone, round which was wrapped a pamphlet, entitled "The Life of Jonathan Martin." He also found in the parcel a letter, sealed with cobbler's wax, and addressed to the clergy of York. He read and exhibited both the letter and pamphlet at the house where he was stopping, but they were thought of no consequence. Fortunately, unimportant as they were considered, he did not destroy them. The letter was couched in the same strain as that already given.

In other MSS. dropped in or near the Minster, and bearing the signature of "M.," the following expressions were found:—

"Your great churches and minsters will fall down on your guilty heads;" but no sort of suspicion was entertained that anyone was wicked or mad enough to cherish the determination of destroying one of the finest existing specimens of the munificence and piety of our ancestors; therefore no precautionary measures were taken.

On the 27th of January, Martin left York with his wife, stating that they were going to Leeds to reside, and his luggage was sent off accordingly to that place. They arrived in Leeds on the 28th, and Martin remained there till the Saturday following. They lodged at the house of John Quin, No 6, Brick Street. His conduct is described as having been most orderly and decorous. He attended worship at a chapel of the Primitive Methodists one evening; his conversation was cheerful and perfectly rational; he appeared to be kind and affectionate to his wife, and spent the time while he was in the house chiefly in singing hymns, reading the Scriptures, and conversing on sacred subjects. The principal part of Thursday and Friday he was engaged in vending his pamphlet. When he left Quin's house on Saturday morning, between nine and ten o'clock, he seemed perfectly tranquil, and said he was going to fulfil an appointment that he had in the neighbourhood of Tadcaster, and that he should return to his wife at Leeds on Monday by dinner-time. Instead of stopping at Tadcaster, he came back to York, and went to his old lodgings in Aldwark. He told Mr. and Mrs. Lawn that he and his wife had been no further than Tadcaster, and that he was going to stop in that neighbourhood for the purpose of hawking books. He asked if he could sleep there that night, and on being answered in the affirmative, he took possession of the room he had before occupied. In the afternoon he went out and was observed perambulating the Minster-yard, and taking special note of the building. His attention appeared particularly directed to the western towers. He returned to Mr. Lawn's in the evening, and remained till eleven o'clock on Sunday morning, when he went out – and returned no more.

This wretched incendiary had then, no doubt, laid all his plans for the destruction of the Minster; a project which, to judge from his subsequent communications to Mr. Wilson, a local preacher at the Wesleyan Methodist Connexion at Hexham, he seems to have entertained for some time. The motives which prompted him to attempt the destruction of this beautiful church were the fanatical antipathy he entertained towards the clergy of the Church, whom he condemned as "blind guides" – to whom, however, he said he felt no ill-will, malice, or personal hostility, but he was sorry for them, as he believed they were leading the higher ranks in society astray; and the destruction of the Minster, he was of opinion, "was for the glory of God, the good of the people of England generally, and for the good of the inhabitants of York in particular, as when the Cathedral was destroyed they would be compelled to disperse themselves to other places of worship, where they would hear the Gospel preached." When he had fully made up his mind on the subject, he began to apprehend opposition from his wife; and he told Mr. Wilson that he adopted the following extraordinary mode of neutralising it:—"He took the ring from her finger whilst she slept, and though she manifested much concern at the loss of her ring, he allowed her to vent her feelings in unavailed regrets, until he thought her sufficiently moulded to his purpose. He then exacted a vow from her that she was to keep his secret, and he would restore her ring. This being agreed to, he told her his intention, on which she seemed greatly disturbed, and they went to Leeds."

After Martin left his lodgings on Sunday morning he went to the Minster and heard the sermon. In the afternoon he repaired there again, and entered the south transept as soon as the doors were open. He walked about till after the service began; and the sexton (Job Knowles) noticed him passing several times as he was ringing the bell for prayers. Before he entered the Minster in the afternoon he had provided himself with a "razor with a white haft, the back of which he used instead of a steel; a flint, tinder, matches, and a penny candle cut in two." This, however, soon burnt out, and he replaced it with one of the wax candles which had been used in the Minster the previous evening. During service he concealed himself behind a tomb – probably Archbishop Grinfield's, in the north transept – muttering to himself as the organ played, "Buzz, buzz – I'll teach thee to stop thy buzzing." There he remained till all the people had left. He then quitted his place of concealment and walked about, looking where he could find best make the fire. The ringers were in the belfry in the evening, and from behind a column he watched them go out. And here it may be remarked that very important consequences often result from apparent accidents. If the ringers had locked the door of the belfry after them, in all probability he could not have made his escape from the Minster, but would have been compelled to remain till the doors were opened in the morning; when mingling with the crowd, in the hurry and confusion, he might not have been noticed, and the calamity would always have been ascribed to accident.

After the ringers left, Martin went into the belfry and struck a light. A gentleman who was passing the Minster about half-past eight o'clock, saw a light in the belfry at that time; but as the ringers had been there, he thought they were about ringing again, and took no notice of the circumstance. Two persons who were confined in Peter Prison also saw a light in the belfry after nine o'clock. At this time the incendiary was busy preparing his means of escape. He cut about ninety feet off the rope attached to the prayer-bell, which passed through a hole in the floor of the belfry into the aisle below, and having pulled it up, he formed it into a ladder by doubling it and tying knots at regular distances. After he had worked some time, he put out his light, and finished his ladder in the dark. When this was completed he left the belfry, and having climbed over the iron gates which separate the nave from the north-east aisle, he used the rope-ladder to get over the gate leading from that aisle into the choir, which is usually kept fast. He then struck a light the second time, and with the razor cut three yards of gold fringe, two gold tassels, &c., from the pulpit, and the crimson velvet curtains from the dean's and precentor's seats at the bottom of the choir, and those from the archbishop's throne. He also took a small Bible, and as he expected to be taken and imprisoned, he brought away the Bible that it might be a comfort to him in his confinement. He then piled the cushions and Prayer-books in two heaps, on each side near the carved work, and set them on fire by introducing matches among them.

Having done this, he set about his escape. He had brought with him a pair of shoemaker's pincers, which Mr. Lawn had left in the room where he slept on Saturday night, and having tied one end of his rope to the machine used for cleaning the Minster, he dragged it under the window in the west aisle of the north transept, which he broke with the pincers; and having seen that one of the piles (that by the archbishop's throne) to which he had set fire was burning briskly, he descended, and left the Cathedral a little after three o'clock in the morning of the 2nd of February, taking with him the articles before mentioned, and also some purple silk – a part of one of the robes of the clergy.

During the time he was in the Minster he says he felt no fear, but was, ''on the contrary, quite happy; sometimes he prayed, and sometimes he praised God, because, as he said, He had strengthened him to do so good a work!''

The incendiary had left the Minster several hours before the fire was discovered. The patrol left the Minster-yard about half-past two o'clock, before he had made his escape, and they saw no indications of anything unusual when they left. About four o'clock a man going past saw a light in the Minster, but he thought the workmen were preparing a vault, and unfortunately passed on without endeavouring to ascertain what was really the cause of so unusual an occurrence as a light burning in the sacred edifice at that early hour.

At five o'clock a series of reports, resembling repeated explosions, were heard. The parties who heard them wondered what they meant, but never thought of tracing them to their source. The discovery at last took place in the following singular manner: – A lad named Swinbank, one of the younger choristers, whose duty it was to go and practise at the Minster early every morning, went as usual a little before seven o'clock on the morning of the 2nd of February. He found the doors were not open, and began to slide on a piece of ice in the Minster-yard to amuse himself. Whilst so doing he fell on his back, and before he recovered himself from that position he saw smoke issuing from the roof of the Minster. Alarmed at the sight, he went to Job Knowles, the sexton, for the keys. On his return he found the doors had been opened by some of the workmen, and Mr. Scott, the builder, entered the building at the south door, but had scarcely got in when he was compelled to retreat – so dense was the smoke that respiration was impossible. A gentleman with difficulty then made his way to the organ screen; but was compelled to retreat to avoid suffocation. By the vestry-door, however, access was obtained to the choir – the gates from the vestry, and also those leading from the aisle into the choir, being fortunately open. The fire, which originated at one end of the stalls, had consumed the whole row, with all their tabernacle work; and about half-an-hour after it was first discovered, the flames had spread to the stalls on the other side. One of the Minster engines was kept in the vestry, and this was immediately placed in the aisle, where it played on the place where the communion-plate was kept, and around which the flames were raging with great intensity: the tabernacle screen was in this spot burnt to the ground, and the plate was melted into one mass. As soon as this engine was got to work, several individuals succeeded in carrying out the whole of the cushions and books from the north side of the choir; the cushions and part of the hangings of the Cathedral were also saved, as was the curious old chair which stood within the rails. The next effort was to remove the brass eagle or lectern. This was effected with great difficulty, owing to its weight, by the few persons who had the courage to brave the suffocating effects of the smoke. They were driven back three times before they succeeded in carrying off the upper part of the eagle, which was taken into the vestry; the other portion was afterwards carried out at a door on the chapter-house side. All this was the work of a few minutes; and at this time (perhaps about a quarter after seven), the organ screen, the north side of the choir, and the roof, were to all appearance untouched by the fire. At this period, if a few firemen had been present who understood their business, this part of the church might have been saved. Shortly after, however, the flames spread round the south-west corner of the choir and reached the organ; and when this noble instrument caught fire, an appalling noise – occasioned by the action of the air in the pipes upon the flames – resounded through the building, and struck with awe all who heard it.

Whilst this was passing in the interior of the building, the alarm had been spread through the city by the ringing of the bells of St. Michael-le-Belfry, and the Yorkshire Insurance Company's engine was soon on the spot. It was placed at the south door, and the pipes were carried into the Minster, and directed over the organ upon the fire which was then raging in the choir. The city engines arrived soon after, and were stationed at different parts of the building. An express was sent to the barracks, and the barrack engine arrived about eight o'clock. Major Clark and several officers accompanied it with a file of the 7th Dragoon Guards, who were of great use in facilitating the operations of the persons employed in extinguishing the flames.

About ten minutes before eight o'clock another engine was brought into the Minster; but the roof having caught fire from the organ – the flames from the latter igniting some of the bosses of the groining, which were of maple-wood – the melted lead and pieces of burning timber began to fall so rapidly that the men were compelled to abandon their positions, and the engine was stationed further off, in the nave, whence it continued to play over the screen upon the burning ruins in the choir for several hours. Previous to the removal of this engine, an attempt was made by two or three gentlemen to cut down the great gates leading from the choir into the north-east aisle, with a view to cut off the communication with the altar: the molten lead and burning rafters, however, fell about them so rapidly that they were obliged to desist.

By eight o'clock, or a little later, the organ – one scarce equalled for tone and power by any instrument in the world – was totally consumed, together with the valuable collection of music which was deposited in the organ loft; and much of which, being in manuscript, could not be replaced.

By the exertions of Mr. Plows, stone-mason, a number of men were about this time got upon the roof of the side of the aisle; by means of ropes, buckets and the pipe of an engine were hoisted up, and from this elevation a torrent of water was discharged upon the flames beneath. A number of men were also employed in cutting away the roof towards the east window, who continued their exertions as long as they were practicable. About a quarter past eight o'clock the flames burst through the roof, near the lantern tower, and the spectacle from the exterior was awful and impressive in the extreme, whilst the effect of the scene in the interior was magnificent beyond description. Immediately in front of the screen which divides the nave from the choir, the engine already alluded to was playing directly upon the fire, but with little effect, owing to the magnitude of the space over which the flames had spread themselves. From the screen to the altar the vast area had the appearance of an ignited furnace; and the men who were employed in working the engines, and in various other ways endeavouring to stop the progress of the flames, resembled beings of another world rather than inhabitants of this material globe. Their voices, as they shouted to their comrades for "water" or for more assistance, fell in harsh and discordant tones on the ear; they moved enveloped in an atmosphere so dense that it was scarcely possible to breathe in it, partially illuminated by the flames and partly by the rays of the sun, which now streamed in through the painted windows, producing altogether an effect indescribably beautiful and grand. A number of bats and other birds, burnt out of their retreats, were now seen flitting about, unable to find an outlet, and many perished in the flames.

About half-past eight o'clock an express was sent by Archdeacon Markham to the Mayor of Leeds, informing him that the Minster was on fire, and requesting that two of the largest engines belonging to that town might be sent off immediately. This was shortly followed by another express from Mr. Newman, the actuary of the Yorkshire Fire Office, requesting that two more engines might be immediately forwarded to York. At this period serious fears were entertained that the fire would extend over the whole of this immense fabric; the flames were rapidly gaining ground at the east end, and the engines had not the least effect in allaying their progress. The lantern tower, and the whole of the roof of the nave appeared to be saturated with smoke, which also poured out of the windows of the western towers. The knotted rope having been discovered by which Martin made his escape, and not satisfactorily accounted for, and its being rumoured that a bunch of matches had also been found which had been lighted at both ends, the opinion that the fire was not caused by the gas, or by candles being left in the organ-loft or in the clergyman's robing-room, which had at first been entertained, began to give way to the idea that this was the work of an incendiary; and when the smoke was seen issuing from the places we have mentioned, it was at once said that a train had been laid, and that it was breaking out in different places. This, providentially, was not the case; the smoke penetrating the roof, &c., was merely occasioned by the denseness of the volume of vapour collected in the church before the doors were opened, and which at last found vent in that manner; and the fire never extended beyond the lantern tower.

At ten minutes past nine a portion of the burning roof fell in with a tremendous crash. For an instant the whole area was illuminated, and the next moment a volume of smoke and ashes was sent forth which involved for a short time everything in darkness and obscurity. From that time till half-past ten portions of the roof kept falling in, till from the lantern tower to the east window the blue vault of heaven was the only canopy. The molten lead from the roof during this period poured down in torrents.

Soon after ten o'clock an engine arrived from Escrick Park, near York, the seat of Paul Beilby Thompson, Esq., M.P. That no time might be lost, that gentleman's beautiful grey carriage horses were yoked to his engine, and it was driven into the city with the utmost promptitude. About half-past ten another engine arrived from Tadcaster, and was immediately got to work. One of these engines was brought to the east end, and played into the choir through an aperture made in the lower department of the window; another also played for a short time through the farthest window at the north-east end.

As great alarm was felt lest the east end of the Minster should fall, a part of the staff of the 2nd West York Militia was placed to prevent the public from passing in that direction; the inmates of the opposite houses had previously removed their families. Providentially, however, this alarm turned out to be unfounded. This fine window – the largest, we believe, in England, if not in the world – was only very partially injured.

The floor of the choir was strewed with fierce-burning timbers, and resembled a liquid lake of fire; it was heated completely through, and the vaults below glowed with a radiance that occasioned a general cry from those who could get near, of "The vaults are on fire." But the heat now began sensibly to abate, owing partly to the quantity of water poured upon the burning timbers which covered the floor of the choir and the Lady's Chapel behind the altar screen, and partly to the removal of the burning rubbish from the bases of the pillars, which latter being of limestone, were very much injured by the action of the fire. The rafters of the roof, and other immense pieces of timber, were converted literally into charcoal, and were removed to the nave and into the Minster-yard.

About noon the fears of the fire spreading any farther were removed; but the engines continued to play for hours after upon the mass of fire and flame on the floor of the church. Great efforts were also made to save the beautiful screen

which divides the nave from the choir, and this was effected, for that ornament of the Minster was only very slightly injured.

About two o'clock the engine of the Norwich Union Company, with the requisite number of men, arrived from Leeds. They had been barely two hours on the road, and in less than three minutes after the engine stopped in the Minster-yard it was at work. Two other engines arrived from Leeds shortly after. A fourth arrived about four o'clock.

When the fire was so far got under that no fears were apprehended of its extending beyond the choir and chancel, several parties were admitted into the nave to view the spectacle. Some ladies were amongst them, one of whom was heard to exclaim, on viewing the awfully splendid yet distressing scene, "What a subject for Martin!" alluding to the celebrated painter. Little did she think then that Martin's brother had occasioned this terrible conflagration.

The crowds of people who flocked to the scene of this calamity continued to increase all the afternoon, and it was found necessary to place constables at the Minster doors, to prevent the influx of persons desirous of seeing the state the edifice; many arrived from a considerable distance, and it was quite impossible that more intense feelings of anxiety and distress could have been evinced than were displayed by the inhabitants of York, who from their infant days had been accustomed to consider the Minster as their boast and glory.

A great-aunt of mine has often described to me the overwhelming sensation it caused. Her father, a man of remarkable self-restraint, wept like a child. The feeling in many a home was as if some accident had befallen and carried off a dearly-loved relation.

There was gloom that day on every countenance, and in the early part of the day a sort of stupor appeared to pervade all ranks; people were overcome by the greatness of the unexpected calamity, and seemed scarcely to know whether to consider as real the events which were passing around them, or whether they were under the influence of a dream.

During the whole afternoon the workmen and others were busily employed in removing the fallen rafters and other rubbish from the choir. Most of these were carried out into the Minster-yard, which was thickly strewed from the south door to the vestry with the fragments of the roof, blackened and reduced to charcoal. Within the nave a detachment of the Dragoon Guards was drawn up to prevent intrusion there, and a guard of the staff of the 2nd West York was mounted for the same purpose, as well as to secure the ornamental portions of that part of the structure from damage. The floor of the nave was strewn with fragments of the roof which had been brought from the choir; and against one of the pillars lay the remains of the organ – a few fragments of the gilt pipes and a portion of the iron work. A dense mass of smoke still rose from the embers, on which several of the engines continued to play during the night. The fire was not totally extinguished when the shades of evening drew on, for occasionally a fitful flash of lambent flame was seen struggling with the gloom, but was quickly extinguished by the water from the engines directed to the spot.

During the evening the silence which reigned around, only broken at intervals by the tread of the sentinels or the occasional remarks of a passenger, formed a striking contrast to the bustle and confusion which had prevailed during the day. About ten o'clock men were observed with lanterns visiting every part of the roof, to see that all was safe; and the night was passed without any further alarm.

A word as to the extent of injury which the sacred building sustained. The roof of the central aisle, which was of exquisite workmanship, was entirely destroyed from the lantern tower to the east window; this roof occupied a space of 131 feet in length by 45 in breadth, and was 99 in height from the floor to the choir. In the interior, from the organ screen to the altar screen, all the beautiful tabernacle work, the stalls, galleries, bishop's throne, pulpit, &c., were entirely consumed. The altar screen was so much injured that it was obliged to be taken down. Of the monuments, several were damaged either from the effect of the fire or the falling of the timbers of the roof.

It is impossible to conclude this part of the subject without alluding to the remarkable circumstance that one of the lessons appointed to be read on the Sunday after this calamity at the evening service was the 64th chapter of Isaiah, being the Church's prayer to God. It was singularly applicable to the fire which destroyed the Cathedral; one verse especially – "Our holy and our beautiful house, where our fathers praised Thee, is burned with fire: and all our pleasant things are laid waste." Few in the congregations assembled in the numerous churches of York on the Sunday evening heard it unmoved. Another thing, thought to be a coincidence, but which is certainly a very remote one, was that the Cathedral was fired by Martin on Candlemas Day, using one of the wax-candles employed in the choir during evensong.

Various reports as to the origin of the fire circulated in York. Some supposed it originated from the gas, others attributed it to the candles left alight in the organ loft or in the vestry of the clergy. But others suspected it was the work of an incendiary, and they were confirmed in this belief by finding the knotted rope which had been left by Martin, and was discovered early in the morning.

On Monday evening a committee of inquiry was formed, consisting of clergy and gentlemen. They met at the Residence; and the vergers, workmen, and other individuals connected with the Minster, underwent a rigorous examination. The investigation was continued on Tuesday and Wednesday, and the strictest secrecy was observed in the proceedings; in the course of which it was ascertained that the rope was cut from the one which is attached to the prayer-bell, and that not with a knife, but by being chafed with a sharp stone. It was also ascertained that the window was opened from the interior; and a bunch of matches, burnt at both ends, was found amongst the rubbish, and afterwards a pair of shoemaker's pincers. The matches were found under the rubbish of the burnt organ; the pincers on the stool of the window out of which the knotted rope was suspended. The fact was also proved that several anonymous letters had been sent to the vergers; and also that the parcel, with the letter and pamphlet before alluded to, had been found in the Minster by a person from Hull. A gentleman was despatched to Hull to obtain possession of these documents; but in the meantime they had fallen into the hands of Mr. Isaac Wilson, of that place, who with great promptitude came to York and laid them before the committee.

Mr. Pardoe, the active police officer of York, was employed to ascertain to whom the shoemaker's pincers belonged, and they were owned by Mr. Lawn, at whose house Martin had lodged. Other circumstances formed a chain of evidence so complete and conclusive as to leave no doubt that Jonathan Martin was the incendiary, and hand-bills were issued on Thursday offering a reward for his apprehension. Pardoe had been despatched to Leeds in pursuit the previous day, with a warrant from Archdeacon Markham, which on his arrival was instantly backed by the Mayor of the borough. For the rest of the day and during the night Pardoe and the whole force of the police were employed in endeavouring to find a clue to the retreat of the incendiary. They were not successful; but on Thursday morning his wife was taken into custody while vending the "History of his Life." When discovered by the officers, she expressed her surprise at the charge against her husband; and after admitting that he left that town on Saturday morning, said that she understood, on his departure, he was going into the neighbourhood of Tadcaster; that she had not heard of him since; and that she had experienced great uneasiness at his long absence. She added that his place of concealment, or anything further connected with the affair, was totally unknown to her. She was kept in custody at Leeds, in her own house, in the charge of two constables, who obtained possession of all Martin's books and papers.

On Thursday morning information was received which caused an express to be sent off to the neighbourhood of Pontefract, where an active and diligent search was commenced. A clue was obtained, which led to the belief that the incendiary had passed through Pontefract on the road to Wakefield. The Mayor of Pontefract ordered the police of that town to afford every assistance to the gentlemen in pursuit, and he was traced to Polston toll-gate. From the information there obtained it was supposed he had taken the direction to Heath; and the pursuit was immediately followed up in that direction, and continued through most of Friday. It was reported in the evening about seven o'clock that Martin had been captured about five miles from Bedale, and would be brought into York by the Carlisle Express coach. The coach was half-an-hour beyond its time, and the streets were filled with crowds of anxious spectators, who waited in the expectation that the incendiary would arrive by it. Many persons went out of Micklegate Bar, and ran alongside of the coach till it stopped in Coney Street. It was then found that the report was an erroneous one, for Martin was not there; nor was it true that he had been captured.

On Saturday morning it was ascertained that the police had been on a wrong scent, as Martin had proceeded to the north instead of to the west; and about half-past nine o'clock that morning an express was received stating that he had been asrrested the previous evening near Hexham. The following are the particulars of his flight and capture:

Martin left the Minster, as has been stated, a little after three o'clock in the morning. He proceeded to Easingwold and got a pint of ale; from thence to Thirsk, at which place he arrived at eleven o'clock; from Thirsk he went to Northallerton, where he arrived about three o'clock in the afternoon in a state of apparent fatigue. He remained till evening with a brother-in-law who resided there, and expressed great anxiety to get on to Hexham to see a friend. At nine that evening he left Northallerton in a coal cart, in which he travelled all night till he arrived at Joft-hill pit, near West Auckland, on the Watling Street road. The next morning he proceeded to Alensford, on the Derwent, where he slept on the Tuesday evening. He left Alensford about eight o'clock on the Wednesday morning, and stopped at the Riding Mill, where he had a pint of ale; from thence he proceeded to Corbridge, and had half-a-pint of ale; then to Cadlaw Hill to his friend Mr. Kell, where he arrived about two the same afternoon, being the same place where he sought refuge when he escaped from the asylum at Gateshead. Martin remained there till eleven o'clock on Friday morning, and during his stay he expressed a great anxiety to see newspapers.

The handbills giving a description of Martin's person, and offering a reward for his apprehension, were circulated in all parts of the North; and one of them fell into the hands of Mr. Stainthorpe, a sheriff's officer, of Newcastle, who knew him. Mr. S., on Friday, the 6th, having to go to Corbridge, heard that Martin had returned home, but did not at that time know there was any charge against him. Returning to Hexham, where he kept a public-house, Mr. S. found the handbill lying on the table; and he immediately saddled his pony and set off to Mr. Kell's, where he felt satisfied he would find him. The house, called Cadlaw Hill, is situated between Stagshaw Bank and Hexham, on the north side of the Tyne. It Is a house situated by itself, and had Martin not been well known in the neighbourhood, it might have afforded concealment for some time. On alighting he inquired of a young woman who was standing at the door if Jonathan Martin had got home. The family, it would seem, were not aware of the crime he had committed, as the bailiff was readily answered in the affirmitive. On receiving this information he bolted in, and found Mr. Kell and Martin sitting together, the latter engaged in reading a hymn-book. They both rose on his entrance, and he, accosting Martin, asked, "Is not your name Jonathan Martin?" He immediately replied, "Yes, it is." On which Mr. Stainthorpe said, "You are my prisoner." Martin displayed very little emotion, nor did he even ask why he was made a prisoner. Mr. Kell was greatly surprised, and asked Mr. Stainthorpe what Martin was charged with. He replied he was not at liberty to tell him; but that he should require his assistance to convey the prisoner to Hexham, on reaching which place he would give him every information necessary. Mr. Kell readily agreed, and the prisoner as readily seemed disposed to take the road. The first question he asked Mr. Stainthorpe was, "Do you belong to York?" Mr. Stainthorpe replied in the negative, and cautioned him not to say anything that might criminate himself. On their coming in sight of Hexham, from which Cadlaw Hill is distant nearly four miles, Martin, pointing to Highside House, two miles from Hexham, said, "Yonder is the house in which I was born;" and seeing the church of Hexham, he exclaimed, "That is a fine old church. Did the Catholics build that too?" On the way Martin asked if any York papers came to Hexham. And also he said to Mr. Stainthorpe, "Am I advertised in the Newcastle papers?" On being told he was, and also that he was charged with burning York Cathedral, he readily said *he had done it;* and he added, "As soon as I knew I was advertised, I intended to tell everything." On reaching the House of Correction, Martin's bundle was opened, when it was found to contain part of the valuable crimson fringe, &c., which he said he had cut away from the pulpit, or some part of the Minster, a small Bible which he had brought away at the same time, and a piece or two of the painted glass of the Minster. An old razor was found in his pocket, with which he said he cut the crimson fringe, &c., and with which also he struck the fatal light by which he was able to fire the Minster. There were found also seven copies of his Life, but only one penny of money. He appeared up to the moment of his apprehension to have been profoundly ignorant of the extent of the injury he had occasioned; but on a gentleman telling him he had totally destroyed the Cathedral, his countenance brightened, and the news seemed to exhilarate him. He exclaimed, seemingly pleased, "Have I?" After he was lodged in the House of Correction an express was sent off to York with the intelligence.

It was whilst he was in the House of Correction at Hexham that Mr. Wilson (of whom mention has been made) visited him, in company with Mr. Stainthorpe. Mr. Wilson asked him whether his desire to see the newspapers at Cadlaw Hill arose from an anxiety for self-preservation. He replied, "None whatever;" but as he was ignorant what effects had been produced by the fires he had kindled, he was anxious to know; on which Mr. Stainthorpe said the damage was estimated at £100,000. He coolly said, "If it were not for the glory of God, if that could be promoted, £200,000 would not have been too much, and that in his opinion it would have been well if all the Minster had gone together, as the worship carried on in it was idolatrous and superstitious." He declared that he was quite happy and fully resigned to his situation, and "would give himself up into the hands of the Lord."

Such had been the demonstration of popular feeling shown by the persons collected at different times to wait the coaches coming in when Martin was expected, that the magistrates very prudently arranged that he should arrive in York early on Monday morning, and that the examination should take place immediately on his arrival. It was as near as possible half-past three o'clock when Mr. Newstead and Pardoe arrived with their prisoner in a post-chaise at the Session House in the Minster-yard. He was taken into the room occupied by Harrison, the keeper of Peter Prison, where he seated himself on a chair with his hands clasped, his feet elevated on the fender, and his eyes closed. Mr.

Pardoe asked him if his feet were cold; to which he replied "Yes"; and this was the only word he spoke till the examination commenced. He was dressed in a blue coat and trousers, with a drab great-coat. He had by no means the appearance of a "stout man," as described in the bill; but the person where he lodged said he had fallen away very much in that short period.

It was half-past four o'clock when everything was arranged for examination. The magistrates took their seats on the bench, and Martin was placed at the bar; the warrant under which he was apprehended was read over to him, and the depositions of witnesses were also read.

It is unnecessary here to give the evidence either on this occasion or at the subsequent trial. On being asked what he had to say for himself, he made the following confession in a firm voice:—

"The reason that I set fire to the Cathedral was on account of two particular dreams. In the first dream I dreamed that a man stood by me with a bow and a sheath of arrows. He shot an arrow, and the arrow stuck in the Minster door. I then wished to shoot, and the man presented me the bow, and I took an arrow from the sheath and shot, and it struck on a stone and I lost it. In the second dream I dreamed that a cloud came down on the Cathedral, and came over to the house where I slept, and it made the whole house tremble. Then I woke; and I thought it was the hand of God pointing out that I was to set fire to the Cathedral. And those things which were found on me I took to bear witness against myself; I cut the hangings from the throne, or cathedra, or whatever you call it, and tore down the curtains."

Here he stopped rather abruptly, and being asked whether he had anything more to say, he replied "No."

During the whole of the proceedings Martin appeared perfectly calm, and stood with his eyes closed nearly the whole of the time, his head inclining over the right shoulder.

His committal was then made out, and signed by Mr. Dickens, the chairman, and the Rev. D.R. Currer, and he was removed to the City Gaol, and given into the custody of Mr. Kilby, to remain till the Assizes.

After Martin was committed to the charge of the gaoler on the morning of the 9th of February, he breakfasted and went to bed. His sleep was sound and tranquil, and he awoke much refreshed and in good spirits.

Strangers were not admitted to see him. Next day he appeared greatly depressed, and was very anxious to avoid public observation. He attended prayers in the chapel during the morning. The next day, however, he refused to attend the chapel. Subsequently he was visited by the Rev. G. Coopland, the chaplain, in his day-room, who found that so deeply rooted was his aversion to the Liturgy of the Church of England as to leave him no reason to doubt that a forced attendance during the chapel service would much more likely to prove injurious than beneficial to his own mind. Besides, he thought it not all improbable that were he compelled to attend, he might consider it his duty to interrupt the service, and publicly to protest against a mode of worship which he deemed unscriptual. Under these circumstances his attendance at chapel was not enforced. He frequently prayed and sang hymns, and when the order was relaxed by which strangers were prohibited from seeing him, he entered very freely into conversation with them. He still pretended to be favoured with extraordinary visions. On one occasion he said he dreamed that two angels appeared to him in prison, one of whom he told him to apply his lips to the tip of his wings, which he did, when he was immediately conveyed beyond the walls of his prison.

His brother arrived in York about ten days before the Assizes commenced, to make preparations for his defence. The defence intended to be set up was insanity; and a number of witnesses were collected with a view to support this plea. Dr. Wake, at the request of his brother, visited him on Friday, the 20th. Up to this period his conduct had been extremely mild, and his feelings composed; but a little change had not been observed for a day or two previous, and that night, about twelve o'clock, he attempted to make his escape. He slept in what was called the Hospital Room – a room in which there were two beds, a person who was appointed as his guard sleeping in one of them, and Martin in the other. The guard fell asleep about half-past eleven o'clock, and was soon after awoke by a knocking, apparently outside the room. Not apprehending anything, he went to sleep again; and Martin, having torn his bed-rug into lengths, tied them together, and formed a rope about nine yards long. He fastened this round his ankles, and having on only his shirt and his drawers, he ascended the chimney. An iron gate which was fixed in near the top prevented him, however, from getting to the outside of the prison, and he was obliged to descend again. He then placed his sooty shirt under the bed, swept the soot into the same place, and put on his flannel dress, and retired to bed. The attendant, on awakening about two o'clock, found him up, but he soon lay down again; and both rose at half-past six o'clock. Almost as soon as the door was opened Martin bolted out, and went into the yard. His attendant, alarmed, followed him, and found him washing himself. The state of the room and of his person, together with two bricks laid in the fire-place, proved the fact that an escape had been attempted. Indeed, when charged with it, he did not deny it. He said, if he had been a smaller person he should have effected his escape; but that it was the "will of God" he should make the attempt, and be frustrated.

Of course, after this, a closer watch was kept upon the actions of the prisoner.

On Monday, March 23rd, he was brought before Mr. Justice Bayley at the Guildhall, and true bills were found against him for arson and sacrilege. He is described during the examination at the Guildhall as having been perfectly placid, and as having smiled occasionally.

When the Court adjourned for rest and refreshment to the Mansion House during the proceedings, he engaged in conversation with the parties near him, and laughed at their observations. A lady said to him – "In destroying that beautiful pile of buildings you inflicted no real punishment on its clergy."

Martin laughed, and answered – "Eh, but it may mak' them stand and consider their ways. All those who are really converted will think I've done right enuff."

The trumpets soon after sounded, heralding the approach of the judge. The prisoner said – "Hark, how the watchman cries. Oh! attend to the sound." The crowd was so dense in the hall that it was with difficulty a passage could be made for his lordship. Martin laughed, and observed to Mr. Kilby, "They'll have t' ould man down." A gentleman asked him if he was not afraid. He said, "No, not at all."

The populace entirely filled the hall and part of the yard; and Jonathan turned his face towards them, frequently laughing, and talking to those with whom he came immediately in contact. He said he "believed he was the most righteous man in court", adding, "I have made as much noise as Bonaparte ever did. I think this is a very throng day." He then turned round to the counsel and reporters, and said, "I keep them very busy; I have given them all a job. I'll put their hands in by-and-bye." When the judge returned he said, "Here's t' ould man coming again." He seemed quite pleased at being the object of such universal interest, and repeatedly laughed at the attempts of the people to get a sight of him.

The trial of Jonathan Martin took place in the Crown Court of York Castle before Mr. Baron Hullock, on Monday, March 30. The Court was crowded. When placed at the bar and the first charge, that of having feloniously set fire to the Cathedral Church of St. Peter's, York, had been read to Martin by the clerk of arraigns, and he had been asked the usual question whether he were "guilty or not guilty," he placed himself in a theatrical attitude, and said, "It was not me, my lord, but my God did it. It Is quite common to Him to punish to the third and fourth generation, and to show mercy to all that fear Him and keep His commandments."

A plea of "Not guilty" was entered.

The second indictment was then read over to him, charging him with feloniously stealing a quantity of crimson velvet and gold fringe and two gold tassels, the property of the Dean and Chapter of the Cathedral and Metropolitical Church of York. He was asked whether he was guilty or not guilty. Throwing out his left hand, he replied—

"My God gave me that for my hire. The Lord gave the silk to mak' a robe, like David the King, and the velvet to mak' a cap, and the tassels I took from the pulpit to hang down over my right and left ear."

THE CLERK OF INDICTMENTS. – "Are you guilty or not guilty?"

MARTIN. – "I had it give me for hire."

This was taken as a plea of "Not guilty;" and Mr. Baron Hullock addressing him, said, "You will be tried to-morrow morning at nine o'clock." He bowed, and said, "Very well, my lord;" and was removed from the bar.

The crier of the Court then announced, at the desire of the judge, that the trial of Jonathan Martin would not take place till Tuesday morning at nine o'clock.

On Tuesday, March 31st, the Court was crowded as on the preceeding day, and great confusion was the result; this seemed to cause Martin much amusement, and he laughed repeatedly at the struggles of the crowd at the door, and leaped on a seat to observe it.

After the hearing of the evidence, the substance of which has been incorporated in the narrative, Jonathan Martin was called upon for his defence. Martin, who had become very listless during the examination, seemed at this movement full of animation, and in a very vehement manner uttered in broad Northern dialect the following words in his defence:—

"The first impression that I had was by two particular dreams, sir; and after I had written five letters to warn the clergy. I think the last I wrote a very severe one. I believe I wrote in it all the curses of the Scripture to warn them, and likewise signed my name to every letter, and the place I lodged at, No. 60, Aldgate. I never received any letters, which I was anxious to have from these clergymen, to speak to them by mouth, but there was found none among them that dared to answer me. I prayed to the Lord what I was to do. The next night I dreamt that a wonderful thick cloud came from heaven and rested upon the Minster." (Here the prisoner gave a long account of his dream, mentioned above, and about the cloud resting over the house.) He continued: – "The house was so shook that it awoke me from sleep. I was astonished, and began to ask the Lord what it meant. I felt a voice inwardly speak that the Lord had chosen me to destroy the Cathedral for the wrong that was doing by the clergy in going to plays, and balls, and card-tables, and dinners. Different things impressed my mind that the Lord has chosen me, because the house shook and trembled. I thought it resembled the pillar of smoke, and fulfilled the prophecy of Joel, that God would pour out His Spirit upon all flesh, and the old men should see visions, and the young men dream dreams, and that there should be signs in the heavens, blood and fire, and vapour and smoke. I thought that I should be fulfilling the word of God, and it was so impressed on my mind I had no rest night or day; for I found the Lord had determined to have me to show this people a warning to flee from the wrath to come. I was rather at a loss, and astonished about my wife lest she should attack me, for I could not do it without being all night from her. After I had considered a while and got everything in order, I began to think it was impossible for me to do it, as if I was away without my wife knowing where, she might conceive I was about the Cathedral, and come and put me out. Therefore I thought of this, to take my wife's ring off her finger, and tie her over to this concern, which I did, as I have mentioned before, and the circumstance of my wife's keeping the vow. After I told her the circumstance she was much grieved, and strove to get me away to Leeds, to get me from the purpose I had informed her of. We went to Leeds and stayed a few days there, but I could get no rest to my mind till I had accomplished the deed. I was obliged to take leave of her on the Saturday morning. I had a severe contest between flesh and blood. It was a sair contest, especially when she asked what was to become of her, and of my child Richard

I had at school at Lincoln. I thought she would have nailed me to the spot; but for a moment a passage of Scripture struck my ears, and it cried out like a whisper, 'What thou doest, do quickly.' I heard another – 'He that loveth father or mother more than me is not worthy of me.' And I heard a third whisper – 'Even thine own life.' I tore myself from her arms. I said – 'Lord, not my will, but thine be done.' I then felt the love of God in my heart. I thought I would go to Tadcaster, and took twenty books with me. When I got them the Spirit told me to go forward. I had no money to keep me over the Sunday. I had only fourpence-halfpenny.'' The prisoner then gave a minute detail of his proceedings, and the different expedients resorted to in order to set fire to the building, which he described as having been a work of great labour and difficulty. He said, at the evening service he was "very much vexed at hearing them sing the prayers and amens; he thought the prayer of the heart came from the heart, and that they had no call for prayer-books." He observed – "The organ then made such a buzzing noise, I thought, 'Thou shalt buzz no more – I'll have thee down to-night.' Well," he continued, "they were all going out, and I lay down aside of the bishop, round by the pillar." (The prisoner concealed himself behind a tomb.) "I lay here till all went out. I thought I heard the people coming down from ringing the bells; they all went out, and then it was so dark that I could not see my hand. Well, I left the bishop, and came out and fell upon my knees, and asked the Lord what I was to do first, and he said – 'Get thy way up into the belfry and cut a rope;' and I had never been there, and I went round and round; I had sort of a guess of the place from hearing the men, as I thought, came down. Then the Spirit said, 'Strike a light.' And I then struck a light with a flint and razor that I had got, and some tinder that I had brought from my landlord's. I saw there were plenty of ropes: then I cut one, and then another; but I had no idea they were so long, and I kept draw, draw, and the rope came up till I daresay I had near 100 feet. I have been a sailor, and thought to myself, this will make a man-rope, a sort of scaling rope, and I tied knots in it. Aye, this is it, I know it well enough (pointing to the rope which lay upon the table). So I went down to the body of the Cathedral, and bethought me how I should go inside. I thought if I did so, by throwing the rope over the organ, I might set it *ganging*, and that would spoil the job. So I made an end of the rope fast, and went hand-over-hand over the gates, and got down on the other side, and fell on my knees, and prayed to the Lord, and He told me that do what I would they would take me. Then I asked the Lord what I was to do with the velvet, and He told me,'' (the prisoner here repeated what he had before stated in his plea about the robe, cap, and tassels.) "The fringe, I thought, would do for my hairy jacket that I have at Lincoln. I have a very good sealskin one there; I wish I had it with me, that I might show it you. Then I got all ready. Glory to God! I never felt so happy; but I had a hard night's work of it, particularly with a hungry belly. Well, I got a bit of wax-candle, and I set fire to one heap, and with the matches I set fire to the other. I then tied up the things that the Lord had given me for my hire in this very handkerchief that I have in my hand." He then observed that he had "hard work" while engaged in making his preparations; "but," said he, "I had a glorious time of it; and many a time I called 'Glory be to God' in a way which I wonder they did not hear on the outside." He left the pincers, he said, because the old man with whom he lodged could not afford to lose them, and he knew he would get them again. He thought it a work of merit to burn prayer-books and music-books, but not to burn the Word of God, and he appeared to regret that he could not save the large Bible by getting it over the gates and putting it outside. He detailed the particulars of his journey to the North; and described himself as having, from his arrival at York till he reached Northallerton, had very little food, but "t' Lord refreshed my soul on t' road wi' t' snow upon t' ground." He then went on with his story till he reached Mr. Kell's house, and "t' Hexham man came, tapped me on t' shoulder, and took me to t' lock-up." He concluded, after speaking twenty minutes – "I am almost tired of talking, but I will efterwards tell ye a bit more."

A minute or two after, he said to the reporters – "An' you have been writing down what I said – I think I talked o'er fast for thee!" He then espied one of his publications, and said – "I see the'se gotten one of my bukes. I wrote mysen at different times, and have sold 10,000 copies."

The defence set up for the prisoner by Mr. Brougham, acting for Jonathan Martin's brother, was that Jonathan had perpetrated the deed when in an unsound state of mind. The jury returned the verdict – "We are of opinion that he set fire to the Cathedral, being at the time insane, or of unsound mind."

Baron Hullock: – "Then your verdict must be *not guilty* on the ground of insanity; and the prisoner must remain in close custody during his Majesty's pleasure."

Martin was highly irritated at the line of defence adopted by Mr. Brougham; but that some suspicion of his lunacy was entertained by himself at an early period appears from his own words in his autobiography, written before he set fire to York Minster: – "The devil suggested to me that the people would think me mad. My wife endeavoured to comfort me, as she feared for my head."

After the sentence he was handcuffed and conveyed into the Castle. He made no observation, but was evidently disappointed and dejected at the result. For some days after this Martin seemed rather despondent, but he soon resumed his activity, pacing up and down at the rate of five miles an hour, and at an average of twenty miles per day. He asked someone he knew, who visited him, after his son, who was at school at Lincoln, and said – "I'm thinking that God ha' used me varry badly."

He was removed from York Castle to St. Luke's Hospital in London, where his conduct is described as having been generally rational. He seldom spoke on the subject of his crime. Towards his brother he entertained the bitterest enmity for having had him proved insane. But he consoled himself in his confinement with the thought, "The Lord will take His own time to deliver me, and that will not be long, for He has a great work which cannot be done without me."

When he heard of the death of Baron Hullock, before whom he was tried, and which took place the same year, he seemed much agitated, walked about a while, as if talking to himself, but made no observation. It transpired afterwards that he looked on this as a signal instance of the Lord punishing one of his enemies.

BROTHER JUCUNDUS.

AT York were two religious houses – St. Mary's Abbey and St. Leonard's Priory – so close together that their walls abutted. The magnificent ruins of St. Mary's Abbey Church, the heavy fragments of the Priory Church of St. Leonard's, now stand in the gardens of the Botanical Society, and resound no longer to the sound of psalmody, but to the strains of the band playing marches, waltzes, and overtures.

At the close of the fifteenth century, before the Disssolution was thought of, there lived, and fasted, and prayed in St. Leonard's Priory a fat monk named Brother Jucundus. He had not been long in the house. He had joined the order in a fit of headache and remorse, after heavy potations on the occasion of the installation of a new Lord Mayor, and it is possible – probable, I suspect – that he somewhat regretted his precipitancy. Yet there was no escape. The irrevocable vows were on him; for life he was bound to eat only vegetables and bread, drink very small beer, and sleep only six hours in the night.

Convivial songs floated through his mind when he ought to have been chanting the Psalms of David, and the flavour of old sack rose upon his palate when he looked dolefully down at dinner-time into his mug of "swipes."

A year passed. The full paunch of Brother Jucundus began to subside; his fat cheeks to fall flabby, like the dewlaps of a cow; a dispirited expression took the place of the watery twinkle which had once animated his eye.

Come what might, Brother Jucundus felt he must have a fling. He should die without it. Just one jollification in the twelvemonth, and then he would put up for the rest of the year with beans and cabbage, small beer and matins before dawn.

York fair approached. York fair! of all that is ravishing! The shows of dancing dogs, the whirli-go-rounds, the giantesses and dwarfs, the "spice" stalls, the drinking-booths! To York fair he must, he would go, if condemned to a bean and a thimbleful of water for fasting dinner ever after.

And go he did. He managed it in this way: – After dinner the whole community took an hour's sleep. As they rose at midnight and dined at midday, this was very necessary, and the Priory was silent, save for snores, from one o'clock to two. At half-past one Brother Jucundus stole to the porter's lodge, found the porter asleep in his chair – so took possession of his keys; went to the Prior's apartment; the Prior was asleep; pocketed a crown from his money-box, and left the Priory.

At two o'clock the community awoke. The porter missed his keys. The Prior missed the crown. All the monks were summoned into the chapter-house, and all missed Brother Jucundus.

After long deliberation it was decided that two sedate and trusty brothers should be sent out in quest of him.

It was a bright, sunny afternoon. Jucundus had enjoyed himself amazingly. The amount of gingerbread horses and men he had consumed was prodigious. He had seen "The Spotted Boy" and "The Bearded Woman;" he had gone round in the whirligig on the back of a wooden horse; he had shot for nuts at a mark, and won his pocket full, which he cracked every now and then, and washed down with a draft of really good ale. And now, just now he was going up in the boat of a great see-saw, with a foaming tankard in his hand, his jolly red face illuminated with glee, and his ample throat thundering forth—

> "In the dulce jubilo-o-o,
> Up, up, up we go-o-o,"

when his sweet jubilee was cut short by the sight of two monks from his Priory, with grim faces, making their way towards the see-saw.

Brother Jucundus tried to scramble out, and in so doing tumbled down. He was picked up. Either his libations, or the fall, or disinclination to return to St. Leonard's weakened his legs, and he tottered so much that the reverend fathers were obliged to put him in a wheelbarrow and roll him to the Priory gate. At the entrance stood the Prior with a brow of thunder.

Brother Jucundus looked pleasantly up in his face from out of his conveyance, smiled benignantly, and piped—

> "In dulce jubilo-o-o,
> Up, up, up we go-o-o."

The chapter was still sitting, stern and threatening.

The helpless monk was trundled in his barrow into the midst of the assembled fathers, to be tried and sentenced.

He had been caught, *flagrante delicto*, in a see-saw, drunk, riotous, and incapable. Nevertheless, Brother Jucundus was not disposed to view his case unfavourably. He looked round on the chapter with an affectionate glance from out of his watery eye, and the kindest, most winsome smile on his ruddy cheeks.

He was asked at once for his defence. He murmured with a hiccup—

> "In dulce jubilo-o-o."

The sentence was unanimous, and unfalteringly given. He was to be walled alive into a niche in the Priory cellar. The execution was to be carried into effect immediately.

As he was helped down the cellar stairs, some glimmering of his situation came in on the mind of Jucundus, and he sadly trolled out—

"Down, down, down we go-o-o."

A convenient niche was soon found. A cruse of water and a loaf of bread, with cruel mockery, were placed in the recess. The ready hands of zealous monks mixed the mortar, brought the bricks, and in a quarter of an hour Brother Jucundus was firmly walled in to his living grave.

Now for the first time did the extreme inconvenience of his position break upon the unfortunate monk. In the wheelbarrow he had been able to sit; here he was walled upright. It was cramping, intolerable. He kicked, he pressed backwards with all his might; and suddenly, with a crash, the wall behind him gave way, and he rolled backwards over a heap of fallen bricks into a cellar.

The shock brought him completely to his senses. Where was he? Now he saw the gravity of his offence – the terrible fate that had been prepared for him. Escape was fortunately open to him. He ran up the cellar stairs, and found himself in the Abbey of St Mary's. The cellars of the two monasteries had adjoined; a wall alone had divided them. He had tumbled out of St. Leonard's into St, Mary's.

St. Mary's Abbey belonged to the severe Cistercian Order. Complete silence was one of the rules of the society. Except on Easter day, no monk might speak; on Easter day every one talked, and nobody listened. When Brother Jucundus accordingly appeared in the cloisters, no monk turned to look at him, or asked him "how the saints he had come there?" but swept by him like a ghost. Jucundus made himself as much at home as was possible. He took his place at the table, and ate and drank what was set before him, occupied a pallet in the common dormitory, lifted his voice in concert with the others in the Abbey choir, and nobody meddled with him. The monks, if they thought about him at all – and it was against their rules to think of anything but their own spiritual affairs – thought he was a new monk just joined in the usual accepted manner.

A twelvemonth passed. It had been dull in St. Leonard's; it was duller in St. Mary's. The day came round on which York fair was held, the day, that happy day, which had ended so dolorously.

Now the day before York fair the office of cellarer fell vacant in St. Mary's Abbey by the death of the monk who had presided over the wine and beer. The Abbot by a happy inspiration committed the keys to Brother Jucundus. Here was an opportunity! If York fair might not be enjoyed in the market-place and the Pavement, he would at least commemorate it in the Abbey cellar.

On York fair day, accordingly, Brother Jucundus, after having seen all his fellow monks safe in bed, stole down the stone steps into the vault where were the barrels, with a tankard in his one hand and a lantern in the other.

St. Mary's Abbey was often called upon to receive noble, even royal guests, and entertain them nobly and royally. It therefore contained barrels of very prime wine and very strong audit ale. Brother Jucundus went along the range of barrels trying one tipple after another. There is nothing so dangerous as mixing your drink, and this the reverend brother discovered at last, for he sat down, unable to proceed further, by the best cast of Malmsey, and turning the tap, filled his tankard.

Next day at noon the Cistercians assembled in the refectory for their frugal repast, dinner and breakfast in one: and as they had been up since midnight, and had eaten and drunk nothing for twelve hours, were tolerably hungry and dry. But the mugs were empty. At the Abbot's table even was neither wine nor beer. The silent fraternity bore with this some time, but at last even the rules of the Order could not keep them perfectly silent. They shuffled with their feet, growled and grunted discontentedly. At last the Abbot, in a voice of thunder, shouted—

"I want my beer!" and the example of the head becoming infectious, "Beer, beer, beer! we all want our beer!" resounded from every part of the refectory.

"Where was the cellarer?" Nobody knew. At last two brothers were commissioned to go to the cellar and fetch ale. They presently returned with awe-struck countenances, beckoned to the Abbot to follow them, and led the way along the cloisters down the cellar stairs. Curiosity, though against the rule, was infectious, and all the monks crept *en queue* after the Abbot. When they reached the vault a shocking sight presented itself to their eyes. Brother Jucundus lay with his head against the butt of Malmsey, flourishing his tankard over his head, and feebly, incoherently, trolling forth—

"In dulce jubilo-o-o,
Up, up, up we go-o-o."

It was too flagrant an offence to be passed over. A chapter of the Order was at once constituted in the cellar itself. All the monks were present. Unanimously it was decided that after solemn excommunication with bell, book, and candle, the guilty brother should be walled up alive on the scene of his crime in that very cellar.

The awful scene of excommunication was proceeded with. It took some time, and during the ceremony Brother Jucundus gradually resumed consciousness – the fumes of the Malmsey slowly evaporated. A convenient recess was found, where a heap of crumbling bricks lay prostrate. It was the identical nook out of which a year and a day before Brother Juncundus had escaped into the Cistercian Order and Abbey of St. Mary.

Into this niche therefore he was built. His terrible position had not, however, as yet forced itself on the monk's brain; he still tasted Malmsey, still was his heart buoyant, and swelling lungs he roared forth his song—

"In dulce jubilo-o-o,
Up, up, up we go-o-o."

Now, it happened that the clocks in St. Leonard's and St. Mary's differed by a quarter of an hour. That of St. Leonard's was slower than that of St. Mary's. Consequently it was only just dinner-time in St. Leonard's Priory, and the cellarer, pitcher in hand, had just descended the stairs, and was filling his vessel with small beer, when he heard close to his ear, from behind the wall, a stentorian voice thunder forth—

"In dulce jubilo-o-o,
Up, up, up we go-o-o."

The voice, the strain, the words were those of Brother Jucundus, who a year and a day before had been immured at that very spot.

Down went the pitcher, and away fled the monk – amazement, admiration in his countenance, "A miracle! a miracle!" in his mouth – to the monks, just issuing from the church and the recitation of Sext and the office for the dead around the body of their Prior, lately deceased, and that day to be buried.

The whole community rolled like a tidal wave down the cellar-stairs, and stood with breathless awe in a circle about the spot where twelve months and a day before they had walled in Brother Jucundus.

It was a miracle – there could be no doubt of it. Eager hands tore down the wall, and revealed the reverend brother, and rosy as of yore, and at his side a loaf as fresh as when put in, and a pitcher still full to the brim.

There could be no doubt but that this was a special interposition to establish the innocence of the monk, and to indicate to the community who was to be their future Prior.

With one voice they shouted, "Jucundus our Prior! Saint Jucundus our head and father!"

On the shoulders of the enthusiastic brethren the miraculous monk was carried up-stairs and installed in the Prior's seat in the chapter-house.

Under him St. Leonard's jogged along very pleasantly, and he did much in his long rule of the monastery for its discipline and good order, if not to justify, at least to excuse the dissolution which fell on it immediately after his death.

MARY BATEMAN

WITCH AND MURDERESS.

MARY HARKER was the daughter of a small farmer at Aisenby, in the parish of Topcliffe, near Thirsk, where she was born in 1768. From an early age she exhibited great quickness, which, instead of taking a direct course and developing into intelligence, was warped into low cunning.

She received, for one in her situation, a good education – was taught to read, and write, and cypher. But she very early showed a want of moral principle, very possibly because it was never instilled into her by her parents, and her first petty thefts having been pardoned or laughed at, she grew bolder, and what had been occasional grew to be frequent, and matured into a habit of peculation. Her father sent her into service at the age of thirteen, in Thirsk, and for a while she either concealed or did not yield to her propensity for theft. At all events, if she did pilfer, she was neither suspected nor discovered.

At the age of twenty she left Thirsk for York, and after a year's sojourn in that city, was detected in an attempt at robbery, and ran away to Leeds, where, in 1788, she worked as a mantua-maker; but as her knowledge of dress-making was imperfect – she had only acquired it during he twelvemonth at York, where her mistress had been a dress-maker – she was able to work for the lower classes alone. She lived in Leeds for four years, following this occupation and occasionally telling fortunes. Her professed calling admirably served to introduce dupes to her, and the servant-girls for whom she worked infrequently introduced her to their young mistresses.

In the year 1792 she married an honest, hard-working man named John Bateman, who had made her acquaintance only three weeks previously. This man, there is no reason for believing, was, at first at all events, an accomplice in, or acquainted with, the crimes committed subsequently by his wife, though afterwards it is scarcely possible to exculpate him from connivance in them.

She now began openly to profess fortune-telling, the removal of spells, the power of controlling the future, &c., in which, however, she did not act in her own name, but as the deputy of Mrs. Moore, whom she represented as a person endowed with the supernatural powers belonging to the seventh child of a seventh child.

Whether such a person existed or not was never ascertained, but it is certain that Mary Bateman, at the outset of her career, had some accomplice, and she was from her youth fond of associating with gipsies and other vagrants, from whom she learned the art she afterwards practised.

The Bateman's lodged in High Court Lane, Leeds and she stole from a fellow-lodger a silver watch, a spoon of the same metal, and two guineas. The theft was discovered, and she was made to restore what she had taken, but she was not prosecuted.

Several charges of obtaining silk goods under various names of persons with whom she was acquainted were made and substantiated at this time, but the shopkeepers, with mistaken clemency, regarding her as a poor milliner, forgave her.

A poor man, a neighbour, who earned his living and supported his family with the assistance of a horse and cart, sickened and died, leaving a widow and four children, the eldest a boy about fifteen years of age. The widow, who was only the stepmother of the children, was persuaded by Mary Bateman that the eldest boy meant to sell all the little property his father had left, and appropriate the money to his own use, to prevent which she advised the mother to sell the horse, cart and furniture as soon as possible, and to quit Yorkshire. This advice the infatuated woman took, turned everything into money, left a share with Mary for the children, and departed. Mary Bateman appropriated the sum entrusted to her, and sent the children to the union.

A gentleman living in Meadow Lane, in Leeds, bought a leg of mutton at the shambles, and requested that it might be sent home immediately. Mary, ever on the watch for her prey, hastened to the bridge over which the butcher's boy had to pass, and when she saw him approach, made towards him in a great hurry, pretending she was the gentleman's servant, scolded the boy for being so long upon the road, and taking the mutton by the shank, gave him a slap on the back, telling him she would carry it home herself. It is needless to say that carry it home she did, but not to the gentleman's house. When dinner-time came the joint had not arrived. The gentleman went to his butcher to inquire about the neglect, but he was informed that the meat had been sent an hour ago, and was taken from the boy by a woman, whom the butcher described, and whom the gentleman recollected to have seen at the stall when he was buying the meat, and whose residence he luckily knew to be in the Old Assembly-Room Yard, in Kirkgate. He accordingly posted down to her house, and the first object that presented itself to his eyes on entering it was his leg of mutton roasting before Bateman's fire. After upbraiding Mary, she agreed to pay for the mutton, and the matter was thus compromised.

In 1793 Bateman took a small house in Well's Yard, and furnished it decently – by what means, unless from the proceeds of her frauds, it is difficult to say, though it is due to the husband to admit that he was never proved to be cognisant of any of her malpractices, and was sometimes the victim of them. She once went into his workshop and took with her a letter representing that his father, who was then town-crier at Thirsk, was at the point of death.

Her husband instantly set off for that town, and had scarcely entered it when he heard his father's voice in the market-place announcing an auction. He hurried back to Leeds to inform his wife of the hoax that had been practised upon them; but on his return he found his house stripped of every article of furniture, which Mary had sold, in all probability to hush up some robbery she had committed.

After some time they jointly found means to get fresh furniture, and they took in lodgers, one of whom, a Mr. Dixon, discovered Mary in the act of purloining money from his box. She was forced to refund it, and make good several losses that Mr. Dixon had before sustained, but for which he had not been able to account.

In the year 1796 a tremendous fire broke out in a large manufactory in Leeds, and by the falling of one of the walls many unfortunate people lost their lives. This calamity Mary Bateman turned to her own advantage. She went to Miss Maude, a lady known for her charitable disposition, and telling her that the child of a poor woman had fallen a victim, and that she had not linen to lay the child out on, begged she would lend her a pair of sheets. This request was complied with; but the sheets, instead of being turned to such a benevolent purpose, were pledged at a pawn broker's shop. Three similar instances occured at the same time, and all the sheets were disposed of in the same way. Nor did her frauds on the plea of this calamity end here. She went round the town representing herself as a nurse at the General Infirmary, and collecting all the old linen she could beg to dress the wounds, as she said, of the patients who had been brought into the infirmary, but in reality to dispose of them for herself.

Bateman, ashamed of the disgrace caused by his wife's conduct, entered the supplementary militia, but he took with him his plague – his wife. And here a wide field opened for a woman of her disposition. She practised her old arts and learnt fresh ones. Of her exploits while in this situation we have no information; but when she quitted the army with her husband in the year 1796, on their return to Leeds, they took up their residence in Marsh Lane, near Timble Bridge. Mary then began to practise on a large scale. She herself, as she said, had no skill in casting nativities or reading the stars, but a certain Mrs. Moore was a proficient in this art, and to Mrs. Moore she referred all knotty points. It is hardly necessary to say that Mrs. Moore had no existence whatever.

The first experiment in witchcraft was made upon a Mrs. Greenwood, whom she attempted to persuade that she, Mrs. Greenwood, was in danger of committing suicide on account of domestic misfortunes, and that the skill of Mrs. Moore would be necessary to prevent so dire a catastrophe. Next she informed her that her husband, who was then from home, was taken up for some offence, and placed in confinement; that four men had been set to watch him; and that if four pieces of gold, four pieces of leather, four pieces of blotting-paper, and four brass screws were not produced that night, and placed in her hands to give to Mrs. Moore to "screw down" the guards, her husband would be a dead man before morning. In vain did Mrs. Greenwood plead that she had no pieces of gold; this difficulty Mrs. Bateman proposed to overcome by suggesting to her that she might borrow or steal them; the latter proposal startled her intended dupe, and, fortunately for her, she had fortitude enough to emancipate herself from the witch's trammels.

The family of Barzillai Stead, a person who had been unsuccessful in business, next became the object of Mary's iniquitous exactions. Upon the husband's fears she contrived to work with so much success, by representing the bailiffs to be in continual pursuit of him, that she obliged him to enlist, and to share his bounty with her and her imaginary wise-woman. Her next object was to arouse the jealousy of the wife: this she did by assuring her that it was the intention of Barzillai to take with him, when he went to his regiment, a young woman out of Vicar Lane, Leeds. In order to prevent this it became necessary to "screw down" the rival queen; this was to be effected by the agency of Mrs. Moore, but Mrs. Moore's screws would never drive without money – three half-crowns were to be produced for this purpose, and two pieces of coal; the coals were to be placed at the woman's door in Vicar Lane; they were then to be laid on the fire – the woman was to be thrown into a sound sleep – the fire was to communicate to her clean clothes, which had been washed in contemplation of the intended journey, and, the clothes being consumed, she could not of course elope without them. The morning after this charm had taken effect, Stead left Leeds to join his regiment, and left the imaginary woman of Vicar Lane behind him. Mary was then left at liberty to play off the whole artillery of her frauds upon the unsuspecting wife of Stead. To enter into all expedients she adopted to fleece this poor woman would swell this article to an inconvenient length; suffice it to say that she obliged her to sell or pawn every article in her house that would raise money, and drove her to such a state of desperation as to lead her victim to attempt suicide. While Mary Bateman was practising upon this woman, her dupe was confined, and the Leeds Benevolent Society, finding her in a state or destitution, determined to apply a guinea to the relief of her wants. This sum was given to her in three payments of 7s., and out of this guinea Mary Bateman had the inhumanity to exort 18s. by persuading the credulous woman that she would "screw down" the Benevolent Society, so as to force the managers to give her more alms.

The furniture and clothes were now all gone, and nothing remained but a few tools left by Stead when he went into the army, but even these could not escape the avarice of Mary Bateman, who was never at a loss for expedients to effect her purposes. She persuaded Stead's wife that it was in the power of Mrs. Moore – Mrs. Moore again! – to "screw down" all the officers in her husband's regiment, and so to screw them that they could not avoid giving him his discharge; but then money must be raised, and how, when nothing remained in the house but the tools? They of course must be sent to the pawnbroker's and every farthing they fetched was paid to Mary to get her friend Moore to interpose her kind offices for the liberation of the soldier. This charm failed, as the officers were too much for the witch.

Mary Bateman next became acquainted with a tradesman's wife of the name of Cooper. She persuaded this woman that her husband was about to abscond, and take with him all the property he could raise, and that she might not be left quite destitute, Mary prevailed upon her to convey as much of the furniture as she could out of the house, including an excellent clock, and to lodge all this furniture at Bateman's. There it did not remain long. Mary took it all to the pawnbroker's, got for it what it would fetch, and left the abused husband and his credulous wife to redeem it at their leisure.

Blown upon as the credit of Mrs. Bateman's witchcraft then was, she removed from Timble Bridge to the Black Dog Yard, at the Bank. While she lived here one of her hens laid a wonderful egg, remarkable for bearing this inscription—

"CHRIST IS COMING."

But as so singular a phenomenon was not likely to obtain all the credit necessary for carrying into effect her fraudulent intentions unless supported by some kind of proof, she had the ingenuity and cruelty to contrive that two other eggs, bearing similar inscriptions, should be deposited in the nest by the same unfortunate hen. Persons flocked from all quarters to see the wonderful eggs, and they who dared to disbelieve stood a good chance of being maltreated by the credulous multitude. Mary's motive for producing those eggs is not well made out, but it is supposed that she had at that time a notion of following the example of Joanna Southcote, as she was then in the habit of attending the meetings of the sect founded by that extraordinary woman. Mary succeeded in realising no inconsiderable sum by means of these eggs, for she made those who came to see the miracle pay a penny each for the gratification of their curiosity.

Shortly after the subject of this narrative contrived to ingratiate herself, as she well knew how, into the good graces of a family of the name Kitchin, two maiden ladies of the Quaker persuasion, who kept a small linen-draper's shop near St. Peter's Square, in Leeds. There is every reason to suppose that she had deluded these unfortunate young women with some idea of her skill in looking into futurity, or, at least, that some of her friends – a Mrs. Moore or a Miss Blythe perhaps – could read their destiny in the stars! For some time Mary was the confidant of the Misses Kitchin. She was frequently at their house; she assisted in their shop; and her interference extended even to their domestic concerns. In the early part of September, 1803, one of the young women became very ill; Mary Bateman procured for her medicines, as she said, from a country doctor. These medicines, like those administered afterwards to Perigo and his unfortunate wife, were of powerful efficacy, and in the course of less than one week Miss Kitchin died. In the meantime her mother, hearing of her dangerous situation, came from Wakefield, and though in good health when she left home, the other as well as the second daughter took the same illness, and in a few days both were laid in the grave, at the side of their ill-fated relation.

Previous to the death of one of the sisters a female friend of the family was sent for, and when she arrived the poor sufferer seemed oppressed with some secret that she wished to communicate, but her strength failed her, she expired without being able to do so.

Only ten days sufficed to carry off the mother and two sisters. The complaint of which they died was said to be *cholera* – a complaint, let it be remembered, attended by symptoms resembling those produced by poison. It did not, however, suit the purposes of Mary Bateman to give the disorder so mild a name. She represented it to be the plague, and the whole neighbourhood shunned the place, and would as soon have entered the most infectious wards of a pest-house as this dwelling. Mary alone, in the face of all danger, was ready to afford her friendly offices; and when the persons composing this unfortunate family were buried the door was closed, and a padlock placed upon it.

A physician of eminence in the town, on being called in to visit the last surviving sister, was so strongly impressed with the opinion that her sickness and sudden death had been caused by poison, that he examined with much care many of the vessels in the house, inquired if any water for poisoning flies had been used, and expressed a wish to open the body; but the family being all dead, and no persons at hand who thought themselves authorised to give that permission, the corpse was interred unopened, and with it the opportunity for detection. During the time of the fatal illness in the Misses Kitchin's house, Mary Bateman was unremitting in her attention; she administered their food, and from her hands the medicine was conveyed to their lips. Some time after the death of these ladies their creditors looked over their effects, when it was found that their house and shop had been plundered of almost everything they contained: and to add to the embarrassment of their affairs, the shop books were missing. The creditors only divided eightpence in the pound.

Two young women, then servants in Leeds, had long been in Mary's toils, and she had fleeced them pretty handsomely; and not only them, but their friends, for she had prevailed upon one of them to rob her mother of several articles, and amongst the rest of a large family Bible. When she had got all from them that could be extorted without awakening the suspicions of their friends, she sent both these deluded girls, at different times, to seek service in Manchester, cautioning them, if they met, not to speak to each other, on pain of breaking the charm. When they arrived in Manchester, Mary contrived to keep up a correspondence with them, and got from them even the clothes they wore, so that they were almost reduced to a state of nakedness. One day these poor destitute girls met in the streets of Manchester; the meeting being quite unexpected, they both burst into tears, and their emotions became so violent that further concealment was out of the question. They thereupon related to each other their sad history, and by comparing notes, found that they were both the dupes of Mary Bateman. They then wrote to Leeds, and laid their case before their friends, who interfered in ther behalf, and got from the witch part of the property she had so wickedly extorted.

The witch also contrived to ingratiate herself into the good opinion of another young woman, and got from her several sums of money for the purpose of curing her of an "evil wish" laid upon her by an old beggar-woman whom she had refused to relieve. The cure was to be effected by Miss Blythe, to whom a pocket-handkerchief was to be sent. In due course the directions arrived, and Miss Blythe, who, like Miss Moore, could never put her charms in motion without money, required that different sums, amounting in all to five guineas, should be produced, and as much wearing apparel as was worth about the same sum; but this money and these clothes were only to be kept till the evil wish was removed, and then to be restored to the owner. The period fixed for the opening of the mysterious bags, in which these articles were deposited, had arrived, when one day a person brought a fruit-pie to the young woman, telling her that her sweetheart had sent it. This pie she tasted, and let a fellow-servant partake with her, but though very nice in appearance, the taste was hot and offensive; they in consequence desisted from eating it, and the young woman took it down to Mary Bateman to ask her opinion. Mary affected that she knew nothing herself of such things, but she would send it to the sagacious Miss Blythe. This, as the simple girl supposed, was done, and Miss Blythe informed her that it was very well she had not eaten much of the pie, for if she had, it would have been her last, as it was "full of poison!" Soon after the girl opened the bags, and found that her guineas had turned to copper and her clothes to old rags!

In the year 1807, Bateman, who, owing to the conduct of Mary, never remained long in one place, removed into Meadow Lane. While living in this situation a very extraordinary circumstance occurred, and it is not improbable that Mary was in some way privy to the transaction. A man of the name Joseph Gosling, a cloth-dresser, had been long out of employ, and his family, which consisted of a wife and four children, was reduced to great extremity. One day the whole of the family had been out for some time, when one of the children, a boy about seven years of age, returned, and found on the table a small cake; the mother and other children soon after returned, and partook of this cake. They immediately became so sick as to render medical aid necessary. Mr. Atkinson, the surgeon, was then sent for, and by administering emetics saved the lives of the family. On analysing the cake it was found to contain a large quantity of arsenic. It is impossible to say why or by whom this poisonous bread was placed in the situation in which the boy found it, and the only reason why it is supposed to have been placed there by Mary Bateman is the knowledge that poisonous drugs were much in use by her, that human life was in her estimation of little value; and that the cries or tricks of the children may have inconvenienced her.

In the month of April, 1807, Judith Cryer, a poor old washerwoman, and a widow, was occasioned uneasiness by the misconduct of her grandson, a boy about eleven years of age. Winifred Bond, a person who had some dealings with Mary Bateman, either as her dupe or her agent, recommended the old woman to apply to Mary, as a person who could remove the causes of her distress. Judith consented to consult her; Mary soon found out the foible of the poor woman. An inordinate fear about the future fate of this darling grandson was the spring in Judith's mind on which the witch found she could play with success. She recommended that an application should be made to Miss Blythe, a lady of her acquaintance, who she said lived at Scarboro', but who, in fact, had no more real existence than the invisible Mrs. Moore. She then undertook to write to her dear friend. In a few days an answer was received from this lady, which shocked Judith beyond description. The letter contained the representation of a gallows, with a rope dangling from it. The letter also stated that the grandson would be executed before he attained the age of fourteen years, unless the catastrophe was prevented by the old woman rising four guineas, and applying them as Miss Blythe should direct. To raise such a sum seemed as impossible to Judith as to pay the National Debt. At last, however, she contrived to scrape it together with the utmost difficulty. When raised, it was, as Mary pretended, to remain unapplied till she received further instructions from Miss Blythe. The instructions at length arrived, and ordered that three guineas should be put into a leathern bag, and sewed up in Judith's bed, where they were to remain untouched till the boy had attained the age of fourteen. The former part of these directions were, as far as concerned Judith, faithfully complied with – Mary, as she thought, deposited the money as directed; but when the witch was afterwards apprehended, Judith opened her bed, took out the bag, and found it empty.

Mary having embraced the faith of the followers of Joanna Southcote, got introduced to the houses of many of them, and invariably robbed them: sometimes by practising on their fears, and at others by absolute theft.

In the year 1808, Bateman's family removed to Camp Field, in Water Lane, and there Mary met with a new and profitable subject for the exercise of her villainous arts. The wife of James Snowden, a neighbour, had a sort of presentiment that one of her children would be drowned; but whether this notion proceeded from morbid fancies originating in her own mind, or was suggested to her by Mary Bateman, is not known. Mary Bateman offered her service, or rather the services of Miss Blythe, to save the child from a watery grave. Miss Blythe was then represented as living at Thirsk, and a letter was received from her, directing that James Snowden's silver watch should be sewed up in the bed by Mary Bateman. This was accordingly done.

Next, money to the amount of twelve guineas was required. Letters were received from Miss Blythe, directing that this money should be sewn up in the bed, to be restored when the charm had taken effect. By-and-bye it was found necessary to increase the terrors, and in addition to the death of the son, Miss Blythe suggested that ill would befall the daughter, unless the family left Leeds, and removed to Bowling, near Bradford. The bed containing the charms they were allowed to take with them, but it was thought expedient to leave a considerable portion of their property in the house, and deposit the key with Bateman.

At length they expressed a wish to be allowed to rip open the bed and take out the watch and money, but the proper time, they were told, had not yet arrived; and before the property was taken out, the family of Snowden was to take a DOSE, which was at that time in preparation for them, and was to have been administered about the end of October, 1808. Happily for them this dose was never taken.

At this juncture, so critical to the family in question, Mary Bateman was apprehended for her frauds committed on William Perigo's family, and the wilful murder of Perigo's wife, by administering poison, of which she had died nearly two years before. This event naturally created a good deal of interest, and a narrative of the transaction was published in the *Leeds Mercury* of the 22nd of October. On the evening of that day Snowden was sitting in a public-house at Bradford when the *Mercury* was produced, and the narrative read by some person in the company. Snowden heard the relation with violent emotion, and as soon as it was finished, started from his chair and hurried home with all possible expedition. His first care was to give his wife a hasty and confused notion of the imposition that had been practised upon them, and next to unrip the folds of the bed; when, instead of watch and money, he discovered – a coal! He then went to Leeds, and found his house, which he had left in the care of Mary Bateman, plundered of almost everything it had contained, and on a search-warrant being procured, part of the property was found in Bateman's house.

John Bateman, the husband, was in consequence apprehended and committed to prison, to take his trial for the offence, either as a principal or as an accomplice. At the following Sessions his trial came on, and he was acquitted.

A brother of Mary Bateman, who had deserted from his Majesty's navy, had come with his wife to live in Leeds, and lodged with Bateman. Mary finding that her lodgers were a restraint upon her, determined to quit of them. For this purpose she wrote, or procured to be written, a letter to her sister-in-law, stating that her father was on the point of death, and summoning her to attend to receive his last blessing. The affectionate daughter answered the summons instantly, but when she arrived at Newcastle, where her father lived, she found him in perfect health. In the absence of his wife, Mary contrived to persuade her brother that she was inconstant, and was plunging him into debt, and so far succeeded as to induce him to write to his wife and tell her she need not return, for he would not receive her. She did, however, return, and convinced him of her innocence; when on examining their trunks it was discovered that Mary had, in the wife's absence, stolen their clothes, and disposed of them for what they would bring. This, as might be expected, roused the brother's indignation; but Mary soon got him out of the way, for she actually went before the magistrates and lodged an information against him as a deserter. He was in consequence obliged to quit Leeds, and afterwards entered military service. This did not, however, content Mary. She wrote to his mother, and told her that her son had been apprehended as a deserter, and that if she could send £10, a substitute was ready to go, and would be accepted in his stead. The ten pounds were sent, and Mary pocketed the money.

On the 21st of October, 1808, Mary Bateman was apprehended by the Chief Constable of Leeds on a charge of fraud, and was, after undergoing several long examinations before the magistrates of the borough, committed to York Castle on suspicion of the wilful murder of Rebecca Perigo, of Bramley.

A poor family of the name of Perigo, living at Bramley, near Leeds, had been defrauded by Mary Bateman of money to the amount of nearly £70, and of clothes and furniture to a considerable amount. These frauds were committed under the pretence of engaging Miss Blythe to relieve Mrs. Perigo from the effects of an "evil wish" under which she was supposed to labour. The money was all represented as sewn up in the bed, and was to be at the disposal of the Perigo's when the spell was broken. But when the appointed time for restoring the property approached, Mary Bateman conveyed poison to Perigo and his wife in their food. The woman died, but providentially Perigo recovered, and was able to bring the prisoner to justice.

It is unnecessary to give the particulars of the series of extortions committed on the Perigos. When nothing could be extracted from the unfortunate people, and Mary saw the time was come when she must refund or be exposed, the following letter reached her victims, purporting to come from Miss. Blythe.:—

"My Dear Friends,—

"I am sorry to tell you you will take an illness in the month of May next, either one or both, but I think both; but the work of God must have its course. You will escape the chambers of the grave; though you seem to be dead, yet you will live. Your wife must take half a pound of honey down from Bramley to Mary Bateman's at Leeds, and it must remain there till you go down yourself, and she will put it in like stuff as I have sent from Scarboro' to her, and she will put it in when you come down and see her youself, or it will not do. You must eat pudding for six days, and you must put in such like stuff as I have sent to Mary Bateman from Scarboro', and she will give your wife it, but you must not begin to eat of this pudding while I let you know. If ever you find yourselves sickly at any time, you must take each of you a teaspoon of this honey. I will remit £20 to you on the 20th day of May, and it will pay a little of what you owe. You must bring this down to Mary Bateman's, and burn it at her house when you come down the next time."

The rest shall be told by Perigo himself, as given in his evidence at the trial. Pursuant to the directions in this letter, witness stated that his wife took the honey to Mary Bateman's; that when she returned she brought six powders with her. The witness went to Mary Bateman's house, and talked to her about the letter he had received, and said it was a queerish thing that Miss Blythe should be able to forsee that they should be ill. Mary explained that she (Miss Blythe) knew everything relating to them, and that if they followed her directions all would be well. Mary also told him that they were to do with the powders each day as they were marked, or it would kill them all. Mrs. Bateman then mixed a powder in the honey in his presence, and he took the honey home. On the 5th day of May witness received another letter from Mrs. Blythe, but after reading it over one or twice, and copying a few lines from it, he destroyed it. He said the copy he had taken was also destroyed. The witness was then desired to state the contents of this letter, which he recited, as he did all the letters that had been destroyed, from memory, as follows:—

"My Dear Friends,—

"You must begin to eat pudding on the 11th of May, and you must put one of the powders in every day as they are marked, for six days; and you must see it put in yourself every day, or else it will not do. If you find yourself sickly at any time, you must not have no doctor, for it will not do, and you must not let the boy that used to eat with you eat of that pudding for six days; and you must make only as much as you can eat yourselves; if there is any left it will not do. You must keep the door fast as much as possible, or you will be overcome by some enemy. Now think on and take my directions, or else it will kill us all. About the 25th of May I will come to Leeds, and send for your wife to Mary Bateman's. Your wife will take me by the hand, and say, 'God bless you that I ever found you out.' It has pleased God to send me into the world that I might destroy the works of darkness. I call them the works of darkness because they are dark to you. Now, mind what I say, whatever you do. This letter must be burnt in straw on the hearth by your wife."

The witness proceeded to state that in consequence of these directions, on the 11th of May (Monday) they began to eat of the pudding, a powder being put in each day as marked on the paper, and that they found no particular taste in the pudding for five days. And that on Saturday the witness was coming to Leeds without seeing the powder put in, when his wife reminded him that it was necessary he should see it put in. Witness said his wife had made the pudding earlier than usual for that purpose. Witness saw the powder put in, which was four or five times larger than any of the other powders. On his return from Leeds, about twenty minutes after twelve o'clock, his wife had prepared a small cake from some of the dough which was left after making the pudding; this she broke in two pieces, and he ate one of them. Witness said the cake tasted very keen, and observed to his wife if the pudding tasted as bad he would not eat it. When the pudding was ready he ate a single mouthful, but it was so nauseous that he could eat no more of it; his wife, however, swallowed three or four mouthfuls, but was unable to eat more, and she carried the pudding into the cellar, and was there seized with the most violent vomitings. His wife said this was the illness predicted by Miss Blythe, and they should take the honey. Witness took two spoonfuls of it, and his wife took six or seven. This made them worse than before. The vomiting continued incessantly for twenty-four hours. His wife would not hear of a doctor being sent for, as that was contrary to Miss Blythe's directions, who had assured them that their sickness should not be unto death, and though they might seem to be dead, yet should they live, for that she was sent to destroy the works of darkness. Witness said a violent heat came out of his mouth, which was very sore, that his lips were black, and that he had a most violent pain in his head, twenty times worse than a common headache; everything appeared green to him. Witness had also a violent complaint in his bowels; he could eat nothing for several days, and began to get better only by hairbreadths. The witness then proceeded to detail the symptoms of his wife, which were similar to his own, only more violent. Her tongue swelled so that she could not shut her mouth, she was constantly thirsty, entirely lost her strength, and expired on Sunday, the 24th of May. Before she died he sent for Mr. Chorley, a surgeon from Leeds, but as she died before his arrival, a messenger was sent to acquaint him with this circumstance, and therefore he did not come. His wife before she died made him promise not to be rash with Mary Bateman, but to wait the appointed time. Witness himself went to Mr. Chorley on the day after the death of his wife. Mr. Chorley having examined him and heard his account of the symptoms, expressed his opinion that he had received poison into his stomach. Witness said that his wife was perfectly well immediately before eating of the pudding on Saturday. By the directions of Mr. Chorley, a paste was made of the flour of which their pudding had been made and given to a fowl; but it received no injury, and the witness said it was alive to this day. A part of the fatal pudding was also given to a cat, which it poisoned, but the result of this experiment was detailed by another witness.

Witness now went into a detail of transactions subsequent to the death of his wife. In the month of June, a short time after that event, the witness went to the prisoner's house, and acquainted her with the death of his wife, and told her he was sorry they had not sent for a doctor when they were sick, but that they had acted according to the directions of the letter. Mary Bateman said, "Perhaps you did not lick up all the honey as directed in the letter;" and I said, "No; I am afraid it is that honey that has done our job."

About the beginning of June, Perigo received a letter to the following effect, purporting to be from Miss Blythe:—

"My Dear Friend,—

"I am sorry to tell you that your wife should touch of those things which

I ordered her not, and for that reason it has caused her death. It had likened to have killed me at Scarboro' and Mary Bateman at Leeds, and you and all; and for this reason she will rise from the grave, she will stroke your face with her right hand, and you will lose the use of one side, but I will pray for you. I would not have you to go to no doctor, for it will not do. I would have you eat and drink what you like, and you will be better. Now, my dear friend, take my directions, do, and it will be better for you. Pray God bless you. Amen, amen. You must burn this letter immediately after it is read."

Soon after this, witness was ordered by Mr. Chorley to Buxton, and having on his return called on the poisoner, she expressed her surprise that he should have gone to a doctor contrary to Miss Blythe's command, and said that had she known he had been going to Buxton, she would have given him a bottle that would have cured him on the road.

William Perigo proceeded to relate that on the 19th of October, 1808, he unripped the bed in which all the bags were sewn up, and having opened the whole of them, he found no money whatever. In the bags in which he expected to find guinea-notes, he found only old waste paper, and where he expected to find gold, he found only a half-penny or a farthing. But the four silk bags in which he saw four guinea-notes put, he could not find at all, nor could he give any account as to how or where they were gone. Upon making this discovery the witness went to Leeds, and saw Mary Bateman, and said to her, "I am sorry to think you should use me in this manner; " to which she replied, "How?" He then said, "I have opened the bags, and there is nothing in them but bits of lead, plain paper, and halfpennies, and bad farthings." At which she did not seem at all surprised, but said, "You have opened them too soon." He answered, "I think it is too late." He then said he would come down to her house in the morning with two or three men and have things settled. The prisoner begged that he would not, and said if he would appoint a time and place to meet her alone, she would satisfy him. To this the witness consented, and the Leeds and Liverpool canal bank, near the bridge, was fixed as the place of meeting.

The officers of justice arrested Mary Bateman at this meeting.

The trial was conducted at York before Sir Simon Le Blanc on the 17th March, 1809; she was found guilty, and condemned to death.

During the brief interval between her receiving sentence of death and her execution, the Rev. George Brown took great pains to prevail upon her to acknowledge and confess her crime. On his touching upon the subject of the Quaker ladies, whose death had been so sudden and mysterious, she seemed perfectly to understand his meaning, but said that she knew nothing about it, as at the time she was confined in childbirth.

Though the prisoner behaved with her usual decorum during the time that remained to her, and joined with apparent fervour in the customary offices of devotion, she exhibited no compunction for crimes of which she would not acknowledge herself to be guilty. She maintained her caution and mystery to the last. On the day preceding her execution she wrote a letter to her husband, in which she enclosed her wedding-ring, with a request that it might be given to her daughter. In this letter she lamented the disgrace she had brought upon her husband and family, but declared her entire innocence of the crime laid to her charge, and for which she was about to suffer, though she acknowledged – what, indeed, she could not deny to her husband – that she had been guilty of several frauds. "I have made my peace with God, and am easy in mind. To-morrow will end all here, and the Lord will care for me hereafter."

It will hardly be credited, though it is a certain fact, that this unhappy woman was so addicted to fraud that even then she was incapable of refraining from her trickery and deception. A young female prisoner had, in her presence, expressed a wish to see her sweetheart. Mary Bateman took her aside, and said that if she could procure a sum of money to be made into a charm, and sewed into her stays, the young man would be compelled to visit her. The simple girl complied, and Mary Bateman having prepared a potent spell, it was bound round the breast of the young woman. No sweetheart made his appearance, and the girl's confidence beginning to waver, she unbound the charm to take out her money, and found that it had vanished.

The circumstance having been reported to the Governor of York Castle, where Mary Bateman and the girl were confined, part of the spoil was refunded, and Mary Bateman directed to balance the account by giving to the dupe some of her clothes. Exhortations and remonstrances failed to move her to confess her crimes. At five o'clock on the morning of Monday, March 20th, 1809, she was removed from her cell and from her infant child, which lay sleeping on the bed, unconscious of the fate of its wretched mother. She stopped and kissed it for the last time, but without showing any emotion at having to leave it for ever. Every possible effort, every religious influence was brought to bear on her to make her confess, but in vain. At twelve o'clock she was led forth to execution. On the scaffold she again denied her guilt, and with this denial on her lips was launched into eternity.

Her body was taken to the General Infirmary at Leeds. Though the hearse did not reach Leeds till midnight, it was met by a considerable number of people waiting for it. At the Infirmary her body was exhibited at the charge of 3d. a head to visitors for the benefit of the institution. At this rate 2500 individuals were admitted, and upwards of £30 was realised. Her body was afterwards dissected, and in compliance with a favourite Yorkshire custom, her skin was tanned and distributed in small pieces to various applicants.